Hossein Bidgoli

California State University, Bakersfield

Information
Systems
Literacy

Paradox for Windows

Macmillan College Publishing Company
New York

Maxwell Macmillan Canada
Toronto

Maxwell Macmillan International
New York   Oxford   Singapore   Sydney

Cover photo: Copyright © Douglas E. Walker/Masterfile.
Cover photo insets: Courtesy of International Business Machines Corp.

Editor: Charles E. Stewart, Jr.
Production Editor: Stephen C. Robb
Photo Editor: Chris Migdol
Text Designer: Anne Flanagan
Cover Designer: Russ Maselli
Production Manager: Pamela D. Bennett
Electronic Text Management: Marilyn Wilson Phelps, Matthew Williams, Jane Lopez, Karen L. Bretz

This book was set in ITC New Baskerville and Swiss 721 Condensed by Macmillan College Publishing Company and was printed and bound by Von Hoffman Press, Inc. The cover was printed by Von Hoffman Press, Inc.

The Publisher offers discounts on this book when ordered in bulk quantities. For more information, write to: Special Sales Department, Macmillan College Publishing Company, 445 Hutchinson Avenue, Columbus, OH 43235, or call 1-800-228-7854

Macmillan College Publishing Company
866 Third Avenue
New York, New York 10022

Macmillan College Publishing Company is part of the
Maxwell Communication Group of Companies.

Maxwell Macmillan Canada, Inc.
1200 Eglinton Avenue East, Suite 200
Don Mills, Ontario M3C 3N1

Library of Congress Cataloging-in-Publication Data
Bidgoli, Hossein.
    Information systems literacy. Paradox for Windows / Hossein Bidgoli.
        p.   cm.
    Includes index.
    ISBN 0-02-309571-7
    1. Data base management. 2. Paradox for Windows (Computer file) I. Title
QA76.9.D3B5265 1994   93–41017
005.75'65—dc20   CIP

Printing: 1   2   3   4   5   6   7   8   9   Year: 5   6   7   8

To so many fine memories of my brother, Mohsen,
for his uncompromising belief in the power of education.

Preface

Information Systems Literacy: Paradox for Windows is a component of a modular series of textbooks developed for use in introductory computing courses. This Paradox for Windows text is written for first courses in database design and use or for use in conjunction with texts in any course where a database tutorial is required.

Chapter 1, "The World of Microcomputers," takes a comprehensive look at microcomputer hardware and software and their applications. This chapter provides a thorough discussion of the types of application software used today and lays the foundation for the hands-on section of the text.

Chapter 2 gives a quick review of MS-DOS and PC-DOS. This presentation should assist readers to use their PC and Paradox for Windows more effectively.

Chapter 3 provides an overview of Windows 3.1. This presentation should prepare students for a better understanding of Windows principles and Paradox for Windows.

Chapter 4 is an overview of databases and database management systems. This presentation provides a theoretical background for the design and implementation of a database using Paradox for Windows.

The software tutorials in this book (Chapters 5 through 11), organized into manageably sized chapters, are designed to give the student comprehensive training and reference. This approach lets the instructor choose which and how many topics to cover, and it gives the student a valuable reference to use long after the class is completed. Advanced topics not covered in many texts are included here, as a growing number of students are coming into introductory computing courses with some software literacy; this book allows students to go further in their studies.

The software chapters are pedagogically designed with the student in mind. Features include:

- Introductory sections that explain, in basic terms, what the software is, why it was developed, and how it is used. Too many books "jump right in" without giving the student a sense of context.
- Frequent use of computer screen illustrations to augment written instruction.
- Twenty to 30 review questions, 5 to 8 hands-on experience assignments, and 10 multiple choice and 10 true/false questions at the end of each chapter.
- A complete summary of key terms and key computer commands in each chapter.
- When appropriate, a unique section entitled "Misconceptions and Solutions." Common errors, improper operating procedures, and ways to avoid or solve them are highlighted for the student.

Appendix A includes answers to selected end-of-chapter review questions. Appendix B provides a quick review of file transfer among Windows applications. Ancillary materials for instructors are:

- Instructor's Manual, including Test Bank, Transparency Masters, and data disk, that enables students to access the programs and exercises included in the text. The manual also has lecture outlines, answers to review questions/exercises, and guidelines for projects.
- Computerized Test Bank.

In any hands-on computer lab, having an accurate text makes managing the lab far easier. The best way to make a text accurate is to use it. During the two years I spent developing this text I have received corrections and suggestions that make this book one you should find both easy to use and reliable.

ACKNOWLEDGMENTS

Several colleagues reviewed different versions of this manuscript and made constructive suggestions. Without their help the manuscript could not have been refined. The help and comments of the following reviewers are greatly appreciated: Kirk Arnett, Mississippi State University; Tom Berliner, University of Texas, Dallas; Glen Boswell, San Antonio College; Gary Brent, Scottsdale Community College; Chris Carter, Indiana Vocational Technical College; Michael Davis, Texas Technical University; Steve Deam, Milwaukee Area Technical College; Beth Defoor, Eastern New Mexico University, Clovis; Richard Ernst, Sullivan Junior College; Barbara Felty, Harrisburg Area Community College; Pat Fenton, West Valley College; Phyllis Helms, Randolph Community College; Mehdi Khosrow-pour, Pennsylvania State University, Harrisburg; Candice Marble, Wentworth Military Academy; Ramon Mata-Toledo, James Madison University; John Miller, Williamsport Area Community College; Charles McDonald, East Texas State University; Sylvia Meyer, Community College of Vermont; J. D. Oliver, Prairie View A&M University; Greg Pierce, Penn State University; Eugene Rathswohl, University of San Diego; Mary-Ann Robbert, Bentley College; Herbert Rubhun, University of Houston, Downtown; R. D. Shelton, Loyola College; Sandra Stalker, North Shore Community College; Maureen Thommes, Bemidji State University; G. W. Willis, Baylor University; and Judy Yeager, Western Michigan University.

Many different groups assisted me in completing this project. I am grateful to over four thousand students who attended my executive seminars and various classes in information systems and software productivity tools. They helped me fine-tune the manuscript during its various stages. My friend Bahram Ahanin helped me to improve many concepts of hardware/software and put them in a non-technical and easy-to-understand format. My colleague and friend Dr. Reza Azarmsa provided support and encouragement. I am grateful for all of his encouragement. My colleague Andrew Prestage assisted me in numerous trouble-spots by running and debugging many of the screens presented in the book.

I am indebted to Jacki Lawson, Denise Candia, Julie Gunn, and Vivian Cochneuer, who typed and retyped various versions of this manuscript. Their thoroughness and patience made it easier to complete this project. They deserve special recognition for all this work.

A team of professionals from Macmillan College Publishing Company assisted me in this venture, including Charles Stewart, senior editor; Steve Robb, production editor; and Jane Lopez and Pete Robison, art coordinators.

Finally, I want to thank my family for their support and encouragement throughout my life. My two sisters, Azam and Akram, deserve my special thanks and recognition. My wife, Nooshin, has been very supportive and patient. My little baby, Morvareed, has been very patient throughout this work. I extend my deepest love and appreciation to both.

Dr. Hossein Bidgoli is professor of management information systems at California State University, Bakersfield. He holds a Ph.D. degree in systems science from Portland State University with a specialization in design and implementation of MIS. His master's degree is in MIS from Colorado State University. Dr. Bidgoli's background includes experience as a systems analyst, information systems consultant, financial analyst, and he was the Director of the Microcomputer Center at Portland State University, where the first PC Lab in the United States was started.

Dr. Bidgoli, a two-time winner of the MPPP (Meritorious Performance and Professional Promise) award for outstanding performance in teaching, research, and university/community service, is the author of forty-two texts and numerous professional papers and articles presented and published throughout the United States on the topics of computers and MIS. Dr. Bidgoli has also designed and implemented over twenty executive seminars on all aspects of information systems and decision support systems.

Paradox for Windows

Contents

Contents

Contents xiii

Contents

The World of Microcomputers

1–1   INTRODUCTION

In this chapter we discuss microcomputer fundamentals. Hardware and software for micros are described. Different classes of application software are introduced. Guidelines for successful selection and maintenance of micros are highlighted. A brief explanation of the advantages of micros compared with mainframes is presented. The chapter also includes a hands-on session with a microcomputer. The chapter concludes by defining these important concepts: computer files; types of data, values, and formulas; and priority of arithmetic operations. The information in this chapter should help you to be a more effective microcomputer user.

1–2   WHAT IS A MICROCOMPUTER?

The terms **personal computer** (PC), **micro**, or **microcomputer** refer to the smallest type of computer when measured by such attributes as memory, cost, size, speed, and sophistication. Although small, these computers are so powerful that sometimes the difference between PCs and larger computers is blurred. The reason for such confusion is the ever-increasing power and capability of PCs.

Since the beginning of the microcomputer era in roughly 1975, the capability of these computers has improved beyond imagination. Still, some experts believe this is only the beginning—there is a lot more to be done by micros.

A microcomputer consists of input, output, and memory devices. Figure 1–1 illustrates a typical microcomputer system. The **input device** is usually a keyboard. A PC keyboard is similar to a typewriter but with some additional keys. Figure 1–2 displays an IBM enhanced keyboard and a standard keyboard. In the future, voice input devices may be part of the system. Other input devices include a mouse, touch technology, light pen, graphics tablet, optical character reader (OCR), magnetic ink character recognition (MICR), camera, sensor, and bar code readers.

The common output devices for microcomputers are a cathode-ray tube (CRT) monitor, sometimes called video display terminal (VDT), and the printer. The

Figure 1–1
Typical microcomputer system (courtesy of Radio Shack, a division of Tandy Corp.).

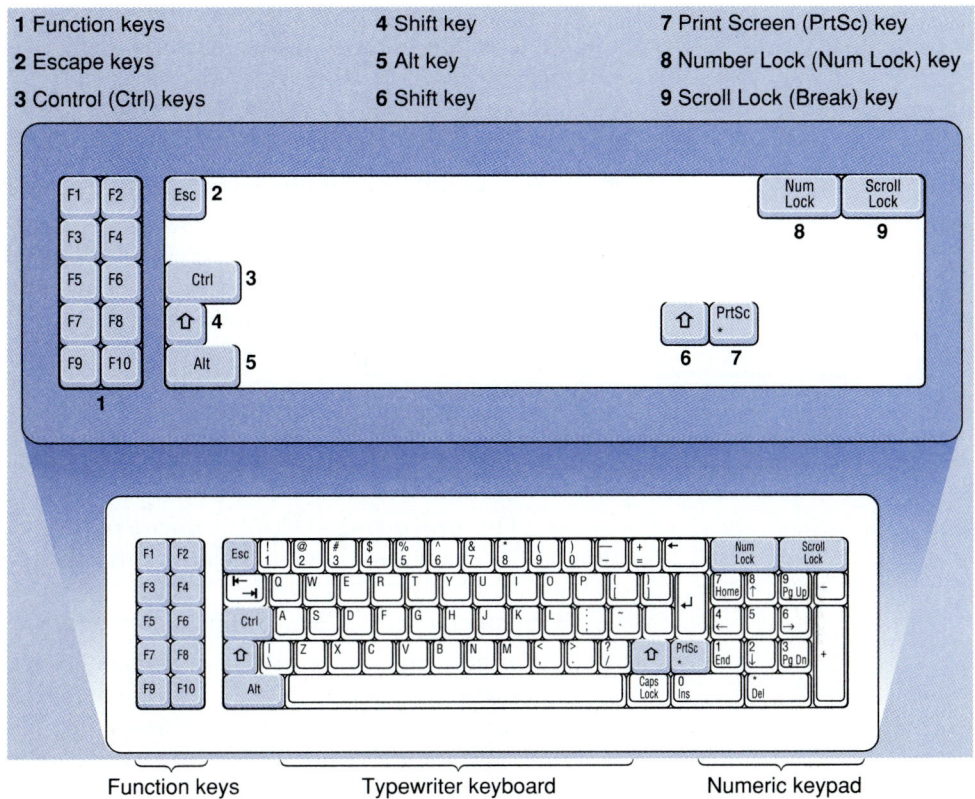

1 Function keys   4 Shift key   7 Print Screen (PrtSc) key

2 Escape keys   5 Alt key   8 Number Lock (Num Lock) key

3 Control (Ctrl) keys   6 Shift key   9 Scroll Lock (Break) key

Function keys   Typewriter keyboard   Numeric keypad

A.

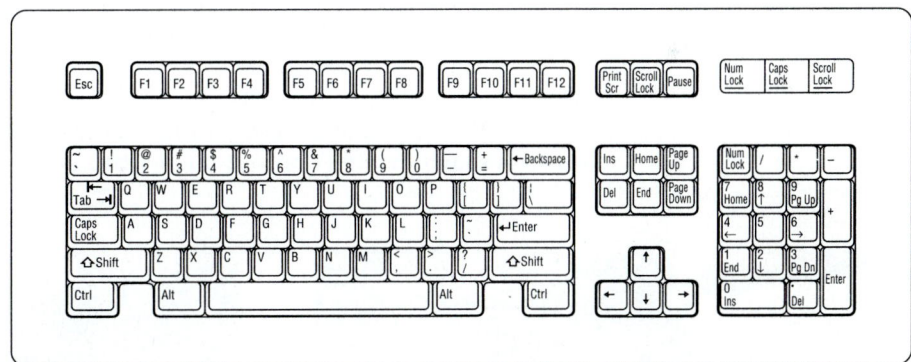

B.

Figure 1–2
A. IBM standard keyboard. B. IBM enhanced keyboard (courtesy of International Business Machines Corp.).

output generated on the monitor is called soft copy and printed output is referred to as hard copy. Other output devices include cameras, floppy disks, and plotters.

Two types of monitors display output. Some microcomputers utilize a monochrome-type screen. As the name indicates, this type of screen generates one color, such as green, although some screens are amber (orange). Either type of monochrome monitor can generate graphic output if accompanied by a graphics card or graphics adapter. The other type of monitor is called a color monitor (sometimes referred to as an **RGB** monitor—red-green-blue monitor). It shows data in a color format.

The sharpness of images on the display monitor is referred to as resolution. The intersection of a row and a column is called a pixel. The higher the number of these pixels, the higher the resolution. Color monitors come in various levels of resolution such as CGA, EGA, VGA, super VGA, and XGA:

- A color graphics adapter (CGA) displays 320-by-200 (pixels) resolution in 4 colors
- An enhanced graphics adapter (EGA) displays 640-by-350 resolution in 16 colors. More advanced versions of EGA display 640-by-480 resolution in 16 colors and 320-by-200 resolution in 256 colors.
- A video graphics array (VGA) displays 640-by-480 resolution in 16 colors and 320-by-200 resolution in 256 colors. Super VGA and XGA monitors display more than 640-by-480 resolution in many different colors. The exact resolution depends on the specific type of the monitor.

The processing part of a microcomputer, that is its **central processing unit** (CPU) or microprocessor, includes three components:

1. **Main memory** stores data, information, and instructions.
2. **Arithmetic logic unit** (ALU) performs arithmetic and logical operations. Arithmetic operations include addition, subtraction, division, and multiplication. Logical operations include any types of comparisons, such as sorting (putting data into a particular order) or searching (choosing a particular data item).
3. **Control unit** serves as the commander of the system. It tells the microcomputer what to do and how to do it.

Figure 1–3 illustrates two different microprocessor chips, or microchips, which contain the electronic components necessary for processing.

Microcomputers are getting smaller but more powerful. Among the various types are portable (laptop) micros and notebook micros (see Figure 1–4).

A.

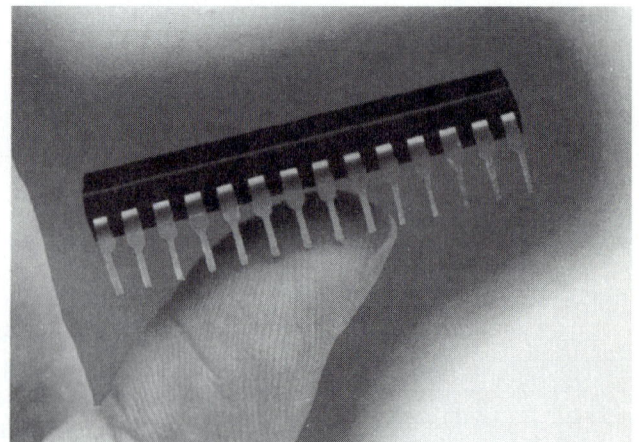

B.

Figure 1–3
A. Motorola MC 68020 microprocessor in its protective ceramic package (courtesy of Motorola, Inc.).
B. AT&T Bell Labs microprocessor (courtesy of Radio Shack, a division of Tandy Corp.).

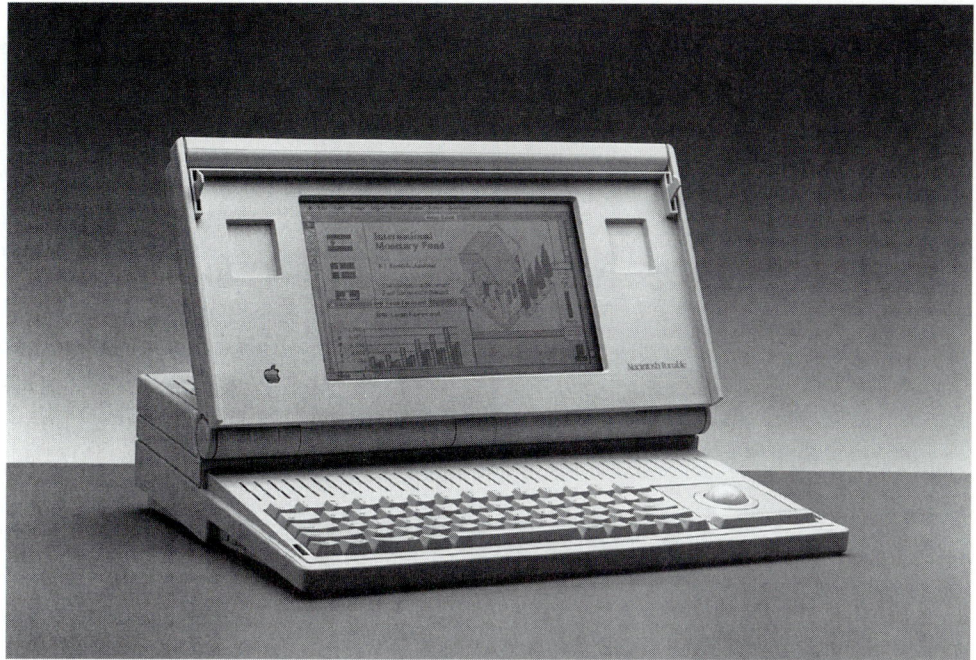

A.

B.

Figure 1–4

A. The all-in-one design of the Apple Macintosh Portable integrates the CPU, Active Matrix Liquid Crystal Display, keyboard, pointing device, battery and disk storage into a single easy-to-carry package. B. With the Macintosh PowerBook computer, customers can take advantage of notebook convenience and Macintosh power anywhere, whether at home, school or on the road for business (courtesy of Apple Computer, Inc.).

1–3   THE KEYBOARD

As you can see in Figure 1–2B, an enhanced keyboard is divided into three sections. On the top are 12 function keys. In a standard keyboard, there are only 10 function keys. Some keyboards have the function keys on the left (Figure 1–2A). With most application software, these keys perform special functions, or they can be programmed to perform a particular task. For example, Lotus 1-2-3, Quattro Pro, dBASE, and WordPerfect effectively use 12 keys (F1 through F12) for performing different tasks.

The middle part of the keyboard is similar to a typical typewriter. However, notice some special keys that a typewriter does not have (e.g., the Alt key).

The right section has a numeric key pad similar to that of an adding machine. It is used to facilitate numeric data entry (when the Num Lock key is pressed down) or for cursor movement.

The purpose of function keys and some of the special keys varies in different application programs. For example, F1 in WordPerfect 5.1 cancels a selection or performs "undelete" operations. In Lotus 1-2-3, Quattro Pro, or dBASE, it accesses the online help command.

1–4   IMPORTANT AUXILIARY DEVICES

Besides the obvious input/output devices, some additional devices are required for effective utilization of a microcomputer. Disk drives and adapter cards are two of the most important devices.

1–4–1   Disk Drives

Disk drives enable the microcomputer system to retrieve data from a disk into main memory and to store data from main memory to a disk. Disk drives come in various capacities. Your system may have one or more floppy disk drives. It may also have a hard disk drive. As you will see later, **hard disks** are capable of storing masses of information. The capacity of a hard disk is many times greater than that of a **floppy disk** (also called a diskette or just a floppy). A floppy disk can hold from 360 kilobytes (K) to 1.44 megabytes (MB) of data. Some new floppies are capable of storing 2.88 MB. The capacity of a hard disk varies from 5 to 600 MB or more.

The capacity of a storage device is measured in terms of bits or bytes of data stored on that device. Table 1–1 summarizes the memory equivalents.

1–4–2   Adapter Cards

Adapter cards are installed in expansion slots (channels) inside the computer (see Figure 1–5). These cards are used to attach a particular option to the system unit. Table 1–2 summarizes typical adapter cards.

Table 1–1
Memory Equivalents

0 or 1 is equal to one bit

8 bits is equal to one byte

1,024 (2^{10}) bytes is equal to one kilobyte

1,048,576 (2^{20}) bytes is equal to one megabyte

1,073,741,824 (2^{30}) bytes is equal to one gigabyte

10,995,627,776 (2^{40}) bytes is equal to one terabyte

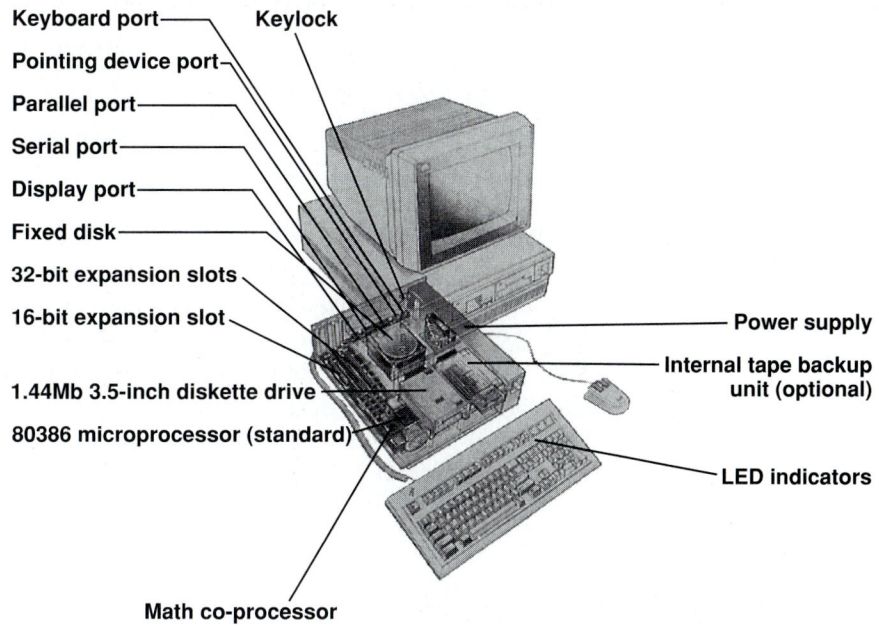

Keyboard port — Keylock
Pointing device port
Parallel port
Serial port
Display port
Fixed disk
32-bit expansion slots
16-bit expansion slot

1.44Mb 3.5-inch diskette drive
80386 microprocessor (standard)

Power supply
Internal tape backup unit (optional)

LED indicators

Math co-processor

A.

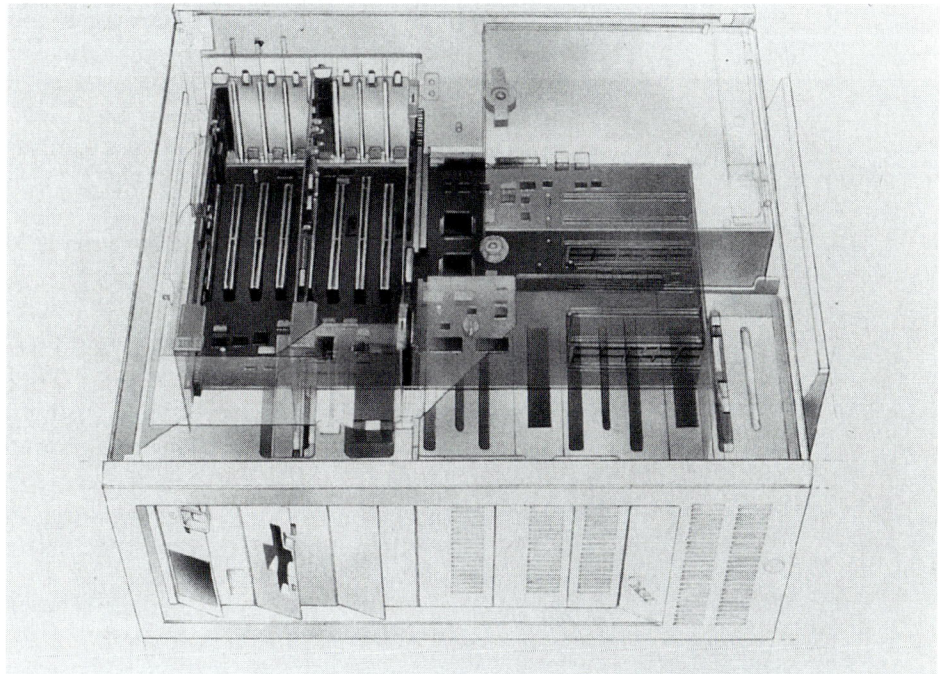

B.

Figure 1–5
Inside your PC. A. Port and expansion slots in a microcomputer (courtesy of International Business Machines Corp.). B. Inside a microcomputer. This model is IBM's PS/2 95XP 486 (courtesy of International Business Machines Corp.).

Table 1–2
Commonly Used Adapter Cards

- Disk drive card for connecting disk drives to the system unit
- Display card for connecting the CRT to the system unit
- Memory card for connecting additional RAM to existing memory
- Clock card for connecting a clock to the system unit
- Modem card for connecting the PC to the outside world
- Printer interface card for connecting a printer to the system unit

The original IBM PC has five expansion slots; the IBM XT and AT have eight slots. Adapter cards usually have outlet ports that are accessed at the back of the system unit. It is important to know that the newer PCs do not require as many adapter cards. Ports, which are either parallel or serial, connect devices to the system unit. You must connect a serial device to a serial port and a parallel device to a parallel port. Serial devices transfer one bit of data at a time; parallel devices transfer a series of bits of data at a time.

1–5   TYPES OF PRIMARY MEMORY

Computers store data in two kinds of memory: main, or primary memory, and auxiliary, or secondary memory. **Primary memory** is the heart of the microcomputer; it is usually referred to as **random-access memory** (RAM). This is a volatile memory. Data stored in RAM will be lost in the event of a power failure. To avoid this type of loss, always save your work on a permanent memory medium (i.e., secondary memory), such as a diskette.

Three other types of memory also can be referred to as main memory, but the user cannot have direct control over them:

1. **Read-only memory** (ROM): A prefabricated ROM chip is supplied by vendors. This memory stores some general-purpose instructions or programs. For example, some commands of the Disk Operating System (DOS) and some versions of the BASIC language are stored on ROM chips. DOS is the operating system for IBM microcomputers and compatible systems.
2. **Programmable read-only memory**: By using a special device, the user can program this memory. However, once programmed, the user cannot erase this type of memory.
3. **Erasable programmable read-only memory**: This type of read-only memory can be programmed by the user and, as the name indicates, erased and programmed again.

1–6   CONVENTIONAL, EXPANDED, AND EXTENDED MEMORIES

With the introduction of 386- and 486-based computers and the Pentium (the new high-powered microprocessor introduced by Intel), two new types of main memory have entered the market and have made the memory discussion even more confusing. The next few paragraphs briefly describe these two new memories and differentiate them from conventional memory.

Conventional memory, or RAM, is the first 640 K of the memory of your computer. The majority of XT-type machines come with 1 MB of memory; however, DOS can only directly reach the first 640 K of this memory. The other 384 K (1024 K–640 K) is used (as shown in Figure 1–6) by ROM BIOS (Basic Input Output System), adapter ROM, video memory, and the EMS (Expanded Memory Specification) window.

Expanded memory is located outside of the conventional memory and works based on a technique called bank switching. Lotus, Intel, and Microsoft (LIM) corporations devised the LIM Expanded Memory Specification (EMS) for expanded memory. This is like a memory storage area on an EMS-compatible expansion card inside your computer. To utilize expanded memory on your computer, you need both an EMS-compatible memory expansion card and a device driver known as Expanded Memory Manager (EMM). The EMM helps the microprocessor find a page(s) of data that your software is looking for and puts the data into a 64-K page frame as four 16-K pages. DOS can then locate the data, and your software program can use it. Expanded memory is useful for designing large spreadsheets.

Extended memory is also outside of conventional memory, but it functions basically as additional RAM and is accessible to your computer directly. No bank switching occurs with extended memory. This means that after DOS addresses the first 640 K of conventional memory, it then automatically accesses the next chunk of the memory, which is the extended memory (see Figure 1–6). A 286-based PC can access up to 16 MB of RAM, and 386- and 486-based PCs can access up to 4,096 MB of RAM.

Which memory should you get, expanded or extended? Well, the software in use dictates the type of memory. Earlier software requested expanded memory. Today's graphical environments, such as Windows, prefer extended memory. In fact, your additional memory can be configured either way using special software.

Figure 1–6
Conventional, extended, and expanded memories.

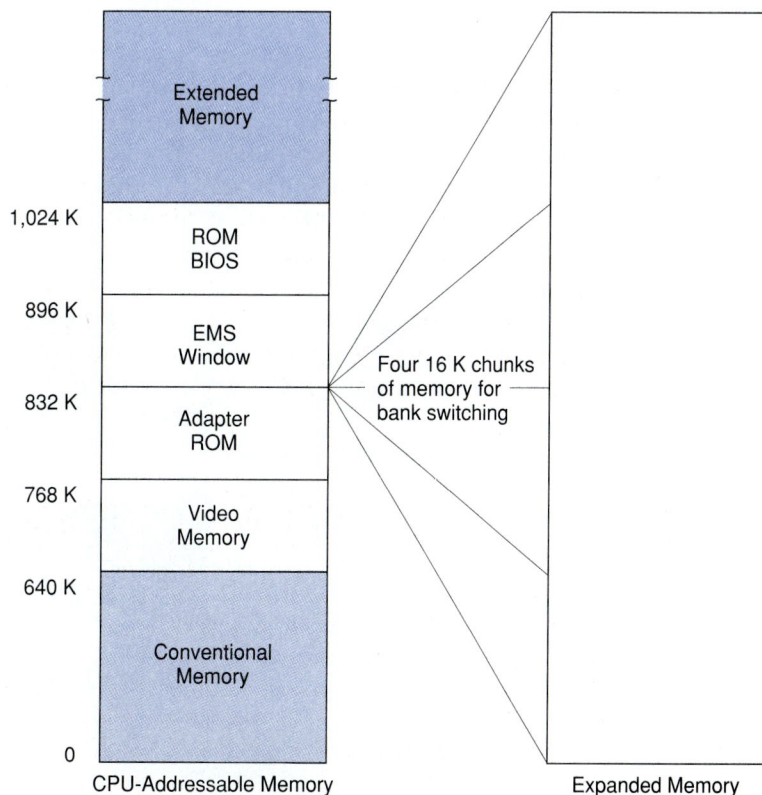

	Extended Memory
1,024 K	ROM BIOS
896 K	EMS Window
832 K	Adapter ROM
768 K	Video Memory
640 K	Conventional Memory
0	

Four 16 K chunks of memory for bank switching

CPU-Addressable Memory

Expanded Memory

1–7   TYPES OF SECONDARY MEMORY

Since the main memory of a microcomputer is limited, expensive, and volatile, **secondary memory** storage devices are needed for mass data storage. Secondary storage is nonvolatile. Secondary storage devices are broadly classified into magnetic and optical. Let us briefly consider each group.

1–7–1   Magnetic Storage Devices

Magnetic storage devices include the diskette, mini floppy, hard disk, and Bernoulli box. The capacity of a diskette or a hard disk depends on its technical features.

There are three types of standard diskettes: 3½ inches, 5¼ inches, and 8 inches. The most recent floppy disk is a 2-inch floppy. Diskettes can be single density, double density, or high density. Density refers to the amount of information that can be stored on a disk. Diskettes can also be single sided or double sided. A 5¼-inch, single-sided, single-density floppy can hold roughly 125 K; a 5¼-inch, single-sided, double-density floppy can hold roughly 250 K; a 5¼-inch, double-sided, double-density floppy can hold roughly 360 K; a high-density (sometimes called quad-density) diskette can hold up to 1.2 MB. A 3½-inch, low-density floppy disk can store 720 K of data and a 3½-inch, high-density floppy can store 1.44 MB of data.

A hard disk (also called fixed disk or Winchester disk) can be 14, 8, 5¼ or less than 4 inches in diameter. The capacity of this device varies from 5 MB to 1 gigabyte.

A **Bernoulli box** is a removable medium. After finishing your computer work, you can pull this device out and store it in a safe location, which is not possible with a hard disk. A Bernoulli box uses high-capacity floppy disks to store 10 MB of data or more. Generally speaking, it is less prone to damage than a hard disk. This is true because the drive head of a Bernoulli box does not move as a hard disk head moves, often resulting in head crashes. In a Bernoulli box, the floppy disk moves toward the stationary read/write head through air currents. Figure 1–7 displays a Bernoulli box.

At the present time, the most commonly used secondary storage device is a 3½-inch floppy disk. However, at the beginning of the PC era, 5¼-inch floppy

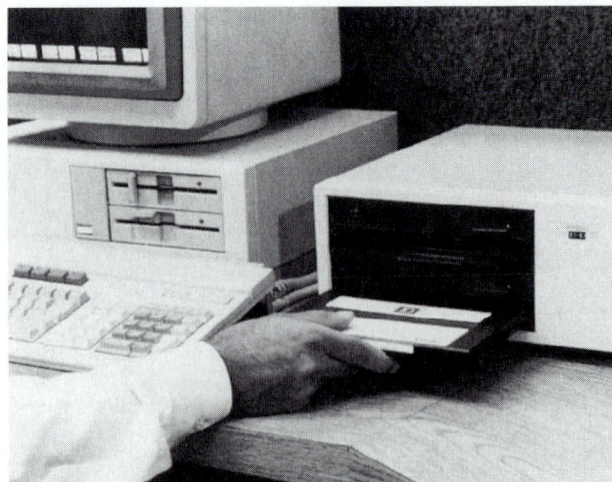

Figure 1–7
A Bernoulli box.

Figure 1–8
A 5¼-inch floppy disk.

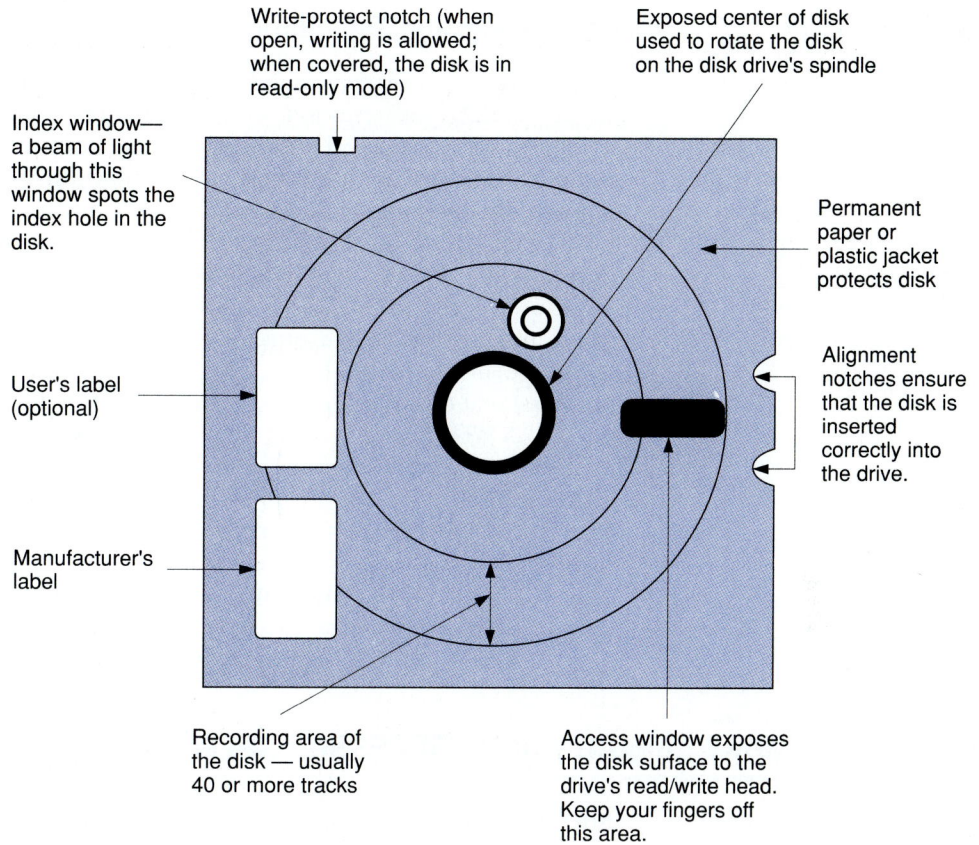

Write-protect notch (when open, writing is allowed; when covered, the disk is in read-only mode)

Exposed center of disk used to rotate the disk on the disk drive's spindle

Index window— a beam of light through this window spots the index hole in the disk.

Permanent paper or plastic jacket protects disk

User's label (optional)

Alignment notches ensure that the disk is inserted correctly into the drive.

Manufacturer's label

Recording area of the disk — usually 40 or more tracks

Access window exposes the disk surface to the drive's read/write head. Keep your fingers off this area.

disks were the most commonly used secondary storage devices. A floppy disk is made of plastic material coated with magnetic material. A 5¼-inch disk is enclosed in a permanent vinyl jacket to protect the disk. After using a floppy disk, you should put it back in its paper cover to protect it from dirt and dust. Do not touch exposed portions of the disk or data loss may result. Figure 1–8 highlights important areas of a 5¼-inch diskette. Figure 1–9 displays a 3½-inch diskette. The 3½-inch diskettes are more durable and easier to handle than the 5¼-inch disks. They also store more information.

Figure 1–9
A 3½-inch floppy disk.

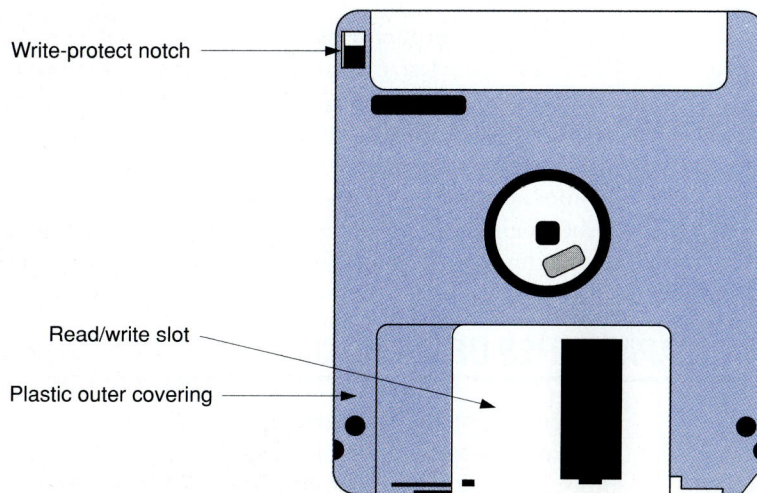

Write-protect notch

Read/write slot

Plastic outer covering

1–7–2   ## Optical Storage Technologies

Three types of optical storage have attracted much attention in recent years: CD-ROM, WORM, and erasable optical disk. The major advantages of optical technology devices are durability and massive storage capacity. The major drawback of optical technology is its slow speed; however, vendors are working rapidly to improve the technology. Let us briefly look at each type.

CD-ROM (compact disk, read-only memory), as the name indicates, is a permanent medium. In CD ROM, information is recorded by disk-mastering machines. A CD-ROM, which is similar to an audio compact disk, can be duplicated and distributed throughout an organization. Its major application is for large, permanent databases, for example, public domain databases such as libraries, real estate information, and corporate financial information.

A **WORM** (write once, read many) disk is also a permanent medium. Information can be recorded once and cannot be altered. A major drawback compared with CD-ROM is that you cannot duplicate a WORM disk. Its major application is for storing information that must be kept permanently, for example, information related to annual reports, nuclear power plants, airports, and railroads.

An **erasable optical disk** meets the needs of high-volume storage and updating. Information can be recorded and erased repeatedly.

Figure 1–10 illustrates each of the three types of optical storage.

1–8   MEMORY CAPACITY AND PROCESSOR SPEED

Microcomputer RAM capacity used to start at 512 or 640 K. Now PCs with capacities of 4 to 16 MB are becoming more common, and in the future, micros will approach minicomputer capacity.

For present and future planning, you should be able to calculate the memory requirements for your computing needs. For example, if you have a PC with 640 K of RAM, all of that memory may not be accessible to you. A large portion of that memory may be needed by software you use to carry out applications. As an example, Lotus Release 2.01 needs almost 200 K of RAM. So in your 640-K PC, you are left with only 440 K of memory to use (640 − 200 = 440).

Another consideration regarding memory is speed. The speed of the processor is measured in megahertz (MHz) and usually varies from 4 to 66. Vendors are rapidly extending this technology also. Soon, speeds of 100 MHz or more will be available. The higher the processor speed, the faster the computer.

Another factor that has direct impact on speed is the word size of the processor. Word size indicates the number of characters that can be processed simultaneously. Word size varies from 8 to 32 bits for microcomputers. The bigger the word size, the faster the computer.

The speed of your microcomputer may have a direct impact on your business operation. With a faster computer, you can process more information in a shorter period of time. However, always consider the additional cost incurred by buying a more powerful PC and the marginal benefit to be gained.

1–9   GENERAL CAPABILITIES OF MICROCOMPUTER SOFTWARE

A microcomputer can perform a variety of tasks by using either commercial software or software developed in-house. In-house developed software is usually more expensive than commercial software. However, software developed in-house

A.

CD ROM

B.

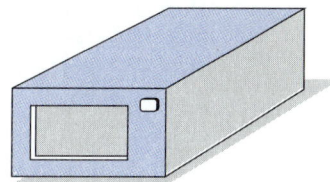

WORM disk

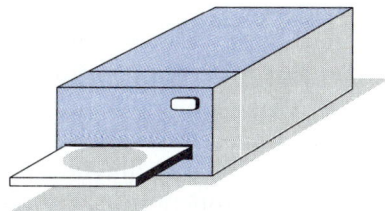

Erasable optical disk

C.

Figure 1–10
Optical storage devices for microcomputers. A. Close-up of CD-ROM (courtesy of Radio Shack, a division of Tandy Corp.). B. Disks and disk drive B (courtesy of NEC). C. Erasable optical disk.

is more customized and should better fit users' needs. Several thousands of software packages are available for PCs. For any task that can apply to several users, there is a software package on the market. The following are typical commercial packages and applications available for microcomputers.

1–9–1   Word Processing Software

A microcomputer that functions as a word processor is similar to a typewriter with a memory. With such a facility, you can generate documents, make deletions and insertions, and cut and paste. **Word processing software** is becoming more sophisticated. Some of the programs now provide limited graphics and data management features. Word processing programs allow users to save hundreds of hours by not typing the same document repeatedly. For example, organizations do not need to retype the letter that is sent to many of their customers. They need only change the names and addresses in the letters. Numerous word processing programs fill the marketplace. Some of the popular ones are WordPerfect (WordPerfect Corp.), Word (Microsoft Corporation), AmiPro (Lotus Development Corporation), and Wordstar (MicroPro International Corporation).

1–9–2   Grammar Checker Software

The ever-increasing speed and memory of microcomputers are promoting a new type of software. Most word processors now include spelling checkers, which are able to correct most of the typos in a document. The next challenge is the creation of documents that include correct verbs, subjects, adjectives, and a smooth style. Also, the creation of simple, easy-to-read, and simple sentences is of prime importance. **Grammar checker software** promotes good writing techniques.

Grammar checkers perform text analyses through linguistic analysis, parsing, and rule matching. Parsing means simply breaking long sentences into shorter ones. More sophisticated software includes more sophisticated parsers. Grammar checkers play an especially important role when multiple authors are involved in a project. In such cases, grammar checkers help create uniformity of tone, level, style, and usage. Grammar checkers are not 100 percent perfect yet, but they have come a long way. Among the more popular grammar checkers are Grammatik Windows and Grammatik IV (Reference Software International), PowerEdit (Artificial Linguistics, Inc.), and Correct Grammar for DOS (Writing Tools Group, Inc.).

1–9–3   Spreadsheet Software

A spreadsheet is a table of rows and columns. **Spreadsheet software** can be broadly classified into two types. One type is a dedicated spreadsheet; this means the program performs only spreadsheet functions. The other type of spreadsheet package can perform more than one type of function. Lotus 1-2-3, for example, is capable of performing spreadsheet functions as well as database and graphics functions. Other popular spreadsheet packages include Symphony (Lotus), Excel (Microsoft), SuperCalc (Computer Associates International, Inc.), and Quattro Pro (Borland International).

The number of jobs that can be performed by a spreadsheet program is unlimited. Generally speaking, any application suitable for analysis by row and column is a candidate for a typical spreadsheet. For example, say you decide to use a spreadsheet to prepare a budget. As soon as you have completed your budget, you can perform some impressive what-if analysis. This means you can manipulate variables on the spreadsheet. For example, reduce your income by 2 percent and direct the spreadsheet to calculate the effect of this change on other items in the spreadsheet.

1–9–4 Database Software

Database software is designed to perform database operations such as file creation, deletion, modification, search, sort, merge, and join (combining two files based on a common key). A file is a collection of a series of records. A record is a collection of a series of fields. A field is a collection of a series of characters. For example, the names, GPAs, and majors of all the students in our computer class constitute a student file. The name, GPA, and major of each student make up the record of each student. The name, GPA, or major is a field.

Popular database programs include dBASE III PLUS and IV (Borland), PC-File III (Buttonware, Inc.), Q&A (Symantec), Paradox (Borland), Omnis Quartz (Blyth Software), FoxBase and Fox Pro (Microsoft), and R-BASE (Microrim Corporation).

Think of a database as a table of rows and columns. The rows correspond to the occurrence of a record. The columns correspond to the fields within the record. Two common applications of database software are sorting and searching records. In sort operations, the user enters a series of records in any order, then asks the database program to sort the records in ascending or descending order based on the data in the fields. Search operations are even more interesting. You can search for data items that meet certain criteria, for example, all the MIS students who have GPAs greater than 3.60 and are younger than 20 years of age. Some databases (such as Q&A) allow you to search for key words within a text file.

1–9–5 Graphics Software

Graphics software has been designed to present data in graphic format. Data can be converted into a line graph to show a trend, to a pie chart to highlight the components of a data item, and to other types of graphs for various analyses. Masses of data can be converted to a graph and, in a glance, the reader can discover the general pattern of the data. Graphs can easily highlight patterns and the correlation of data items. They also make data presentation a more manageable job. Graphics can be done with integrated packages such as Lotus 1-2-3 or Quattro Pro or with dedicated graphics packages. Five popular graphics packages are Aldus Persuasion (Aldus Corporation), Hollywood Graphics (IBM Corporation), Harvard Graphics (Software Publishing Corporation), Freelance (Lotus), and Power Point (Microsoft Corporation).

1–9–6 Communications Software

Through a modem and **communications software**, your microcomputer can easily connect you to a wealth of information available in public and private databases. For example, several executives in different states or countries can work expeditiously on the same report by using communications software. The report is sent back and forth on computer to each location until it is completed. Communications software and a modem also make remote data entry an easy task. A modem converts computer signals (digital signals) to signals transferable on a telephone line (analog signals). Some software packages, such as Symphony by Lotus, include a communications program within the package itself. However, there are many communications software products on the market, among them Crosstalk

(Microstuf, Inc.), On-Line (Micro-Systems Software, Inc.), Pfs: Access (Software Publishing Corp.), and Smartcom II (Hayes Microcomputer Products, Inc.).

1–9–7   Desktop Publishing Software

Desktop publishing software allows you to produce professional-quality documents (with or without graphics) using relatively inexpensive hardware and software. All you need is a PC, a desktop publishing software package, and a laser or letter-quality printer. Desktop publishing has evolved as a result of three major factors: inexpensive PCs, inexpensive laser printers, and sophisticated and easy-to-use software.

With desktop publishing software, you can produce high-quality screen output and then transfer it to a printer—what you see is what you get (WYSIWYG). Today, newsletters, brochures, training manuals, transparencies, posters, and books are produced by means of desktop publishing.

Several desktop publishing software packages are available on the market. Pagemaker (Aldus) and Ventura Publisher (Xerox Corporation) are two popular ones. See Figure 1–11 for some of the output of desktop publishing software.

1–9–8   Financial Planning Software

Financial planning software works with large amounts of data and performs diverse financial analyses. These analyses include present value, future value, rate of return, cash flow analyses, depreciation analyses, and budgeting analyses. There are several packages for financial planning on the market. Among them are DTFPS (Desk Top Financial Solutions, Inc.), Excel (Microsoft), Finar (Finar Research Systems, Ltd.), Javelin (Javelin Software Corporation), Micro-DSS/Finance (Addison-Wesley Publishing Co.), Lotus 1-2-3 (Lotus), Quattro Pro (Borland), IFPS (Comshare), and Micro Plan (Chase Laboratories, Inc.).

Using these packages, you can plan and analyze your financial situation. For example, you can determine how much your $2,000 IRA will be worth at 5 percent interest in 30 years. Or, you can discount all future cash flows into today's dollars. You will know how much you have to deposit in the bank to have $90,000 in 10 years for your child's education.

1–9–9   Accounting Software

In addition to spreadsheet software which has widespread applications in the accounting field, there are dedicated **accounting software** packages that are able to perform many accounting tasks. The tasks performed by such software include general ledgers, account receivables, account payables, payrolls, balance sheets, and income statements. Depending on the price, these software packages vary in sophistication. Some of the popular accounting software packages are Business Works PC (Manzanita Software Systems), 4-in-1 Basic Accounting (Real World Corporation), Peachtree (Peachtree Software, Inc.), and DacEasy Accounting (Dac Software, Inc.).

1–9–10   Project Management Software

A project consists of a series of related activities. Building a house, designing an order entry system, or writing a thesis are examples of projects. The goal of **project management software** is to help decision makers keep time and budget under control by resolving scheduling problems. Project management software helps managers to plan and set achievable goals. Project management software highlights the bottlenecks and the relationships among different activities. This

A.

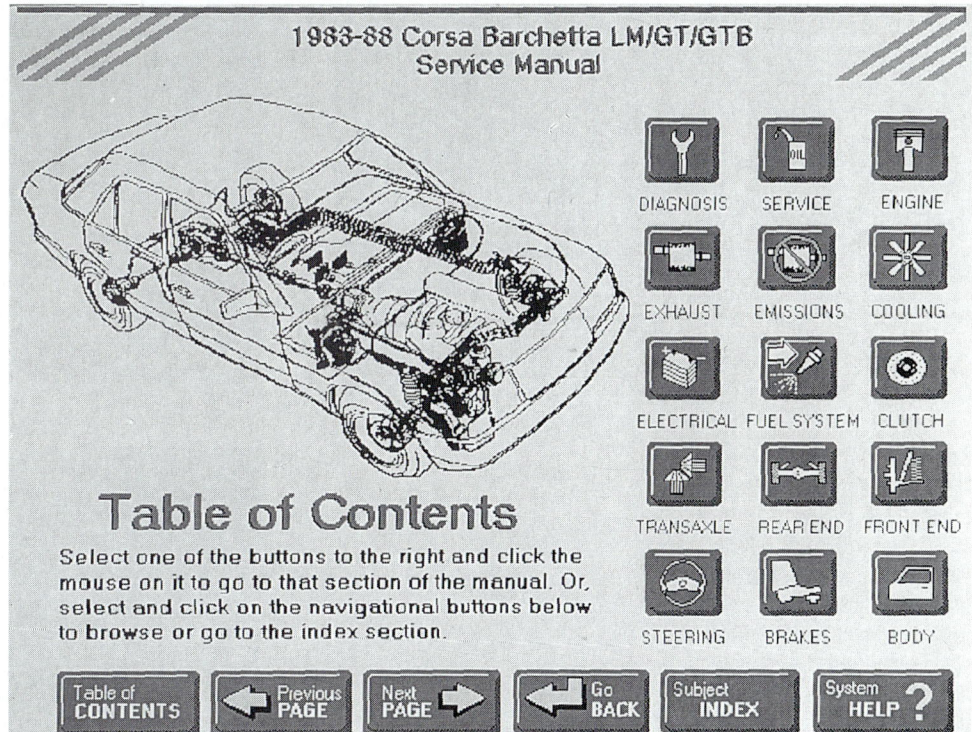

B.

Figure 1–11

Desktop publishing output. A. Desktop publishing combines text, graphics, and illustrations (courtesy of Aldus). B. With desktop publishing, business professionals can prepare high-quality documents on their own (courtesy of Ashton-Tate Corp.).

software allows the user to study the cost, time, and resource impacts of any change in the schedule. Several project management software packages are on the market: Harvard Total Project Manager (Software Publishing), Micro Planner 6 (Micro Planning International), Microsoft Project (Microsoft), Superproject Expert (Computer Associates) and Time Line (Symantec).

1–9–11

Computer-Aided Design (CAD) Software

Computer-aided design (CAD) software involves drafting and design. CAD software has replaced the traditional tools of drafting and design such as the T-square, triangle, and paper and pencil. It is used extensively in the architectural and engineering industries. CAD software no longer belongs only to large corporations. Because of the 386- and 486-based PCs and significant price reduction, small companies and individuals can afford this software. These new PCs have larger memory and are significantly faster than earlier PCs. With their enhanced power and sophistication, they are able to take advantage of most of the features offered by CAD programs. The home use of CAD software includes diverse architectural and engineering applications. There are several CAD programs on the market: AutoCAD (Autodesk), Cadkey (Cadkey), and VersaCAD (VersaCAD). See Figure 1–12 for some output from a CAD system.

A.

B.

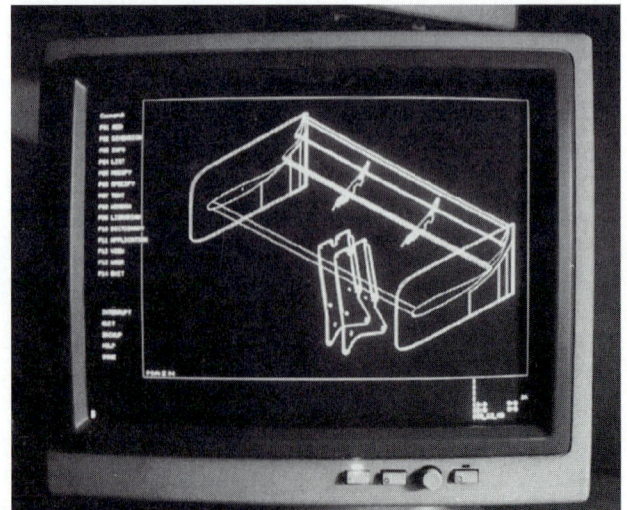
C.

Figure 1–12
A. CAD System for detailed architectural design (Larry Hamill/Macmillan). B. CAD system for design of a multicomponent product (courtesy of International Business Machines Corp.). C. CAD-supported design of aircraft landing gear (courtesy of International Business Machines Corp.).

1–9–12 Other Popular Software for Microcomputers

In addition to the 11 types of software just described, there are some others commonly used with microcomputers. Let us briefly consider them.

Utility software. These programs or utilities provide various DOS operations. Their goal is to simplify DOS operations for PC users. Depending on the sophistication of the program, various tasks are offered such as hard disk management, recovering a damaged disk or file, menu design, condensing a hard disk, and so forth.

Terminate & Stay Resident (TSR) Software. These programs are loaded when you start your PC and they stay in the background while other software applications are being used. TSR programs offer various features including screen printing, calendar, memo pad, and online calculator.

Investment Analysis Software. In addition to spreadsheet software, several other types of software are designed for investment analysis. By means of these programs, the user can track stocks, bonds, and other investment portfolios. Some of the programs are able to download financial data from public databases or stock exchanges. Others allow users to input their own financial data; then the programs perform financial analysis.

Tax Preparation software. This software assists a PC user in preparing taxes in a fairly straightforward manner. Some of the software packages enable the user to electronically download prepared tax forms to an IRS office.

Games software. Games probably form the oldest group of software for microcomputers, and they cover a broad range of activities. Although games are losing their popularity, they are still played by many PC users.

1–10 GUIDELINES FOR SUCCESSFUL SELECTION OF A MICROCOMPUTER

Because of the many microcomputers on the market, making a selection is a difficult task. The general guidelines provided here regarding the purchase and maintenance of a microcomputer may help you to choose a suitable computer and maintain it more easily.

Before you start the selection process, define your requirements. Sometimes this is called the "wish list" approach. You should have a clear idea of the type of microcomputer you *need* and the specific applications you want it to handle.

After you define your needs, think about software. Remember, if there is software on the market, there must be hardware to run it; but the reverse is not necessarily true. After defining the software and hardware you need and want, consider the technical support provided by vendors and reputation of vendors.

Important factors regarding selection and maintenance of a microcomputer are summarized next.

Software Selection

Good software should

- be easy to use
- be able to handle the business volume
- have good documentation
- have training available

- have updates available (free of charge or for a minimum charge)
- have local support
- come from a reputable vendor
- have a low cost

Hardware Selection (Processor and Keyboard)

Good hardware should

- have a comfortable keyboard
- have function keys
- have a general operating system (e.g., OS/2, MS-DOS, PC-DOS, Windows, or UNIX)
- have 16-bit or bigger processor (word) size
- have a high speed
- be expandable (memory and peripheral)
- have enough channel capacity or expansion slots (for attachment of peripherals)
- have a low cost

Hardware Selection (CRT)

A good monitor should

- have a separate CRT (not a built-in one)
- be easy to read (high resolution, super VGA or higher)
- have a standard number of characters per row and column

Hardware Selection (Disk Drive and Hard Disk)

A good disk drive should

- have a built-in, not separate, disk drive
- have adequate storage capacity (to load and run popular software)
- have a hard disk option

Hardware Selection (Printer)

A good printer should

- have a standard printer interface (without additional devices)
- produce high-quality output
- have high speed
- have a reasonable amount of noise suppression
- let you change tape, ribbons, or toner cartridge easily
- have a low cost

Vendor Selection

A good vendor should

- have a good reputation
- have a knowledgeable staff

- have training available for hardware and software
- have a hot line available
- support newsletters and user groups
- provide a "loaner" in case of breakdown
- provide updates (e.g., trade-in options)

Maintenance Contract Selection

A good contract should

- have a warranty period
- state a flexible time for repair
- limit downtime and inconvenience by providing flexible repair visits and timely repair of the computer
- have reasonable terms for contract renewal
- allow relocation and/or reassignment of the present contract
- observe confidentiality issues

1–11　TAKING CARE OF YOUR MICROCOMPUTER

To maintain the health of your microcomputer, consider the following factors:

- Protect your microcomputer against dirt, dust, and smoke.
- Make backup copies for security reasons and keep backups in different locations.
- Avoid any kind of liquid spills.
- Maintain steady power. Use surge protectors for power fluctuations and use lightning arresters in mountainous areas.
- Protect the system from static by using humidifiers or antistatic spray devices.
- Do not start your computer with a disk that you are not familiar with (avoid computer virus—the deadly program that erases and/or corrupts all your data).
- Do not download information to your computer from unknown bulletin boards. Downloading means importing information from other computers by using a modem and telephone line.
- Acquire insurance for your computer equipment.

1–12　ADVANTAGES OF MICROCOMPUTERS COMPARED WITH MAINFRAMES

Generally speaking, a microcomputer offers several advantages over a mainframe computer. Because of their extended memory and increased speed, microcomputers can perform many of the tasks performed by a mainframe but on a smaller scale. The advantages of microcomputers in comparison with mainframes follow:

- They are easier to use.
- They are less threatening to those who are not computer experts (e.g., they are smaller).
- They give the user more control.

- They are relatively inexpensive.
- They can be portable.

1–13   YOU AND YOUR PC: A HANDS-ON SESSION

If you place the DOS diskette or "boot disk" (disk that can be used to start the computer) in drive A, when you turn the computer on, your microcomputer will ask for the date. Remember, the majority of IBM or IBM-compatible systems come with a DOS disk. Either type the date in the desired format or press the Enter key to bypass the date. The computer then asks you for the time. Either type the time in the desired format or press the Enter key to bypass the time. Now you are at the A> prompt. This means your default drive is A.

If your computer has a hard disk, this start-up procedure is slightly different. You will get the system started from the hard disk and your prompt will be C> instead of A>. See Figure 1–13.

In any case, from this mode (the DOS mode), you can go to any application software.

For example, if the software (e.g., Lotus 1-2-3) is installed in the hard disk, use the DOS CD command to change to the directory that stores the software; then type *123* and press Enter. From the DOS mode, you can access any application software.

When you are at the C> prompt, you are in RAM. This area is called a working or temporary area. Any work you do in this area will disappear if you turn the computer off. To make your work permanent, you have to transfer it to a **permanent area**. The permanent area usually is either floppy disk or hard disk. Your work stays in the permanent area until you erase it.

While you are at the C> prompt, you can send any information to RAM by using the keyboard. This information can become permanent by saving it into a permanent medium. All application programs include a command for saving your work.

Beginning computer users are always worried about making mistakes! What happens if you make a mistake? Don't panic. Your mistake can be corrected easily. Some application programs have an UNDO command. If you realize you have made a mistake, you can recover from it by using the UNDO feature. All application programs include a feature for correcting mistakes. In the worst case, you can retype the correct statement over your previous material. Remember, any address (or cell) in the computer memory can hold only one value at a time. As soon as you type and enter a new value, the old one disappears.

1–14   WHAT IS A COMPUTER FILE?

A **computer file** is basically an electronic document. One way to create a document is to type and enter it using the keyboard. As soon as you save the document, you have generated a computer file.

To differentiate one file from another, you must save each file under a unique name—a file name. A file name is any combination of up to eight valid characters. Valid characters include letters of the alphabet (upper case or lower-

Figure 1–13
Getting the system started.

```
C>
```

case), digits 0 through 9, the underscore, and some special characters. If you provide a name longer than eight characters, some application programs give you an error message; others truncate the name and accept only the first eight characters.

In addition to a file name, a file is usually saved with a file extension. A file extension is similar to a file name but uses up to three characters. Some application programs automatically provide a file extension when you save the file. In other application programs, providing a file extension is the user's responsibility.

Several characters have special meanings in different application software. The asterisk (*) can represent any number of characters up to eight. The question mark (?) can represent any single character. These two characters are called wildcard characters. These **wildcards** can significantly improve your efficiency while you work with application programs. For example, all your Lotus 1-2-3 graphic files are identified by *.PIC. The * represents any file name and the PIC indicates that your file is a Lotus 1-2-3 graphic file. For example, if you want to copy all your Lotus 1-2-3 graphic files from the disk in drive A to the disk in drive B, type this DOS command at the A> prompt: *COPY *.PIC B:* (follow by pressing the Enter key). If you did not have this wildcard feature, you would have to repeat the COPY command as many times as the number of the graphic files. The file BRANCH?.* represents BRANCH1, BRANCH2, and so on. For example, in DOS if you type *DIR *.WK?* (and press Enter), your Lotus 1-2-3 files from version 1 and 1A (WKS) files, version 2 (WK1) files, version 3 (WK3) files, and student version (WKE) files will be displayed. The asterisk as the file extension indicates that the file can have any extension. Your entire disk can be identified by *.*. Using the COPY command, for example, at the A> prompt, to copy the entire disk in drive A to drive B, type *Copy *.* B:* (and press Enter).

1–15   TYPES OF DATA

Any application program or computer language accepts different types of data. The most commonly used data types are numeric and nonnumeric.

Numeric data include any combination of digits 0 through 9 and decimal points. Numeric data can be integer or real. Integer data include only whole numbers without any decimal points, for example, 656 or 986. Real data include digits and decimal points, for example, 696.25 or 729.793. Real data is sometimes called floating point data. Floating point means that the decimal point can move from right to left, for example, 222.2, 22.22, 2.222. Another type of real data is the fixed point, meaning that the decimal point is always fixed.

Nonnumeric data, or alphanumeric data, is sometimes called labels or strings. Any types of valid characters can be nonnumeric data, for example, Jackson or 123 Broadway Street. You cannot perform any arithmetic operations with nonnumeric data.

1–16   TYPES OF VALUES

Computers usually handle two types of values: variables and constants. **Variables** are valid computer addresses (locations) that hold different values at different times. For example, in A=65, A is the variable and 65 is the **constant.** B = "Brown": B is the variable and Brown is the constant. A variable holds a given value at any given time. As soon as you enter a new value into this variable, the old value disappears. The constant is always fixed. See Figure 1–14.

Figure 1–14
Example of a variable and a constant.

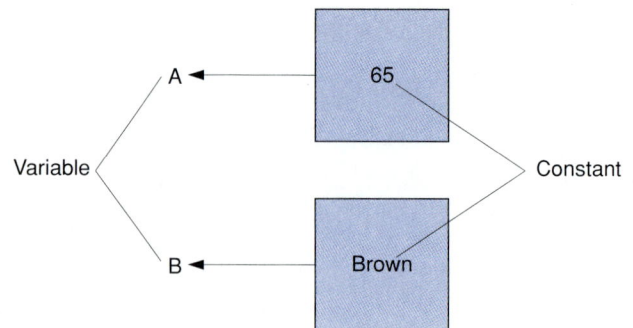

1–17   TYPES OF FORMULAS

Two types of formulas or functions are handled by computers: user-defined and built-in.

User-defined formulas or functions are a combination of computer addresses designed to perform a certain task. For example, the area of a triangle can be presented as A = B*H/2 (meaning base multiplied by height divided by 2). In this case, A is a formula or a function. When you enter different values for B and H, and a different value for A, the area of the triangle, will be calculated.

Built-in formulas or functions are already available within the application program or the computer language. As soon as the user provides values for a given variable or variables, the application program or the computer language dynamically calculates these formulas. For example, SQRT(X) is a function that calculates the square root of a variable, X. The X and any other information needed by these functions are called arguments. As soon as you provide a value for X, the square root is calculated; for example, SQRT(25) is equal to 5. The function FV(payment,interest rate,term) calculates the future value of a series of equal payments with a given interest rate over a period of time (term). This function can help you determine, for example, the future value of an IRA in which you plan to invest $2,000 for 30 years at a 10 percent interest rate.

1–18   PRIORITY OF ARITHMETIC OPERATIONS

When application programs perform arithmetic operations, they follow a series of rules. The rules for priority of arithmetic operations are as follows:

1. Expressions inside parentheses have the highest priority.
2. Exponentiation (raising to power) has the next highest priority.
3. Multiplication and division have the third highest priority.
4. Addition and subtraction have the fourth highest priority.
5. When there are two or more operations with the same priority, operations proceed from left to right.

The following examples should make the rules clear. First, an application program uses * (asterisk) for multiplication, ^ (caret) for exponentiation (raising the power), and / (slash) for division. If A=5, B=10, C=2, calculate the following:

$$A+B/C \quad = \quad 10$$
$$(A+B)/C \quad = \quad 7.5$$

$$A*B/C \quad = \quad 25$$
$$(A*B)/C \quad = \quad 25$$
$$A\char`^ C/2 \quad = \quad 12.50$$

SUMMARY

This chapter focused on microcomputers in general. Input, output, and primary and secondary memory devices for microcomputers were described. The general capabilities of microcomputers were introduced. The chapter presented a series of guidelines for successful selection and maintenance of a microcomputer. It also listed the advantages of micros over mainframes. A hands-on session included the basics for getting started as a computer user. The chapter concluded with a definition of computer files, types of data, types of values, types of formulas, and priority of arithmetic operations.

REVIEW QUESTIONS

*These questions are answered in Appendix A.

1. What is a microcomputer? What are some of the capabilities of a micro?
*2. What are some typical input devices for a micro?
3. What are some typical output devices for a micro?
4. Explain the difference between a primary memory device and a secondary memory device.
5. What is RAM? ROM? PROM? EPROM?
*6. What are the most commonly used secondary storage devices for a micro?
7. What is extended memory? What is expanded memory?
8. Describe optical technologies. What are their advantages and disadvantages?
9. How do you measure the memory capacity of a micro?
10. Besides memory, what other attributes are important when you buy a micro?
11. What is the difference between a floppy disk and a hard disk?
12. Give the speed range for a typical microcomputer.
*13. What is the memory size of a typical micro?
14. What is a good software?
15. What is a good hardware?
16. What is a good maintenance contract? Who are the good vendors?
*17. How should you care for your micro?
18. List some application programs for a micro.
19. What are some of the advantages of a micro compared with a mainframe?
20. What is permanent memory in a PC? What is temporary memory?
21. How do you send information from RAM to a floppy or hard disk?
*22. How do you correct your mistakes?
23. Define a computer file.
24. What is a wildcard character?
25. Describe different types of data.
26. What is a variable? What is a constant?
*27. What is the priority of arithmetic operations?
28. List the symbols used for arithmetic operations.
29. Turn on a PC. What do you see? Turn it off. Insert the DOS disk in drive A and turn the computer back on. What do you see this time?

30. Enter the correct date and time in your computer. What happens if you make a mistake?

31. Type *DIR* and press the Enter key. What is displayed at this time?

32. What types of PCs do you have on your campus? Describe different input/output devices used by the PCs in your school's micro lab. Do you have a Bernoulli box in the lab? What are some of the advantages of Bernoulli box over a hard disk?

33. What are the most commonly used disks on your campus—3½ or 5¼? Compare and contrast these two types of storage devices.

34. Consult computer magazines to find out which computers use optical disks.

35. Which of the types of software packages introduced in this chapter are available on your campus? What are the applications of each?

36. If you want to buy a PC for personal use, how should you start shopping? What attributes makes a PC attractive?

KEY TERMS

Accounting software	EPROM	Personal computer (PC)
Arithmetic logic unit (ALU)	Erasable optical disk	Primary memory
	Expanded memory	Priority of arithmetic operations
Bernoulli box	Extended memory	
Built-in formulas or functions	Financial planning software	Project management software
Central processing unit (CPU)	Floppy disk	PROM
	Grammar checker software	Random-access memory (RAM)
CD-ROM	Graphics software	
Communications software	Hard disk	RGB monitor
Computer-aided design (CAD) software	Input device	Read-only memory (ROM)
	Main memory	Secondary memory
Computer file	Micro	Spreadsheet software
Constants	Microcomputer	User-defined formulas or functions
Control unit	Nonnumeric data	
Conventional memory	Numeric data	Variables
Database software	Output device	Wildcard
Desktop publishing software	Permanent area	Word processing software
		WORM disk

ARE YOU READY TO MOVE ON?

Multiple Choice

1. Choose the correct ranking of monitor display resolutions from lowest to highest.
   a. VGA, CGA, XGA
   b. EGA, VGA, CGA
   c. EGA, CGA, VGA
   d. CGA, EGA, XGA
   e. XGA, CGA, EGA

2. Which of the following is *not* a typical adapter card?
   a. printer interface card
   b. clock card

    c. disk drive card
    d. display card
    e. punch card

3. Of the following types of main memory, which can the user control directly?

    a. ROM
    b. REM
    c. RAM
    d. PROM
    e. all of the above

4. What is now the most commonly used secondary storage device?

    a. 5¼ inch floppy disk and a hard disk
    b. 3½ inch floppy disk and a hard disk
    c. Bernoulli box and a hard disk
    d. hard disk with no floppy disk
    e. none of the above

5. What is the major advantage of optical storage technology?

    a. storage capacity
    b. cost
    c. durability
    d. both A and C
    e. all of the above

6. When we refer to memory and storage capacity sizes, we use kilobytes (as in 360 K). 1 K equals approximately

    a. 1 byte
    b. 1,000 bytes
    c. 1,000,000 bytes
    d. 1,048,576 bytes
    e. none of the above

7. Word size directly affects

    a. the speed of the computer
    b. the ability of the user to understand what is being said
    c. the maximum amount of data that can be displayed on the CRT
    d. the choice of which type of disk drive to use
    e. the meaning of the function keys on the keyboard

8. Which of the following are disadvantages of mainframes when compared with microcomputers?

    a. They are more difficult to use.
    b. They are more threatening to users who are not computer experts.
    c. The user has less control.
    d. They are relatively more expensive.
    e. All of the above are disadvantages.

9. After booting the computer with the DOS disk (loading DOS and entering the date and time), you are at

    a. the Lotus Access menu
    b. the DOS prompt (A> or C>)
    c. the parallel/serial interface
    d. the BASIC prompt
    e. none of the above

10. An example of alphanumeric data would be

    a. 123
    b. 123.25
    c. LOTUS-123
    d. A=(123-2)/4
    e. none of the above

True/False

1. The terms *personal computer*, PC, and *microcomputer* refer to different types of computers.
2. A typical microcomputer consists of input, output, and memory devices.
3. Monochrome CRTs cannot generate graphic output.
4. The purpose of function keys and special keys on a computer keyboard does not vary in different application programs.
5. The capacity of a hard disk is greater than the capacity of a floppy disk.
6. A WORM disk can be recorded and erased repeatedly when high-volume storage and updating are essential.
7. Typical microcomputer software packages and applications include spreadsheet, database, graphics, communications, and word processing.
8. The first step in selecting a microcomputer is to define your needs; then think about software.
9. The commands DIR *.* and DIR ????????.??? produce the same results.
10. Expressions inside parentheses have the lowest priority when it comes to performing arithmetic operations.

ANSWERS

Multiple Choice		True/False	
1.	d	1.	F
2.	e	2.	T
3.	c	3.	F
4.	b	4.	F
5.	d	5.	T
6.	b	6.	F
7.	a	7.	T
8.	e	8.	T
9.	b	9.	T
10.	c	10.	F

A Quick Trip with MS-DOS and PC-DOS

2

2–1   INTRODUCTION

This chapter describes the basics of the Disk Operating System (DOS). The differences between internal and external DOS commands are explained as are the features of system date and time. After file specifications in the DOS environment are reviewed, the DIR command for generating a directory listing is discussed. Next, important keys in the DOS environment and the FORMAT command for creating a usable data disk are highlighted. Other DOS basics covered are the different versions of MS-DOS and PC-DOS, batch and AUTOEXEC files, the process of creating a directory, and commands for directories. Both DOS 5.0 and 6.0 are presented in general. A most useful feature of the chapter is a table summarizing important DOS commands.

2–2   TURNING ON YOUR PC

When you access a personal computer in a computer lab or any other location, the computer is either off or on. This text assumes that your computer has a hard disk and that the Disk Operating System (DOS) files are stored in drive C in the hard disk. DOS disks come with the computer when it is purchased.

Turn the computer on. This procedure is called **cold boot**. Boot means getting the computer started. If the computer is already turned on, press the Ctrl, Alt, and Del keys simultaneously. This procedure is called **warm boot**. The warm boot is faster than the cold boot, because the computer does not check its memory in a warm boot as it does in a cold boot.

If your computer does not have a hard disk and you want to start it from a floppy disk, insert the boot disk in drive A and turn the computer on. When the computer is booted from the floppy disk, it asks you to enter the current date. Type the date in the format requested (mm-dd-yy). After typing the current date, press the Enter key. Your PC now asks for the current time. Type the current time in the format requested (hh:mm:ss). (Note that DOS operates on a 24-hour clock, 2:30 p.m. is 14:30, 9:15 p.m. is 21:15, etc.) After typing the time, press the Enter key. Now you should see the A> prompt. This means the necessary portions of DOS have been loaded into primary memory (RAM) and drive A is the default drive. Default drive means that from this point on this is the drive the computer accesses for executing commands. For example, if you decide to save a file, your file will be saved onto the disk in this drive. If you ask for a directory listing, the directory of the disk in this drive will be highlighted. At this point, you should be able to access any internal or external DOS commands.

If your DOS is installed on the hard disk (which is usually the C drive), your default drive will be the C drive. In a computer with hard disk, the date and time are maintained internally, so you do not need to enter them at boot-up time.

If you boot-up from the floppy disk and do not want to enter the date and time, you can bypass the prompts by pressing the Enter key twice. When the prompts are bypassed, the PC uses the default date and time when saving files. It is a good practice to enter both the correct date and time when you start the PC, so all your programs and data files are saved with this current information. The correct date and time can help you to determine the most or least recent versions of your files listed in the directory. A **directory** is the listing of all your files.

If you forget to enter the current date and time at the boot-up time, or if the date and time of your system are not correct, you can enter this information at any given time by using the DATE and TIME commands. At the DOS prompt, type *DATE* and press the Enter key. The computer will ask you to enter the current date in the format mm-dd-yy. Type the date and press the Enter key. Now type *TIME* and press the Enter key. The computer will ask you to enter the current time in the format hh:mm:ss. After typing the current time, press the Enter key. At this point the computer registers this information in its memory, where it will remain and be updated automatically until you turn the PC off. Computers with a hard disk have a battery-operated clock on their motherboard. The motherboard is where the computer's primary electronic circuitry resides. The date and time are maintained automatically, and user intervention is not required except for correcting the date or time.

Internal commands (sometimes called memory resident commands) are those commands that are loaded into the computer's memory at boot-up time. As soon as you see a DOS prompt such as A> or B> or C>, you can execute any internal command. Internal commands can be used without the DOS disk in any disk drive. CLS (clear screen) is an example of a DOS internal command. If at the DOS prompt you type *CLS* and press the Enter key, the screen will be erased.

External commands (sometimes called non-memory resident commands) are those commands that can only be executed by having the DOS disk in one of the drives. These commands are sometimes called DOS utilities. They are separate programs stored on the DOS disk. For example, DISKCOPY (generates a duplicate of a disk) is an external DOS command. A listing of most of these commands appears at the end of the chapter.

2–3   DIFFERENT DOS PROMPTS

Depending on how you get your PC started, you will see different prompts. If you have a hard disk in your system and you start the system from the hard disk, your prompt may be C>. The prompt indicates the current default drive. The default drive is the disk drive that the PC will access if no other disk drive is specified. If a file is located on a disk that is not in the default drive, the default must be changed or the disk drive containing the file must be specified. Changing the default is an easy task. At the C> prompt type *A:* (remember the colon) and press the Enter key. Now the prompt is A>. You can change this back to C> by typing *C:* and pressing the Enter key. The prompt can be customized by using the PROMPT PG command followed by pressing Enter. This command is useful when you use directories (discussed later in this chapter). By using this command, you know in which drive and/or directory you are at any given time.

2–4   DOS FILE SPECIFICATIONS

DOS files basically follow the same conventions that apply to other software. This means **file names** can be up to eight characters long. File names can contain digits 0 through 9 and some special characters such as underscore (_), pound sign (#), and so forth. To be on the safe side, limit the use of special characters in file names and do not use any space in a file name.

File extensions can be up to three characters long and contain the same characters used by file names. For example, TEST.TEX is a valid file name. Important file extensions in the DOS environment include these:

- BAK (backup): This extension indicates files generated by some word processing, spreadsheet, and database management programs; the files are backup copies of the original files.
- BAT (batch): This indicates a text file generated by the user. The file includes DOS commands and statements that are executed when the name of the file is typed.
- COM (command): This extension identifies files that can be executed by typing the name of the file.
- EXE (executable): Like COM files, files with this extension can be executed by typing the file name.
- SYS (system): This extension identifies files that can be used only by DOS.

2–5   DIR COMMAND

With DOS files installed in the hard disk, you can generate a listing of your current directory by using the DIR command. Type *DIR* and press the Enter key; information similar to Figure 2–1 will be presented to you. At the top of Figure 2–1, the listing indicates the volume in drive C is MS-DOS_6. This is the internal name for this disk. The LABEL command allows you to change this name. To do this, at the C> prompt type *LABEL* and press Enter. Specify the new label (name) of up to 11 characters and press Enter. From now on the internal name of this drive will be the name that you just specified.

The DIR command provides the name of each file, the file extension, the size of the file in bytes, and the date and time that the file was created or changed. At the end of the listing, the DIR command tells you the number of the files and the amount of bytes available on this particular disk. To erase the screen, type *CLS* and press the Enter key. To generate a listing for drive A, type *DIR A:* and press Enter. A listing of drive B can be created by typing *DIR B:* followed by pressing Enter.

The DIR command can be used with wildcard characters. Wildcard characters function as placeholders for other characters in the file name or file extension. The two valid DOS wildcards are the * (asterisk) and the ? (question mark). The asterisk replaces one or more characters in the file name or extension with any valid character. For example, *.COM refers to any file name with the extension COM. The question mark replaces only one character in the file name or extension with a valid character. For example, entering DIR *.COM displays all COM files. DIR *.PIC displays all Lotus 1-2-3 graphic files. DIR *.AB? displays any file that has AB as the first two letters of its extension, while the third character can be any valid character. DIR *.WK? displays Lotus WK1, WKS, WKE, or WK3 files. WKS are Lotus 1-2-3 files before Release 2.0, WK1 are Lotus release 2.0 and 2.01, 2.2, 2.3 and 2.4 files, WKE are Lotus 1-2-3 files in the student version of the software, and WK3 are Lotus 1-2-3 files in Release 3 or higher. It also displays Quattro Pro WKQ files.

2–6   DIR WITH DIFFERENT SWITCHES

The DIR command can be used with different switches (parameters) to provide different types of listings. DIR/W provides a wide directory; this means you get a horizontal listing of your directory. In this case, only file names and extensions

Figure 2–1
Directory listing of MS-DOS 6.

```
Volume in drive C is MS_DOS_6
Volume Serial Number is 1C22-913B
Directory of C:\DOS

.               <DIR>         06-06-92    12:24p
..              <DIR>         06-06-92    12:24p
DBLSPACE BIN       51214      03-10-93     6:00a
FORMAT   COM       22717      03-10-93     6:00a
NLSFUNC  EXE        7036      03-10-93     6:00a
COUNTRY  SYS       17066      03-10-93     6:00a
KEYB     COM       14983      03-10-93     6:00a
KEYBOARD SYS       34694      03-10-93     6:00a
SETUP    EXE       71974      03-10-93     6:00a
DOSSETUP INI        3735      03-10-93     6:00a
ANSI     SYS        9065      03-10-93     6:00a
ATTRIB   EXE       11165      03-10-93     6:00a
CHKDSK   EXE       12907      03-10-93     6:00a
EDIT     COM         413      03-10-93     6:00a
EXPAND   EXE       16129      03-10-93     6:00a
EDLIN    EXE       12642      06-13-91     5:00a
MORE     COM        2546      03-10-93     6:00a
MSD      EXE      158470      03-10-93     6:00a
QBASIC   EXE      194309      03-10-93     6:00a
RESTORE  EXE       38294      03-10-93     6:00a
MIRROR   COM       18169      06-13-91     5:00a
SYS      COM        9379      03-10-93     6:00a
UNFORMAT COM       12738      03-10-93     6:00a
SMARTDRV SYS        8335      06-13-91     5:00a
OS2      TXT        6358      03-10-93     6:00a
NETWORKS TXT       20463      03-10-93     6:00a
README   TXT       44990      03-10-93     6:00a
DEBUG    EXE       15715      03-10-93     6:00a
FDISK    EXE       29333      03-10-93     6:00a
DOSSHELL VID        9462      03-10-93     6:00a
19C1DOSC BAT          16      01-23-93     3:05p
DEFAULT  SET        4207      01-02-94    10:49a
DOSSHELL GRB        4421      03-10-93     6:00a
CHOICE   COM        1754      03-10-93     6:00a
DEFRAG   EXE       75033      03-10-93     6:00a
PACKING  LST        2507      06-13-91     5:00a
DEFRAG   HLP        9227      03-10-93     6:00a
DOSSWAP  EXE       18756      03-10-93     6:00a
EGA      CPI       58870      03-10-93     6:00a
RECOVER  EXE        9146      06-13-91     5:00a
EGA      SYS        4885      03-10-93     6:00a
HIMEM    SYS       14208      03-10-93     6:00a
MEM      EXE       32150      03-10-93     6:00a
XCOPY    EXE       15820      03-10-93     6:00a
MONEY    BAS       46225      06-13-91     5:00a
MSHERC   COM        6934      06-13-91     5:00a
DELTREE  EXE       11113      03-10-93     6:00a
GORILLA  BAS       29434      06-13-91     5:00a
4201     CPI        6404      06-13-91     5:00a
4208     CPI         720      06-13-91     5:00a
5202     CPI         395      06-13-91     5:00a
MOVE     EXE       17823      03-10-93     6:00a
ASSIGN   COM        6399      06-13-91     5:00a
RAMDRIVE SYS        5873      03-10-93     6:00a
BACKUP   EXE       36092      06-13-91     5:00a
SMARTDRV EXE       42073      03-10-93     6:00a
COMP     EXE       14282      06-13-91     5:00a
```

Figure 2–1
(continued)

```
DISPLAY   SYS      15789  03-10-93    6:00a
DOSHELP   HLP       5667  03-10-93    6:00a
DOSSHELL  COM       4620  03-10-93    6:00a
DOSSHELL  EXE     236378  03-10-93    6:00a
FASTHELP  EXE      11481  03-10-93    6:00a
GRAFTABL  COM      11205  06-13-91    5:00a
FASTOPEN  EXE      12034  03-10-93    6:00a
HELP      HLP     294741  03-10-93    6:00a
HELP      COM        413  03-10-93    6:00a
NIBBLES   BAS      24103  06-13-91    5:00a
REMLINE   BAS      12314  06-13-91    5:00a
MODE      COM      23521  03-10-93    6:00a
POWER     EXE       8052  03-10-93    6:00a
EXE2BIN   EXE       8424  06-13-91    5:00a
PRINT     EXE      15640  03-10-93    6:00a
JOIN      EXE      17870  06-13-91    5:00a
LCD       CPI      10753  06-13-91    5:00a
QBASIC    HLP     130881  03-10-93    6:00a
PRINTER   SYS      18804  06-13-91    5:00a
SHARE     EXE      10912  03-10-93    6:00a
DELOLDOS  EXE      17710  03-10-93    6:00a
SETVER    EXE      12015  03-10-93    6:00a
APPEND    EXE      10774  03-10-93    6:00a
APPNOTES  TXT       8660  06-13-91    5:00a
KEYBHP    COM      15997  06-13-91    5:00a
MODEHP    COM      23232  06-13-91    5:00a
SSTOR     SYS      37260  06-13-91    5:00a
DISKCOMP  COM      10620  03-10-93    6:00a
MOUSE     SYS      32730  06-13-91    5:00a
DISKCOPY  COM      11879  03-10-93    6:00a
B         BAT         46  06-06-92    1:53p
589DOSCM  BAT         16  01-23-93    3:01p
D5C0DOSC  BAT         16  01-23-93    6:49p
2688DOSC  BAT         16  01-23-93    3:08p
370CDOSC  BAT         16  01-23-93    4:12p
D923DOSC  BAT         16  01-23-93    5:50p
BA6EDOSC  BAT         16  01-23-93    6:43p
D329DOSC  BAT         16  01-23-93    6:49p
DRIVER    SYS       5406  03-10-93    6:00a
FC        EXE      18650  03-10-93    6:00a
FIND      EXE       6770  03-10-93    6:00a
GRAPHICS  COM      19694  03-10-93    6:00a
GRAPHICS  PRO      21232  03-10-93    6:00a
LABEL     EXE       9390  03-10-93    6:00a
SMARTMON  EXE      28672  03-10-93    6:00a
SMARTMON  HLP      10727  03-10-93    6:00a
SORT      EXE       6922  03-10-93    6:00a
LOADFIX   COM       1131  03-10-93    6:00a
MWBACKUP  EXE     309696  03-10-93    6:00a
MWBACKUP  HLP     400880  03-10-93    6:00a
REPLACE   EXE      20226  03-10-93    6:00a
SUBST     EXE      18478  03-10-93    6:00a
TREE      COM       6898  03-10-93    6:00a
DOSKEY    COM       5883  03-10-93    6:00a
VFINTD    386       5295  03-10-93    6:00a
MWBACKF   DLL      14560  03-10-93    6:00a
MWBACKR   DLL     111120  03-10-93    6:00a
MOUSE     COM      56408  03-10-93    6:00a
MSBACKUP  EXE       5506  03-10-93    6:00a
MSBACKUP  OVL     133952  03-10-93    6:00a
MSBACKFB  OVL      69066  03-10-93    6:00a
```

Figure 2–1
(continued)

```
MSBACKFR OVL      72474 03-10-93     6:00a
CHKSTATE SYS      41600 03-10-93     6:00a
UNDELETE EXE      26420 03-10-93     6:00a
MWUNDEL  EXE     130496 03-10-93     6:00a
MWUNDEL  HLP      35741 03-10-93     6:00a
MWGRAFIC DLL      36944 03-10-93     6:00a
MSBACKUP HLP     314236 03-10-93     6:00a
WNTOOLS  GRP       2205 01-02-94     6:25p
MSBACKDB OVL      63098 03-10-93     6:00a
MSBACKDR OVL      66906 03-10-93     6:00a
MSBCONFG OVL      47210 03-10-93     6:00a
MSBCONFG HLP      45780 03-10-93     6:00a
DBLSPACE EXE     274388 03-10-93     6:00a
MEMMAKER INF       1652 03-10-93     6:00a
INTERLNK EXE      17197 03-10-93     6:00a
INTERSVR EXE      37314 03-10-93     6:00a
MSCDEX   EXE      25377 03-10-93     6:00a
DBLSPACE HLP      72169 03-10-93     6:00a
DBLSPACE INF       2178 03-10-93     6:00a
DBLSPACE SYS        339 03-10-93     6:00a
DBLWIN   HLP       8597 03-10-93     6:00a
DOSSHELL HLP     161323 03-10-93     6:00a
EMM386   EXE     115294 03-10-93     6:00a
MEMMAKER EXE     118660 03-10-93     6:00a
SIZER    EXE       7169 03-10-93     6:00a
MONOUMB  386       8783 03-10-93     6:00a
MSTOOLS  DLL      13424 03-10-93     6:00a
MSAV     EXE     172198 03-10-93     6:00a
MSAV     HLP      23891 03-10-93     6:00a
MSAVHELP OVL      29828 03-10-93     6:00a
MSAVIRUS LST      35520 03-10-93     6:00a
VSAFE    COM      62576 03-10-93     6:00a
MWAVDOSL DLL      44736 03-10-93     6:00a
MWAVDRVL DLL       7744 03-10-93     6:00a
AUTOEXEC UMB        703 01-01-94     5:34p
MOUSE    INI         28 01-01-94     5:34p
CONFIG   UMB        142 01-01-94     5:34p
MEMMAKER STS        851 01-01-94     5:40p
MWAVDLG  DLL      36368 03-10-93     6:00a
MSBACKUP INI         43 01-03-94     4:46p
MWAVSCAN DLL     151568 03-10-93     6:00a
MSBACKUP RST        608 04-13-92     7:07a
MSBACKUP TMP       5014 01-02-94    10:49a
MWAV     EXE     142640 03-10-93     6:00a
MWAVABSI DLL      54576 03-10-93     6:00a
MWAV     HLP      24619 03-10-93     6:00a
MWAVSOS  DLL       7888 03-10-93     6:00a
MWAVMGR  DLL      21712 03-10-93     6:00a
MWAVTSR  EXE      17328 03-10-93     6:00a
COMMAND  COM      52925 03-10-93     6:00a
MSAV     INI          0 01-01-94     3:01p
DEFAULT  BAK       4207 01-02-94     9:56a
MSBACKUP LOG     196811 01-02-94    10:54a
DEFAULT  SLT         64 01-02-94    10:49a
DEFAULT  SAV         64 01-02-94     9:56a
DOSSHELL INI      16424 01-02-94     1:02p
       176 file(s)    6563296 bytes
                    129966080 bytes free

C>
```

are listed. Figure 2–2 was generated by typing *DIR/W* at the C> prompt and pressing the Enter key. *DIR/P* gives you one screen of the file listing. At the bottom of the screen, a prompt tells you to strike a key to see another screen. Figure 2–3 was generated by typing *DIR/P* at the C> prompt and pressing the Enter key. (Notice that this is a partial listing.)

The DIR command enables you to get a listing of files in any drive by specifying the drive. For example, say the current drive is A; type *DIR B:/W* to display a wide directory of drive B. There must be at least one space between the DIR command and a drive name when you issue the command. Remember, to execute any DOS command, you must press Enter after typing the command.

```
C>DIR/W

  Volume in drive C is MS_DOS_6
  Volume Serial Number is 1C22-913B
  Directory of C:\DOS

[.]              [..]             DBLSPACE.BIN     FORMAT.COM       NLSFUNC.EXE
COUNTRY.SYS      KEYB.COM         KEYBOARD.SYS     SETUP.EXE        DOSSETUP.INI
ANSI.SYS         ATTRIB.EXE       CHKDSK.EXE       EDIT.COM         EXPAND.EXE
EDLIN.EXE        MORE.COM         MSD.EXE          QBASIC.EXE       RESTORE.EXE
MIRROR.COM       SYS.COM          UNFORMAT.COM     SMARTDRV.SYS     OS2.TXT
NETWORKS.TXT     README.TXT       DEBUG.EXE        FDISK.EXE        DOSSHELL.VID
19C1DOSC.BAT     DEFAULT.SET      DOSSHELL.GRB     CHOICE.COM       DEFRAG.EXE
PACKING.LST      DEFRAG.HLP       DOSSWAP.EXE      EGA.CPI          RECOVER.EXE
EGA.SYS          HIMEM.SYS        MEM.EXE          XCOPY.EXE        MONEY.BAS
MSHERC.COM       DELTREE.EXE      GORILLA.BAS      4201.CPI         4208.CPI
5202.CPI         MOVE.EXE         ASSIGN.COM       RAMDRIVE.SYS     BACKUP.EXE
SMARTDRV.EXE     COMP.EXE         DISPLAY.SYS      DOSHELP.HLP      DOSSHELL.COM
DOSSHELL.EXE     FASTHELP.EXE     GRAFTABL.COM     EDIT.HLP         FASTOPEN.EXE
HELP.HLP         HELP.COM         NIBBLES.BAS      REMLINE.BAS      MODE.COM
POWER.EXE        EXE2BIN.EXE      PRINT.EXE        JOIN.EXE         LCD.CPI
QBASIC.HLP       PRINTER.SYS      SHARE.EXE        DELOLDOS.EXE     SETVER.EXE
APPEND.EXE       APPNOTES.TXT     KEYBHP.COM       MODEHP.COM       SSTOR.SYS
DISKCOMP.COM     MOUSE.SYS        DISKCOPY.COM     B.BAT            589DOSCM.BAT
D5C0DOSC.BAT     2688DOSC.BAT     370CDOSC.BAT     D923DOSC.BAT     BA6EDOSC.BAT
D329DOSC.BAT     DRIVER.SYS       FC.EXE           FIND.EXE         GRAPHICS.COM
GRAPHICS.PRO     LABEL.EXE        SMARTMON.EXE     SMARTMON.HLP     SORT.EXE
LOADFIX.COM      MWBACKUP.EXE     MWBACKUP.HLP     REPLACE.EXE      SUBST.EXE
TREE.COM         DOSKEY.COM       VFINTD.386       MWBACKF.DLL      MWBACKR.DLL
MOUSE.COM        MSBACKUP.EXE     MSBACKUP.OVL     MSBACKFB.OVL     MSBACKFR.OVL
CHKSTATE.SYS     UNDELETE.EXE     MWUNDEL.EXE      MWUNDEL.HLP      MWGRAFIC.DLL
MSBACKUP.HLP     WNTOOLS.GRP      MSBACKDB.OVL     MSBACKDR.OVL     MSBCONFG.OVL
MSBCONFG.HLP     DBLSPACE.EXE     MEMMAKER.HLP     MEMMAKER.INF     INTERLNK.EXE
INTERSVR.EXE     MSCDEX.EXE       DBLSPACE.HLP     DBLSPACE.INF     DBLSPACE.SYS
DBLWIN.HLP       DOSSHELL.HLP     EMM386.EXE       MEMMAKER.EXE     SIZER.EXE
MONOUMB.386      MSTOOLS.DLL      MSAV.EXE         MSAV.HLP         MSAVHELP.OVL
MSAVIRUS.LST     VSAFE.COM        MWAVDOSL.DLL     MWAVDRVL.DLL     AUTOEXEC.UMB
MOUSE.INI        CONFIG.UMB       MEMMAKER.STS     MWAVDLG.DLL      MSBACKUP.INI
MWAVSCAN.DLL     MSBACKUP.RST     MSBACKUP.TMP     MWAV.EXE         MWAVABSI.DLL
MWAV.HLP         MWAVSOS.DLL      MWAVMGR.DLL      MWAVTSR.EXE      COMMAND.COM
MSAV.INI         DEFAULT.BAK      MSBACKUP.LOG     DEFAULT.SLT      DEFAULT.SAV
DOSSHELL.INI
       176 file(s)      6563296 bytes
                      129966080 bytes free

C>
```

Figure 2–2
Directory listing with DIR/W command.

Figure 2–3
Directory listing with DIR/P command.

```
C>DIR/P

 Volume in drive C is MS_DOS_6
 Volume Serial Number is 1C22-913B
 Directory of C:\DOS

 .              <DIR>         06-06-92   12:24p
 ..             <DIR>         06-06-92   12:24p
 DBLSPACE BIN      51214      03-10-93    6:00a
 FORMAT   COM      22717      03-10-93    6:00a
 NLSFUNC  EXE       7036      03-10-93    6:00a
 COUNTRY  SYS      17066      03-10-93    6:00a
 KEYB     COM      14983      03-10-93    6:00a
 KEYBOARD SYS      34694      03-10-93    6:00a
 SETUP    EXE      71974      03-10-93    6:00a
 DOSSETUP INI       3735      03-10-93    6:00a
 ANSI     SYS       9065      03-10-93    6:00a
 ATTRIB   EXE      11165      03-10-93    6:00a
 CHKDSK   EXE      12907      03-10-93    6:00a
 EDIT     COM        413      03-10-93    6:00a
 EXPAND   EXE      16129      03-10-93    6:00a
 EDLIN    EXE      12642      06-13-91    5:00a
 MORE     COM       2546      03-10-93    6:00a
 MSD      EXE     158470      03-10-93    6:00a
 QBASIC   EXE     194309      03-10-93    6:00a
 Press any key to continue . . .

 (continuing C:\DOS)
 RESTORE  EXE      38294      03-10-93    6:00a
 MIRROR   COM      18169      06-13-91    5:00a
 SYS      COM       9379      03-10-93    6:00a
 UNFORMAT COM      12738      03-10-93    6:00a
 SMARTDRV SYS       8335      06-13-91    5:00a
 OS2      TXT       6358      03-10-93    6:00a
 NETWORKS TXT      20463      03-10-93    6:00a
 README   TXT      44990      03-10-93    6:00a
 DEBUG    EXE      15715      03-10-93    6:00a
 FDISK    EXE      29333      03-10-93    6:00a
 DOSSHELL VID       9462      03-10-93    6:00a
 19C1DOSC BAT         16      01-23-93    3:05p
 DEFAULT  SET       4207      01-02-94   10:49a
 DOSSHELL GRB       4421      03-10-93    6:00a
 CHOICE   COM       1754      03-10-93    6:00a
 DEFRAG   EXE      75033      03-10-93    6:00a
 PACKING  LST       2507      06-13-91    5:00a
 DEFRAG   HLP       9227      03-10-93    6:00a
 DOSSWAP  EXE      18756      03-10-93    6:00a
 EGA      CPI      58870      03-10-93    6:00a
 RECOVER  EXE       9146      06-13-91    5:00a
 EGA      SYS       4885      03-10-93    6:00a
 Press any key to continue . . .

 (continuing C:\DOS)
 HIMEM    SYS      14208      03-10-93    6:00a
 MEM      EXE      32150      03-10-93    6:00a
 XCOPY    EXE      15820      03-10-93    6:00a
 MONEY    BAS      46225      06-13-91    5:00a
 MSHERC   COM       6934      06-13-91    5:00a
 DELTREE  EXE      11113      03-10-93    6:00a
 GORILLA  BAS      29434      06-13-91    5:00a
 4201     CPI       6404      06-13-91    5:00a
 4208     CPI        720      06-13-91    5:00a
 5202     CPI        395      06-13-91    5:00a
 MOVE     EXE      17823      03-10-93    6:00a
 ASSIGN   COM       6399      06-13-91    5:00a
 RAMDRIVE SYS       5873      03-10-93    6:00a
 BACKUP   EXE      36092      06-13-91    5:00a
```

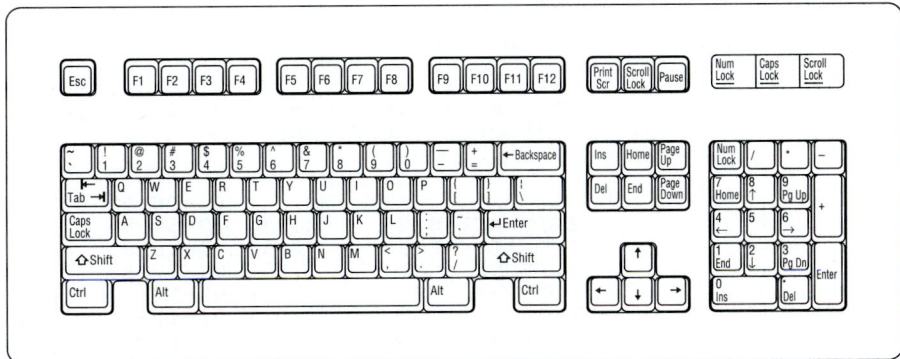

2–7   IMPORTANT KEYS IN DOS ENVIRONMENT

Examine the picture of a typical keyboard in Figure 2–4. Several of the keys perform special tasks in the DOS environment. Table 2–1 briefly explains these keys.

2–8   CREATING YOUR OWN DATA DISK: THE FORMAT COMMAND

Before using a newly purchased floppy disk on your PC, you must format the disk. To format a disk at the C> prompt insert a blank disk in drive A; type *FORMAT A:* and press the Enter key. When the process is finished, DOS asks you if you would like to format another disk. If you answer Y (for yes), you will be prompted to insert a new disk. If you answer N (for no), the C> prompt will return. Various computers use different versions of the FORMAT command. Consult your DOS manual for the specific version of the FORMAT command for your computer.

When you format a disk, the operating system checks your entire disk for defective spots. It tells you if your disk is usable or not. The FORMAT command also divides a disk into tracks and sectors and creates the *File Allocation Table* (FAT). The FAT indicates where data is saved on a disk.

When you format a disk, that disk is completely erased. Make sure the disk you are formatting is either a new disk or an old disk with files for which you have no need. Figure 2–5 shows the formatting procedure. At the C> prompt we typed *FORMAT A:*, pressed Enter, and followed the prompt.

You can format a disk in a different drive than A. For example, at the C> prompt type *FORMAT B:* and press the Enter key; the disk in drive B will be formatted.

Having a formatted disk at hand, you are ready to use it as a data disk or to copy other programs onto it.

2–9   DIFFERENT VERSIONS OF MS-DOS AND PC-DOS

PC-DOS is for IBM microcomputers and MS-DOS is for IBM compatibles. Both of these programs have gone through several revisions. The first version was 1.0 and the latest is version 6.0. Each version has added new commands and corrected some of the bugs in the earlier versions. Major enhancements occurred in version 3.0 and later versions. Versions 3.1 and later include commands for the local area network (LAN) environment. Minor revisions are indicated as .1, .2, and so on. Major revisions are indicated as 2, 3, and so forth.

Table 2–1
Special Keys on the Keyboard

Keys	Description
Backspace	Backs up and erases the character typed
Ctrl+Alt+Del	A key combination used to warm boot the system— equivalent to turning your computer off, then turning it back on (without memory check)
Ctrl+C or Ctrl+Break	Cancels a command while it is being executed (Note: Look for Break on the side of the Pause key.)
Ctrl+Print Scr or Ctrl+P	Sends a copy of each line on the screen to the printer as it is being displayed, assuming you are connected to a printer and the printer is on. This command toggles the printer on. (Toggle means the key combination remains in effect until you press Ctrl and PrtScr or P again.) When the printer is toggled on, everything displayed on the screen will be printed.
Ctrl+S or Ctrl+Num Lock	Pauses the directory listing for viewing
Esc	Erases the current command or statement
F1 (function key)	Displays one character of the previous command by each press. Useful for editing a DOS command.
F3 (function key)	Displays the entire previous command. You can perform editing or just press F3 and then the Enter key to execute the command again.
Print Scr (one key)	In enhanced keyboards, does the same job as Shift+Prtsc
Shift+Prtsc	Sends a copy of the screen to the printer. This command does not toggle the printer on.

Figure 2–5
Formatting procedure.

```
C>FORMAT A:
Insert new diskette for drive A:
and press ENTER when ready...

Checking existing disk format.
Formatting 1.2M
Format complete.

Volume label (11 characters, ENTER for none)?

   1213952 bytes total disk space
   1213952 bytes available on disk

      512 bytes in each allocation unit.
     2371 allocation units available on disk.

Volume Serial Number is 0362-1BEC

Format another (Y/N)?N


C>
```

Versions of MS-DOS and PC-DOS are upwardly compatible: all the commands in earlier versions are available in the newer versions, but not vice versa. To a typical microcomputer user, PC-DOS and MS-DOS are almost identical. To find out which version of DOS you are using, at the DOS prompt, type *VER* and press the Enter key. This command displays the current version of DOS in the default drive. Figure 2–6 illustrates this process. It shows this DOS is version 6.0. In this text, DOS version 6.0 is used. All the commands discussed in the text work with all versions of DOS unless otherwise specified.

2–10   BATCH AND AUTOEXEC FILES

Batch files are disk files designed for a specific use. A batch file can have any standard name, but the extension must always be BAT. In theory, batch files can be of any length. You can include any valid command or statement in a batch file. To enter a command, you must always press the Enter key after the specific command. To generate a batch file you can use EDLIN, the line editor available on DOS prior to version 5.0, or any word processing program. DOS 5.0 and 6.0 include an impressive full-screen editor called EDIT. For simple batch files, you can use a version of the COPY command, which allows you to copy one or a series of files. For example, if the default drive is C, to copy a file named TEST from drive C to drive A, type *COPY TEST A:* and press Enter. To generate a simple batch file using the COPY command, the process is as follows:

```
C>COPY CON MYFILE.BAT       (press Enter)
Command or statement        (press Enter)
Command or statement        (press Enter)
Command or statement        (press Enter)
```

To terminate a batch file, press Ctrl and Z together (or the F6 function key). To execute a batch file, all you need to do is to insert the disk that includes the batch file and type the name of the file at the C> prompt.
A simple batch file follows:

```
C>COPY CON HELLO.BAT        (press Enter)
DIR                         (press Enter)
CLS                         (press Enter)
BASICA                      (press Enter)
                            (press Ctrl and Z keys together or press F6)
```

If you type *HELLO* at the C> prompt, you will see a listing of a directory of drive C, the screen will clear, and BASICA will be loaded to RAM. (The assumption is that drive C includes BASICA, a programming language available in the majority of computers.)

Figure 2–6
Finding out your version of DOS.

```
C>VER

MS-DOS Version 6.00


C>
```

The only limitation with COPY CON is that you cannot edit a file that has been created. For editing, you have to redo the entire file or use EDLIN, EDIT, or use some other word processing or editor-type system.

To stop the execution of a batch file, press Ctrl and Break at the same time.

If you name your file AUTOEXEC.BAT, it will be executed automatically as soon as you start the system. As a matter of fact, DOS always looks for the **autoexec file** first. If you have such a file, all its commands and statements will be executed. This facility can be very helpful. In addition to designing a menu or customizing your system, you can help people who are unfamiliar with computers by providing a question-and-answer type environment. Batch files in general are very helpful if you have to do a series of repetitive operations.

2–11   DEFINING A DIRECTORY

When you format a disk, DOS automatically creates a directory for you. This directory usually is called the **root directory**.

As a result of advances in disk technology, more and more files can be stored on a disk. These files are stored based on the date that they were created. As the number of files increases, it becomes extremely difficult to manage them properly. It becomes a time-consuming process to locate one file among several hundred.

There is a limit to the number of files that can be stored on a floppy disk or a hard disk. The root directory on a single-sided disk can hold up to 64 files; on a double-sided disk there can be up to 112 files. The root directory of a high-density disk can hold up to 224 files, and on a hard disk, up to 512 files. To create a better mechanism for storing and maintaining files and to bypass these file limitations, you can create **subdirectories**. A subdirectory is similar to a folder that contains a listing of files that you have grouped together based on a given scheme. (Subdirectory names follow the same conventions as file names.)

Consider a file cabinet in your office. Suppose that you store all important sales documents in this file cabinet. One method of storage is to throw all the sales documents in the cabinet as they arrive. In this case, retrieving information is a very difficult task. Another method is to divide the file cabinet into three separate parts (three subdirectories) by using some type of folders. You can then divide these folders into more logical parts (lower-level subdirectories). After this segmentation, you can put each document into its proper folder. This method, which is illustrated in Figure 2–7, improves retrieval time.

The directory below the root directory is considered a subdirectory to the root directory. A directory immediately below a subdirectory is considered a subdirectory to that subdirectory. In Figure 2–7, the WEST, SOUTH, and EAST regions are subdirectories to the root directory. OREGON and CALIFORNIA are subdirectories to the WEST region. They can be broken down further into SOUTHERN and NORTHERN (California) and so on.

As another example, suppose that on your hard disk you create four subdirectories for WordPerfect, Lotus 1-2-3, dBASE, and Quattro Pro. All your word processing documents will be saved in the WordPerfect directory, all your spreadsheets will be saved in the Lotus 1-2-3 directory, and so forth. Under Lotus 1-2-3, you may want to create two subdirectories, one for graphics files and one for database files. You can continue this process for several levels based on your specific needs.

The root directory is always identified by a back slash (\). The current subdirectory is identified by a period (.) and the parent subdirectory (the directory immediately above the current directory) is identified by two periods(..).

Figure 2–7
Example of directory structure.

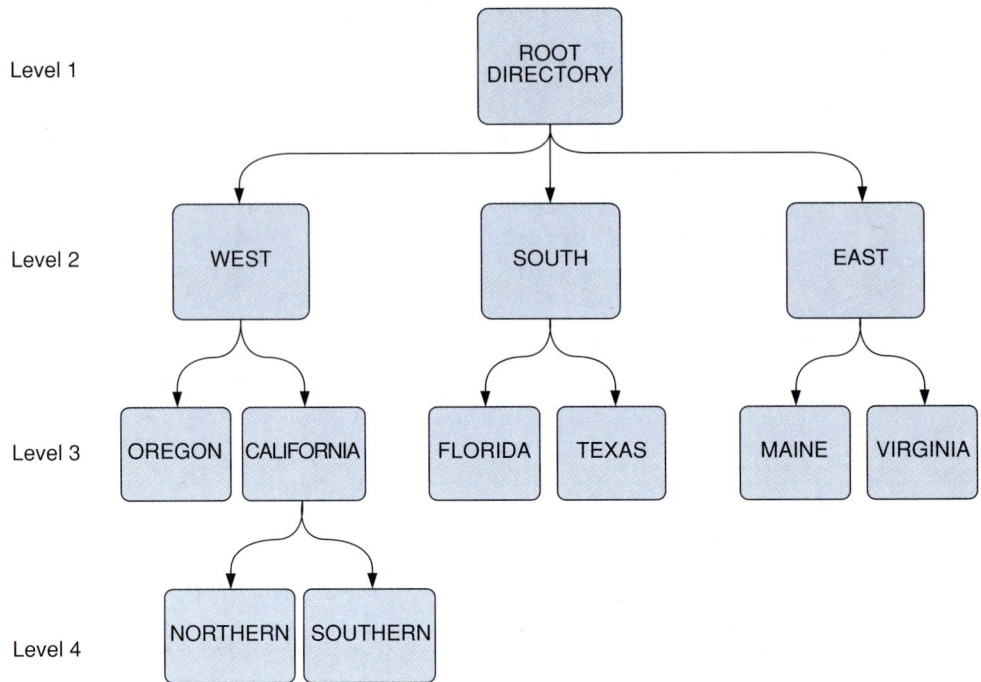

Figure 2–7
Example of directory structure.

2–12   IMPORTANT COMMANDS FOR DIRECTORIES

To create a subdirectory, use the DOS command MKDIR (make directory) or MD. You must be in the directory immediately above the subdirectory you are creating. To change to a subdirectory or make a subdirectory the current directory, use the CHDIR (change directory) or CD command. The CD command uses several different parameters as shown in Table 2–2.

To remove a subdirectory, you first must erase all the files and subsequent subdirectories by using either the DEL or ERASE command. Then get in the root directory and use the RMDIR (remove directory) or RD command.

If you do not know in which directory you are working, use the PROMPT PG command. At the DOS prompt, type *PROMPT PG* and press Enter. The default prompt changes to a prompt that identifies the current directory. For example, if you are working in the OREGON directory, your new prompt will read C:\OREGON>.

To display the structure of your directory, use the TREE command. Type *TREE /F* to display each directory on your disk and the files stored within each directory.

Another powerful command that you can use with directories is the PATH command. This command establishes a search path. Suppose that the DOS disk is in drive A and you are working with a data disk in drive B. If you issue an external DOS command from drive B, you will receive an error message (because the DOS disk is in drive A). When you type *PATH A:* at the *A>* prompt, DOS searches the root directory on drive A for any commands that it cannot find in the current drive or directory (in this case drive B). You also can establish multiple search paths by using the PATH command and a semicolon (;). Suppose that you want to tell your computer to search for DOS commands in drive B and in a subdirectory on drive C called EXTERNAL. Type the following search path to do the job: *PATH B:\; C:\EXTERNAL.*

Table 2–2
Change Directory (CD) Command
Parameters

Parameter	Function
CD.	Displays the current directory
CD..	Moves up one directory level
CD\	Moves up to the root directory from any directory level
CD..\..	Moves up two directory levels
CD\WEST\OREGON	OREGON becomes the current directory

When you establish a search path, it remains in effect until you turn off your PC. To cancel a search path, type *PATH* and press Enter. To make a search path permanent, enter the command into your AUTOEXEC.BAT file. Then, as soon as you start your computer, the search path will be activated.

2–13   DOS 5: AN OVERVIEW

In 1991, Microsoft Corporation released a new version of MS-DOS: **DOS 5.0**. In all ways, this release is a major improvement over the earlier releases of DOS. DOS 5 is uniquely identified by the following features:

■ Memory management. DOS 5.0 allows the memory of your computer to be used more effectively. This is because DOS 5.0 loads itself to memory other than conventional memory. For example, DOS 5.0 loads drivers and TSR programs to the upper memory area, leaving you with more conventional memory.

■ A shell program providing some of the features of Windows 3.0/3.1. Using the shell program, you enter a graphical-type environment. In this environment, you can access various options through the keyboard or simply through the mouse, which simplifies your DOS work.

■ A DOS macro capability. Through a DOSKEY you can assign a series of options to a DOS command and then use this DOS command by only typing its name. This is almost like creating a mini batch file.

■ Support for higher capacity disks. DOS 5.0 basically lets you utilize as much memory as your computer can support.

■ Some command enhancement. Many new commands and new options in existing commands have been added in DOS 5.0. For example, two of the most important new commands are UNDELETE and UNFORMAT, which allow you to rescue your work erased mistakenly.

■ Capability of task swapping. Using DOS 5.0, you can exit one application program such as a word processor and enter another application program such as Quattro Pro and easily get back to the word processor without closing the Quattro Pro program.

■ A new and complete online help facility. DOS 5.0 enables you to receive online help for all DOS commands. At the DOS prompt, type *HELP* and press Enter for complete information on the help facility. Or type *HELP*, then the command name, and press Enter. This provides you with specific help on a given command. For example, type *HELP DIR* and press Enter to receive online help for the DIR command.

■ Full-screen editing feature. DOS 5.0 includes an impressive full-screen editing component that is similar to a word processor. (The EDLIN utility is still available for people who are familiar with it.)

All commands presented in this chapter work in DOS 5.0 and 6.0.. Consult Table 2–3 for summary of important DOS commands. The commands simplify DOS operations and your PC work.

Table 2–3
Important DOS Commands*

Command	Function
ATTRIB +R (Release 3 and higher)	Makes a file a read-only file, e.g., ATTRIB +R COMMAND.COM (press Enter). This makes COMMAND.COM a read-only file.
ATTRIB –R (Release 3 and higher)	Removes the read-only status, e.g., ATTRIB –R COMMAND.COM (press Enter)
CHDIR (CD)	Changes the current directory or displays the current directory path. For example, CD\ changes the current directory of a drive to its root directory
CHKDSK	Displays free space on diskette
CHKDSK B:	Displays free space on diskette in drive B
CLS	Clears the screen
COMP	Compares two files to determine if they are the same or if they are different, e.g., COMP A:TEXT.JOE B:TEXT.JAC
COPY Filename.ext B:	Copies Filename.ext to the B drive
COPY B:Filename.ext	Copies Filename.ext to the C drive
COPY *.ext B:	Copies all files with the same ext from the C drive to the B drive
COPY B:*.ext	Copies all files with the same ext from the B drive to the C drive
COPY *.* B:	Copies all files from the C drive to the B drive
COPY B:*.*	Copies all files from the B drive to the C drive
COPY Filename1.ext Filename2.ext	Copies a file from C to C with a different name
COPY B:Filename1.ext B:Filename2.ext	Copies a file from B to B with a different name
COPY Filename1.ext B:Filename2.ext	Copies a file from C to B with a different name

*To execute all of these commands, the C prompt is assumed. An A stands for A drive; B stands for B drive; ext stands for file extension (any three valid characters). Filename can be any valid file name.

Table 2–3
(continued)

Command	Function
COPY B:Filename1.ext Filename2.ext	Copies a file from B to C with a different name
COPY CON B:Filename.BAT	Creates a batch file in drive B. To terminate the file creation, press F6 then Enter.
CTRL-ALT-DEL	Resets the system (a warm boot)
DATE	Resets the system date
DEL Filename.ext	Erases Filename.ext from drive C
DEL B:Filename.ext	Erases Filename.ext from drive B
DEL B:Filename.*	Erases all Filenames with any extension from drive B
DEL B:*.ext	Erases all files with the same extension from drive B
DIR	Displays a directory of C
DIR B:	Displays a directory of B
DIR/P	Displays a complete directory of drive C with a pause before scrolling off the screen
DIR B:/P	Does the same as above for drive B
DIR/W	Displays a wide directory of drive C
DIR B:/W	Does the same as above for drive B
DIR|SORT (| This character is the broken line found on back-slash key)	Displays a sorted directory of drive C
DIR B:|SORT	Displays a sorted directory of drive B
DISKCOMP	Compares two diskettes track by track, sector for sector, to determine if their contents are identical, e.g., DISKCOMP A: B:
DISKCOPY A: B:	Copies a diskette in drive A to a diskette in drive B. The two drives must be identical.
ERASE Filename.ext	Erases Filename.ext on C
ERASE B:Filename.ext	Erases Filename.ext on B
ERASE *.ext	Erases all files with the same .ext on C
ERASE B:*.ext	Erases all files with the same .ext on B
FORMAT A:	Erases and formats a diskette in drive A
FORMAT B:	Erases and formats a diskette in drive B
FORMAT A:/V	Formats a diskette in drive A with a volume label (a name with up to 11 characters long)
FORMAT B:/V	Formats a new diskette with a volume label (a name with up to 11 characters long) in drive B

Table 2–3
(continued)

Command	Function
LABEL	Creates, changes, or deletes a volume label for a disk, e.g., type *LABEL* and press Enter; follow the prompt
MKDIR (MD)	Creates a subdirectory on C drive, e.g., MD CLIENTS
PATH	Instructs DOS to search a specified directory for a program that cannot be found in the current directory, e.g., PATH C:\
PROMPT	Customizes the DOS system prompt, e.g., PROMPT Hello
PROMPT PG	Displays the current subdirectory that you are in
RENAME Filename1.ext Filename2.ext	Renames a file on C
RENAME B:Filename1.ext B:Filename2.ext	Renames a file on B
RMDIR (RD)	Removes a subdirectory from a disk, e.g., RD C:CPA. Remember, the subdirectory must be empty
SHIFT-PrtSc or Print Scr	Prints a copy of the screen
SYS	Puts a copy of operating system files IBMDOS.COM and IBMBIO.COM on the specified diskette or hard disk, e.g., SYS B:
TIME	Resets system time
TREE	Displays the structure of the current directory
TYPE Filename.ext	Displays the content of Filename.ext
TYPE B:Filename.ext	Displays the content of Filename.ext on B
VER	Displays the DOS version number on the screen
VERIFY	Checks the data just written to a disk to be sure the data has been correctly recorded and then displays if the data has been checked, e.g., VERIFY ON sets verify status on, VERIFY OFF sets verify status off, and VERIFY shows verify status.
VOL	Displays the volume label of a disk, if the label exists

2–14   HIGHLIGHTS OF DOS 6.0

DOS 6.0, which was released in April 1993, offers features not available in the previous versions of DOS. Some of the important features of this release are listed next:

- Disk compression that can almost double the capacity of your hard disk
- Back-up facility for easy backing up of your hard disk
- Antivirus feature which eliminates known viruses. Computer viruses are a series of computer codes that can wipe out your computer hard disk.
- Memory management, more powerful than DOS 5.0, that can increase availability of your RAM by up to 100 K
- Advanced communications capabilities for accessing files and peripherals on other PCs with compatible software.
- Availability of electronic mail (E-mail) program. By means of this feature, you can send and receive mail through your computer
- File sharing utility for exchanging files with another microcomputer.
- Ease of use by improving online help
- New commands such as *MOVE* for moving files and DELTREE for deleting a directory and its contents and all its subdirectories

SUMMARY

This chapter introduced you to elementary DOS operations, beginning with differences between internal and external DOS commands. Types of DOS prompts and file name specifications in the DOS environment were described, and the DIR command with different switches was highlighted. Important keys used frequently in DOS environment were introduced. The chapter also examined the FORMAT command, which is necessary for preparing blank disks. After a brief discussion of different versions of MS-DOS and PC-DOS, DOS 5 and 6.0 were outlined briefly. The chapter featured with a table of the most commonly used DOS commands.

REVIEW QUESTIONS

*These questions are answered in Appendix A.

1. What is a cold boot?
2. What is a warm boot?
*3. Why is it important to enter the correct time and date at boot-up time (if the system does not have an internal battery)?
4. What are internal DOS commands?
5. What are external DOS commands?
6. How many different DOS prompts are there?
*7. How do you change from drive C to A and from A to C?
8. What is the default drive?
9. Describe a valid DOS file name.
10. Give three examples of file extensions.
11. How many different ways can you use the DIR command?
12. Name the two DOS wildcards.

13. Describe the functions of the F1, F3, and F6 keys.
14. Why must a new disk be formatted before it can be used?
*15. What is a batch file? What is an autoexec file?
*16. Give three examples of DOS internal and three examples of DOS external commands.
17. What is a directory?
18. Why should you use directories?
19. List some directory commands.
20. How do you get to the root directory from a three-layered subdirectory?
21. How do you remove a directory?
22. What are some of the features of DOS 5.0?
23. How can you receive online help in DOS 5.0?

HANDS-ON EXPERIENCE

1. Start your computer. At the C> prompt enter the date as *1-1-95*. Change it back to today's date.
2. Change the default drive from C to A or from A to C. Type *DIR* and press Enter. What are the contents of drive A and of drive C?
3. By using Ctrl+Alt+Del, warm boot your computer. Type *DIR* and press Enter. How many different types of file extensions do you see in the directory?
4. Type *DIR/W* and press Enter; then type *DIR/P* and press Enter. What is the difference between these two commands?
5. By using the asterisk wildcard (*), generate listings of all COM files, of all EXE files, and of all SYS files.
6. Format a new disk. Use the COPY command to copy all COM files from drive C to this formatted disk.
7. Use the VER command to determine the version of DOS that you are using.
8. Create two directories on a diskette in drive A; name them TEST1 and TEST2. Copy two COM files from drive C to TEST1. Now copy the contents of TEST1 to TEST2.
9. Remove TEST1 from your disk.

KEY TERMS

Autoexec files	DOS 5.0	Internal command
Batch files	DOS 6.0	Root directory
Cold boot	External command	Subdirectory
Directory	File allocation table (FAT)	Warm boot
Disk operating system (DOS)	File extension	
	File name	

KEY COMMANDS

See Tables 2–1 through 2–3

MISCONCEPTIONS AND SOLUTIONS

Misconception   You turn on your PC and you see a message that is not familiar to you, for example:

`NON-SYSTEM DISK`

> **Solution**   You forgot to put the DOS disk in drive A, or you inserted your disk on the wrong side, or you inserted a data disk instead of the DOS disk. Insert the DOS disk into drive A properly and reboot the system.

Misconception   You are trying to format a disk in the A drive and receive this error message:

`ATTEMPTED WRITE-PROTECT VIOLATION`

> **Solution**   The disk in drive A has the write-protection notch covered. Either remove the protection or insert another disk.

Misconception   You are using the FORMAT command and receive this error message:

`DRIVE NOT READY`

> **Solution**   Either the target drive door is not closed or there is no disk in that drive. Insert a disk in this drive, close the drive door, and press Enter.

Misconception   You are using a DOS command and receive one of these error messages:

`SYNTAX ERROR   BAD COMMAND   FILENAME ERROR`

> **Solution**   Check the spelling of the command. Most likely, you have misspelled a command.

ARE YOU READY TO MOVE ON?

Multiple Choice

1. The procedure known as warm boot means
   a. inserting the DOS disk in drive A and turning on the computer
   b. typing the name of the program to be run and pressing Enter
   c. simultaneously pressing the Ctrl, Alt, and Del keys
   d. formatting a disk
   e. none of the above

2. Which of the following prompts are you most likely to see after performing a cold boot with the DOS disk in drive A?
   a. A>
   b. B>
   c. C>
   d. OK
   e. C:/DOS>

3. If the correct date and time are not entered during the boot process or if you want to change them at any time, the commands are
   a. HOUR and DAY
   b. DAY and HOUR

    c. DATE and CLOCK
    d. DATE and TIME
    e. none of the above

4. To change the default drive from drive B to drive A, what should you type at the DOS prompt before pressing Enter?

    a. *A*
    b. *DRIVE=A*
    c. *B+A*
    d. *GO TO A:*
    e. *A:*

5. File names with these extensions can be executed by typing the name of the file. (Remember, both extensions in each pair must be correct.)

    a. COM and SYS
    b. COM and EXE
    c. EXE and SYS
    d. BAK and SYS
    e. BAK and BAT

6. The command DIR/P will yield

    a. the same as DIR
    b. a wide directory listing
    c. one screen at a time of the file listing
    d. a hard copy output to the printer
    e. nothing—it is not a valid command

7. The command to format a disk in drive B is

    a. ERASE B:
    b. DELETE *.*
    c. SYS B:
    d. FORMAT B:
    e. A or B

8. The file allocation table indicates

    a. where data are saved on a disk
    b. the maximum number of files that can be saved on disk
    c. how much disk space is available
    d. how much memory (RAM) is available
    e. none of the above

9. A typical computer response to the command VER is

    a. Disk Verified OK
    b. MS_DOS Version 5.0
    c. File Verified OK
    d. Insert new disk and strike Enter when ready
    e. A or B

10. When you format a disk,

    a. all data is erased
    b. the file allocation table is created
    c. the operating system checks for defective spots
    d. the disk is divided into sectors and tracks
    e. all of the above occur

True/False

1. If the computer is off and the system does not have a hard disk, the DOS disk must be placed in drive A to boot the computer.

2. A cold boot is faster than a warm boot because the computer does not check the memory.

3. To get back to the root directory from a subdirectory, type *CD* and press Enter.

4. External DOS commands are those loaded into the computer memory at boot-up time.

5. The DOS prompt indicates the current default drive.

6. The DIR command generates a listing of the files in the default directory.

7. DOS wildcards act as placeholders for other characters and include *, ?, @, $, %, and |.

8. DIR and DIR/W yield exactly the same information except that DIR/W places it in a wide format.

9. To move up two directory levels, type *CD..\..* and press Enter.

10. Versions of MS-DOS and PC-DOS are not upwardly compatible.

ANSWERS

Multiple Choice		True/False	
1.	c	1.	T
2.	a	2.	F
3.	d	3.	T
4.	e	4.	F
5.	b	5.	T
6.	c	6.	T
7.	d	7.	F
8.	a	8.	F
9.	b	9.	T
10.	e	10.	F

A Quick Trip Through Microsoft Windows

3–1   INTRODUCTION

This chapter presents some of the unique advantages of Microsoft Windows[1] as a graphical-based environment compared with a character-based environment such as DOS. After discussing how to get in and out of Windows, the chapter looks at the procedures for using a mouse and the keyboard in the Windows environment. Next, the help and tutorial facilities of Windows are introduced. The chapter then describes different parts of a Windows screen, the role of the Program Manager, running applications in Windows, working with the Clipboard, quitting an application, and Windows groups.

3–2   WINDOWS 3.1: AN OVERVIEW

Windows 3.1 is an environment based on a graphical user interface (GUI—pronounced "gooey") that runs on top of DOS (i.e., you must have DOS to run Windows). This graphical environment has several advantages not found in the DOS character-based environment. Let us summarize some of these advantages:

1. Windows is easier to use than DOS because with Windows you do not need to memorize the strict DOS command syntax. In Windows, you can perform all DOS functions and more through a series of pull-down menus.

2. All Windows applications share the same principles. When you learn one Windows application, you can easily transfer some or all of what you have learned to other Windows applications.

3. You can work with Windows applications using a mouse, the keyboard, or shortcut keys for speed (described later in this chapter). All these options enable you to become more efficient as you work with Windows programs.

4. Windows presents a **multitasking** environment. This means that you can run more than one program at the same time. Imagine that you are typing a report using WordPerfect and decide you need a spreadsheet created in Lotus 1-2-3. If you are using Windows, you can easily switch to Lotus 1-2-3 and incorporate the desired spreadsheet into your report. You can even integrate a graph into your report. Perhaps you decide that you need a telephone number out of your online telephone directory. You can easily run your telephone directory software, retrieve the correct phone number, then exit the telephone directory software without ever exiting WordPerfect.

5. Windows applications and DOS applications can be run simultaneously. You can even run multiple DOS programs and multiple Windows programs at the same time.

6. Several files can be linked together. If you change data in one file, the same data in the other file will be changed automatically.

7. Windows allows better memory management. You are not restricted by 640 K, the traditional DOS barrier. Windows enables you to use memory well beyond 640 K. It makes your hard disk an extension of your RAM. If a program does not fit into your RAM, it simply spills over to your hard disk.

8. Windows allows you to display on the screen exactly what will appear on printed output. This is called what-you-see-is-what-you-get (WYSIWYG). By

---

[1] For a detailed discussion of Microsoft Windows, consult *Information Systems Literacy: Windows 3.1* by Hossein Bidgoli, published by Macmillan Publishing Company 1993.

Table 3–1
Unique Advantages of Windows

Ease of use

Shared principles among Windows programs

Use of mouse, keyboard, and shortcut keys

Multitasking

Ability to run Windows and DOS applications at the same time

Linkage of several files

Better memory management

True WYSIWYG

Free accessories

means of this feature, you have a pretty good idea of the output of an application before printing it.

9. Accessory programs are free of charge. Windows comes with a group of accessories that are readily available to you at no extra cost: Windows Write—a simple word processor; Windows Paintbrush—a drawing program; Windows Terminal—a communications program; Windows Print Manager—a program that allows you to work and print at the same time; and other more useful programs such as the Calculator, Calendar, Notepad, Cardfile, and Clock.

The unique advantages of Windows are listed in Table 3–1.

3–3   UNDERSTANDING WINDOWS TERMINOLOGY

Windows, just like other software, has its own terminology. Among the important terms are desktop, icon, and mouse. Let us briefly explain each.

Desktop in Windows is similar to the surface of a desk. All your Windows work takes place in the desktop. When you start Windows you start at the desktop. You can do a number of tasks from the desktop; among the most common are the following:

- Fast application switching—going from one application program to another
- Icon spacing change—moving around the existing icons, deleting the unwanted ones, and so forth
- Displaying your document
- Changing colors

An **icon** is a graphic representation of an application, a document, or an object. You can move the mouse pointer to the desired application icon and double-click the left button of the mouse to start the application or open a document.

The **mouse** will be explained in detail in section 3–5. It is the main interface between you and Windows and Windows applications. Although you can use the keyboard or the shortcut keys, using the mouse is probably the most efficient way to accomplish most Windows tasks.

3–4   GETTING IN AND OUT OF WINDOWS

The first step is to install Windows on a hard disk system. Windows will not run on a floppy system. After installing Windows, switch to the drive and directory containing your Windows files by using the DOS CD command (e.g., type *CD WIN31* and press Enter); then type *WIN* and press Enter. You will be presented with a screen similar to the one shown in Figure 3–1. Your screen might be different from what is presented here depending how Windows has been configured.

Three methods allow you to get out of Windows. The first is to move the mouse pointer (see Section 3–5) to the File option at the upper left of the screen and click the left button of the mouse. You will be presented with a screen similar to the one shown in Figure 3–2. Move the mouse pointer to the Exit Windows option and click the left button. The second method is to move the mouse pointer to the control-menu box, at the extreme upper left of the screen, and double-click the left button of the mouse. The third method is to move the mouse pointer to the control-menu box and click the left button once. You will be presented with a screen similar to the one shown in Figure 3–3. Move the mouse pointer to the Close option and click the left button.

Regardless of which of these three methods you use, you will be presented with a screen similar to the one shown in Figure 3–4. Move the mouse pointer to OK and click the left button of the mouse to leave Windows. If you click with the mouse pointer on Cancel, you have indicated that you changed your mind and wish to stay in Windows. When you exit Windows you exit either to DOS or to your starting menu, depending on how you started Windows in the first place.

You can also use the keyboard to exit Windows. To do so, press Alt+F to open the File menu. Then either press the X key or move the cursor to Exit Windows and press Enter. Press Enter again to exit Windows.

Figure 3–1
Windows starting screen.

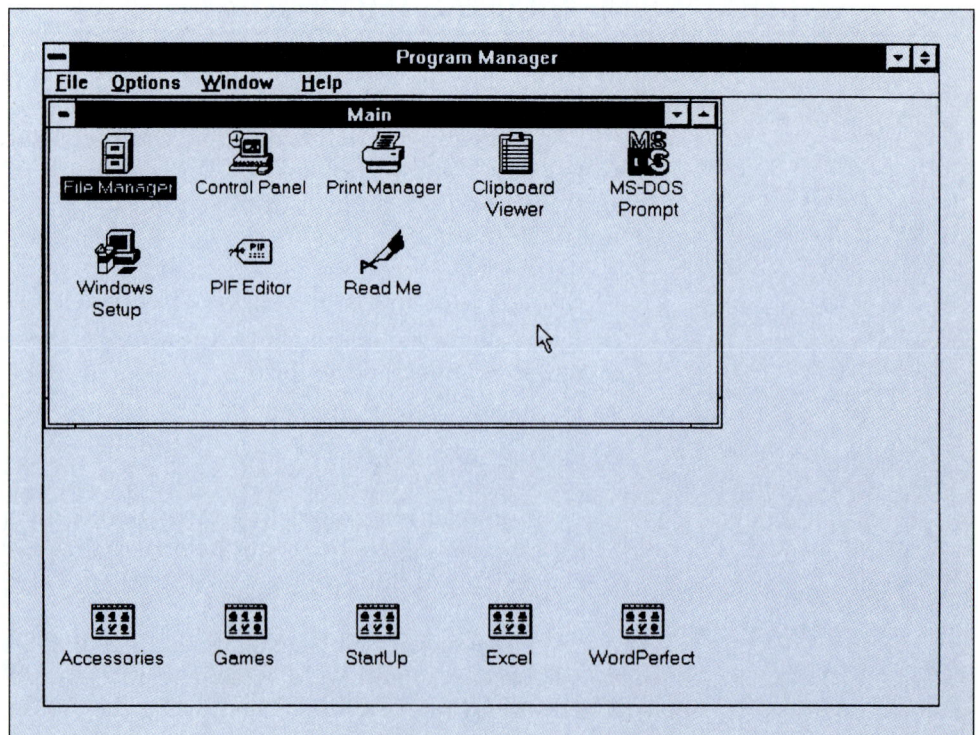

Figure 3–2
File pull-down menu.

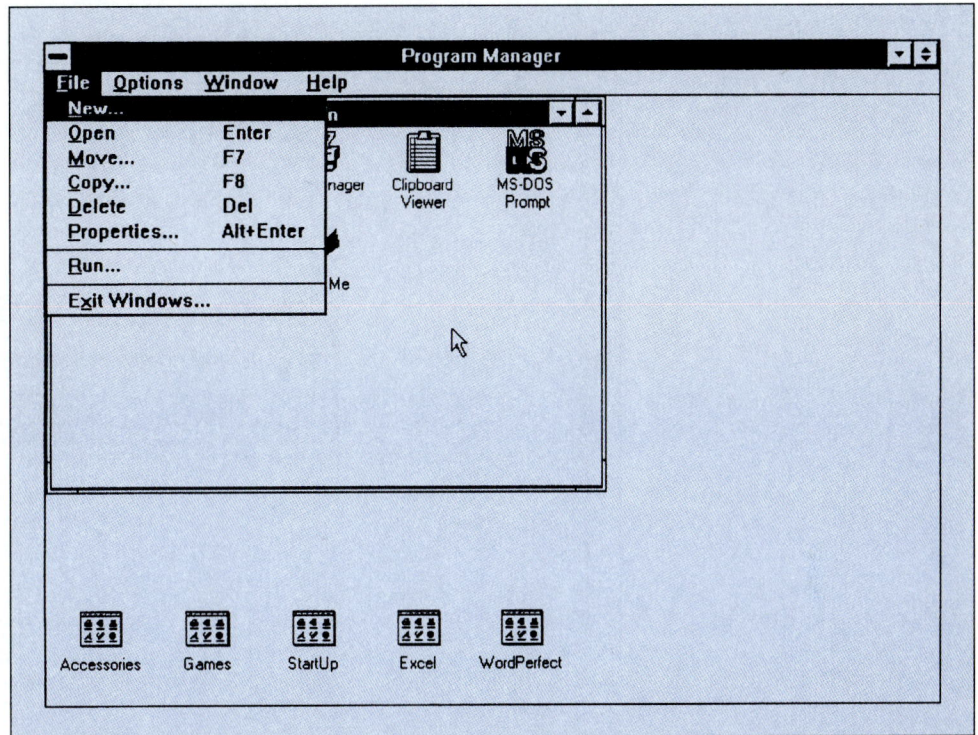

Figure 3–3
Control-menu box options.

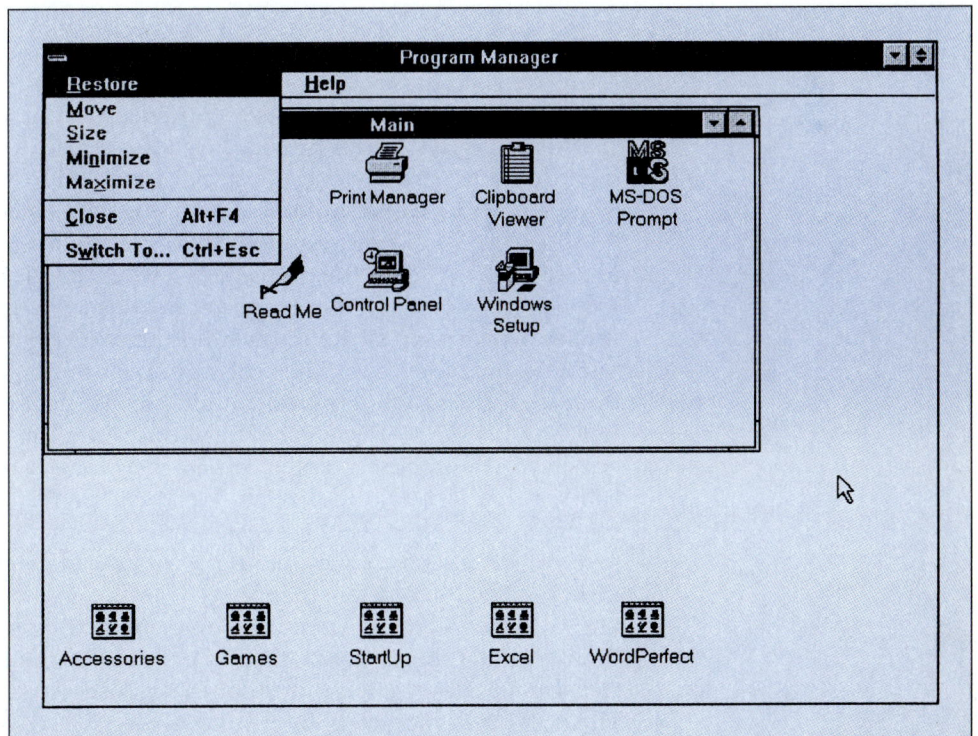

Figure 3–4
Exit Windows dialog box.

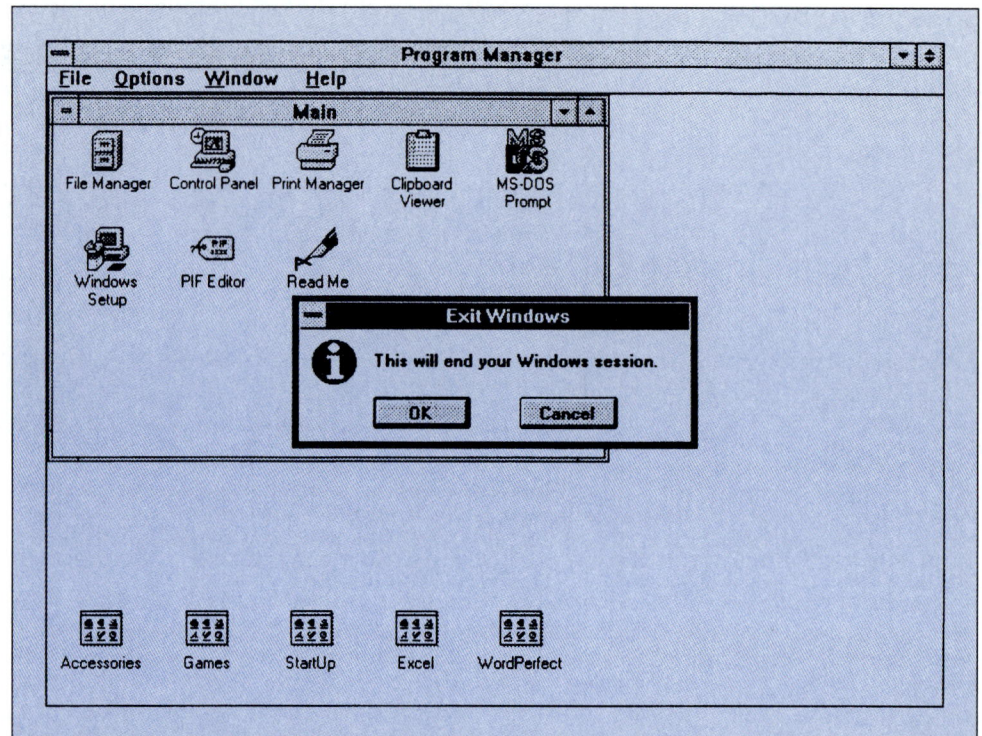

3–5   USING A MOUSE IN THE WINDOWS ENVIRONMENT

Windows offers three user interface options: keyboard, mouse, and shortcut keys. Most users agree that a mouse is preferable to a keyboard in graphical environments such as Windows because of its speed, accuracy, ease of use, and other special functions that it can provide. Using a mouse, you can easily select pull-down menu options, quickly execute application programs, move and/or resize group windows, relocate icons to new locations on the screen, and much more.

If you are right handed, hold the mouse in your right hand, and if you are left handed, hold the mouse in your left hand. Place the mouse on a flat surface (preferably on a mouse pad) and rest your hand on top of it. Place your thumb on one side of the mouse and the two fingers on the opposite end of your hand on the other side. This will leave your index finger and middle finger positioned over the mouse buttons. Lightly rest your fingers on these buttons. To see how the mouse works, move the mouse in a circular motion and look at the screen for the **mouse pointer**, which can be an arrow or some other shape. You will see that it is also moving in a circular pattern, matching the movements of the mouse. If you move the mouse to the left, the mouse pointer moves to the left side of the screen; if you move the mouse away from you, the mouse pointer moves to the top of the screen.

Now let's try selecting some menu items using the mouse. Move the mouse so that the mouse pointer is pointing to the File option at the upper left of the screen; click the left button of the mouse. If you have done this correctly, the File pull-down menu will be displayed (see Figure 3–2). Move the mouse pointer to the Window option and click the left button again to display the Window pull-down menu (Figure 3–5). Notice that positioning the mouse pointer and clicking the left button selects the desired menu item automatically. For now, move the mouse pointer back into the middle of the screen and click the left button to "deselect" any currently highlighted menu items.

Figure 3–5
Window pull-down menu.

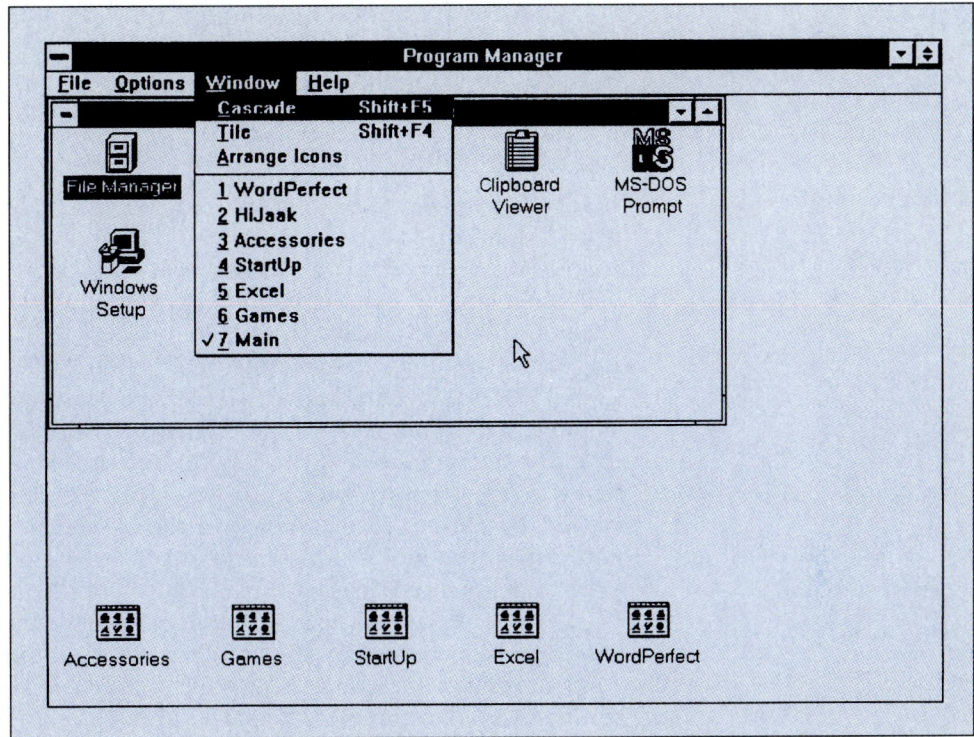

Rapid double-clicking of the left button while pointing the mouse pointer onto an icon automatically executes the application that the icon represents. To see how this works, move the mouse pointer to the accessories icon and double-click the left button. This automatically opens the Accessories window (Figure 3–6). Now you can double-click on any of the options shown to open them.

Figure 3–6
Applications in the Accessories group.

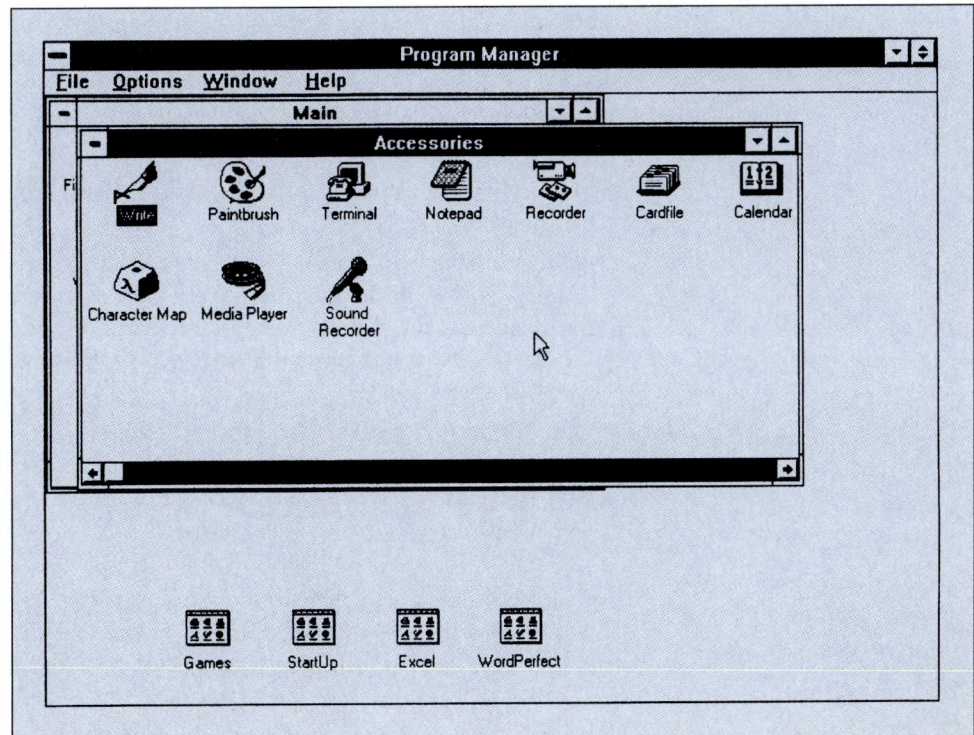

Let's try another example. Move the mouse pointer to the MS-DOS Prompt option in the Main group (see Figure 3–1) and double-click the left button. Windows responds by displaying a DOS prompt. Type the command *EXIT* (press Enter) to return to the Windows main screen.

You can move windows, group icons, application icons, and so forth to other locations on the screen using a method called **click and drag**. To try this, point the mouse pointer onto the title bar of the Main group window (where the word "Main" appears; see Figure 3–1). Click the left button; then, while holding the button down, drag the mouse pointer to a new location on the screen. You will notice that an outline form of the Main group moves with the mouse pointer. When you release the left button, your window will be relocated to the position of the mouse pointer when you released the left button.

Let's try changing the size of the Main group window. Move the mouse pointer to the right edge of the Main group window. Notice that at a certain position over the edge of the window the mouse pointer becomes a double-pointing arrow. When you see this, click and drag a small distance to the right. Again notice the outline form; when you release the mouse button, your window will conform to the size you just constructed by dragging the mouse. If you change your mind, before releasing the left button of the mouse, press the Esc key.

As a final example of moving screen items to new locations, move the mouse pointer onto the MS-DOS Prompt option inside the Main group window. Click and drag the icon to a new location inside of the window, then release the left button of the mouse. The icon will obediently follow your command to position itself in a new location. For now, drag the icon back into its original location.

3–6   USING THE KEYBOARD IN THE WINDOWS ENVIRONMENT

As mentioned, Windows and Windows programs allow use of the keyboard in addition to the mouse. Keyboards are comfortable for experienced typists, and since keyboards have been around for years, people are more familiar with them than with the mouse. If you prefer working with a keyboard, the following areas of it may be used with Windows:

- The typing keys located in the center of the keyboard. These keys are similar to the keys of a typewriter.
- The numeric and cursor movement keys located on the right side of the keyboard. Enhanced keyboards have a dedicated cursor movement pad. For standard keyboards, if you press the Num Lock key, the numeric pad serves as a 10-key machine for entering numbers. Arrow keys are used to move the cursor around.
- The function keys: F1 through F12 located across the top of the enhanced keyboard or F1 through F10 on the left side of the standard keyboard. All these keys perform different functions depending on the application program you are using.

Windows and Windows applications can also be accessed through the combination of keys called shortcut keys. The key-combination method always involves one of the following special keys—Shift, Alt, and Ctrl—combined with another key. For example, Alt+F invokes the File menu. To use a key combination, first press either the Shift, Alt, or Ctrl key and hold it down; then press another key. In this book, the mouse is emphasized as the major Windows interface.

3–7   HELP FACILITIES OF WINDOWS

As you can see in Figure 3–1, one of the options in the Program Manager is Help. The Program Manager, which is the heart of Windows, is used to start other applications and organize applications and files into groups. If you move the mouse pointer to the Help option and click the left button, you will see a screen similar to the one presented in Figure 3–7. You can move the mouse pointer to any of these options and click the left button to execute the desired option. For example, if you click left on the Contents option, you will receive a screen similar to Figure 3–8. As you can see in this figure, the Search option is available; it enables you to search for a particular topic. To exit Search, click on Cancel. You can also select the Glossary option to generate an alphabetized listing of all the topics in Windows. To receive help on commands, click on the underlined command. You can always exit any of these options by clicking the control-menu box and selecting the Close option.

If you select the Windows Tutorial option from the Help pull-down menu, you will be presented with a screen similar to Figure 3–9. The **online tutorial** provides an overview of Windows and mouse operations. If you have not used a mouse before, this tutorial is very helpful.

Figure 3–7
Starting screen of the Help option.

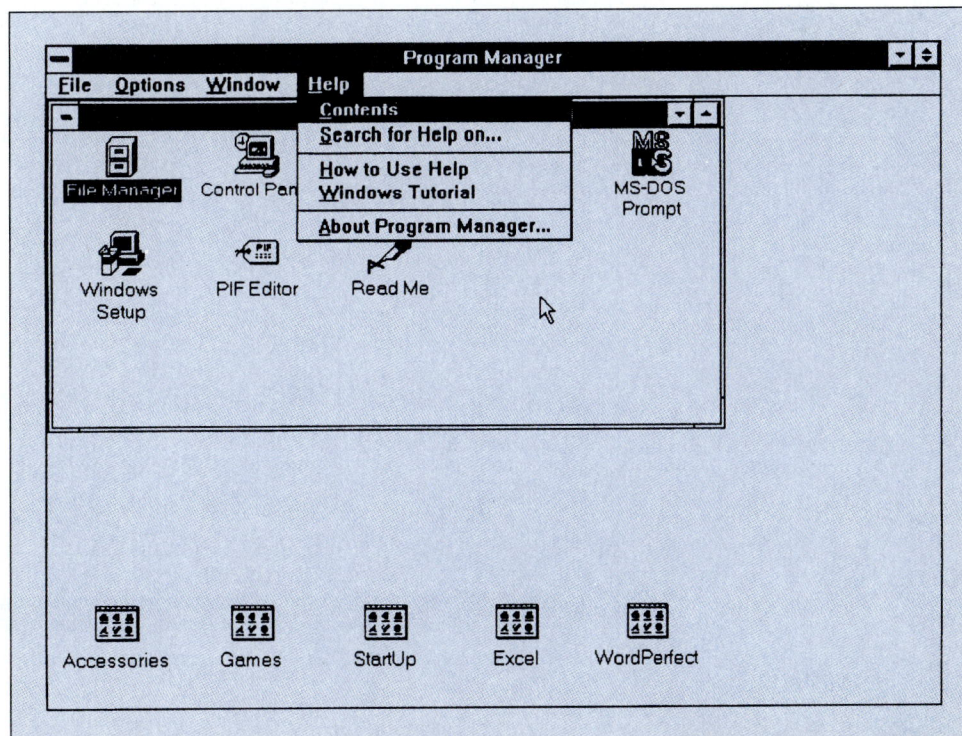

Figure 3–8
Information under the Contents option of the Help menu.

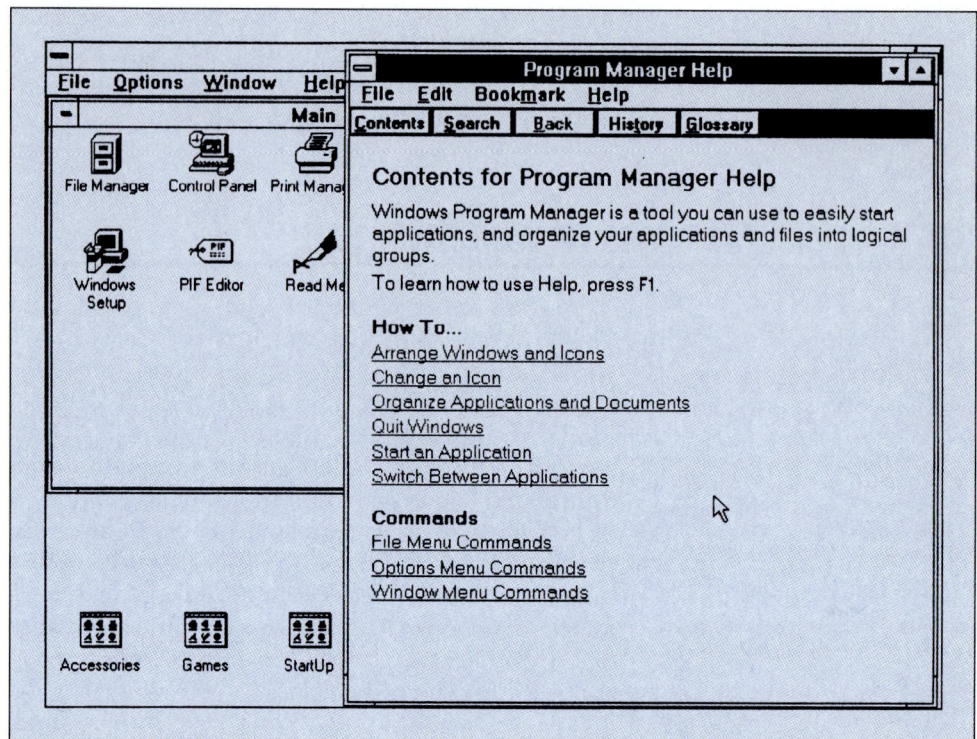

Figure 3–9
Starting screen of the Windows tutorial.

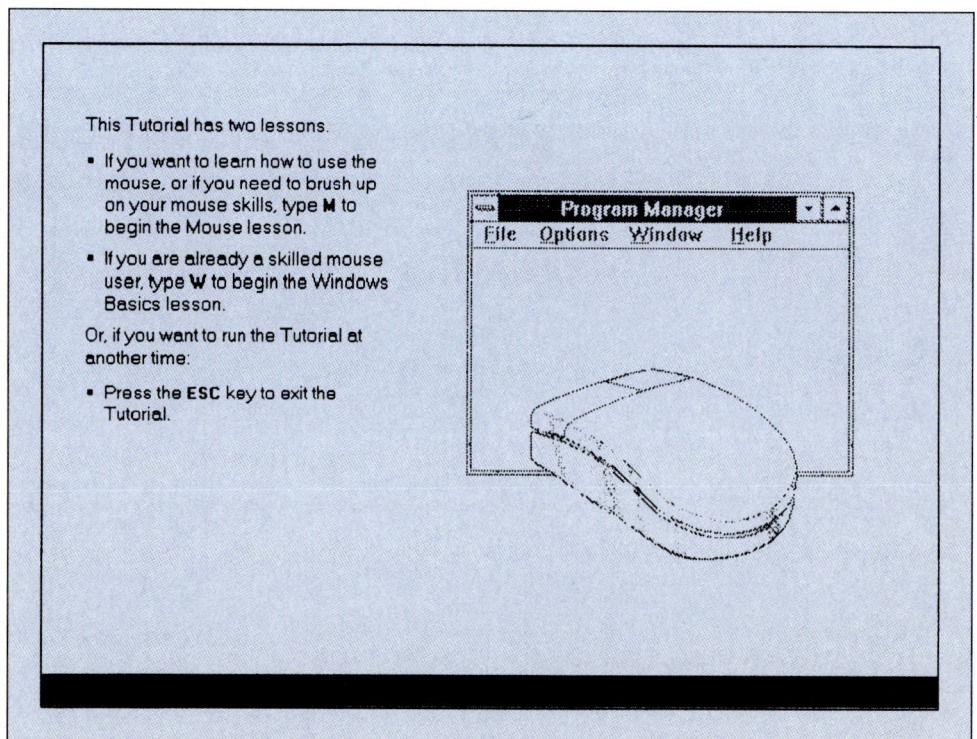

3–8   DIFFERENT PARTS OF A WINDOWS SCREEN

Most Windows screens include the elements illustrated in Figure 3–10. A **window** can be a whole screen or part of a screen. Refer to the figure as you read the following descriptions:

- The window title (in the title bar) is usually the name of the application, name of a document, or name of a file. In Figure 3–10 the title is Notepad - [Untitled] because no document has been opened yet.

- The control-menu box appears at the upper left of each window. The control-menu box is helpful if you are using the keyboard to work with Windows. By using control-menu commands, you can resize, move, maximize, minimize, close windows, and switch to applications. If you use a mouse, you can perform all of the tasks just mentioned by clicking and dragging. Probably the most common application of the control-menu box is closing a window. To do this, just double-click on the control-menu box.

- Insertion point indicates the current position of the cursor at any give time in your document. Text and graphs will be inserted at this point.

- The menu bar lists available menu options. In Figure 3–10, the menu bar includes File, Edit, Search, and Help.

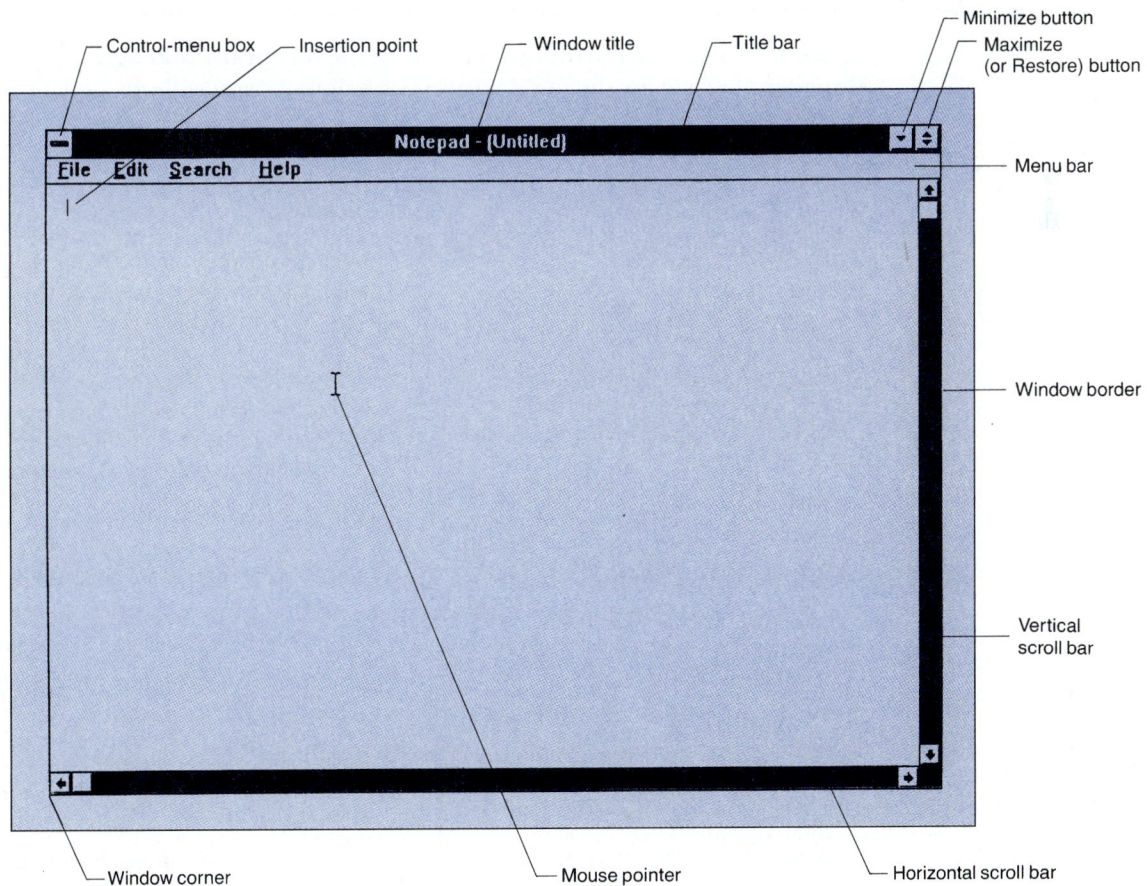

Figure 3–10
Elements of the Windows screen.

- The minimize button can reduce the window to an icon.
- The maximize button can enlarge the active application window so that it fills the entire desktop. After you enlarge a window, the maximize button is replaced by the restore button. You can click the restore button to return a window to its previous size.
- The window border is the outside edge of a window. You can lengthen or shorten the border on each side of a window.
- The vertical and horizontal scroll bars are used to view parts of a document that do not fit on the current screen.
- The mouse pointer is a small arrow that moves on the screen corresponding to the movement of the mouse on your desktop. The mouse pointer changes to a double-pointed arrow when it is moved to the edge of a window. Other common pointer shapes are summarized in Table 3–2.

Table 3–3 summarizes the control menu commands, which are accessible through the control-menu box. Some applications do not have all of these commands. For example, Figure 3–11 does not include all the commands outlined in Table 3–3.

3–9   WHAT IS THE PROGRAM MANAGER?

As soon as you start Windows you start the **Program Manager.** The Program Manager always runs during a Windows session. As you will see later in this chap-

Table 3–2
Mouse Pointer Shapes

Shape	Description	Allows you to
⇒	Arrow	select an option from the menu bar, select an icon, and move a window.
I	I–Beam	enter text.
⧗	Hourglass	do nothing while this shape is visible. Windows is performing a task. You must wait until the pointer changes shape before you can continue.
☞	Pointing hand	jump between Help topics.
☜	Pointing finger	select one or more items in a graph.
✋	Hand	move an item in a graph.
↕	Two-headed vertical arrow	split a worksheet window vertically and resize a row.
⇔	White (with line border) two-headed arrow	adjust the size of a window by "dragging" the side or corner of a window.
↔	Two-headed horizontal arrow (in one color)	split a worksheet window horizontally and resize a column.

Figure 3–11
Control Menu options.

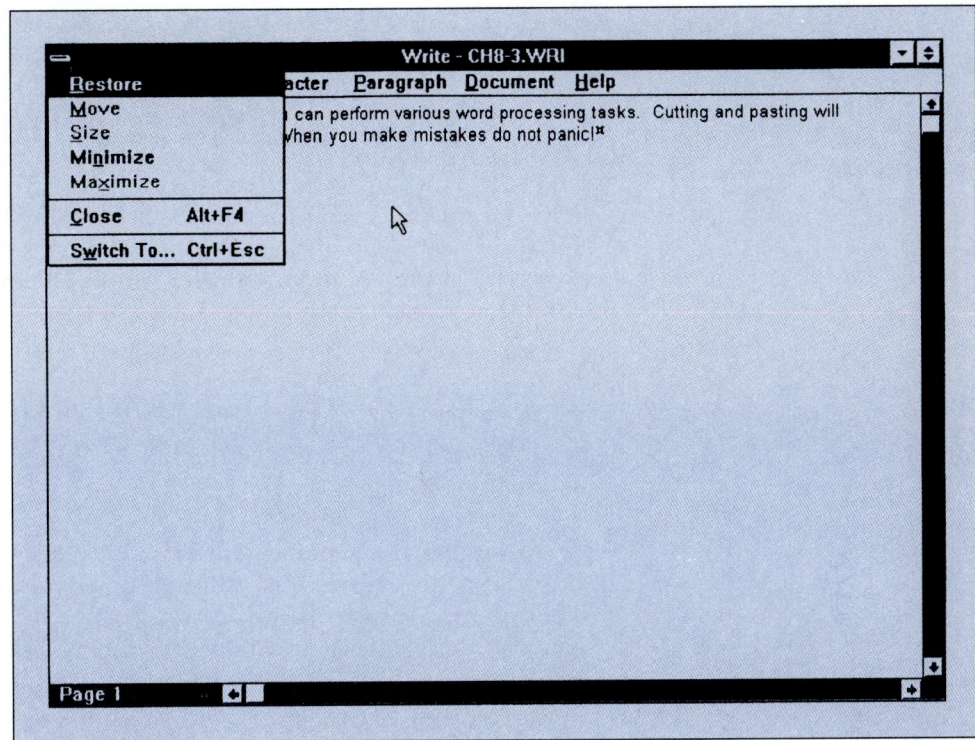

Table 3–3
Control Menu Commands

Command	Function
Restore	Restores the window to its former size after you have enlarged it (by using the Maximize command) or reduced it to an icon (by using the Minimize command)
Move	Uses the keyboard to move a window to another location
Size	Uses the keyboard to change the size of a window
Minimize	Reduces a window to an icon
Maximize	Enlarges a window to its maximum size
Close	Closes a window or a dialog box. You can also use this command to quit an application from an application window.
Switch To	Opens the Task List (discussed later in this chapter). This feature enables you to switch between running applications. It also arranges windows and icons on your desktop.
Next	Switches you between open document windows and icons. This is available for document windows only.
Edit	Displays a cascading menu with additional commands

ter, a variety of tasks can be performed through the Program Manager. When you run other applications, the Program Manager runs either in the background or as an icon on your desktop.

When you first start Windows, the Program Manager opens on your desktop with the Main group window open inside the Program Manager window. See Figure 3–12. This may appear different in your system, depending on how Windows has been configured. The Accessories group, the Games group, the StartUp group, and various applications groups are represented as group icons along the lower border of the Program Manager window. Remember, your screen might be different from what is presented in Figure 3–12.

3–9–1　Different Parts of the Program Manager Window

Refer to Figure 3–13 as you read the following descriptions of the different parts of the Program Manager window:

- **Group window** is a separate window inside the Program Manager window. As you can see in Figure 3–13, this window includes icons that start different applications. Group windows are affected by the commands from the Program Manager menu bar: File, Options, Window, and Help.

- Program-item icons are displayed inside a group window and represent applications, documents, accessories, and so forth. You can select program-item icons to start particular applications; for example, double-click on the File Manager icon to start it.

- Group icon is a minimized group window. These icons are displayed in the lower border of the Program Manager window. Figure 3–13 shows five of these icons.

Figure 3–12
Program Manager window.

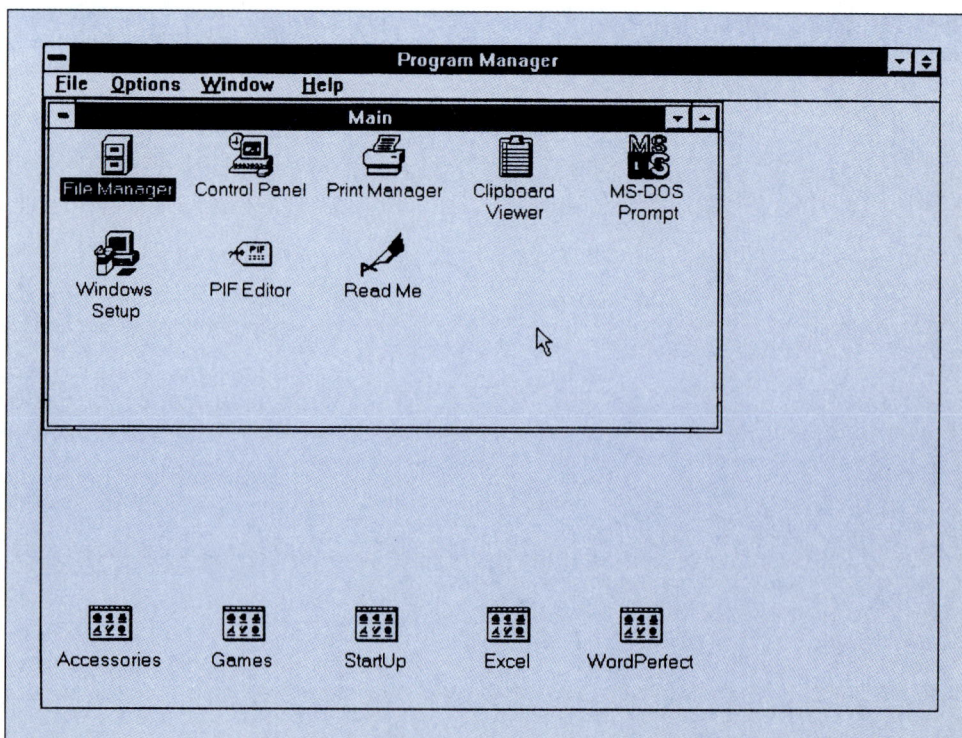

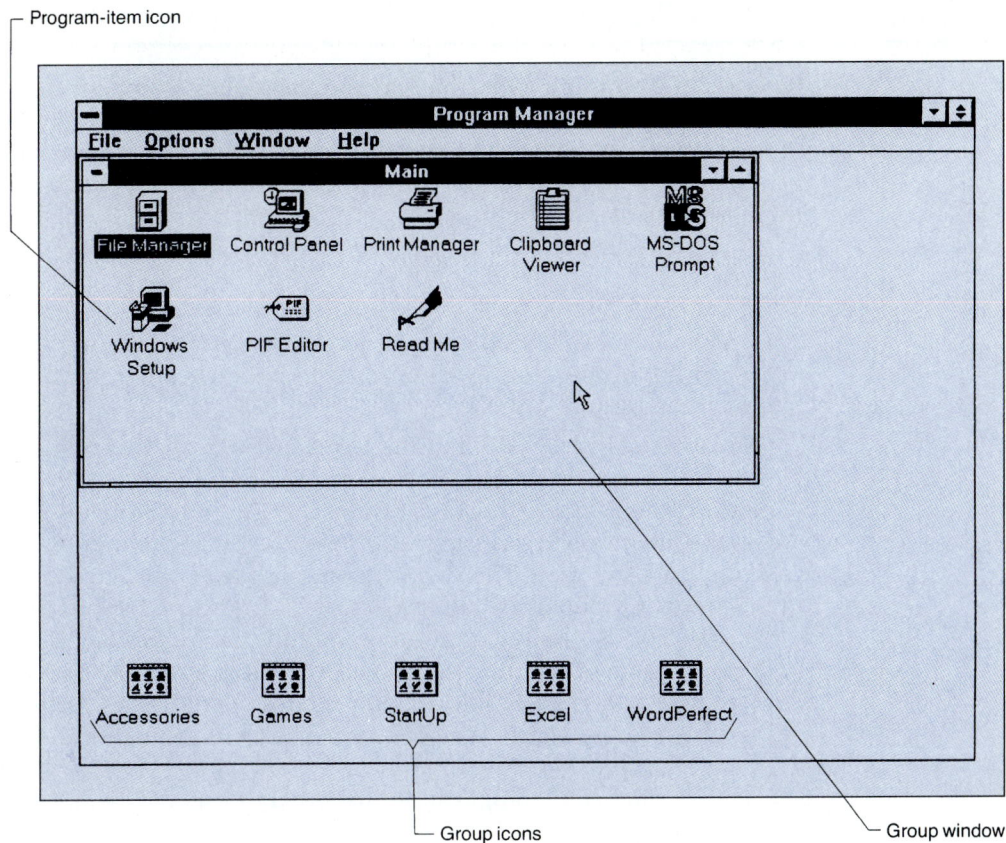

Figure 3–13
Parts of the Program Manager window.

3–9–2   Starting an Application from the Program Manager

Use the mouse and follow these steps to start an application:

1. Open the Program Manager window (if it is not already open).
2. Open the group window (if it is not already open) that includes your desired application by double-clicking on the group icon.
3. Double-click on the program-item icon for your desired application.

3–10   RUNNING TWO OR MORE APPLICATIONS AT THE SAME TIME

Windows allows you to run more than one application at one time. When you run multiple applications at the same time, the processing speed may be slower than normal. Processing speed also depends on the type of computer that you are using. To start several applications, start them in the desired sequence using the method that we just discussed.

3–11   SWITCHING BETWEEN APPLICATIONS

When you are running more than one application at a time, the window in which you are currently working is called the active window. The active window appears in the foreground. It might overlap or completely block other application windows that are also running on your system. To make another application active, you must select its window.

To switch between applications, you can choose one of the following methods:

1. If the application is visible, click the mouse anywhere in the application's window. If the application is running as an icon, click left on its icon, then click left on the Restore option.

2. Display Task List by pressing the Ctrl+Esc keys. A **Task List** is a window that shows all the applications that you have running and allows you to switch between them. Open the Task List by choosing the Switch To option from the Control menu or by pressing the Ctrl+Esc key combination. You will be presented with a screen similar to the one displayed in Figure 3–14. In the Task List window, double-click on the name of the desired application or highlight the name of the desired application and then select Switch To option from the options available in the dialog box. A **dialog box** is a window that appears temporarily to request information. Many dialog boxes include options that you must choose before Windows can execute a command.

To return to the application that you last used, press Alt+Tab.

Figure 3–14
Task List dialog box.

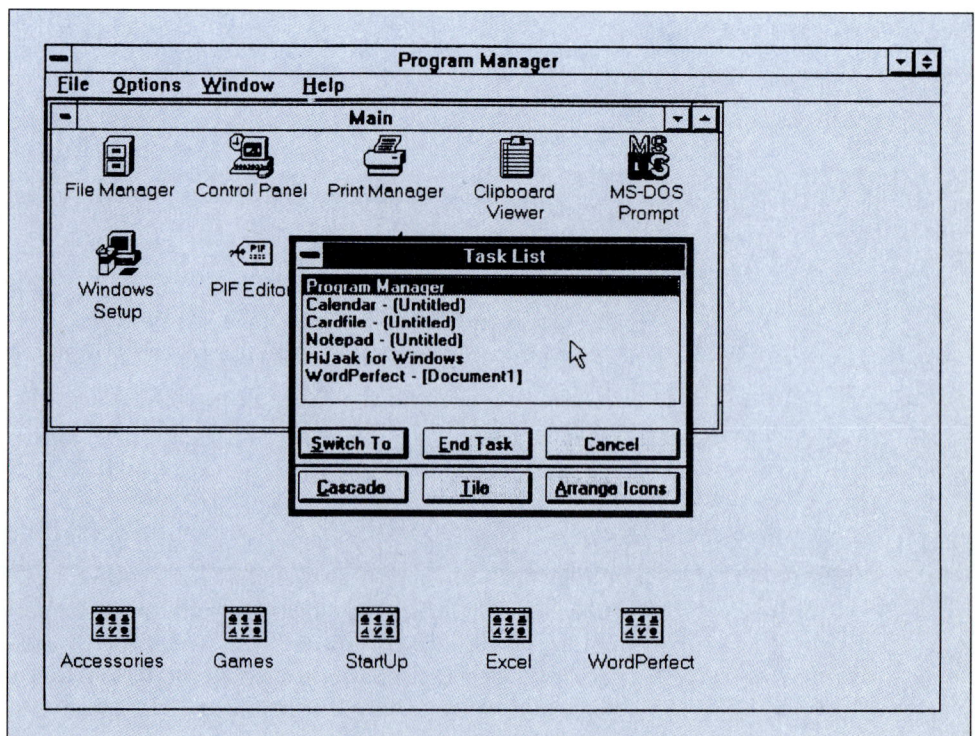

3–12   TRANSFERRING INFORMATION USING THE CLIPBOARD

The Windows **Clipboard** serves as a temporary location that stores information. The Clipboard enables you to copy or move information from one application and then copy ("paste") it in another application. The information that you copy to the Clipboard stays there until you clear the contents of the Clipboard or copy other information to it.

The Clipboard can also serve as a buffer for exchanging information among several applications.

3–12–1   Moving or Copying Information to the Clipboard

How information is moved or copied to the Clipboard depends on the type of application that you are running—a Windows application or a non-Windows application. It also depends on whether your application is running as a window or a full screen.

A Windows application allows you to easily move or copy information or an image to the Clipboard. To copy or move information to the Clipboard, follow these steps:

1. Highlight or select the text or the information that you want to move or copy. (For highlighting text, see the next section.) You can copy or move text, graphics, or both.
2. From the application's Edit menu (e.g., the Edit menu of Lotus 1-2-3), select Cut or Copy. Cut removes the selected text from its current position to the Clipboard. Copy only takes a snapshot for the Clipboard; the existing information remains intact.

You can copy the contents of an entire screen to the Clipboard by displaying the information then pressing the Print Screen key, or Shift+PrtSc or Alt+Prtsc. This process puts a snapshot (also called a bitmap) of the screen onto the Clipboard.

3–12–2   Selecting Text or Graphs

Editing commands can be performed on a block of text instead of on a single character. First you must select (highlight or block) the text. Then you can select various commands such as Cut, Copy, and so forth from the Edit menu of the application software.

To select text using the mouse, follow these steps:

1. Point to the first character of the desired text and click left.
2. Drag the insertion point to the end of the desired text.
3. Release the mouse button.

To cancel the selection, click the mouse button again anywhere in the document. Some applications such as WordPerfect for Windows allow you to select a word by double-clicking on it, a sentence by triple-clicking, an entire paragraph by quadruple-clicking, and so on.

To select a graph in the majority of Windows applications, you can click left on it.

3–12–3   **Transferring Information from the Clipboard**

To transfer the contents of the Clipboard to another application, follow these steps:

1. Start the desired application.
2. Position the insertion point at the place that you want the information from the Clipboard to appear.
3. From the Edit menu of the application (e.g., the Edit menu of Lotus 1-2-3), select Paste.

3–13   QUITTING AN APPLICATION

When you are finished working with an application, you should exit from it. Use one of the following methods to exit a Windows application:

- Select Exit from the application's File menu.
- Press Alt+F4.

To quit a non-Windows application, select the application's Exit or Quit command.

3–14   WORKING WITH GROUPS

Figure 3–15 shows **groups** containing program-item icons that represent applications, accessories, or documents. To start an application from a group, you have to select the application's icon. As you can see in Figure 3–15, Windows includes several predefined groups as follows:

1. The Main group, which is already open in Figure 3–15, contains Windows system applications:
   - File Manager—manages your files and disk drives
   - Control Panel—allows you to change the configuration of your system
   - Print Manager—allows you to install and configure printers
   - Clipboard Viewer—allows you to view, edit, and save the contents of the Clipboard
   - MS-DOS Prompt—allows you to exit to the DOS prompt
   - Windows Setup—displays the system configuration
   - PIF Editor—is a tool for editing program information files
   - Read Me—includes basic information about Windows
2. The Accessories group includes several interesting applications such as word processing, drawing, painting, communications, and so forth.
3. The Games group includes several games that you can use for learning the basics of Windows or for fun.

Figure 3–15
Example of groups.

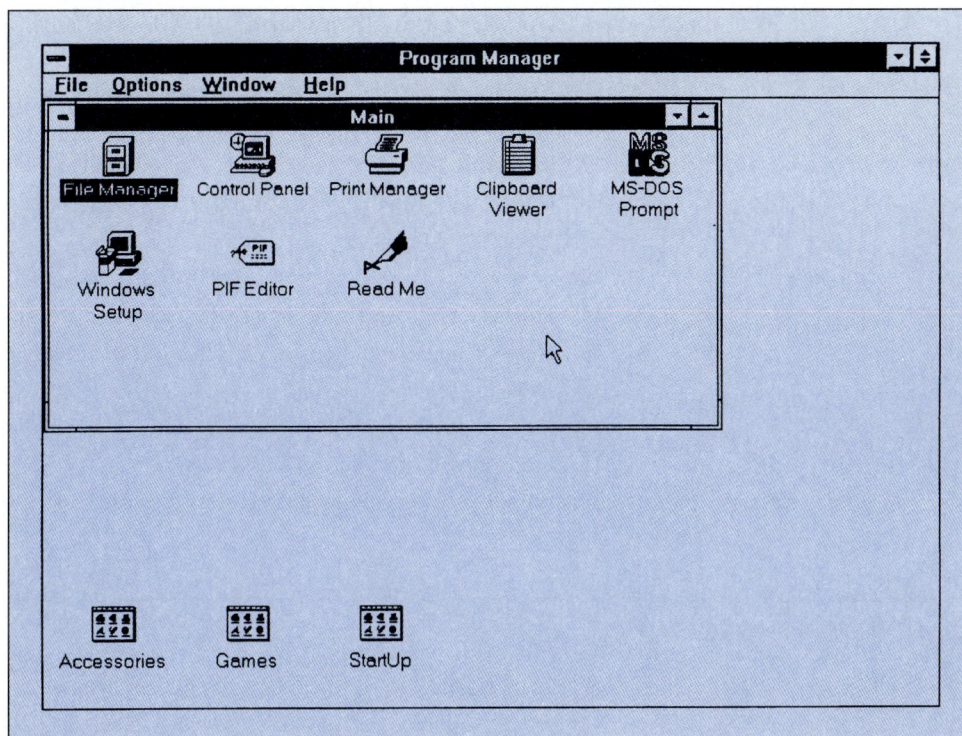

4. The StartUp group contains applications that start when you start Windows. This group is empty until you add applications to it. You can add any application to the group.

5. The Applications group contains applications found on the hard disk during setup. If you select the custom setup, and select not to have Windows set up applications from your hard disk, your Program Manager window will not contain an application group. This is the case in our example.

To start an application, you must first open its group window and select the appropriate program-item icon. To open a group window, double-click on the group icon.

SUMMARY

This chapter provided an overview of the Windows operating environment. The advantages of Windows as a graphical-based environment were highlighted. After the process of getting in and out of Windows was explained, some of the basic features of Windows were discussed: using the mouse, selecting from the Windows screen, using the Program Manager, running an application, working with the Clipboard, and working with a group.

REVIEW QUESTIONS

*These questions are answered in Appendix A.

1. What are some of the advantages of Windows?
*2. How do you start Windows?
3. What is a desktop? What is an icon?

4. How do you use the mouse in the Windows environment? How do you use the keyboard? Which one is easier to use?

5. Explain how to obtain online help in Windows.

6. How is the tutorial facility of Windows started?

7. What is the Control menu? How do you activate it?

*8. Give some of the commands in the Control menu.

9. What is the Program Manager?

10. How do you start an application from the Program Manager?

11. How can you run more than one application in Windows at the same time?

*12. How do you switch between applications?

13. Describe the Clipboard.

14. How do you transfer information from an application to the Clipboard?

15. How do you quit an application?

16. What is a group? How do you start a group?

HANDS-ON EXPERIENCE

1. Start Windows. Use the mouse to invoke the File pull-down menu; select Exit and then OK to leave Windows.

2. Start Windows again. This time exit Windows by means of the keyboard. To do this, first press Alt+F to access the File pull-down menu; then move the cursor to Exit Windows and press the Enter key twice.

3. Start Windows again. Using the mouse, select (one at a time) the File, Options, Window, and Help menus from inside the Program Manager. What is available under each option?

4. By double-clicking the left button of the mouse, open the accessories icon. What is available in this group?

5. Invoke the Windows tutorial program and spend an hour with it. What is available?

6. Use the Glossary option in the Help menu to display the first 20 items in the list.

7. Print the Contents screen by using the Print option from the File menu in the Program Manager Help window.

8. Use the mouse to enlarge the Main group window. Then return it to its previous size.

9. Double-click on the MS-DOS prompt icon. At the DOS prompt, use the DIR command to generate a listing of the current directory. Type *EXIT* and press Enter to return to Windows.

10. Press the Ctrl+Esc key combination to start the Task List. What is available in the Task List dialog box?

KEY TERMS

Click and drag	Group	Mouse pointer
Clipboard	Group Window	Online tutorial
Desktop	Icon	Program Manager
Dialog box	Multitasking	Task List
Graphical user interface (GUI)	Mouse	Window

KEY COMMANDS

Alt+F (to invoke the File menu)

Alt+Tab (to return to the previous application)

Commands for Program Manager (see Figure 3–1)

Ctrl+Esc (to invoke the Task List)

MISCONCEPTIONS AND SOLUTIONS

Misconception   Press the Alt key to activate the menu and move the cursor to an option to execute the option; this is time consuming.

> **Solution**   If a name in the menu bar has an underlined letter, you can press Alt to activate the menu bar and open the desired menu; then press the letter that is underlined. For example, to exit Windows: from the File Manager press Alt+F; then press the X key. An even faster method is to click the left button of the mouse while on the desired menu item.

Misconception   Performing search operations in the Help menu by typing the entire word in the Search for box is time consuming.

> **Solution**   The help facility matches characters you type as closely as possible with the available key words. Just type the closest word or a part of the word that comes to mind.

Misconception   Sometimes you see more than one control-menu box. This is confusing.

> **Solution**   The control-menu box at the far upper left of the screen controls the application (e.g., WordPerfect). The others control the windows inside the application window (e.g., a document in WordPerfect). The extreme upper left control-menu box is usually for the Program Manager.

Misconception   To maximize a window, you click on the maximize button, but this is time consuming.

> **Solution**   You can also maximize a window by double-clicking on its title bar. To restore an application window to its previous size, double-click on the title bar again.

ARE YOU READY TO MOVE ON?

Multiple Choice

1. The following statements about Windows are all true except for which one?
   a. It will run without DOS being in your computer.
   b. It is a graphical environment.
   c. It is a multitasking environment.
   d. It is easier to operate than DOS.
   e. All are true.

2. The following statements about Windows are all true except for which one?
   a. You can run Windows and DOS applications at the same time.
   b. You can link several files together.
   c. Windows provides better memory management than DOS.
   d. All are true.
   e. Only A and B are true.

3. Of the following items, which is not included in the accessories group of Windows 3.1?
   a. File Transfer
   b. Write
   c. Paintbrush
   d. Terminal
   e. Print Manager

4. To start Windows, first change to the drive and directory that contain your Windows files then, before pressing Enter, type
   a. *FILE*
   b. *FUN*
   c. *WIN*
   d. *TEST*
   e. *GO*

5. All the following tasks can be performed from the Windows desktop except
   a. fast application switching
   b. icon spacing changes
   c. displaying your document
   d. changing colors
   e. all are possible

6. The following are all possible applications of a mouse except
   a. invoking a menu
   b. exiting from Windows
   c. deselecting a menu
   d. all are possible
   e. only A and C are possible

7. If you are using a keyboard in the Windows environment, which of the following is *Not* true?
   a. You can use the middle part of the keyboard.
   b. You cannot use the function keys.
   c. You can use the key combinations.
   d. You can use the numeric keypad.
   e. These are all correct.

8. To activate the Task List, which key combination should you press?
   a. Alt+Tab
   b. Ctrl+Esc
   c. Ctrl+Tab
   d. Esc
   e. Alt+F10

9. To start the help facility of Windows,
   a. type *HELP* at the DOS prompt and press Enter
   b. select the Help option from any Windows application menu
   c. type *TUTOR* at the C> prompt and press Enter
   d. select Help from the File menu
   e. none of the above

10. The following are all parts of a Windows screen except
    a. window title
    b. control-menu box
    c. insertion point
    d. title bar
    e. DOS prompt

True/False

1. The minimize button is used to reduce the window to an icon.
2. The window border is the outside edge of a window.
3. The vertical and horizontal scroll bars are used to view only the first five lines of a window.
4. The mouse pointer indicates the present position of the pointer.
5. To return to your previous application, you must press Alt+Esc.
6. Windows applications do not all follow the same principles.
7. Windows presents a multitasking environment.
8. Windows cannot be used to link several files together.
9. The Accessories group is one of the predefined groups in Windows.
10. Application switching is *Not* possible from the Windows desktop.

ANSWERS

Multiple Choice		**True/False**	
1.	a	1.	T
2.	d	2.	T
3.	a	3.	F
4.	c	4.	T
5.	e	5.	F
6.	d	6.	F
7.	b	7.	T
8.	b	8.	F
9.	b	9.	T
10.	e	10.	F

Database and Information Systems

4

4–1   INTRODUCTION

In this chapter we review database principles. The role of the database in design and implementation of a CBIS is emphasized. Types of data models (sometimes called data structures) are introduced, and functions performed by a typical **database management system** (DBMS) are highlighted. The chapter concludes with a discussion of new trends in database design, including distributed databases and database machines.

4–2   DEFINING A DATABASE

A **database** is simply a collection of relevant data stored in a location. In this chapter, an overview of this important component of any computer-based information system is provided, as well as guidelines and instructions for the design and implementation of a database in the CBIS environment.

Databases are used even in manual systems. A file cabinet is a good example of a database. Various information and data are stored in a series of manila folders. In this type of database, however, speed and accuracy are not high. Figure 4–1 shows an example of a manual database. But in this chapter, we are interested exclusively in computerized databases to satisfy the specific need of a CBIS.

In computer terminology, a database is defined as a series of integrated files. A file is a series of related records. A record is a series of related fields. A field is a series of related characters. A character is 8 bits. Figure 4–2 illustrates data hierarchy.

To make these definitions clearer, consider a database as the information related to all the students, faculty, and staff of a state university. One file includes all the student records—their names, Social Security numbers, GPAs, and so forth. Another file includes all the faculty records. And the third file belongs to the staff of the university.

The database is closely associated with DBMS software. A DBMS is a series of computer programs used to create, store, maintain, and access a database. The features offered by a particular DBMS depend on its type and level of sophistication. For example, dBASE is a sophisticated DBMS for microcomput-

Figure 4–1
Example of a manual database

Figure 4–2
Data hierarchy

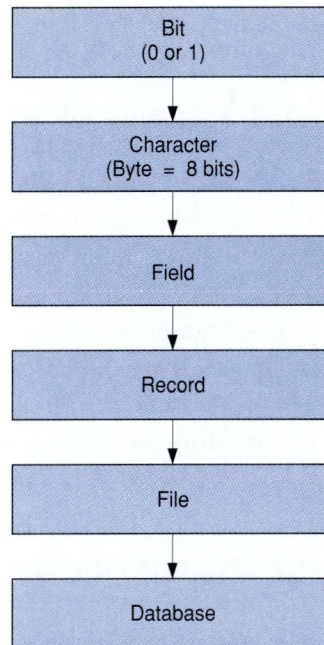

Figure 4–3
Relationship of DBMS, database, and application programs

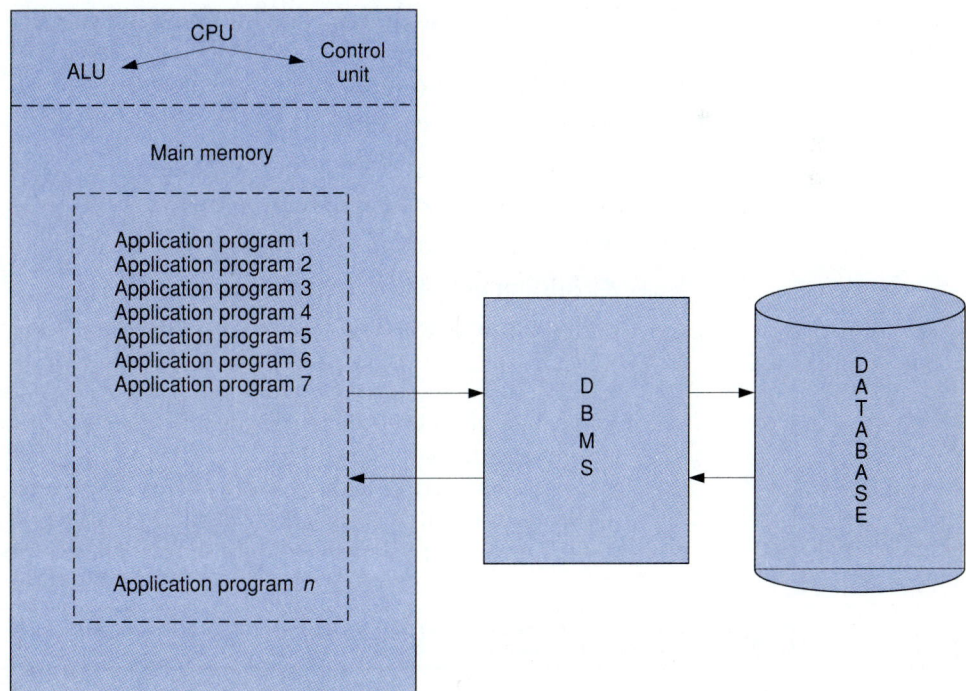

ers. Several other database management systems for microcomputers were highlighted in Chapter 1. Figure 4–3 illustrates the relationship of DBMS to database and application programs. As this figure indicates, an application program written in a high-level language accesses the database through the DBMS software. In other words, DBMS software serves as the gatekeeper for the database.

In comparison with a flat file environment, the database environment offers unique advantages:

- Data and application programs are independent, so the same data can be used by several application programs.
- More information can be generated from the same amount of data. In other words, a given set of data can be manipulated in many ways.
- One-of-a-kind requests can be fulfilled easily.
- Data duplication is minimal. This is true because only one occurrence of each data item is maintained.
- Data management is enhanced and improved. This is possible because there is only one set of data for all users.
- More sophisticated security measures (discussed in the next chapter) can be implemented.

4–3   THE DATABASE ADMINISTRATOR

Design and implementation of a database is done by a **database administrator** (DBA). The scope of the responsibility of a DBA depends on the complexity of the database. Some organizations devote an entire group to database design and maintenance. In smaller organizations, one person may carry the entire responsibility of database design. The following are some of the responsibilities of a DBA:

- Designing and implementing a database
- Establishing security measures
- Establishing recovery procedures
- Documenting the database
- Establishing database performance evaluations
- Adding new database functions
- Fine-tuning existing database functions

In a database environment, both a DBA and database administration are critical. Careful consideration must be given to establishing an effective database administration office and DBA.

Generating a database increases cost and creates more complexity in a CBIS operation. Nevertheless, implementation of an effective CBIS requires an online and comprehensive database regardless of its cost and complexity.

4–4   THE ROLE OF A DATABASE IN CBIS DESIGN AND USE

Any CBIS is designed to provide timely and relevant information by performing data analysis, modeling analysis, or both. Data analysis includes various query operations on a database. Modeling analysis applies some types of models to the data available in the database and provides additional information that is not directly available within the data. To make this discussion clearer, consider the following example.

The data in Table 4–1 was extracted from the corporate database of On-Line Automated, a wholesaler of electronic devices. By manipulating the data, we

Table 4–1

On-Line Automated corporate database

Salespersons	Cities (figures in thousands)				
	LA	Denver	Portland	St. Paul	Detroit
Sue	100	600	680	600	625
Jack	150	510	750	500	980
Bob	180	580	900	480	640
Robin	200	610	830	900	720
Mary	600	920	650	600	690
Becky	250	630	490	400	950
Silvia	350	640	500	600	250
John	750	510	610	720	700
Melanie	550	650	450	950	900

can discover who has the highest total sales, who has the lowest total sales, which city has the highest total sales, and which city has the lowest total sales.

Can anything be predicted about the future by examining these data? Can any statistical conclusion be drawn, either for the salespersons or the sales regions? Based on such simple data analysis, the answer to these questions is no. If we use modeling analysis, however, we can provide answers to these questions and more. With a simple forecasting model, we can generate a forecast for total sales for any city or salesperson. Statistical models can be used to compare the performances of cities or salespersons and to spot significant differences.

As you can see, for any type of analysis, a sophisticated database is essential. A DBMS maintains data as one of the most valuable resources in the organization and provides access to the authorized users.

4–5   A DATABASE AS A CORPORATE RESOURCE

A sophisticated database in a typical business organization may include relevant data related to four major functional areas: finance, marketing, manufacturing, and personnel. Figure 4–4 illustrates a corporate database, and Table 4–2 highlights data items that should be maintained in these individual databases.

4–6   DESIGNING A DATABASE

The first step in designing a database is to identify a data model. A **data model** is a procedure for creating and maintaining a database. A data dictionary must also be defined. A **data dictionary** includes definitions of all the data used in a database—types, sizes, and so forth. Figure 4–5 illustrates a data dictionary.

Finally, the type of organization should be identified. Is it sequential, random, or indexed sequential? In sequential organization, all of the records are stored and accessed one after the other. This method is similar to a cassette tape and is slow. If you want to access the seventh song on the tape, you must either listen to the first six songs or fast forward through them. Typically, this method is used for archiving files. Random organization enables you to access a record

Figure 4–4
A corporate database

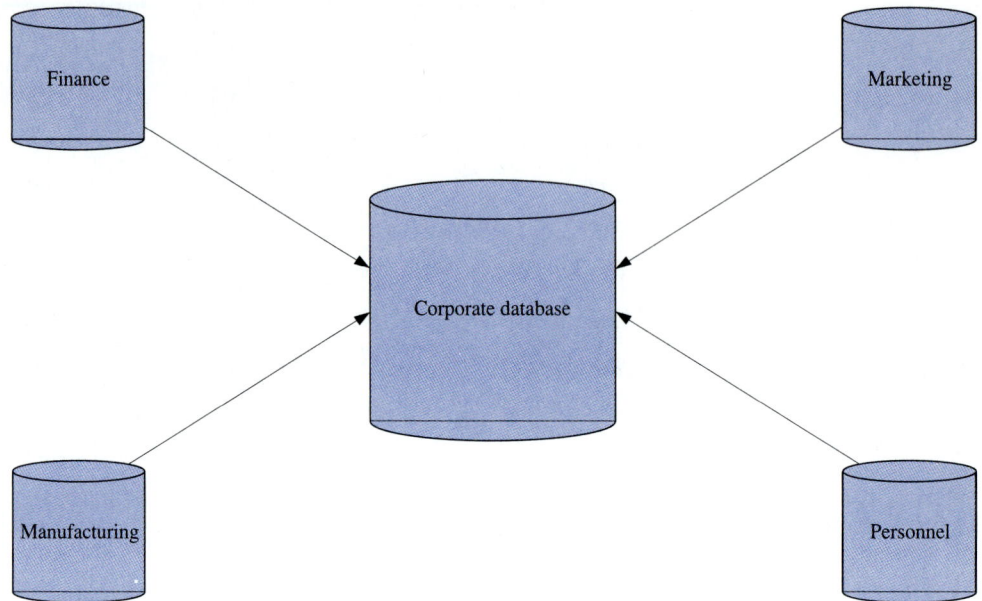

Table 4–2
Corporate database: A typical example

Functional Area	Date to Be Collected and Maintained
Finance	Payroll Costs Taxes Income/loss statements Balance sheets Cash flow Sources of funds Uses of funds
Manufacturing	Warehousing Transportation Purchasing Inventory Production Technology Legal environment
Marketing	Economy Consumer behavior Competitors Sales Promotional activities Advertising
Personnel	Wages and salaries Contracts Skills inventory Personal history Training

Figure 4–5
Example of a data dictionary

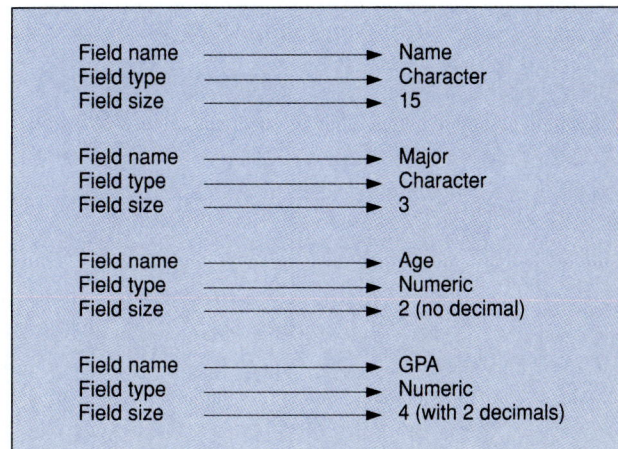

Field name	⟶ Name
Field type	⟶ Character
Field size	⟶ 15
Field name	⟶ Major
Field type	⟶ Character
Field size	⟶ 3
Field name	⟶ Age
Field type	⟶ Numeric
Field size	⟶ 2 (no decimal)
Field name	⟶ GPA
Field type	⟶ Numeric
Field size	⟶ 4 (with 2 decimals)

directly regardless of its storage location. In indexed-sequential organization, you can access a file either sequentially or randomly.

4–6–1   The Flat File Model

A file management system, or a **flat file model,** is simply a file or a series of files that contain records and fields. These files are called flat because there are no relationships between them and because they have no repeating groups. The flat file system does not allow sophisticated database operations performed by other data models. Table 4–3 illustrates an example of a flat file system.

Basic data management operations such as file creation, deletion, updating, and simple data query can be performed using this model. However, as mentioned earlier, this type of data model is limited in its capacity to support complex CBIS requirements.

4–6–2   The Relational Model

A **relational model,** the most popular model, uses a mathematical construct called a relation (table), which is simply a table of rows and columns of data. Rows are records (tuples) and columns are fields (attributes). Different relations can be linked on the basis of a common field (key). To clarify this concept, look at the two relations in Tables 4–4 and 4–5. As you can see, the common field in these two relations is the customer number. A relational DBMS can use these two relations to generate a report like the one in Table 4–6.

The relational model is straightforward. Creation and maintenance of this type of database are easy, as are additions and deletions of records. Overall,

Table 4–3
Example of a flat file

Name	Major	Age	GPA
Mary	MIS	25	3.00
Sue	CS	21	3.60
Debra	MGT	26	3.50
Bob	MKT	22	3.40
George	MIS	28	3.70

Table 4–4
A customer relation

Customer No.	Name	Address
2000	Adams	2020 Broadway
3000	Baker	119 Jefferson
9000	Clark	7521 Madison

Table 4–5
An invoice relation

Invoice No.	Customer No.	Amount	Method of Payment
111	2000	$2000	Cash
222	3000	$4000	Credit
333	3000	$1500	Cash
444	9000	$6400	Cash
555	9000	$7000	Credit

Table 4–6
Invoice and customer relations are joined using customer number

Invoice No.	Customer No.	Amount	Method of Payment	Name	Address
111	2000	$2000	Cash	Adams	2020 Broadway
222	3000	$4000	Credit	Baker	119 Jefferson
333	3000	$1500	Cash	Baker	119 Jefferson
444	9000	$6400	Cash	Clark	7521 Madison
555	9000	$7000	Credit	Clark	7521 Madison

relational models offer a great degree of flexibility. General operations handled by a relational model include the following:

- Creation of relation
- Updating (insertion, deletion, and modification)
- Selection of a relation or a sub-relation
- **Join operation** (putting two relations side by side)
- **Projection** (selection of a subset of a field or a subset of a series of fields)
- General query operation

A major shortcoming of the relational model is in dealing with complex database operations. Establishing many relations, with the key included in each one, may use a great deal of disk space, and modification may be time consuming. This model may limit insertion of new records. Advance planning may resolve some of these problems.

Overall, the relational model is more suitable for applications when a shorter developmental time is needed.

4–6–3

The Hierarchical Model

Like the relational model, a **hierarchical data model** is made up of records (called nodes), each of which can have several fields. The presentation is similar to a one-dimensional array (a table with only one column or one row) or tree structure. The relationships between the records are called branches. The node at the top of the hierarchy is called the root, and every node of the tree except the root node has a parent. The nodes with the same parent are called twins or siblings. For example, P1 and P2 in Figure 4–6 are twins.

In the hierarchical model, the connections between files do not depend on the data contained within the files. The connections are defined initially when the database is designed and are maintained for the entire life of the database. For example, file X is linked to file Y regardless of their contents. The connection between records is hierarchical.

The hierarchical model is sometimes called an upside-down tree (a tree with its roots up). Figure 4–6 illustrates an example of a hierarchical model; it indicates that a supplier may supply three different families of products. In each family, there may be several different product categories. As an example, supplier X may supply soap, shampoo, and toothpaste. Within each product category, there may be many brands of the same product—for example, nine different shampoos or five different toothpastes. Such a relationship is called a one-to-many data structure, which means a parent can have many children; however, each child has only one parent. In the hierarchical model, a search in the parent node can lead you to children nodes and vice versa. Any updating in a parent node should automatically update the children nodes.

The operations associated with the hierarchical model include file creation, file updating (insertion, deletion, addition, and modification), queries, retrieval of the next descendent record, and retrieval of the parent record.

Figure 4–6
Example of a hierarchical model

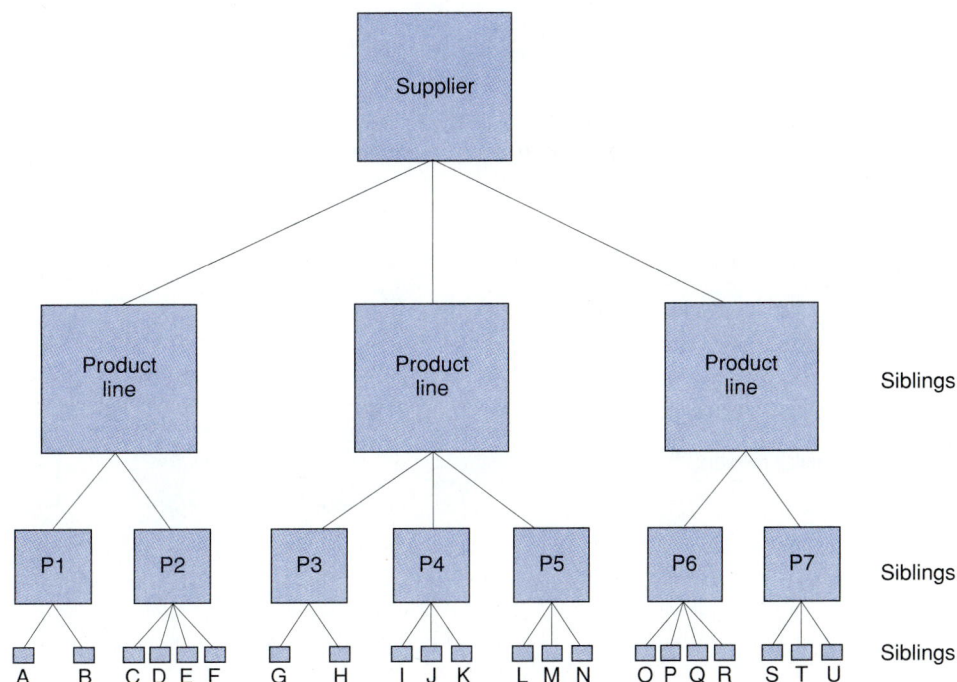

When compared with the relational data model, the hierarchical model is less flexible, primarily because the designer should know the data relationships of a particular system ahead of time.

The Network Model

The **network model** is similar to the hierarchical model. However, the records and fields of a network model are organized differently. Figure 4–7 illustrates customer and invoice relations in a network model. In place of related key fields, there is a connection between the invoice number, the customer number, and the method of payment. In this case, the customer number no longer needs to remain in the invoice record. As Figure 4–7 illustrates, invoice numbers are connected to the customer number in the same order in which they were entered (see Table 4–4).

The network model is not as flexible as the relational model. Also, the data relationships must be defined ahead of time to see if the network model will be suitable for a particular CBIS operation. Operations associated with a network model include file creation, file updating (insertion, deletion, addition, and modification), and queries.

The network model can be considered an enhanced version of the hierarchical model. In this data structure the relationship can be either one-to-many (simple network) or many-to-many (complex network). Figure 4–7 illustrates a one-to-many relationship. Each parent (invoice) has two children (method of payment and customer number). Figure 4–8 illustrates a many-to-many relationship. In a real estate agency, each agent is showing several properties. For example, agent A-1

Figure 4–7
Example of a simple network model

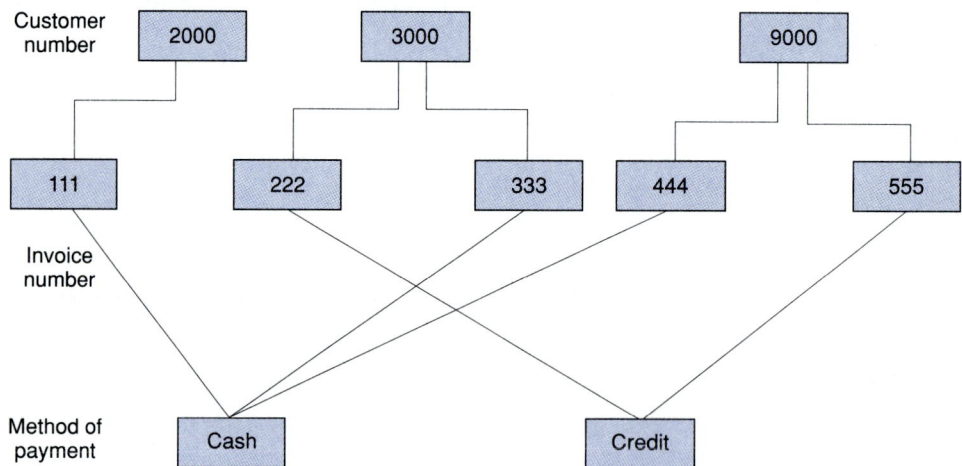

Figure 4–8
Example of a complex network model

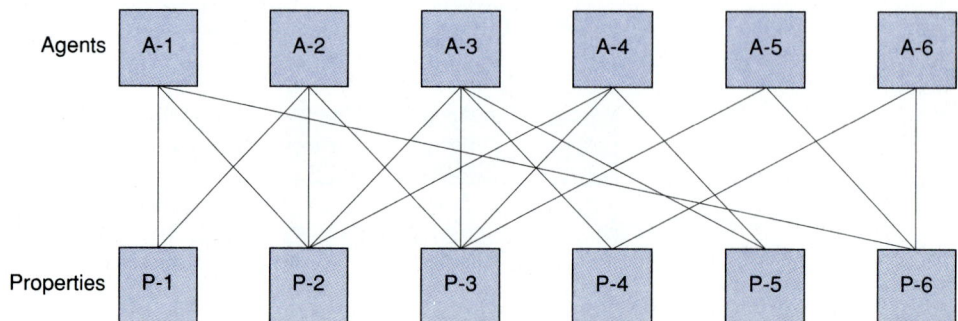

shows properties P-1, P-2, and P-6, but property P-1 is listed with both agents A-1 and A-2. In a many-to-many relationship, the parent-child relationship breaks down, because any record can be the parent and any record can be the child.

4–7   DATABASE MANAGEMENT SYSTEM FUNCTIONS

A database management system, regardless of its data structure (data model), must be able to perform the following operations for effective use in a CBIS environment. In these examples, we use the relational model for simplicity, but these operations are available in other types of data models.

- *Basic data management operations.* The basic data management operations include database creation, modification, deletion, addition, insertion, and maintenance. These operations are supported even in a file (flat file) management system.
- *Basic arithmetic operations.* These include simple arithmetic operations performed on different records and fields in a database, including addition, subtraction, multiplication, and division. These basic operations may be quite useful for simple query operations, such as calculating the average salary for both male and female employees or finding the maximum and minimum salary for each gender.
- *Projection operation.* This function may be a special case of a general query operation that generates a subset of the fields. For example, in a student database that includes each student's name, GPA, age, gender, address, and nationality, a projection operation could generate a listing of the names and GPAs of all these students or a mailing list for mailing the students' transcripts.
- *Search (Query).* This function may include different searches on a database for specific conditions. As an example, a triple-criteria search on our example student database is as follows:

```
DISPLAY ALL STUDENTS FOR GPA >= 3 AND MAJOR = "CS" AND AGE <= 22
```

Query operations can include as many criteria as the number of fields in the database. The search can include an AND search (all criteria specified must be met), an OR search (only one of the specified criteria must be met), or a NOT search (opposite criteria must be met or supply an alternative). AND, OR, and NOT are referred to as Boolean operations.

- *Sort.* **Sort operations** put the database in a specific order. Data can be sorted with one key or multiple keys in ascending or descending order.
- *Summary.* The summary operation may be a special case of basic arithmetic operations and basic query operations. For example, you could generate a subtotal of all MIS students and all accounting students in the student database.
- *Union (merge) operation.* The **union (merge) operation** enables a user to combine two files, tables, or relations, thereby generating a third file, table, or relation that includes all the information from the first two files, tables, or relations. In other words, the union operation does concatenation (joining) over the existing data. Table 4–7 presents this operation on a student database. File 3 is the union of files 1 and 2. Remember, to perform the union operation, the two databases must be **union compatible.** This means they must include the same number of fields and data type.

Table 4-7
Example of a union operation

File 1		File 2		File 3 (union of files 1 and 2)	
Student	**Major**	**Student**	**Major**	**Student**	**Major**
Bob	MIS	Mary	Marketing	Bob	MIS
Barry	CS	Sherry	MIS	Barry	CS
James	MIS	Sandy	Math	James	MIS
Sue	Accounting			Sue	Accounting
				Mary	Marketing
				Sherry	MIS
				Sandy	Math

- *Join operation.* This operation combines two or more files, tables, or relations within a database on a common field in order to generate the third file, table, or relation. Table 4–8 illustrates one example of this operation in which the common key is the customer name.

- *Intersection operation.* The **intersection operation** generates the intersection of two relations in a third relation containing a common tuple(s) (common rows). The relations must be union compatible. Table 4–9 illustrates this operation. The result of the intersection of relations 1 and 2 is relation 3, which contains only one row (tuple), the one belonging to the first two relations.

Table 4-8
Example of a join operation

Relation 1		Relation 2		Relation 3 (joining of relations 1 and 2)		
Customer	**Purchase No.**	**Customer**	**Purchase Amount**	**Customer**	**Purchase No.**	**Purchase Amount**
Barry	112	Barry	$2000	Barry	112	$2000
James	118	James	$5000	James	118	$5000
Susan	129	Susan	$1000	Susan	129	$1000
Bob	135	Bob	$1500	Bob	135	$1500

Table 4-9
Example of an intersection operation

Relation 1			Relation 2			Relation 3 (intersection of relations 1 and 2)		
Student	**Major**	**GPA**	**Student**	**Major**	**GPA**	**Student**	**Major**	**GPA**
Bob	CS	3.60	Tom	ACC	2.90	Tom	ACC	2.90
Bobby	MIS	3.80	Jerry	CIS	3.70			
Tom	ACC	2.90	Don	MGT	3.90			

4–8   NEW TRENDS IN DATABASE DESIGN AND USE

Several new trends, including natural language processing, distributed databases, and database machines, have been occurring in database design and use.

Advances in natural language processing will have a definite effect on the design and use of databases. Natural language processing should give the CBIS user easier access by providing an interface more similar to the user's native language. How nice it would be to pick up a microphone and ask the database to print a listing of overdue accounts! At the present time, no full-featured natural language is available because of the ambiguities in our native languages.

Currently, these trends may be of limited practical importance. In the near future, however, they may be quite significant and may have a direct effect on the design and use of computer-based information systems.

4–8–1   Distributed Databases

So far in our discussion, we have assumed a central database for all the users of a CBIS. However, several factors indicate a database that is a **distributed database** (distributed throughout an organization) is better than a centralized database:

- Economic constraints. For remote users of a CBIS (those users who are not located in the same place where the CBIS is located), it may not be economically feasible to access the central database all the time. It may be more economical to store some of the data at the remote site(s).

- Lack of responsiveness. A centralized database may not be responsive to the immediate needs of a CBIS user. A distributed database provides an immediate response to a user's request.

- Enhanced sophistication in microcomputers. The increasing sophistication and decreasing cost of microcomputers have made distributed processing more feasible and the use of micros a more viable option in a distributed environment. Distributed databases are even more promising with the introduction of multiuser PCs.

- Change in data processing organizational structure. Since the mid-1970s, there has been a trend toward distributed processing. This trend certainly includes database design and implementation. When considering user needs, the responsiveness of this type of system is evidently higher than that of a centralized system.

- Security issues. Although the security of a distributed system versus a centralized system is a debatable issue, in a distributed system the damage and failure may be localized.

These factors support a distributed DBMS. In distributed databases, the data is not located at the same site as the user or the computer. There are some specific advantages of a distributed DBMS: local storage of data decreases response times and communication costs; data distribution involving multiple sites minimizes the effects of a computer breakdown, restricting it to its point of occurrence; the size and number of users are not limited by computer's size or processing power; multiple, integrated small systems might cost less than one large computer; most important of all, a distributed database need not be con-

Figure 4–9
Example of a distributed database

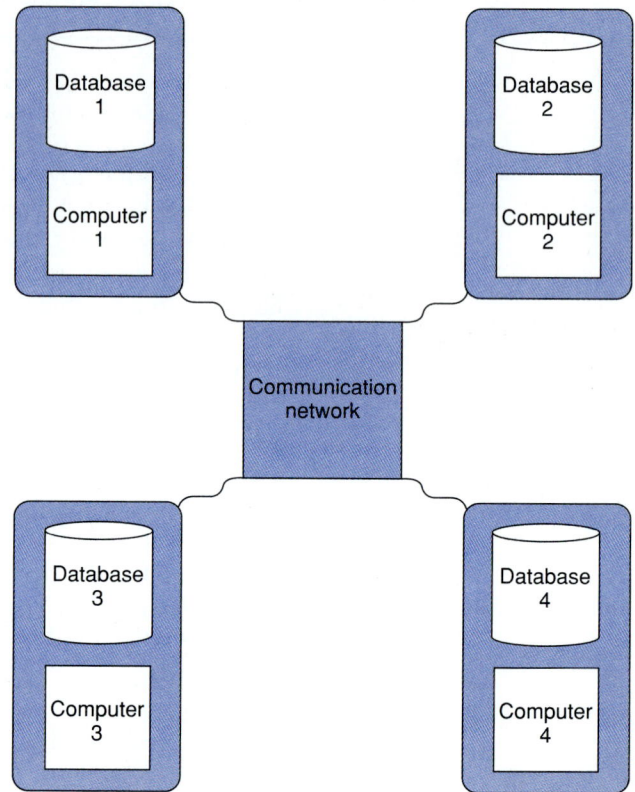

strained by the physical organization of data. Corporate data can be stored in any location and can be accessed from any other location.

A distributed database may follow the data model discussed earlier; however, more than one user can access the same database at the same time. DBAs must design specific features and access codes so that only one user can update the database at any time, otherwise data discrepancies may occur.

Security issues are more important in a multiuser environment, because the system can be accessed from both inside and outside the organization. Security policies must be clearly defined and the authorized users must be identified. The scope of users' access and their times of access also must be clearly defined. Generally speaking, the designer of a database and CBIS must bear in mind that not all applications are suitable for distributed processing.

A distributed database may be designed in several configurations. Figure 4–9 illustrates one example of this type of database.

4–8–2

Database Machines

Database machines have attracted attention in recent years because they enhance efficiency. Database machines simply serve as back-end processors to the main computer system. Because a second processor handles the entire operation related to the DBMS, the first processor (the main computer system) can be dedicated to the application programs. In other words, database machines provide an environment for parallel processing and multitasking (performing more than one task at the same time). This technology has not existed long, so it is difficult to judge its effectiveness. Although it seems to have merit in complex business environments, its real effectiveness is yet to be seen.

SUMMARY

In this chapter we reviewed database and database management systems. The role of a database in the design and use of a CBIS was discussed. We defined database models, including flat file, relational, hierarchical, and network. DBMS functions were explained and we presented several examples. The chapter concluded with a discussion of distributed databases and database machines. In the next chapter, we discuss distributed processing in detail.

REVIEW QUESTIONS

*These questions are answered in Appendix A.

1. What is a database?
2. What are some of the advantages of a database environment compared to flat files?
*3. What are some of the responsibilities of a DBA?
4. Why is a database so crucial in CBIS design?
5. What is data analysis?
6. What is modeling analysis?
*7. What is a data model?
8. What are three types of access methods?
9. Why is the sequential access method slow?
10. Compare and contrast the flat file, relational, hierarchical, and network data models. What are the unique advantages of each type of model?
11. List seven DBMS functions.
12. What is a join operation? Projection? Merge?
*13. What does union compatible mean?
14. For what types of DBMS functions is union compatibility needed?
15. What is a distributed database?
*16. Why and how may a distributed database increase the responsiveness of a CBIS?
17. Is security higher or lower in a distributed environment? Discuss.
18. What is the role of natural language processing in database design and use?
19. What is a database machine?
*20. What are some of the advantages of a database machine?
21. Design a database of the students in your class and perform the seven basic DBMS functions. Hint: You may have to set up several small databases or relations.
22. What is the most logical way to organize a file cabinet? How do you transfer the same principle to a computerized database?
23. Contact a real estate agency in your area and find out how it is managing information related to different properties. What type of report is generated by a computerized database in such a setting? How does the city hall in your area manage its real estate properties?
24. Set up a database similar to Table 4–1. Your table should include 10 student names and 5 test scores. What type of information will be generated by such a table (database)? Who can benefit the most from this table?
25. Assume that you have been asked to set up a database for all the students in your school. What will you include in this database? What type of information will be generated by this database? Who will be the prime user of this database?
26. Computerized search in the library of your school is a good example of an automated database. Consult your librarian and find out how this computerized data-

base works. What type of information is included in this database? Compare and contrast this database with a manual database. What are some of the obvious advantages of this computerized database over the manual database? What type of data model is used by such a database (flat file, hierarchical, relational, or network)?

27. What type of database management system is available in your school? What are some of the functions of this DBMS? Is there a distributed database available? Discuss.

28. Consult computer magazines and find out the strengths and weaknesses of a database machine. Who are some of the vendors of these machines? Who are some of the prime users of database machines?

29. Discuss the role of a natural language processing system in the design and use of a database. Will it become easier to use a database? Discuss.

KEY TERMS

Data dictionary	Distributed database	Projection
Data model	Flat file model	Query operation
Database	Hierarchical data model	Relational model
Database administrator	Intersection operation	Sort operation
Database machine	Join operation	Union (merge) operation
Database management system	Network model	Union compatible

ARE YOU READY TO MOVE ON?

Multiple Choice

1. Which of the following represents the data hierarchy in a computerized database system from smallest component to largest component?
   a. field, record, file, database
   b. record, file, field, database
   c. database, file, record, field
   d. file, record, field, database
   e. file, database, record, field

2. A DBMS is
   a. the database itself
   b. the person in charge of the database
   c. a series of computer programs
   d. a master of science degree in databases
   e. none of the above

3. Responsibilities of the DBA include
   a. designing and implementing the database
   b. documenting the database
   c. adding new database functions
   d. both a and c
   e. all the above

Questions 4 and 5 refer to the following database:

Student	Exam 1	Exam 2	Exam 3	Final
Bill	95	92	95	
Mary	80	86	97	

John	90	95	93
Alice	65	75	85
Bob	85	87	86

4. The results of an analysis are as follows:

   - Bill had the highest score on exam 1.
   - John had the highest score on exam 2.
   - Mary had the highest score on exam 3.

   What kind of analysis was performed?
   a. statistical analysis
   b. modeling analysis
   c. simple data query
   d. sensitivity analysis
   e. none of the above

5. The result of an analysis is as follows:

   Alice has shown constant improvement and will score a 95 on the final exam.

   What kind of analysis was performed?
   a. statistical analysis
   b. modeling analysis
   c. simple data analysis (query)
   d. sensitivity analysis
   e. none of the above

6. In a relational database, different relations can be linked by the
   a. table
   b. tuple
   c. attribute
   d. key
   e. none of the above

7. To be effective, a DBMS must be able to perform the following operation(s):
   a. basic arithmetic operations
   b. search
   c. sort
   d. all of the above
   e. b and c only

8. Boolean operations include
   a. add, subtract, multiply, divide
   b. +, −, *, /
   c. sort, summary, join
   d. flat file, relational, hierarchical
   e. AND, OR, NOT

9. Which of the following is (are) *not* an advantage(s) of distributed databases?
   a. increases response times and communication costs
   b. minimizes the effects of computer breakdown
   c. not constrained by the physical organization of data
   d. size and number of users is not limited by one computer's size or processing power
   e. all the above are advantages

10. The hierarchical database model is sometimes called
    a. a flat file
    b. an upside-down tree
    c. a network model
    d. a many-to-one relationship model
    e. none of the above

True/False

1. A database is a collection of relevant data stored in a location.
2. With a flat file system, data duplication is minimal and data management is enhanced and improved.
3. The database administrator designs and implements the database.
4. When designing a database, a data model must be identified, a data dictionary must be defined, and the type of access must be identified.
5. Sequential access is generally faster than random access.
6. Flat files allow highly sophisticated database operations because there are no relationships between them.
7. The hierarchical database model is less flexible than the relational database model.
8. The relationships in the network model are always one-to-many.
9. In distributed databases, the data is always located at the same site as the user or the computer.
10. Database machines serve as back-end processors, providing an environment for parallel processing and multitasking.

ANSWERS

Multiple Choice		True/False	
1.	a	1.	T
2.	c	2.	F
3.	e	3.	T
4.	c	4.	T
5.	b	5.	F
6.	d	6.	F
7.	d	7.	T
8.	e	8.	F
9.	a	9.	F
10.	b	10.	T

Paradox for Windows at a Glance

5

5–1   INTRODUCTION

This chapter reviews the basics of Paradox for Windows. It defines the general concept of a database and explains the process of getting Paradox for Windows started. The chapter briefly explains the Paradox for Windows desktop and then introduces the help facilities and some general applications of Paradox for Windows. Next there is a brief discussion of file names and data types supported in the Paradox for Windows environment. The chapter concludes with an overview of the Paradox for Windows terminology.

5–2   WHAT IS A DATABASE?

In simple terms, a **database** is an organized collection of data stored in a central location. We all have used many databases but we may not have called them that. A telephone directory is a good example of a database that has been organized alphabetically.

A better example of a database is the Yellow Pages. This database is also organized alphabetically; however, it is organized internally as well. If you are looking for a restaurant, you turn to the R section, find *Restaurants*, and then search alphabetically for a particular restaurant.

In computer terminology we call a database a collection of files, or more specifically, a collection of a series of integrated files. A **file** is a collection of records. A **record** is a collection of related fields treated as a unit, and a **field** is a collection of characters. In other words, records contain the individual information about the entity being described in the database and the fields are the data items of interest about the entity.

Your name, age, and occupation are all examples of fields. If you put name, age, and occupation fields together, you have constructed a record. Putting several student records together would establish a student file. You can have a staff file, a faculty file, and so on. The collection of all these files is called a database. Throughout this book we use the words file, table, and database interchangeably. Please do not get confused! Figure 5–1 is an example of a simple student file. This file includes 10 records with 5 fields per record. The name, major, age, GPA, and gender are field names. Bob, MIS, 22, 2.90, and M are the contents of these fields for the first record.

Most small and medium-size businesses use file cabinets to store their data. File cabinets are organized using a series of file folders. Data in each folder is organized alphabetically, numerically, or by some other ordering scheme. Such a file cabinet and the information it contains can be called a **manual database**.

There are several differences between a manual and an automated database. An automated database is faster, more accurate, and occupies less space than a manual database. Paradox for Windows offers comprehensive database capabilities. We will talk about most of these capabilities in this text.

5–3   GETTING IN AND OUT OF PARADOX FOR WINDOWS

You start Paradox for Windows the same way you start all Windows applications: by double-clicking the program icon in the Windows Program Manager. To display the Paradox for Windows desktop follow these steps:

Figure 5–1
An example of a student database.

Name	Major	Age	GPA	Gender
Bob	MIS	22	2.90	M
Mary	CS	25	2.20	F
Sue	CS	31	2.60	F
Tom	MIS	19	3.80	M
Harry	ACC	26	3.40	M
Sherry	MKT	35	3.90	F
Ray	MGT	41	3.70	M
Terry	ACC	21	2.40	M
Susan	MIS	23	3.80	F
Pam	MIS	29	3.30	F

1. Start the Program Manager.
2. Double-click the Paradox for Windows group icon.
3. In this group double-click the Paradox for Windows icon. At this point the Paradox for Windows desktop appears (see Figure 5–2).

To leave Paradox for Windows click on **File,** then on **Exit.** This will return you to the Paradox for Windows group. You can also double-click the control menu box (discussed in Chapter 3) or press the **Alt+F4** key combination.

Figure 5–2
The Paradox for Windows Desktop.

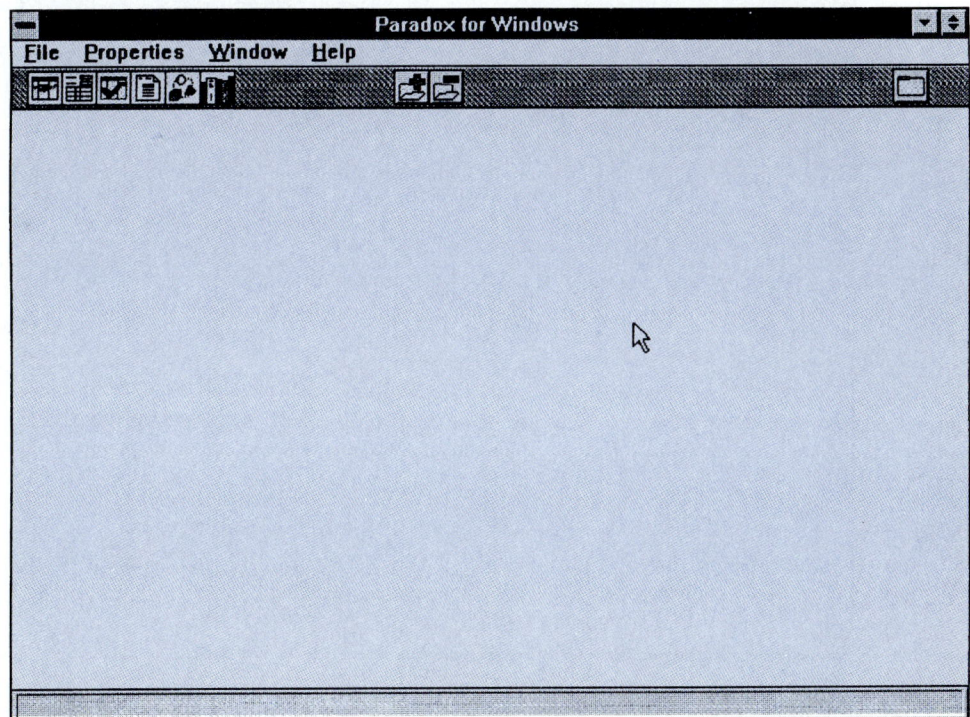

5–4   FIRST LOOK AT THE PARADOX FOR WINDOWS DESKTOP

As you can see in Figure 5–3, the Paradox for Windows desktop includes several distinct areas. Let us briefly explain each area:

1. The title bar. The Paradox for Windows title bar is the uppermost line of the screen. The Title Bar indicates the name of the program, which in this case is Paradox for Windows.

2. The control menu. In the extreme upper left corner of Figure 5–3 is the control menu icon. The Control menu includes several commands. For example, you can double-click the control menu icon to exit Paradox for Windows or you can use the control menu to switch to another Windows application.

3. The minimize and maximize icons. In the upper right corner of the screen you see the minimize and maximize (or restore) icons. These are triangles pointing down and up. The minimize icon is the down-pointing icon used to reduce the desktop to an icon. This is a small graphical representation of the window. If you click on the minimize icon, the desktop is reduced to an icon. To restore the icon to a window, just double-click it. The maximize icon is used to enlarge the window to its maximum size. When you maximize a window, the maximize icon is restored by the restore icon (two small triangles on the top of each other). Clicking the restore icon returns the window to its previous size. Also, you can double-click the title bar in order to maximize or restore a window.

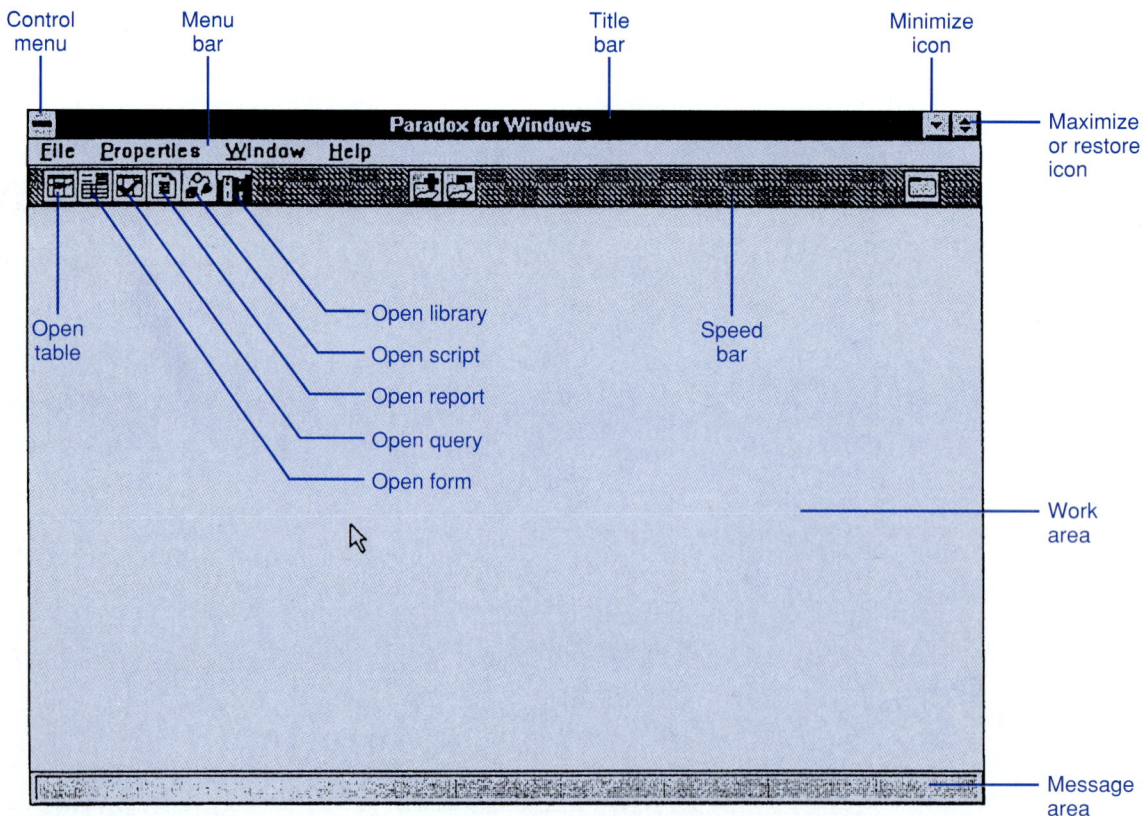

Figure 5–3
Paradox for Windows desktop components.

4.   The menu bar. The Paradox for Windows menu bar is right below the title bar. The initial menu includes four options: File, Properties, Window, and Help. You can select an option from the menu bar by clicking on the option. You can also press the **Alt** key and then press the underscored letter of the menu. For example, to activate the File menu, press the Alt key, and then press the letter F. You will see a screen showing a pull-down menu similar to the one presented in Figure 5–4.

When a pull-down menu is displayed, you can click any of the options or you can move the cursor to the desired option and then press the Enter key.

Menu options can be active or inactive. The options displayed in bold are active. The dimmer options (usually gray) are inactive, meaning they cannot be used at this time. A menu option followed by three dots (. . .) indicates that a dialog box is displayed if that option is chosen. The menu option followed by a pointing triangle indicates that a pull-down menu will be displayed if the option is chosen.

5.   The SpeedBar. Right below the menu bar you see the Paradox for Windows SpeedBar. The SpeedBar displays icons that Paradox for Windows calls buttons or tools. Figure 5–5 provides a summary of Paradox for Windows Speed-Bars. For now remember that the SpeedBar buttons are used as a shortcut for commonly used Paradox for Windows tasks. The tools and buttons available in a SpeedBar depend on which window is active. For example, the SpeedBar for the Paradox for Windows desktop is different from the SpeedBar for a table. We will introduce these individual buttons (tools) as we encounter them.

6.   The Message Area. At the bottom of the desktop (not visible in Figure 5–3) you will see an area for different messages. For example, an error message may be displayed in this area.

The message area is divided into three sections. The left section displays SpeedBar help and status information. For example, if you position the mouse pointer on a button, the name of the button will be displayed here. The middle

Figure 5–4
Options under the File menu.

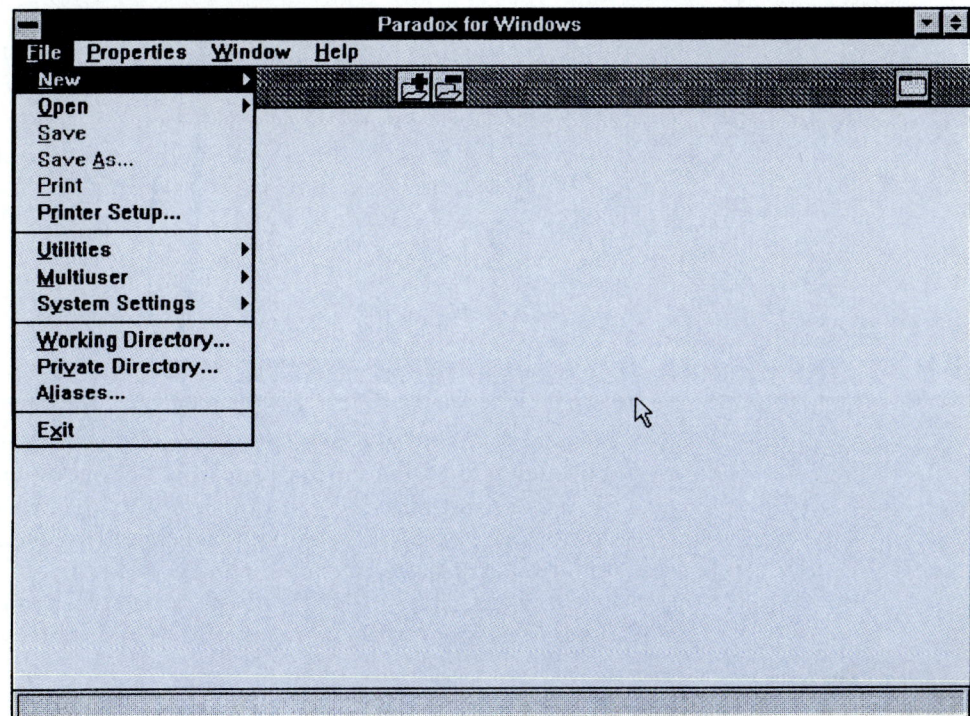

Figure 5–5
Paradox for Windows SpeedBars.

section of the message area displays the record number that you are viewing or editing. The right side of the message area displays the mode, for example, Edit, View, Locked, and so forth.

7. The Work Area. The middle section of the desktop is the Paradox for Windows work area. This is the area that you use to create tables, edit tables, view tables, and so forth.

5–5   THE HELP FACILITY IN PARADOX FOR WINDOWS

Paradox for Windows includes a comprehensive online help facility that can be activated at any time during your work. When the desktop is displayed, press the **F1** function key and a screen similar to the one in Figure 5–6 will appear. You can choose any help facility section by clicking that section. For example, if you click on Keyboard you will see a screen similar to the one in Figure 5–7. If you click on Essentials (in Figure 5–6), you will get a screen similar to the one presented in Figure 5–8. You can click on any of the underlined words to find out exactly what

Figure 5–6
Paradox for Windows help contents.

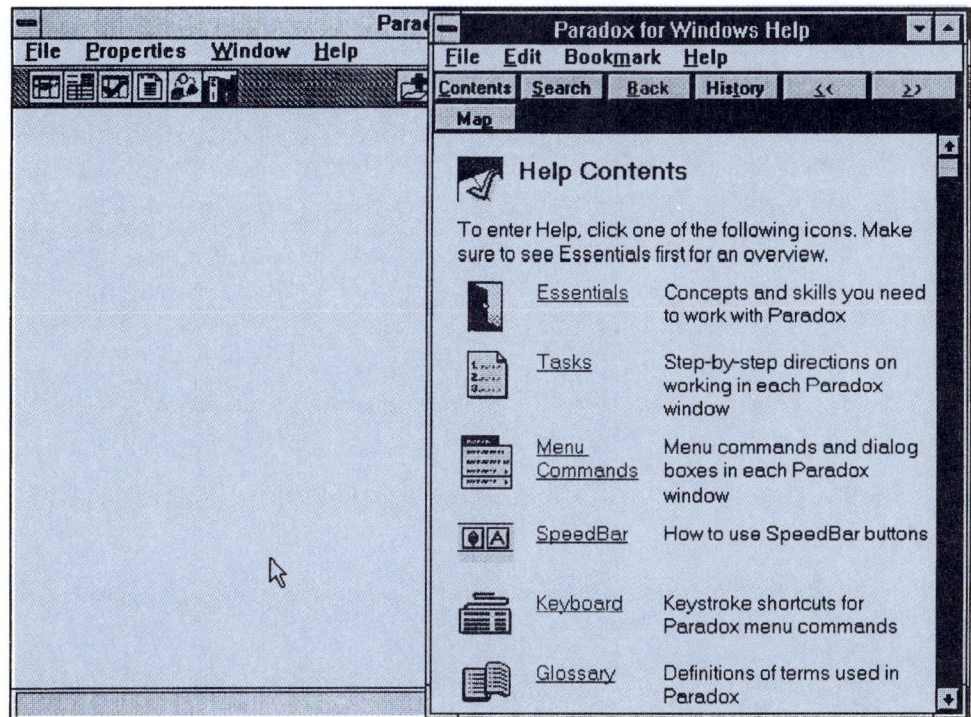

Figure 5–7
Online Help on keyboard.

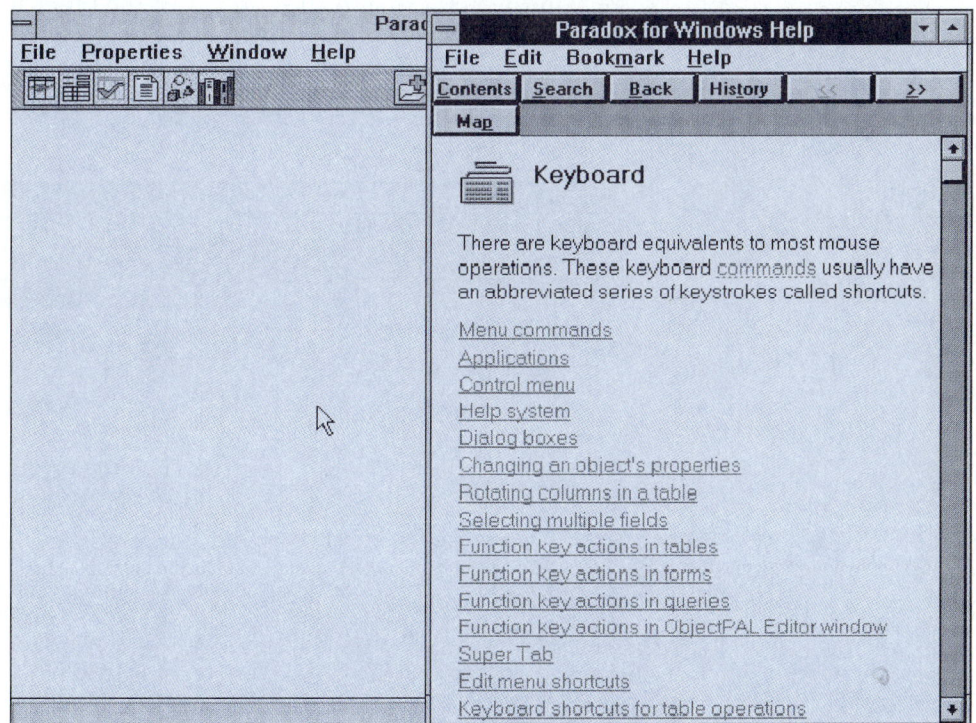

Figure 5–8
Online help on essentials.

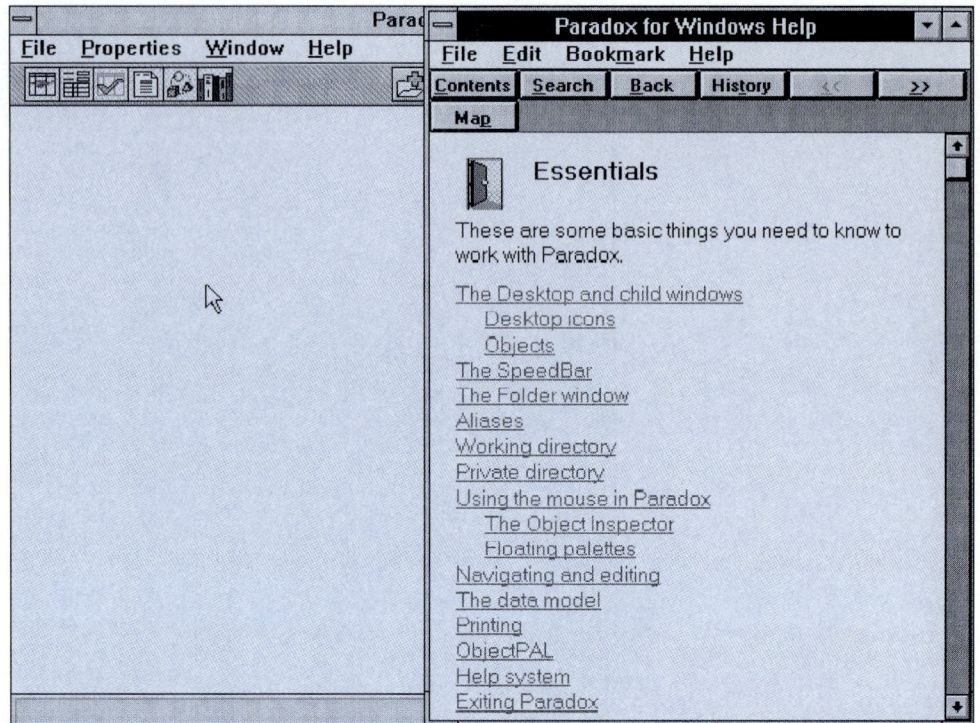

they mean. You can also click on any of the other topics in this window to receive online help. For example, if you click on Objects (in Figure 5-8) you will see a screen similar to the one in Figure 5–9. If you click on Desktop icons (in Figure 5–8) you will see a screen similar to the one in Figure 5–10.

Figure 5–9
Online help on objects.

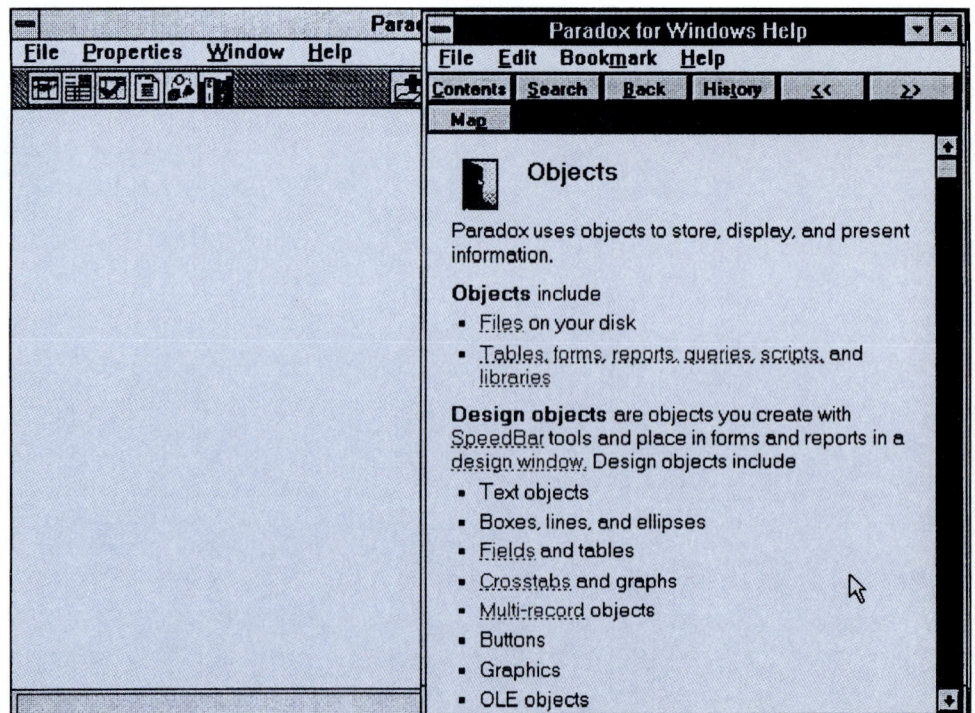

Figure 5–10
Desktop icons.

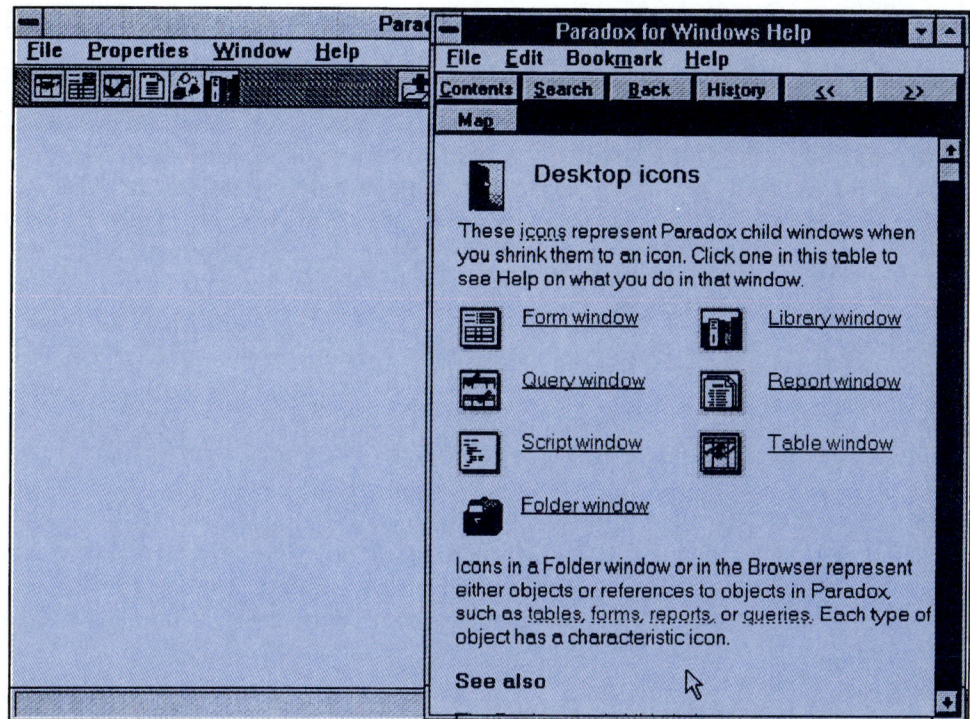

The rest of the help facility of Paradox for Windows is similar to the Windows help facility discussed in Chapter 3. Remember that the Paradox for Windows help facility is **context sensitive**. This means that by pressing the F1 function key from anywhere in the program you will receive help related to your current Paradox for Windows activity. And from the desktop you can click on the Help option to display the Help pull-down menu.

5–6   PARADOX FOR WINDOWS SELECTED APPLICATIONS

The number of tasks performed by Paradox for Windows is virtually unlimited. Generally speaking, in any situation involving data management, Paradox for Windows can be of significant assistance. The following are specific applications of Paradox for Windows that are frequently used.

1. Mailing list generation and maintenance. A comprehensive and up-to-date mailing list can assist any organization in serving its customers. With Paradox for Windows you can create a database with clients' names and addresses. You can make additions, deletions, and modifications to the mailing list, ensuring the creation of correct, easily updated mailing labels in a variety of formats.

2. Automated database for city hall. The city planner of a large Southern California city maintains records on more than 50,000 pieces of property with descriptive information about each parcel. The 14 pieces of information relating to each property (14 fields) include the size of the property, the location, its ownership, and so forth. The city planner can use this automated database and Paradox for Windows to generate numerous reports, each with a unique combination of information for the individual properties. For example, the base may be searched for those properties that cover less than five acres, are in the southwest part of the city, are close to a major highway, and so on. It would be very time-consuming to perform such a task manually. Aside from being slow, a manual database can also result in the generation of erroneous reports.

3. Affirmative action statistics. Paradox for Windows can be used to generate comprehensive reports regarding affirmative action. For example, Paradox for Windows can provide a report listing the number of female employees versus the number of male employees, the average salary of male employees versus the average salary of female employees, and so forth.

4. Equipment rental information. Paradox for Windows can effectively store records on thousands of pieces of equipment. At the end of a given period, Paradox for Windows can generate important reports regarding the performance of each piece of equipment. For example, reports could show how many times a particular item was rented out, or how much income was generated by a particular piece of equipment.

5. Inventory management. Paradox for Windows can be used in any inventory management task. You can generate various statistics regarding on-hand inventory, such as determining the fast-moving items, the slow-moving items, the quantity on hand of each item, and so forth.

5–7   FILE NAMES AND DATA TYPES IN THE PARADOX FOR WINDOWS ENVIRONMENT

A Paradox for Windows file name (or table name) (similar to DOS files) can consist of up to 8 characters. Alphabetic characters, the dash, digits 0 through 9, and the underscore can be used as part of the file name. A file or table name must start with a letter of the alphabet. Try to use file names that have special meaning for the task or function being performed. For example, MAIL, DIVISION, and CUSTOMER are examples of meaningful file names. Field names follow the same rules as table names and can be up to 25 characters long.

Paradox for Windows accepts and manipulates 10 different data types: alphanumeric, numeric, currency, date, short number, memo, formatted memo, graphic, OLE, and binary.

- **Alphanumeric (A** for short) data can be any combination of valid characters. The minimum size of an alphanumeric field is one character; the maximum size is 255 characters. The following are some valid examples:

```
3100 Broadway
ABC–6921
Happy Ending
Good Morning
```

- **Numeric (N** for short) data can include numbers with or without decimals. A minus sign can also be included. You can enter up to 15 significant digits (including decimal places). Numbers with more than 15 significant digits are rounded and displayed in scientific notation. The following are some examples:

```
692185
241.143
.0005
-312.417
```

- **Currency ($** for short) data is similar to the numeric type; however, Paradox for Windows displays a dollar sign to the left of the number, adds commas to separate every three digits, and rounds the number to two decimal places. Negative numbers are displayed in parentheses. You do not type the dollar sign when entering currency data, but you can type commas. The following are some examples:

```
625
17.291
693,752
5296
```

- **Date (D** for short) data include any date between January 1, 100, and December 31, 9999, typed in the form mm/dd/yy, dd-mm-yy, or dd.mm.yy. If you want to enter dates that do not fall within the twentieth century, include the full year. Following are some valid examples:

```
9/31/92
25-Mar-52
31.3.93
```

- **Short number (S** for short) data is used by advanced Paradox for Windows users who need to conserve disk space. This data type can contain only whole numbers (integers) in the range of –32,767 to 32,767. The following are some examples:

```
–625
25
12632
5555
```

- **Memo (M** for short) is used to add long text entries to a record without adding a series of fields to the table. Up to 255 characters of a formatted memo (see below) or 240 characters of a memo field may be stored in the table itself. The rest of the text will be stored in a file with the MB extension. Paradox for Windows automatically opens the MB file. Memo field is mainly used for documentation purposes. For example, you may add certain information related to a record in order to refresh your own memory, for example, information about an apartment that was recently painted in your apartment complex table.

- **Formatted memo (F** for short) is similar to a memo field; however, it gives you more flexibility because you can format the text. This is not possible with a memo field.

- **Graphic (G** for short) contains graphic images, which can be a chart, a graph, clip art, and so forth. When you use this type of field, remember that it requires a lot of disk space.

- **OLE (Object Linking and Embedding—O** for short) contains objects from other Windows applications, enabling you to use data from more than one application program in a table. For example, using this feature, your Paradox for Windows table may utilize data from a spreadsheet program.

- **Binary (B** for short) fields store binary information (zeros and ones). You must access a binary field through ObjectPAL, the programming language of Paradox for Windows.

5–8   PARADOX FOR WINDOWS TERMINOLOGY

Paradox for Windows, like other software applications, uses its own terminology. To be able to work effectively with Paradox for Windows you should become familiar with the terms discussed in the following sections.

5–8–1   Paradox for Windows Desktop: A Second Look

When you start Paradox for Windows, you will see a screen similar to the one presented in Figure 5–11. As you see in this figure, the Paradox for Windows menu is displayed at the top of the screen. Just below the menu you see a blank area. This blank area is called the **desktop** or work area or workspace. The work area is similar to the spreadsheet area in a typical spreadsheet program such as Lotus 1-2-3 or Quattro Pro for Windows.

Figure 5–11 illustrates a blank workspace. Figure 5–12 shows a workspace with one image. An **image** is similar to a spreadsheet. An image is one of your Paradox for Windows data tables or files. At any given time you can have an unlimited number of images on your desktop. Naturally you will not be able to see all your images at the same time. Figure 5–13 illustrates a desktop with two images. Only one of your images is active at any given time. This means you can work with one image at a time. To make an image active you can click anywhere in its window (if the image is visible). If it is not visible you can press **Alt+Tab** repeatedly to navigate through all the open images and windows.

You can also arrange the available images in cascade or tile format. Just select the Window Tile or the Window Cascade commands. In tile format you see the images side by side (see Figure 5–14). In cascade format you see the images layered on top of each other (see Figure 5–15).

Figure 5–11
Paradox for Windows desktop.

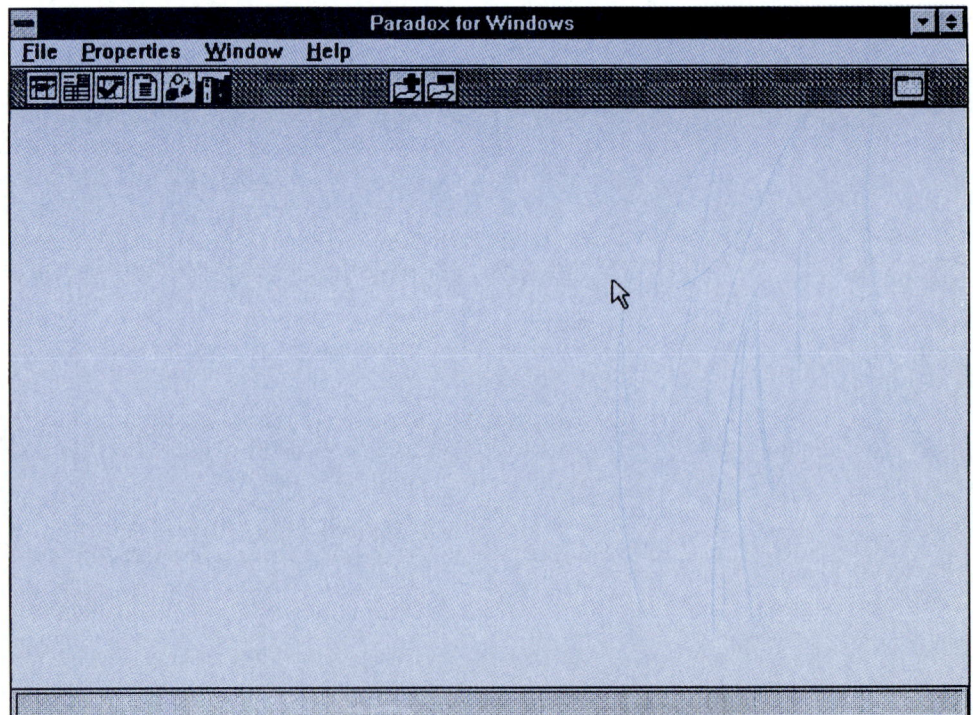

Figure 5–12
Desktop with one image.

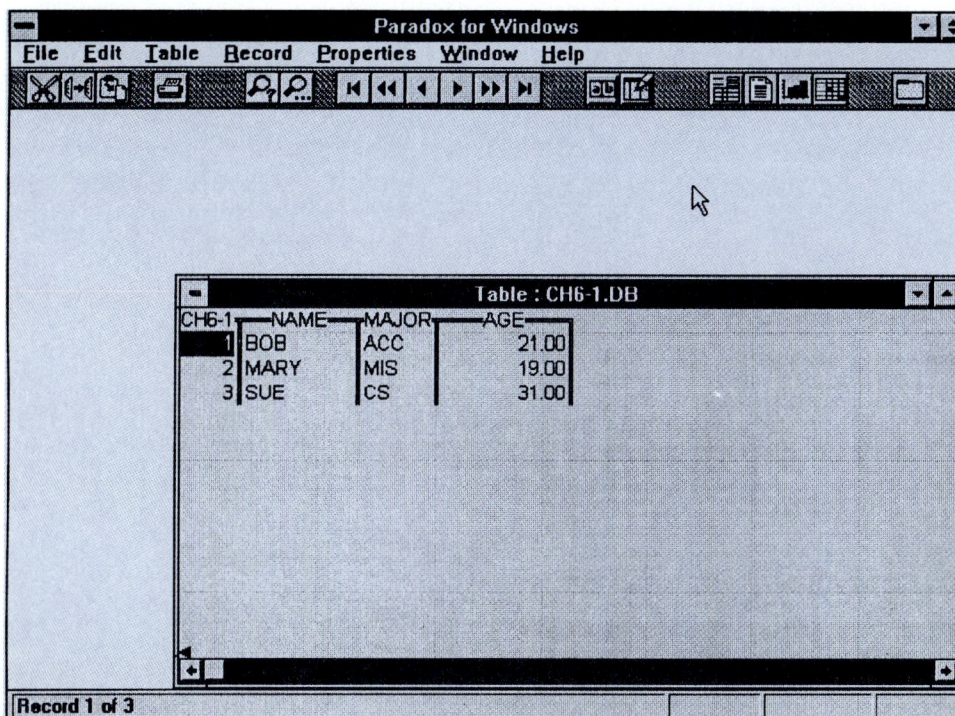

Figure 5–13
Desktop with two images.

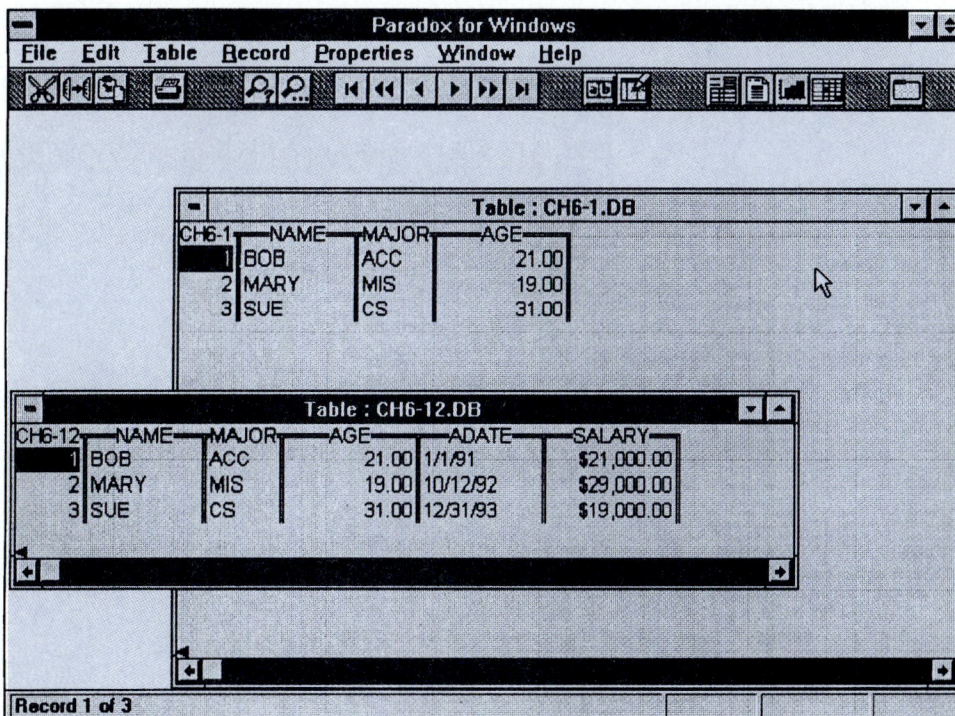

Figure 5–14
Two images in tile format.

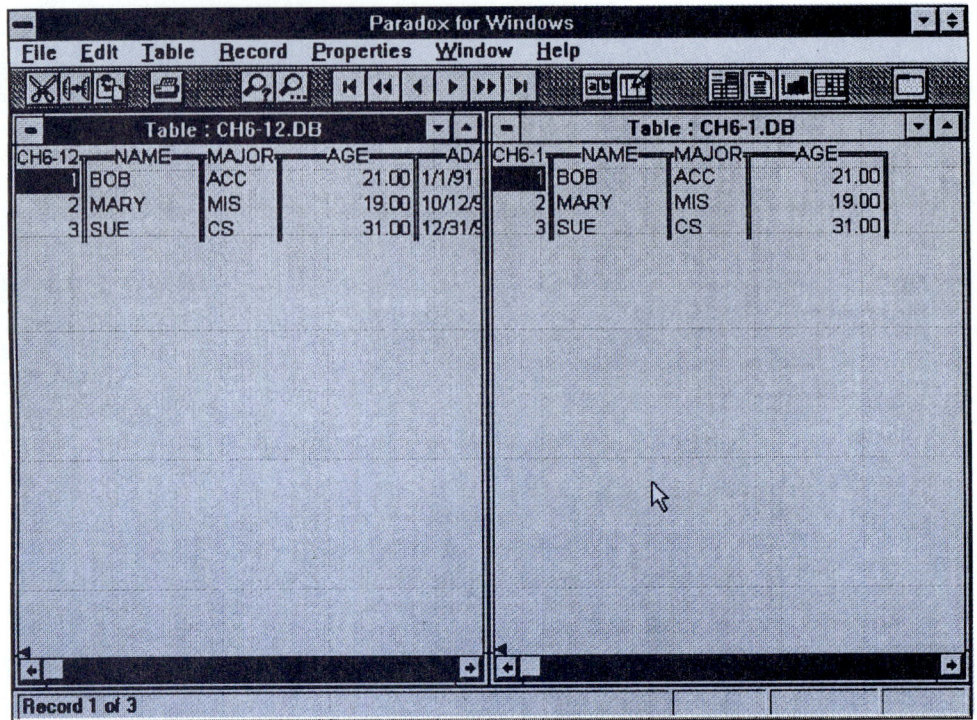

Figure 5–15
Two images in cascade format.

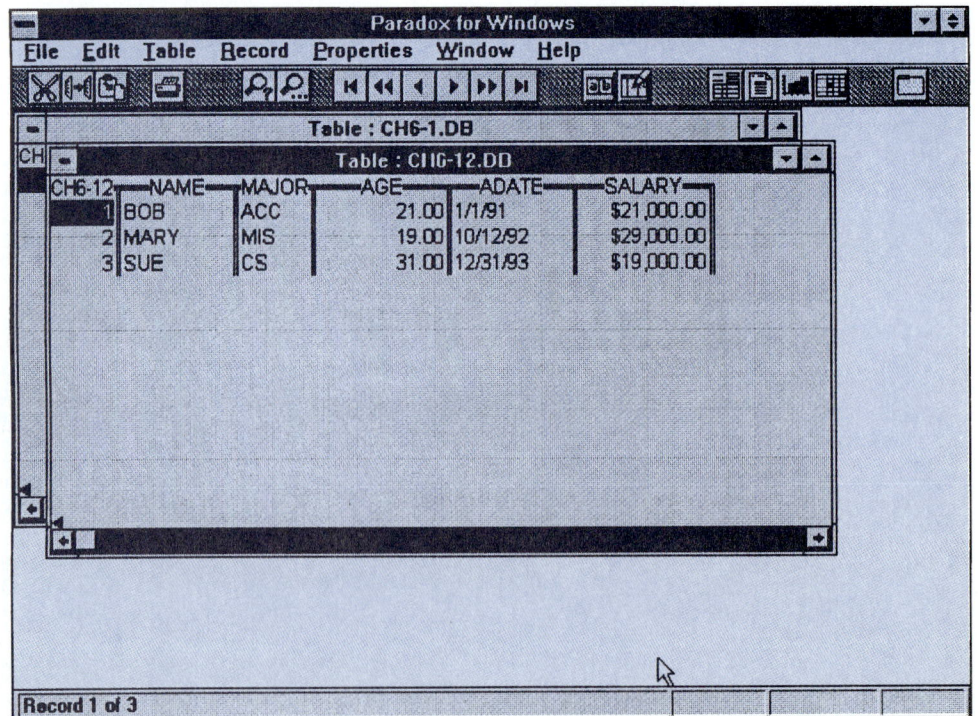

5–8–2   Paradox for Windows Objects

The term **object** in Paradox for Windows refers to many different things. The following are some examples of objects:

- a data table
- a field in a data table
- a record in a data table
- a report—a hard copy generated by your printer
- a form—similar to a report, but includes specific information in a specific format
- a script—an electronic document that stores a series of Paradox for Windows commands. You can store a series of commands and then play them back by using a script file.

An object can be temporary or it can be permanent. As you will see later, Paradox for Windows generates several different types of temporary objects. After your current session these objects will no longer exist. However, Paradox for Windows provides a facility to convert these temporary objects to permanent ones. We will talk more about this later.

Understanding the object concept in Paradox for Windows is very important. Paradox for Windows treats all of its objects in the same manner. For example, the Copy command can be used to make a copy of the following objects: tables, forms, queries, reports, scripts, and libraries. In the same way, you can use the Delete command to delete an object.

An object may include a series of related objects in a larger object called a family. For example, a data table may include a form, a report, and a script. These three objects together are called the family for the table object.

5–9   AN OVERVIEW OF THE PARADOX FOR WINDOWS DESKTOP MENU

As you saw in Figure 5–11, the Paradox for Windows desktop includes four options.

The File menu (in Figure 5–4) includes commands for opening, saving, and printing various objects. It includes commands for printer and system setup. It also includes a series of utilities for copying, deleting, and renaming various objects.

The Properties menu provides information regarding the desktop properties. You can use this menu to change the way your Desktop looks. For example, using this menu you can create another title to appear on the desktop title bar.

The Window menu (see Figure 5–16) includes commands for arranging open windows and icons. You can arrange the open windows in tile or cascade format (as we just did in Figures 5–14 and 5–15).

The Help menu (see Figure 5–17) includes online help for Contents, SpeedBar, the keyboard, using the help facility, and support from Borland, the vendor of Paradox for Windows. We will talk about these menu options in more detail later.

Figure 5–16
The Window menu.

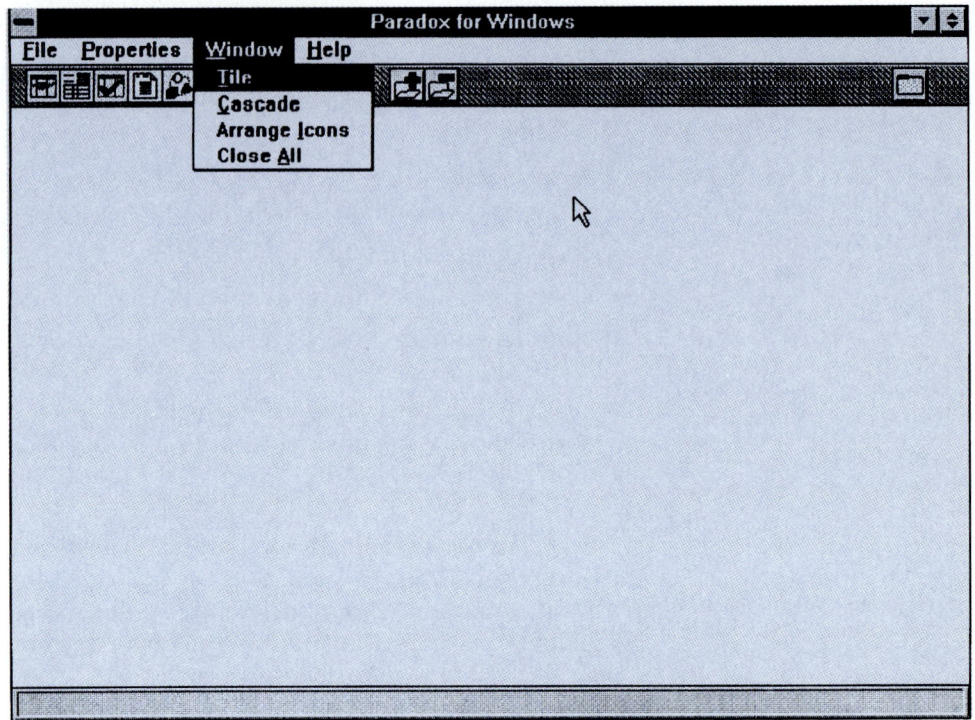

Figure 5–17
The Help menu.

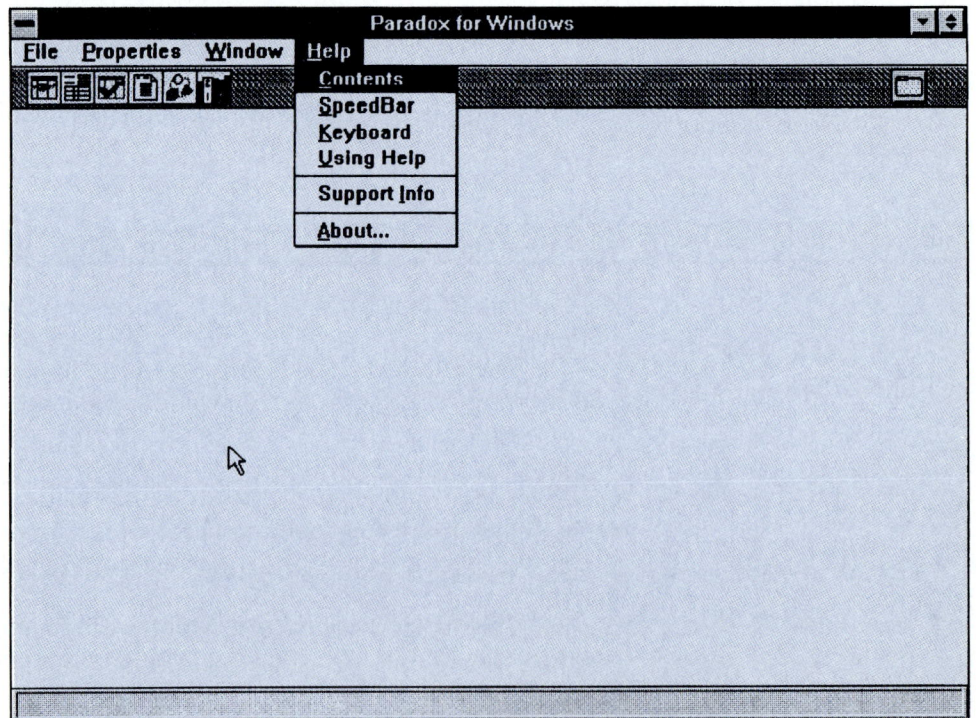

SUMMARY

This chapter reviewed the basics of Paradox for Windows. The process of starting Paradox for Windows was introduced, and Paradox for Windows help facilities were highlighted. Some selected applications of Paradox for Windows were presented along with a brief discussion of data types in the Paradox for Windows environment. The chapter introduced Paradox for Windows terminology, including workspace, image, and object. It provided an overview of the Paradox for Windows starting menu. In the next chapter we will discuss the data management cycle.

REVIEW QUESTIONS

*These questions are answered in Appendix A.

1. What is a database?
*2. What are the differences between a manual and an automated database?
3. How do you start Paradox for Windows?
4. How do you exit Paradox for Windows?
5. In which area are the messages displayed?
*6. How many options are available in the Paradox desktop?
7. How do you select an option from the desktop?
8. What are some examples of Paradox for Windows objects?
9. What are Paradox for Windows SpeedBars?
10. How do you ask for help in Paradox for Windows?
*11. How do you ask for help on a specific command?
12. Describe three Paradox for Windows applications.
13. What can Paradox for Windows do for you as a student?
14. What are the requirements of a Paradox for Windows file name?
*15. How many data types are supported by Paradox for Windows?
16. What is the difference between a currency field and a numeric field?
17. What are short number fields? What are their advantages compared with numeric fields?
18. What is the desktop? How many tables can be displayed in the workspace?
19. What is a Paradox for Windows object? What are some examples of objects?
20. What is a Paradox for Windows image?
21. What option from the Paradox for Windows desktop allows you to arrange various images?
*22. What option in the Paradox for Windows desktop includes commands similar to those in DOS?

HANDS-ON EXPERIENCE

1. Start the Paradox for Windows online help facility. What is available?
2. Get the Paradox for Windows help facility started. Display online help for the keyboard.
3. Walk through the options included in the Paradox for Windows desktop. What is available under File? Under Properties? Press the F1 function key to display the online help for each menu option.
4. Exit Paradox by using the File menu.
5. Start Paradox again. This time exit by pressing the Alt+F4 key combination.

KEY TERMS

Alphanumeric	Field	Memo
Binary	File	Numeric
Context sensitive	Formatted memo	Object
Currency	Graphic	OLE
Database	Image	Record
Date	Manual database	Short number
Desktop		

KEY COMMANDS

Alt (to activate the Paradox for Windows menu)

Alt+F4 (to exit Paradox for Windows)

Alt+Tab (to navigate through open Windows)

F1 (Help) (to ask for online help)

File Exit (to exit Paradox for Windows)

MISCONCEPTIONS AND SOLUTIONS

Misconception   When you finish your Paradox for Windows work, you may terminate the session by pulling your data diskette out and turning the computer off. This may result in data loss.

> **Solution**   Before turning the computer off, always select Exit from the file menu and select Y (for yes).

Misconception   You have installed Paradox for Windows on your computer, and although you have enough memory on your computer, still the processing power is not high enough.

> **Solution**   Install a math coprocessor. Also, configure your additional memory as extended rather than as expanded memory. (See Chapter 1 for the definition of each type of memory.)

Misconception   You are using Paradox for Windows menu options by moving the cursor to the desired option and pressing the Enter key. This may not be very fast.

> **Solution**   Press the underlined letter of each menu option for quick and accurate menu selection. You can also click the desired option using the mouse.

ARE YOU READY TO MOVE ON?

Multiple Choice

1. A computerized database is composed of
   a. fields
   b. records
   c. files
   d. characters
   e. all of the above

2. Compared to a manual database, an automated (computerized) database is

   a. slower
   b. more accurate
   c. less efficient
   d. both a and b
   e. none of the above

3. To start Paradox for Windows from the Windows Program Manager

   a. click on the Paradox for Windows group icon
   b. type Paradox for Windows
   c. click on Run
   d. type *DB*
   e. none of the above

4. You can issue Paradox for Windows commands through the

   a. Paradox for Windows menu
   b. shortcut key
   c. both a and b
   d. DOS prompt
   e. all of the above

5. What should you select from the File menu to exit Paradox for Windows?

   a. F1
   b. *
   c. Ctrl
   d. Exit
   e. none of the above

6. How many options does the Paradox for Windows desktop include?

   a. 4
   b. 3
   c. 2
   d. 5
   e. 10

7. A Paradox for Windows field name can be up to how many characters long?

   a. 10
   b. 25
   c. 15
   d. 20
   e. none of the above

8. To request help, you can

   a. press F1
   b. type *HELP* and press Enter
   c. type *HELP* and the name of the command and press Enter
   d. either a or b
   e. any of the above

9. The following statements are true of valid Paradox for Windows file names except:

   a. they can have up to eight characters
   b. digits 0 to 9 can be used as part of the name
   c. the underscore character can be used as part of the name
   d. the name must start with a letter
   e. all of the above are true

10. Paradox for Windows accepts how many data types?

   a. 8
   b. 7
   c. 10
   d. 6
   e. none of the above

True/False

1. Queries are an example of a Paradox for Windows object.
2. A character field in Paradox for Windows can include up to 200 characters.
3. The Paradox for Windows desktop includes four menu options.
4. To exit Paradox for Windows, select Exit from the File menu.
5. Paradox for Windows includes only two SpeedBars.
6. Access the help facility by pressing the F1 function key.
7. The desktop can include several images at the same time.
8. Paradox for Windows supports six different data types.
9. Date fields are always 10 characters long.
10. Numeric fields always include the $ (dollar sign).

ANSWERS

Multiple Choice		True/False	
1.	e	1.	T
2.	b	2.	F
3.	a	3.	T
4.	c	4.	T
5.	d	5.	F
6.	a	6.	T
7.	b	7.	T
8.	a	8.	F
9.	e	9.	F
10.	c	10.	F

Data Management Cycle

6

6–1   INTRODUCTION

This chapter reviews the major functions performed by Paradox for Windows. File creation and data entry processes are introduced. The processes of adding data to and deleting data from a table are highlighted. The chapter discusses modifying the structure of a database, including adding and deleting fields. The chapter also explains the creation of quick reports, introduces the undo feature of Paradox for Windows, and concludes with a discussion of sort operations.

6–2   IMPORTANT DATABASE OPERATIONS

To refresh your memory, we will briefly summarize the important database operations.

File creation is the first task performed using a database management system such as Paradox for Windows. File creation simply means storing a database electronically. Once a file is created, other database tasks can be easily performed. Paradox for Windows uses the New Table command from the File menu for creating a file.

File **modification** is done whenever you want to change some of the data in the database. You may want to correct a mistake or change some of the existing information in the database, for example, changing a customer's address. Paradox for Windows uses various editing commands in Edit mode for file modification. To get into Edit mode if your table is displayed on the screen, press F9.

File **addition** takes place when you have to add new information to an existing file. Suppose a business starts with 100 customers and later attracts 50 more customers. These new customers can be easily added to the existing file. Paradox for Windows uses various commands in Edit mode for adding new information to an existing file. You can also use the File Utilities Add command to add tables.

File **deletion** is performed whenever you have to delete an entire file. Paradox for Windows provides the File Utilities Delete command. In some cases you may want to delete just a portion of a file, such as one or a series of records or one or a series of fields. To do this you can use various commands in Edit mode.

The **sort** operation is used for organizing a database based on some criterion or a series of criteria, such as sorting the sales force based on their sales totals or sorting the students in the Paradox for Windows class based on their GPAs. Paradox for Windows uses the Sort command from the Table menu for organizing data in the database. During the file creation process you can identify a **key.** A key is a unique field used to identify a record, for example, the last name or the GPA. Paradox for Windows always keeps your table sorted based on this key.

The **search** operation is used to locate specific record(s) in the database. For example, you may be interested in all the MIS students who have a GPA of 3.80 or higher and speak Spanish. Paradox for Windows uses various commands for these search operations. Through the Query option from the File New menu, various search operations can be done.

Report generation is used to generate a hard copy of your Paradox for Windows work. Paradox for Windows provides a powerful Report command for report generation, which is part of the built-in report generator. We will explain this feature in detail in Chapter 9.

6–3   SETTING UP THE WORKING DIRECTORY

By default Paradox for Windows uses the current directory to store the files that you will create. To change this directory to drive A, follow these steps:

1. From the Paradox for Windows desktop select the File option.
2. From the File menu select Working Directory.
3. In the Working Directory box type *A:* and click on OK.

From now on all your work will be saved in drive A. This will help you to keep from cluttering the hard disk with your data files. If you change your mind, you can always go back and change this directory to another.

6–4   YOUR FIRST DATABASE

Your first database table keeps track of three students, their majors, and their ages. Following the directions in Chapter 5, start Paradox for Windows. When the Paradox desktop is displayed, select the **File** option, and then select **New**. Paradox for Windows displays six different objects that can be created. Select **Table**. You will see the Table Type dialog box as displayed in Figure 6–1. If you click the down arrow icon in the Paradox for Windows box, you will see other table types supported by Paradox for Windows (see Figure 6–2). Click on the Paradox for Windows option, and then click on OK to accept Paradox for Windows as your table type. Naturally, if you want to create other table types you have to click on the desired type. At this point you will see a screen similar to the one shown in Figure 6–3. As you see in this figure, the table is called [Untitled]. When you save

Figure 6–1
Table Type dialog box.

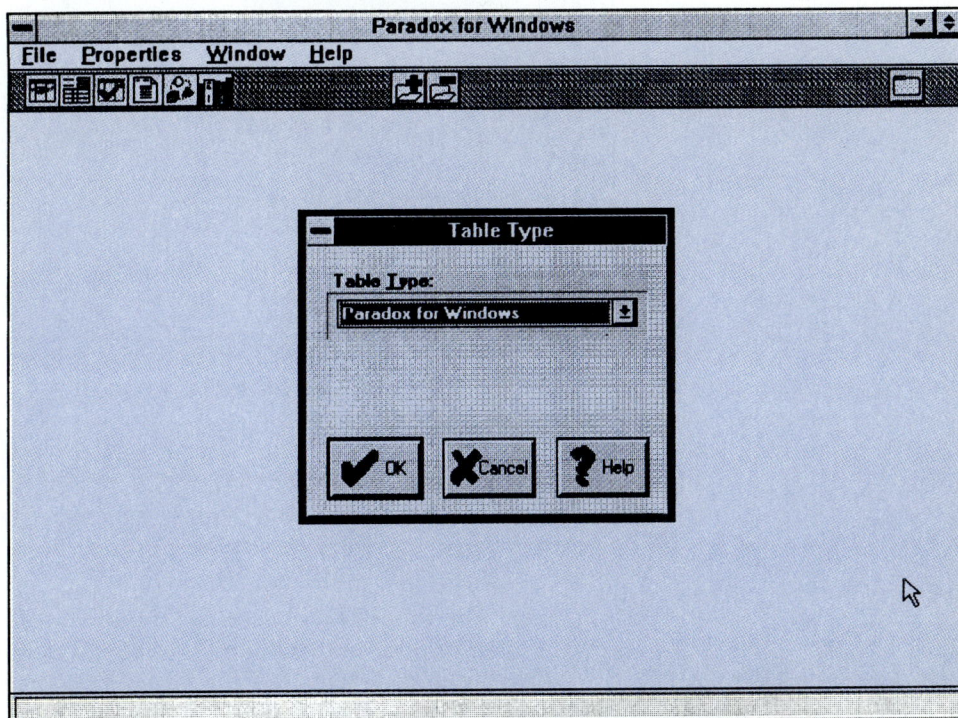

Figure 6–2
Table types supported by Paradox
for Windows.

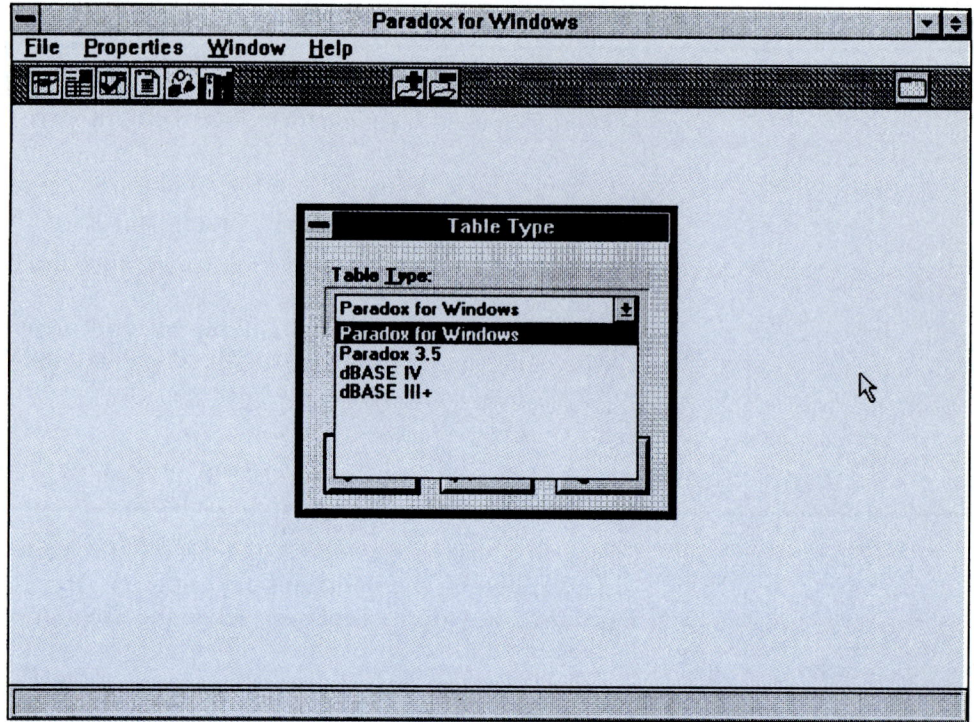

Figure 6–3
The Create Paradox for Windows
Table dialog box.

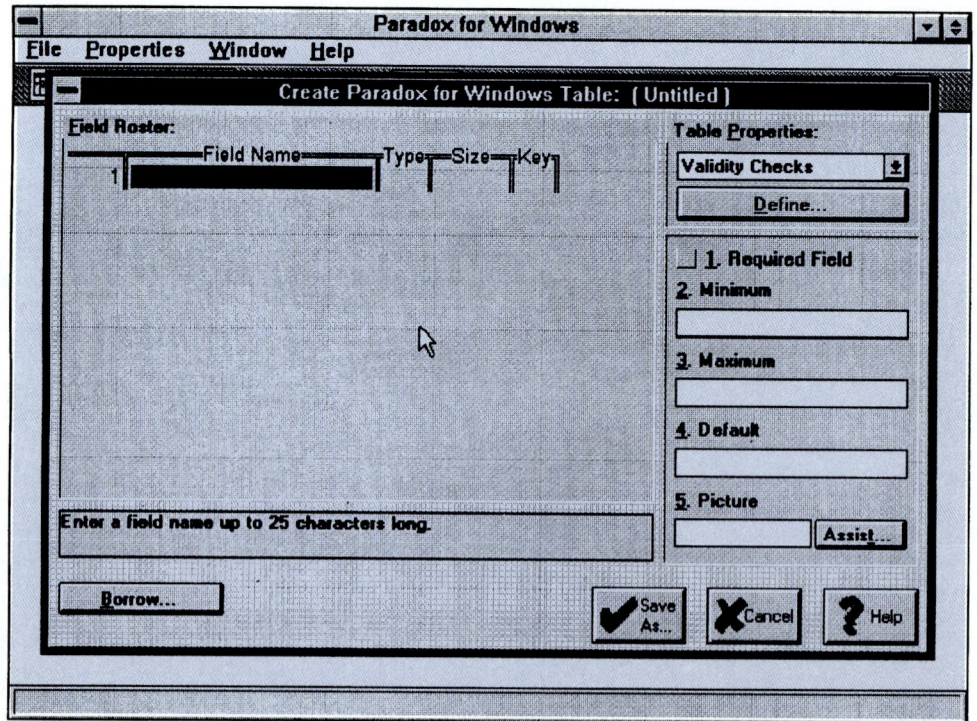

your table, the name you choose for the table will replace [Untitled]. There are
several other options in this dialog box, which we will explain later.

You can also right-click the Open Table button (the first button) from the
desktop to create a table. When you click this button, you are given two options:
New or Open. Click on New. The rest stays the same.

In the field name column type *NAME* and press Tab, → (right arrow), or Enter. For field type enter *A* and press Enter. For size enter *10* and press Enter. This means the NAME field will be alphanumeric and 10 characters wide. Uppercase or lowercase are considered the same. We use uppercase for field names just to make them more distinguishable. While you are in the key field, double-click the mouse button to enter an asterisk (*) in this field. The asterisk means this field will be used as the key field. Paradox for Windows will keep your table sorted based on this field. If you do not want to have the key field, press the Enter key.

Now you are ready to specify your second field. For the name of the second field type *MAJOR* and press Enter, then type *A* and press Enter. Next type *3* and press Enter twice. This means the MAJOR field is alphanumeric with a width of three characters. When you are specifying a field type you can either right-click the mouse button or press the spacebar to generate a listing of all the field types supported by Paradox for Windows.

For field 3, type *AGE* and press Enter, then type *N* for numeric. For numeric fields you do not need to specify the size. At this point you have established the **structure** for your sample database. Your screen should be similar to the one presented in Figure 6–4. To save this structure, click on the Save As button. You will see the Save Table As dialog box as presented in Figure 6–5. In the New Table Name box type CH6–1 and click on OK. You will return to the Paradox for Windows desktop. Paradox for Windows has created a table named CH6–1.DB on the disk in drive A. This table does not yet contain any records. Paradox for Windows automatically attaches a DB extension to the table name.

6–5 ENTERING DATA INTO YOUR DATABASE

To enter data into your database structure, from the opening menu select File, then select Open, and then select Table. Paradox for Windows will display the

Figure 6–4
The Structure of the sample database table.

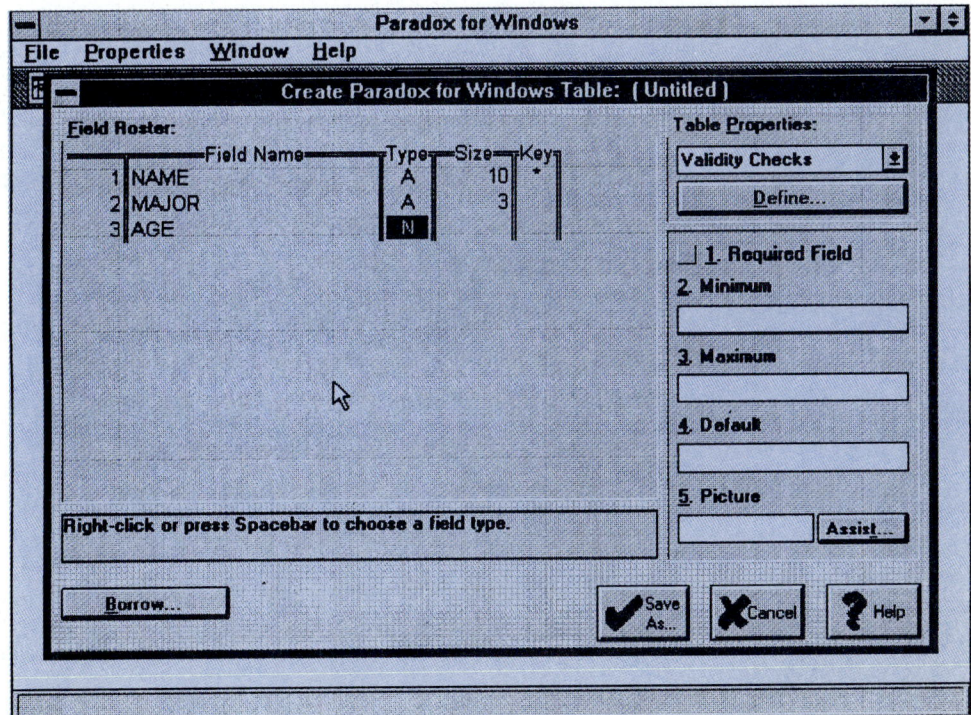

Figure 6–5
The Save Table As dialog box.

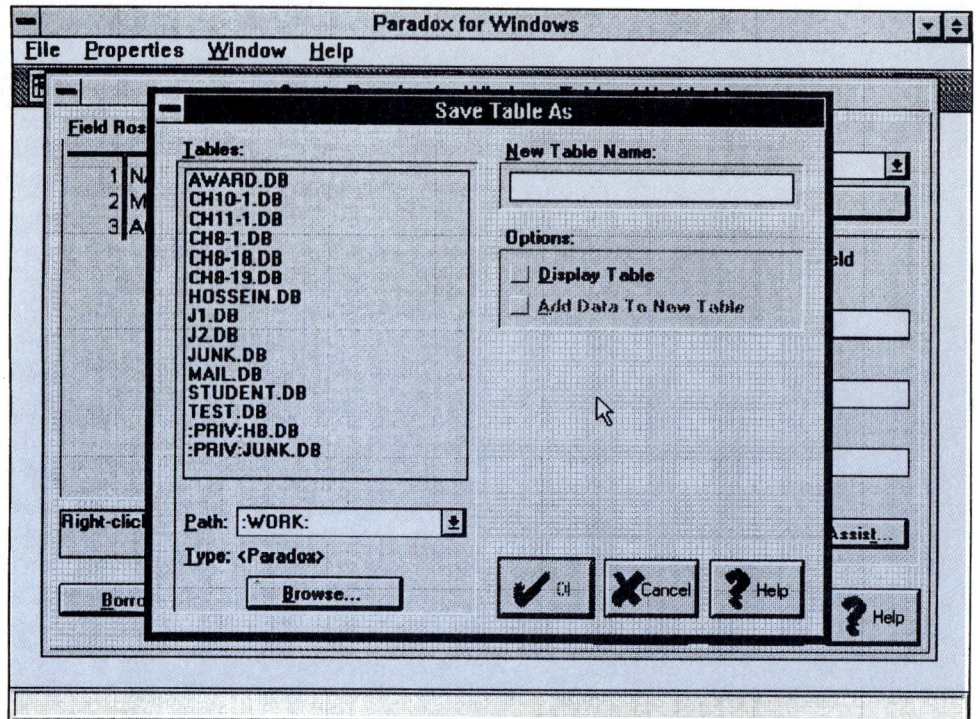

Figure 6–5
The Save Table As dialog box.

Open Table dialog box, which includes all the tables in the **default** drive (see Figure 6–6). Type CH6–1 and press Enter. You can also double-click the table name, or you can highlight the table name and click on OK. You will see a screen similar to Figure 6–7. This is called View mode or the Data Entry window. You can maximize this window by clicking the maximize button (this is what we did). To enter or edit data you must be in Edit mode. To enter Edit mode press the **F9** function key. As soon as you press F9, the word Edit is displayed in the lower right of the screen. As you see in Figure 6–7, the first line indicates that you are working with table CH6–1. The table has three fields: NAME, MAJOR, and AGE. The indicator at the lower right indicates that you have not entered any records yet (zero records). Enter the following three records in the NAME, MAJOR, and AGE fields and make sure to press the Enter, Tab or right arrow key after each entry. Don't press Enter after completing the third record.

BOB	ACC	21
MARY	MIS	19
SUE	CS	31

Paradox for Windows saves your work as you go along. While you are entering your data, Paradox for Windows sorts the table based on the NAME field (key field). When you are done entering these three records, your screen should be similar to the one presented in Figure 6–8. (Note that Paradox automatically adds two zeros after the numbers you entered.)

When you save a table, the table is saved under the given name with DB as its extension. This is how Paradox for Windows differentiates objects. For example, the extension for Saved Forms is .FSL, and the Scripts extension is .SSL. (The script files allow you to store a series of commands, then play them back later.)

Figure 6–6
Open Table dialog box.

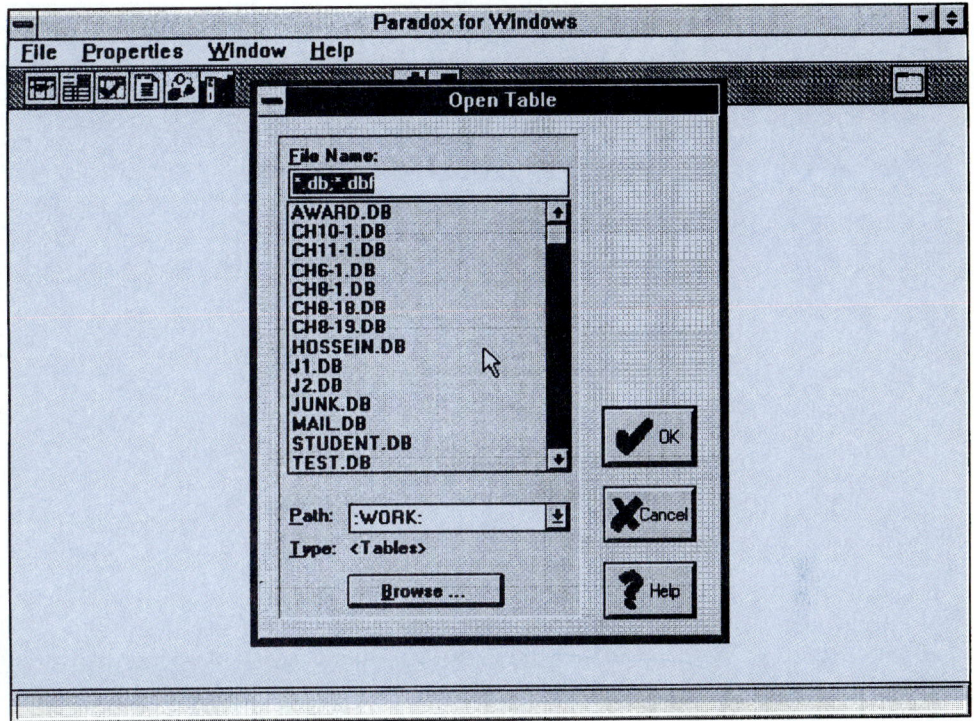

Figure 6–7
Data Entry window.

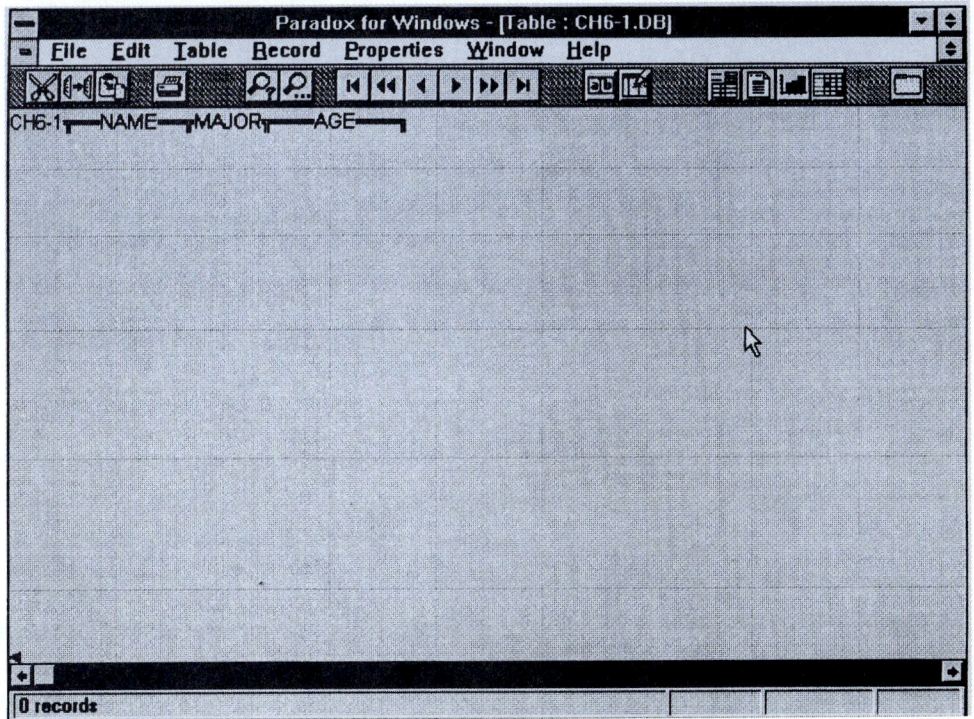

Figure 6–8
Three records have been entered.

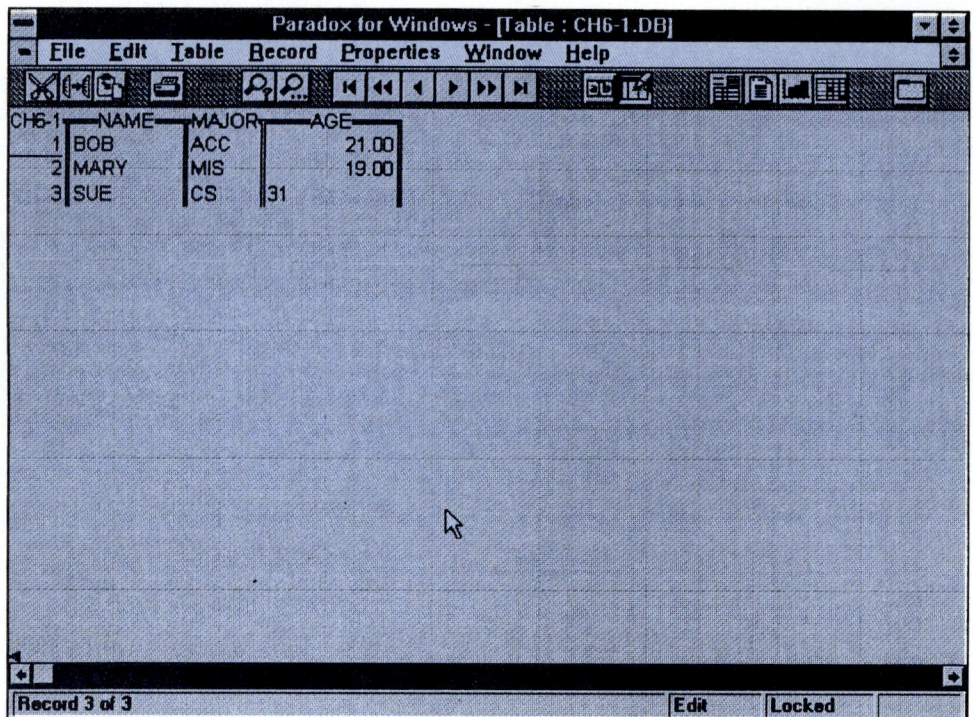

6–6   CLOSING THE TABLE WINDOW

When you are done entering data, you can use one of the following three methods to close the table window:

1. Double-click the table control menu box.
2. Click the control menu box and then click on Close.
3. From the File menu select the Exit option.

Options 1 and 2 return you to the Paradox for Windows desktop. Option 3 returns you to the Paradox for Windows group. Obviously, if you are planning to continue working with Paradox for Windows, do not use option 3.

6–7   PRINTING A QUICK REPORT

In Chapter 9 we will talk about report generation in detail. For now let us use a simple method for **printing reports** from our sample database table named CH6–1 and shown in Figure 6–8. Do the following:

1. Use the File Open Table command to open the CH6–1 table (if it is not already opened).
2. Press **Shift+F7** or Table Quick Report, or click the Quick Report button in the SpeedBar (this icon is the fourth button on the right side of the SpeedBar; it looks like several lines on a piece of paper).
3. Click on the Print button.
4. Click on OK. In a few seconds you will be see a report similar to the one in Figure 6–9.

Figure 6–9

A quick report generated from the sample database table CH6–1.

Saturday, January 01, 1994		CH6-1	Page 1

NAME	MAJOR	AGE
BOB	ACC	21.00
MARY	MIS	19.00
SUE	CS	31.00

As Figure 6–9 shows, the standard report includes the system date and page number and displays your table name.

6–8 INSERTING AND DELETING RECORDS WITHIN A TABLE

SpeedBar ✓ ⟶

To insert a record in a table, you must first be in Edit mode. To get into Edit mode if your table is displayed, press F9. If the table is not displayed, first open the table, then press F9. You can also click the Edit Data button (which looks like a pencil on a ledger—the sixth button from the right on the speed bar), or you can select Table from the menu and then select Edit. To get out of Edit mode, select Table and click on End Edit or just press F9 again.

After entering Edit mode, position the mouse pointer on the record that you want, and then press the **Ins** key. If you have a newer system with an extended keyboard, Num Lock may be on by default. In that case, press the dedicated insert key labeled "Insert" or turn Num Lock off.

Starting at the cursor position, Paradox for Windows moves all the records down by one and makes room for the new record. Your existing records are renumbered. Now you can enter the new record. Try these steps in the table presented in Figure 6–8 and add one record of your choice.

To remove a record, enter Edit mode, move the cursor to the desired record, and press **Ctrl+Del**. Your existing records will be renumbered to reflect the deletion. Using these steps remove the record that you just added to the table in Figure 6–8.

To remove all the records from a table, follow these steps:

1. Select Empty from the Table menu.
2. Click on Yes. At this point all the records are deleted from your table. The table itself remains on the disk; however, it does not have any data in it.

6–9 ADDING RECORDS TO THE END OF A TABLE

To add a record to the end of a table, enter Edit mode and press the down-arrow key (↓) to pass the last record. Paradox for Windows adds a new blank record, giving it the next record number in sequence. You can now enter data in this blank record.

6–10 ADDING AND DELETING FIELDS WITHIN A TABLE

To add a new field to your database, select Restructure from the Table menu. You will see a screen similar to the one in Figure 6–10. At this point you can move the cursor to any field, then press the Ins key to add a new field. To insert a new field

Figure 6–10
Restructure Paradox for Windows
Table.

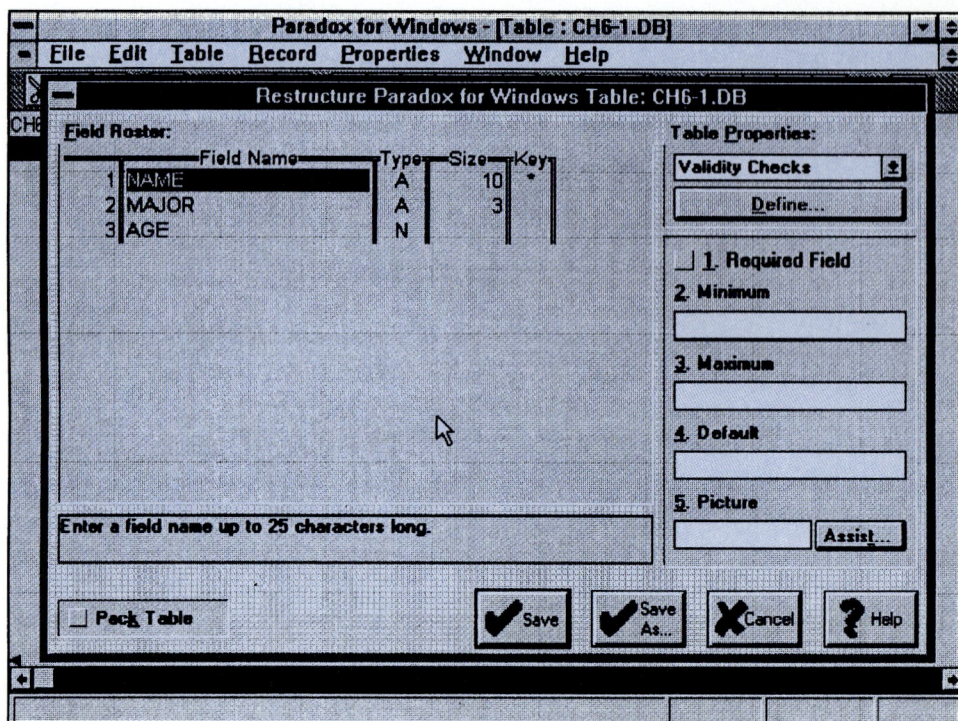

before field number 1, move the cursor to field number 1 and then press Ins. To insert a field after the last field, press the down-arrow (↓) to pass the last field, and then enter your new field.

To delete a field in the Restructure dialog box, move the cursor to the field number of any desired field, and then press the Ctrl+Del key combination. After doing any of these tasks, you must click Save or Save As to save your final work.

Using the Restructure Paradox for Windows table dialog box (Figure 6–10), you can easily change the field type. Just highlight the desired field type, click to display all the field types, and then click on the new field type. Remember to be very careful when you restructure a table because you could permanently damage it. To guard against data loss, make a backup of your database table before you perform any restructuring task.

6–11   CHANGING THE STRUCTURE OF A TABLE USING THE MOUSE TECHNIQUES

While your table is displayed you can change the column width by using the mouse technique. To do this, move the mouse pointer to the border of the desired column. When the mouse pointer touches the border it becomes a two-headed arrow. Click and drag to the desired size, then release the mouse button.

To move a column, position the mouse pointer at the desired column heading (field name). As soon as the mouse pointer touches the field name you will see a small rectangle. Click and drag to the new location, then release the mouse button.

You can also move columns by using the Ctrl+R key combination, which rotates the column you select to the far right end of your table and advances all the other columns. You can repeat this action as many times as necessary to achieve the column order you want.

6–12   MODIFYING THE STRUCTURE OF A TABLE: AN EXAMPLE

Suppose that in the database table presented in Figure 6–8, you would like to add two more fields: ADATE (Admission Date), which is date type, and SALARY, which is currency type. To do this follow these steps:

1. Use the File Open Table command to open the table.

2. Choose Table.

3. Choose Restructure. You will see a screen similar to the one presented in Figure 6–10.

4. Move the cursor to field 4 (a new field). Type ADATE and press Enter. For field type press D (for Date) and then press Enter.

5. Now you are at field 5. For this field, type SALARY and press Enter. For type press $ (for currency). Now the structure of the new table is constructed (see Figure 6–11). At this point click on the Save As button to save this structure. For the new table name, type *CH6–12* and click on OK.

After you click the OK button, in a few seconds Paradox for Windows presents you with the new table structure. This table includes two empty fields (see Figure 6–12). Now press F9 to enter the Edit mode then enter the following data for these three records:

    1/01/91   21000
    10/12/92   29000
    12/31/93   19000

Figure 6–11
The new structure of the sample table.

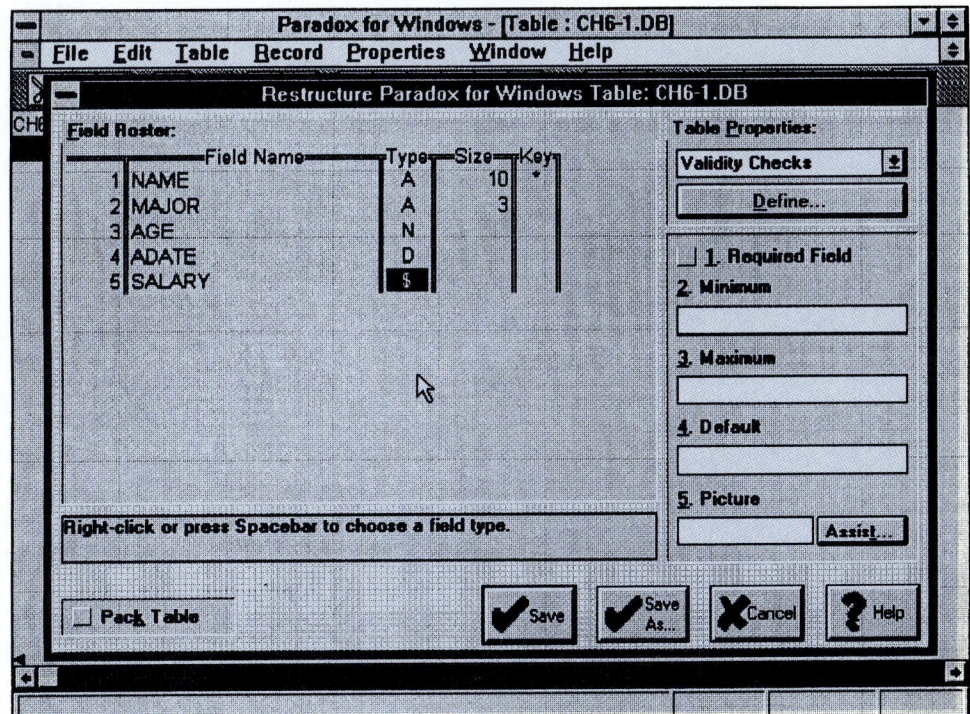

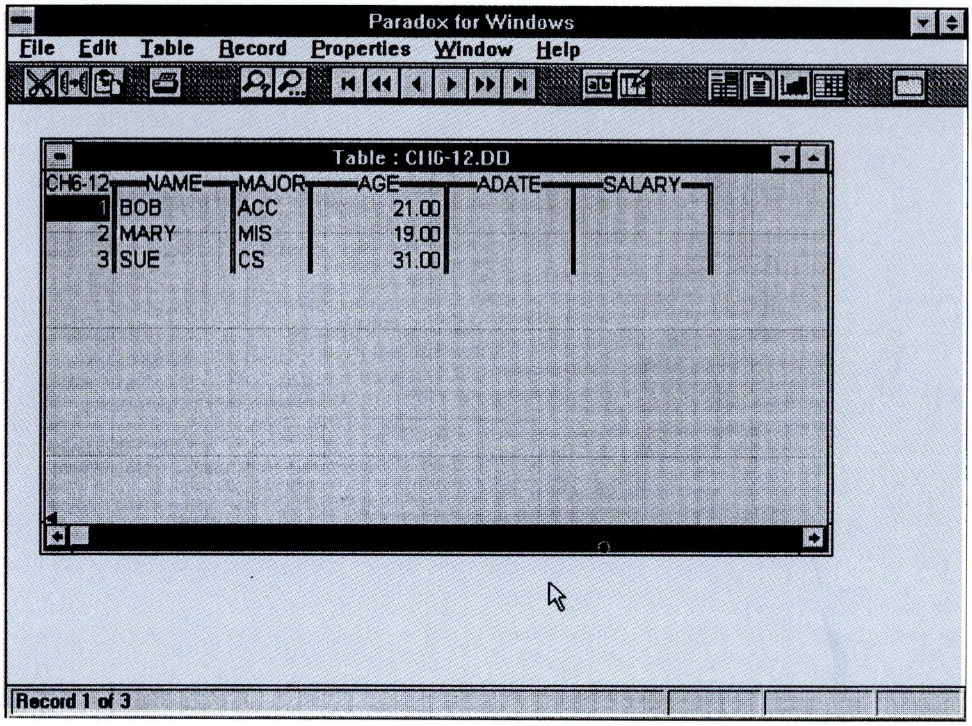

Figure 6–12
The new table with two empty fields.

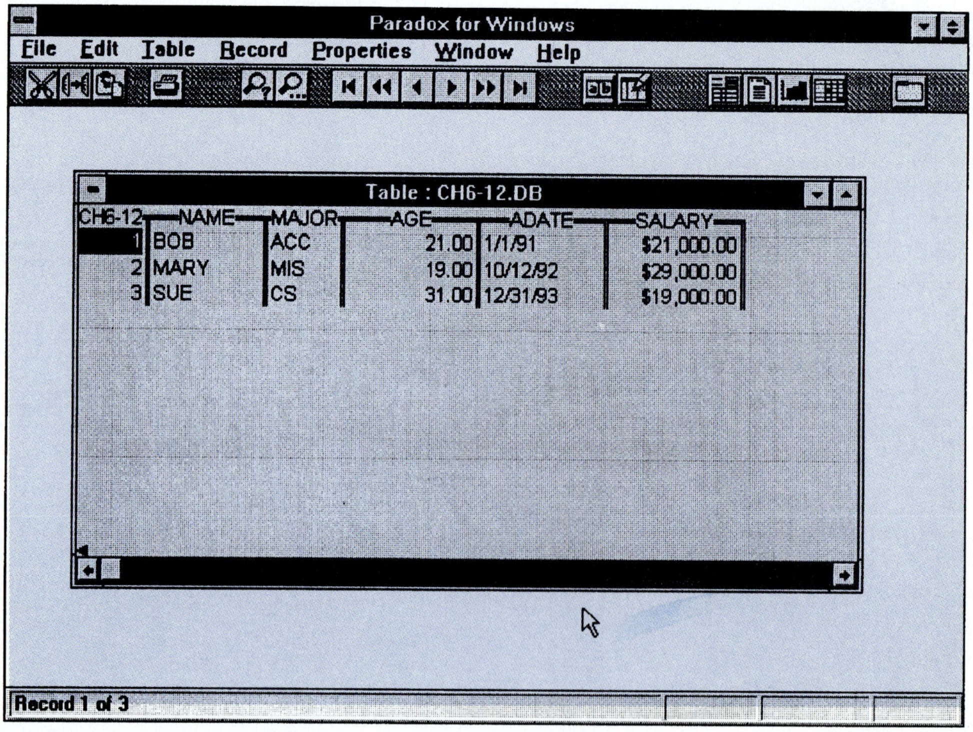

Figure 6–13
The new table.

While the cursor is at the end of record 3, double-click the control menu box to finalize the data entry process. If you view the new table, you will see a screen similar to Figure 6–13.

6–13   THE UNDO FEATURE OF PARADOX FOR WINDOWS

Paradox for Windows offers a powerful **Undo** facility. Using this facility you can reverse certain actions. The Undo command allows you to change your mind and undo changes to a record (before it is finalized). To perform an Undo operation, you can either choose Undo from the Edit menu or press **Alt+BKSP** (Backspace) simultaneously.

You can select the Undo command to undo all changes to all fields in the current record. If the current record has not been changed, Edit Undo does nothing. Since Paradox for Windows updates data as soon as you move off a record, you must use Undo before you leave the record.

To reverse changes to a single field, press the Esc key before you leave the field. Paradox for Windows restores the original contents of the field.

Remember that you cannot undo a record that has been deleted. Once a record is deleted in a table, there is no way to get it back except to reenter it. Also remember that the Undo feature works only while you are still in the field that you changed. When you move to the next field or record, any changes are saved. Paradox for Windows remembers only the previous field value until you leave the field. If you change a field twice, you can undo your second change but not your first change.

6–14   SORTING YOUR DATABASE

Sorted databases are easier to access. For example, you might organize all the students in our Paradox for Windows class based on their grades or all the customers based on their credit limit. As you saw earlier in this chapter, while you are constructing a table you can specify a key field. If you select such a key, Paradox for Windows constantly maintains your table sorted based on this key. However, if you forget to do this or if you want to change the sort order or the sort key, you can always select the Sort command. To sort our sample database table (Figure 6–8) by age, do the following:

1. Open the table.
2. From the Table menu select Sort.
3. Paradox for Windows displays the Sort Table dialog box as displayed in Figure 6–14. The Same Table option places the results of the sort operation in the same table. This means you will end up with a sorted table. No new table will be generated. A keyed table (indicated by key) can be sorted only to a new table (this is the case in our example). The new table option places the results of the sort operation in a New Table. This is the default for keyed tables.
4. Paradox for Windows requests a table name. In the New Table box type *CH6–15*.
5. By default, Paradox for Windows sorts in ascending order based on the values in the key field. Your table can have one primary key and as many secondary keys as the number of your fields minus one (the primary field). The secondary key is usually a tie-breaker. For example, if you sort based on last name, and you have five last names of Smith, these Smiths will be sorted

Figure 6–14
Sort Table dialog box.

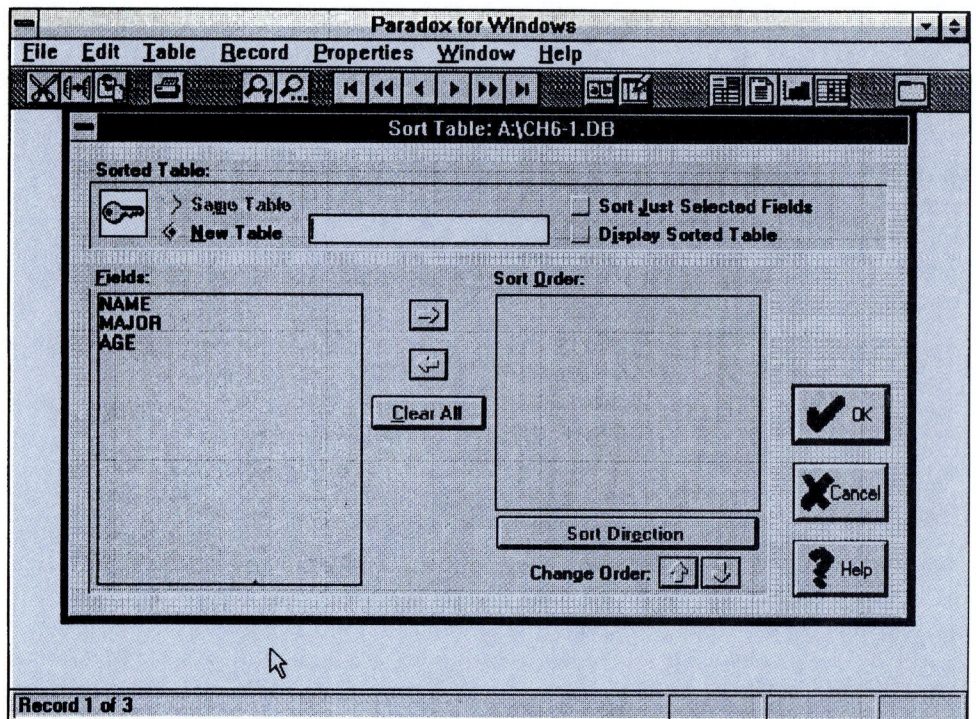

based on their first names *if* you select the last name as the primary key and the first name as the secondary key. To change to descending order, double-click the field name and then click the Sort Direction button in the bottom of the Sort Order box. If you do this, 123 changes to 321, indicating descending sort order. In our example we want to have the AGE field as key number 1 and MAJOR and NAME as key numbers 2 and 3, respectively.

6. Double-click the AGE field in the Fields box and then double-click the MAJOR and NAME fields, respectively. At this point, your screen should be similar to Figure 6–15.

7. Click on OK. Your table will be sorted from youngest person to oldest. To see the sorted table, either open it or click on Display Sorted Table in the Sort Table dialog box. The sorted table is displayed in Figure 6–16. If you select the Sort Just Selected Fields option, Paradox for Windows sorts only on the fields in the sort order list. If two or more records have identical values in these fields, Paradox for Windows cannot resolve the tie, so it places the records together as a group, unsorted. The Clear All option removes all the fields.

When you work with a keyed table, remember the following facts:

1. You can use only alphanumeric, date, and numeric fields as key fields. You cannot use a memo, binary, or graphic field as a key field because the contents of these fields are stored outside of the table, and Paradox for Windows cannot evaluate those contents to determine their uniqueness.

2. Key fields must appear before nonkey fields in the table structure. If you make the second field in a table the key field, Paradox for Windows also makes the first field the key field.

3. If you use keyed tables, you do not have to sort your tables. If you use unkeyed tables, you must resort them whenever you add records. Also, unkeyed tables cannot detect duplicate entries.

Figure 6–15

The completed sort screen for the table presented in Figure 6–14.

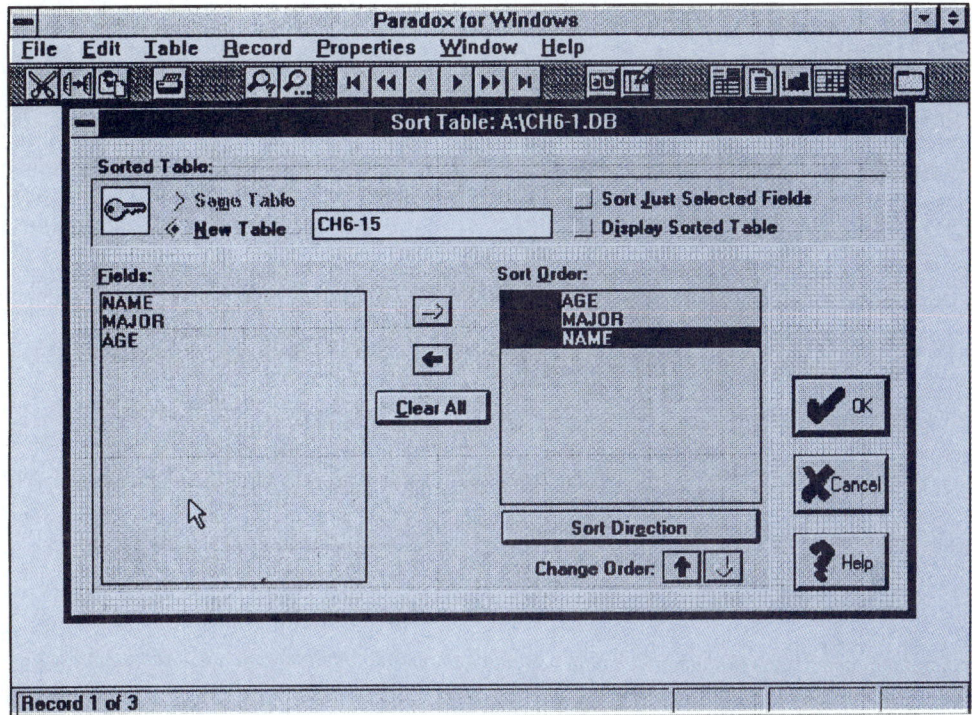

Figure 6–16

A sorted database table.

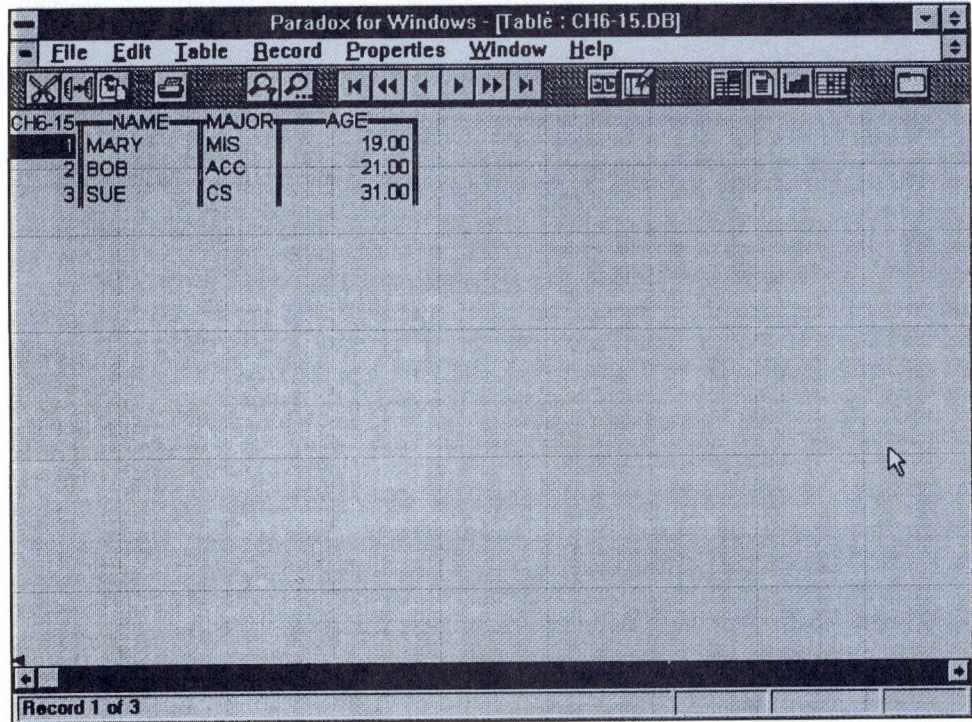

SUMMARY

This chapter reviewed important tasks performed by Paradox for Windows. The process of creating a database was explained. Steps for adding and deleting records and changing the structure of a database were highlighted. The process of creating quick reports was introduced, along with the Undo feature of Paradox for Windows. The chapter also highlighted the sorting procedure. In the next chapter we will discuss various editing tasks in Paradox for Windows.

REVIEW QUESTIONS

*These questions are answered in Appendix A.

1. What are major operations performed by a DBMS?
2. When you specify a table name, in which drive will this table be saved? How do you change the working directory?
*3. What command is used to create a database?
4. What is a valid database name?
5. What is the convention for choosing field names?
6. How do you save the structure of your database?
*7. What is the difference between the Save and Save As commands?
8. What are some of the keys for cursor movement in editing mode?
9. How do you correct your mistakes?
10. How do you add more records to your active database?
*11. How do you delete a record? How do you erase all records in the current database?
12. What command is used for changing the structure of a database?
*13. How do you add two new fields to a database?
14. How do you delete two fields from a database?
*15. Is it necessary to specify a width for a date field? For a numeric field?
16. What are some of the data types supported by Paradox for Windows?
17. While using the Del or Ctrl+Del commands, is it possible to change your mind and undelete the object?
*18. How do you create an quick report?
19. How do you activate a file, that is, bring a file from disk to memory?
20. How do you add more records to the bottom of your current table?
21. How many keys can be included as sort keys?
22. How do you change the sort order?

HANDS-ON EXPERIENCE

1. Start Paradox for Windows and insert a formatted disk in your default drive. Do the following:
    a. Create a file called CH6EX-1 with three fields: CUSNAME (alphanumeric, width 10), CREDIT (numeric), and ADATE (date). Use the following data:

    John, 2000, 01/09/92
    Terry, 5000, 06/06/93
    Sue, 2500, 07/07/91

    b. Save this database to your disk.

    c. Change the CREDIT for Terry from 5000 to 6500.

    d. Add another record to this database: Mary, 1700, 02/09/93.

    e. Display the final database.

    f. By double-clicking the control menu box close this table.

2. Retrieve CH6EX-1 from your disk by using the File Open command and do the following:

    a. From the Table menu select the Restructure option and then add AGE (numeric) as a new field to this database:

Customer 1	30
Customer 2	40
Customer 3	55
Customer 4	60

    b. Delete the ADATE field from the database.

    c. Display the new database.

    d. Delete record 3.

    e. Display the new database.

    f. By double-clicking the control menu box close the table.

3. Create the following database under CH6EX-2 with three fields: CUSNAME (alphanumeric width 10), CREDIT (numeric), and ADATE (date). Use the following data:

    Bob, 5000, 01/01/93

    Tom, 6000, 01/01/90

    a. Save this file on your disk.

    b. By using the File Open command, activate CH6EX-1.

    c. By using the Save As command, save this table under TEST.

    d. By using the File Utilities Delete command, erase TEST.

4. By using Shift+F7 create a paper output of your last database.

5. Sort the last table based on the credit to a new table named SCHEX-2. Sort it again based on name in descending order into a table named SNCHEX-2.

KEY TERMS

Database addition	Database search	Default setting
Database deletion	Database sort	Printing reports
Database key	Database structure	Undo feature
Database modifications		

KEY COMMANDS

Alt+BKSP (to undo your last action)	F9 (to enter Edit mode)	Ins (to insert a new record in Edit mode)
Ctrl+Del (to delete a record in Edit mode)	File New Table (to create a database Table)	Shift+F7 (to generate a quick report)

MISCONCEPTIONS AND SOLUTIONS

Misconception   You save a Paradox for Windows table, but when you try to retrieve it, you can't.

> **Solution**   You have probably saved your table in a directory other than the default directory. To retrieve such a table you must type the drive and/or the directory name before typing the table name, or use File Working Directory to change the default. Also, in the Open Table dialog box you can click on the Browse button to search other directories.

Misconception   You are trying to come up with a table name and you do not know the names that you have already used.

> **Solution**   When Paradox for Windows requests a table name, if you respond with the name that has already been used, Paradox for Windows warns you that you are overwriting an existing table. Just choose a different name.

Misconception   You are viewing a table and you see a series of asterisks (*) displayed in some of your fields.

> **Solution**   The column for a numeric field is not wide enough. You have to extend the column. The simplest way is to use the mouse, click the column border, and drag it to the right.

ARE YOU READY TO MOVE ON?

Multiple Choice

1. You can sort a table
   a. to itself
   b. to a new table in the default drive
   c. to a table in any drive
   d. all of the above
   e. none of the above

2. To create a new database (one that does not yet exist), select the following from the Paradox for Windows opening menu:
   a. File
   b. Modify
   c. View
   d. Forms
   e. none of the above

3. To choose the field type, you can
   a. type the first letter of the desired type
   b. right-click to display all the field types, then select the desired one
   c. press the spacebar for different types and select the desired one
   d. all of the above
   e. a or c

4. The field names, field types, field widths, and number of decimal places (if applicable) are known collectively as the file
   a. structure
   b. database
   c. name
   d. record
   e. none of the above

5. When you are finished with data entry and you want to close the data entry window you can
   a. double-click the control menu box
   b. click the control menu box, then click Close
   c. select Exit from the file menu
   d. all of the above
   e. only a and b

6. To permanently remove record number 4 from your file, in Edit mode, you must move the cursor to record 4, then
   a. type *DELETE RECORD 4*, and press Enter
   b. type *DELETE ALL* and press Enter
   c. type *PACK* and press Enter
   d. press Del
   e. press Ctrl+Del

7. To add new records to your file, which mode must you be in?
   a. REPORT
   b. RECORD
   c. EDIT
   d. FORMS
   e. none of the above

8. To retrieve and view the file STUDENTS from disk, select the following from the Paradox for Windows opening menu:
   a. File
   b. Properties
   c. Window
   d. Forms
   e. none of the above

9. One of the following keys allows you to switch between Table View and Edit mode:
   a. F1
   b. F2
   c. F10
   d. F5
   e. F9

10. To print a quick report while the table is displayed, press
    a. Alt+F1
    b. Ctrl+F2
    c. Alt+F5
    d. Shift+F7
    e. none of the above

True/False

1. Paradox for Windows qualifies as a DBMS because it can do basic database management operations, including file creation, file modification, and sort operations.
2. Paradox for Windows attaches the extension DBF to the name of your database (table) file.
3. Field names can contain only letters; no other characters may be used.
4. The sort order cannot be changed once it is established.
5. Paradox for Windows generates only two different file extensions.
6. The File Open command displays all fields; it cannot be used to view data fields selectively.
7. You always have to specify the field width for the date field type.

8. New records can always be added to your file by typing in the data from the keyboard.

9. The Restructure command can be used to add or delete field names in an existing file.

10. The INS and DEL keys can be used to edit and correct mistakes in your database.

ANSWERS

Multiple Choice		True/False	
1.	d	1.	T
2.	a	2.	F
3.	d	3.	F
4.	a	4.	F
5.	d	5.	F
6.	e	6.	T
7.	c	7.	F
8.	a	8.	T
9.	e	9.	T
10.	d	10.	T

Editing, Organizing, and Managing Your Database

7

7–1   INTRODUCTION

This chapter presents various editing features of Paradox for Windows. It highlights Table View, Form View, and Field View as three different methods for editing your database tables. The chapter discusses the Locate command for locating and editing different records; explains borrowing a table structure for creating similar database tables; and covers key rules for the various Paradox for Windows Sort operations. Next, the chapter discusses the export and import features of Paradox for Windows; explains the process of adding and subtracting tables; and concludes with some of the most important "utility" commands for easy data maintenance in the Paradox for Windows environment.

7–2   PARADOX FOR WINDOWS EDITING FEATURES

In the last chapter you saw some of the **editing features** of Paradox for Windows. In this chapter we will go into detail about these editing features.

7–2–1   Editing in Table View

Paradox for Windows displays data by default in **Table View** mode. In this view you can see up to 20 rows (records) of data; up to 80 characters per record can be displayed. If the records in your data table include more data than 80 characters, the last column is abbreviated and filled with asterisks. In Table View only one record is active at a time, which means you can work with only one record at a time. The message in the lower left corner of the screen always keeps you informed regarding the active record. For example, in Figure 7–1, record number 1 is your active record. In Table View you can use various keys for moving around

Figure 7–1
A sample data table showing that record number 1 is the active record.

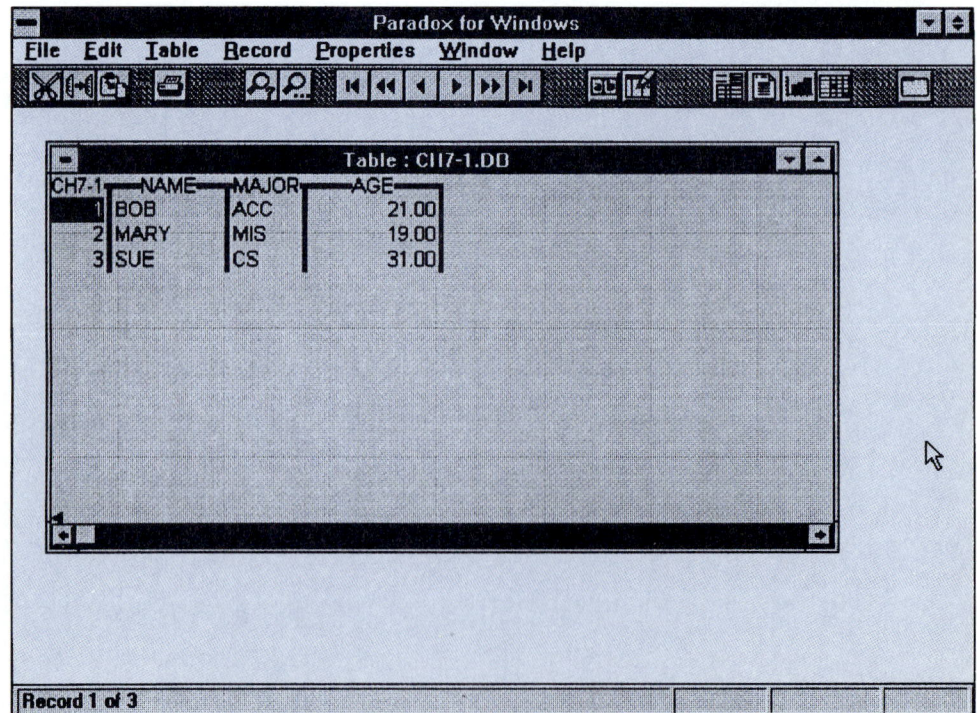

(Table 7–1 lists these keys). To perform any editing task in Table View you must first enter Edit mode. To enter Edit mode if your image is displayed, press F9. If the image is not displayed, open it first, then press F9. To enter Edit mode, you can also click the Edit Data button in the SpeedBar. This button looks like a pencil on a ledger. You can also select Table from the menu, and then select Edit Data. To exit Edit mode, select Table, then click on End Edit.

7–2–2   Editing in Form View

You may prefer to work with one record at a time. This is possible by switching from Table View to **Form View.** To do this, while your table is displayed press the **F7** function key (Form Toggle). Figure 7–2 shows the first record of Figure 7–1 in Form View. Paradox for Windows automatically builds a form for you in Form View. As in Table View, in Form View you can also use various arrow movement keys (Table 7–2 lists these keys). To return to Table View, press F7 again. Remember, to perform any editing task, you must enter Edit mode first.

7–2–3   Editing in Field View

So far you have learned that to change a data item from the end of a record, you can back up by using the backspace key and retype the correct data. This method may not be efficient in all cases. To edit a specific field, you can move the cursor to the field, press the **F2** function key (**Field View**), and then perform the editing task.

When you press F2, the cursor is positioned at the end of your desired field. In Figure 7–3, we put the cursor at the end of record 1. You can use any of the keys listed in Table 7–3 to move the cursor in a given field. You can also use the Ins (Insert) key for adding characters or the Del (Delete) key for deleting characters. When you are finished editing, press the Enter key to finalize the editing task.

For moving around in a table you can also use the options in the Record menu. If you select the Record option you will see a screen similar to the one in Figure 7–4.

Table 7–1

Cursor-Movement Keys in Table View

Key	Function
Ctrl+End	Moves the cursor to the last field of the table
Ctrl+Home	Moves the cursor to the first field of the table
Ctrl ← (left arrow)	Moves the cursor left by one screen
Ctrl → (right arrow)	Moves the cursor right by one screen
↓ (down arrow)	Moves the cursor down by one record
↑ (up arrow)	Moves the cursor up by one record
Enter	Moves the cursor right by one field
→ (right arrow)	Moves the cursor right by one field
← (left arrow)	Moves the cursor left by one field
End	Moves the cursor to the last field of the record
Home	Moves the cursor to the first record of the record
PgDn	Moves the cursor down by one screen
PgUp	Moves the cursor up by one screen

Figure 7–2
A record displayed in Form View.

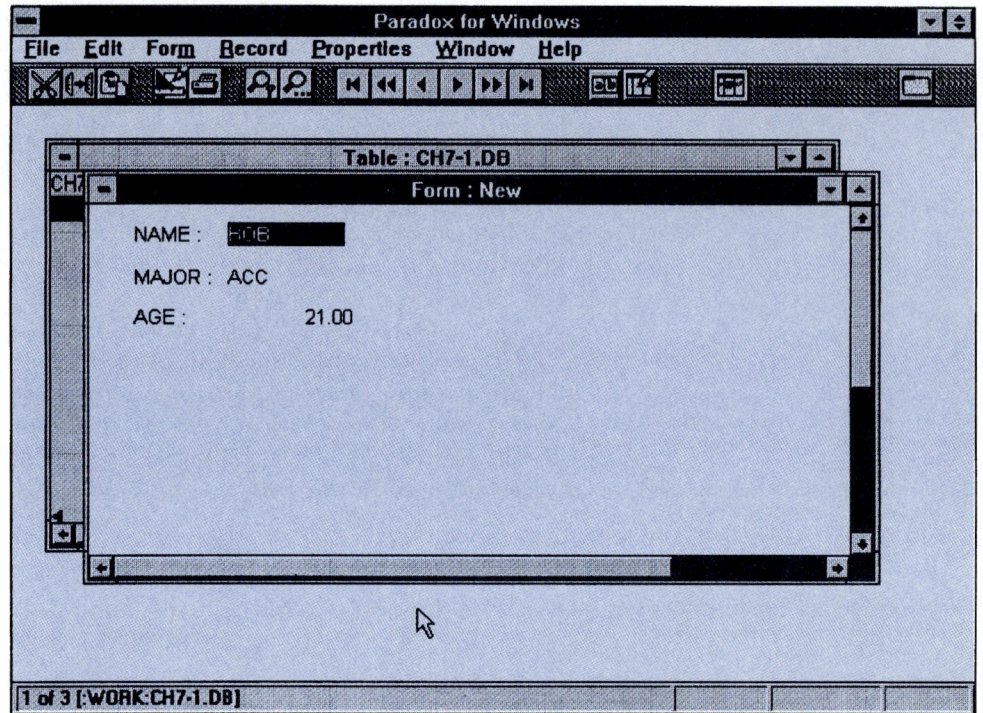

Table 7–2
Cursor-Movement Keys in Form
View

Key	Function
Ctrl+End	Moves the cursor to the last field of the record
Ctrl+Home	Moves the cursor to the first field of the record
PgDn (F12)	Moves the cursor to the same field of the next record
PgUp (F11)	Moves the cursor to the same field of the preceding record
↓ (down arrow)	Moves the cursor down by one field
↑ (up arrow)	Moves the cursor up by one field
Enter	Moves the cursor to the next field
End	Moves the cursor to the last field of the record

7–2–4

Editing a Record with the Locate Command

Sometimes you may want to look for a record in a large database; however, you may have little information about this record. Paradox for Windows provides several methods for locating such a record. The Locate command is probably the fastest method, especially if your data table includes a single key.

To use the Locate command from the Record menu (Figure 7–4), select Locate. You will see a screen similar to the one in Figure 7–5.

If you choose the Field option, Paradox for Windows displays all the fields in the current table. In this list click on the desired field, and then click on OK. This will put you in the specified field of the current record.

Figure 7–3
Record Number 1 in Figure 7–1 is displayed in Field View.

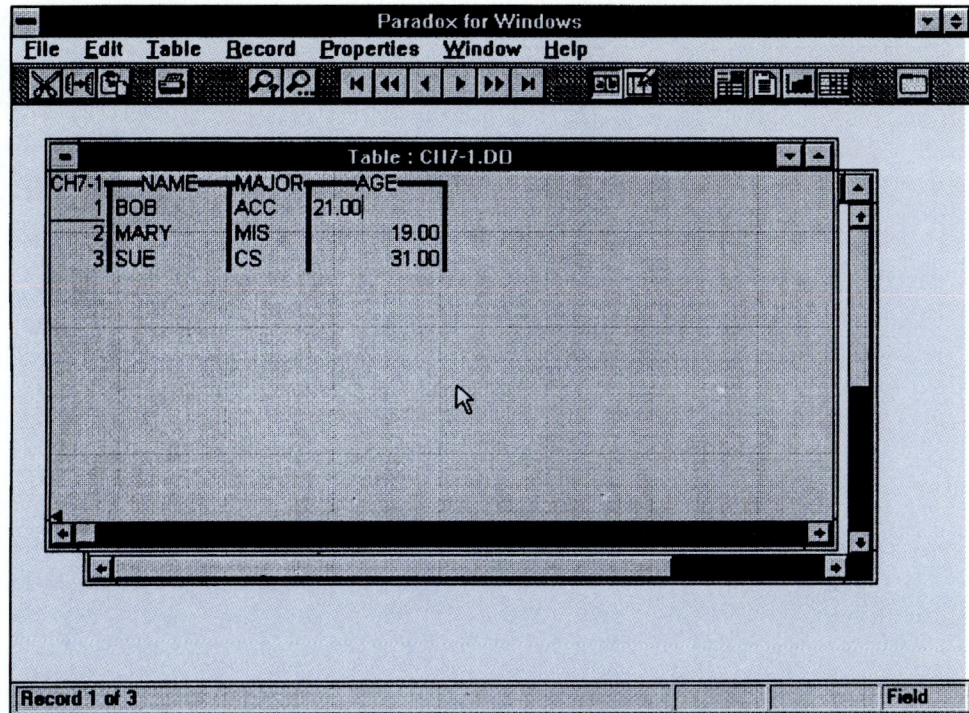

Table 7–3
Cursor-Movement Keys in Field View

Key	Function
Ctrl+left arrow (←)	Moves the cursor one word to the left
Ctrl+right arrow (→)	Moves the cursor one word to the right
↓ (down arrow)	Moves the cursor down one line (in wrapped fields)
↑ (up arrow)	Moves the cursor up one line (in wrapped fields)
→ (right arrow)	Moves the cursor one character to the right
← (left arrow)	Moves the cursor one character to the left
End	Moves the cursor to the last character of the field
Home	Moves the cursor to the first character of the field

If you choose the Record Number, Paradox for Windows displays the Locate Record Number dialog box. Type the desired record number and click on OK.

If you choose the Value (**Ctrl+Z**) option, Paradox for Windows displays the Locate Value dialog box (Figure 7–6). In the Value box type the desired value and click on OK. This will put you in the record that includes this particular value in the specified field.

You can also use the Replace option (**Shift+Ctrl+Z**) (from the Locate menu) to find and replace a particular data item in a table. When you do this, Paradox for Windows provides a confirmation box. Click on Yes to finalize the Replace operations. To perform the Replace operations you must be in Edit mode.

Note that the Value (Ctrl+Z) feature is case sensitive. You must type the exact phrase you want. Uppercase and lowercase are considered to be different. If

Figure 7–4
Options in the Record menu.

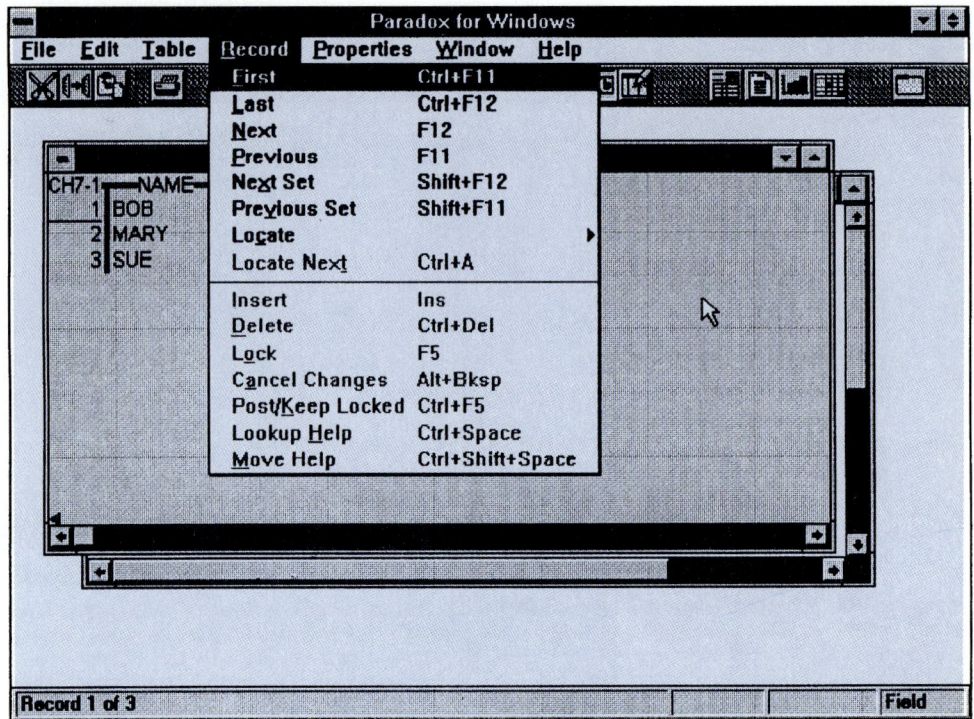

Figure 7–5
Options under the Locate command.

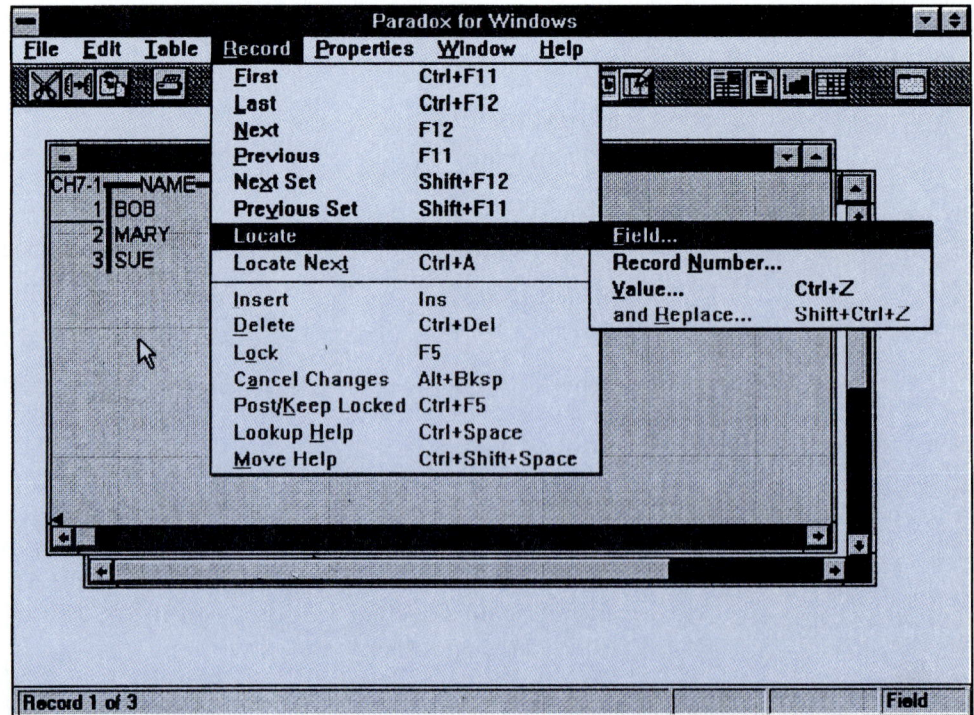

Figure 7–6
Locate Value dialog box.

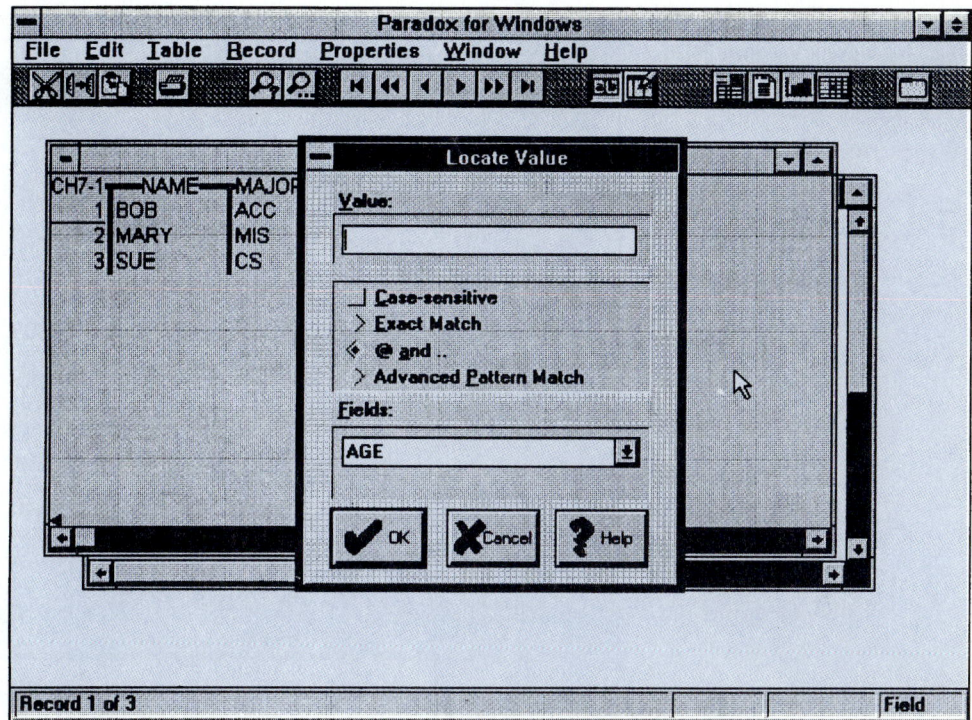

you have more than one candidate for the search, Paradox for Windows moves the cursor to the first record. To see the next record, press the **Ctrl+A** (Locate Next) key. As soon as you find the desired record, you can perform the editing task.

In the Locate Value dialog box you can specify Case-sensitive, Exact Match, or even wildcard characters (discussed in the next chapter).

7–3   BORROWING A TABLE STRUCTURE

To save time you may want to borrow the structure of an existing table for your new table. To do so, from the desktop menu choose File New, then click on Table. Click on OK to accept Paradox for Windows as your table type. You will be presented with the Create Paradox for Windows Table dialog box (see Figure 7–7).

If you click on the Borrow button in the lower left corner of this screen, you will see the Borrow Table Structure dialog box, as displayed in Figure 7–8.

As you see in this dialog box, all the tables in the current directory are displayed. Click the desired table and then click on OK. As soon as you do this the structure of the selected table is displayed in the Create Paradox for Windows Table box and the Borrow button becomes dimmed (unavailable). You can accept this structure as is or you can modify it and then, by using the Save As command, you can save it under a new name.

Let us walk through an example. Choose File New Table from the desktop menu and click on OK. Click on Borrow. Click on CH7-1.DB and then click on OK. The structure of Figure 7–1 is displayed. At this point, you can accept this structure as is or you can modify it. To accept this structure as is, click on the Save As button and specify a new name. To add more fields to this structure, move the cursor to the end of the structure and specify your new fields. To change a field name or type, move the cursor to the desired location (either to the name column or to the

Chapter 7

Figure 7–7
Create Paradox for Windows Table
dialog box.

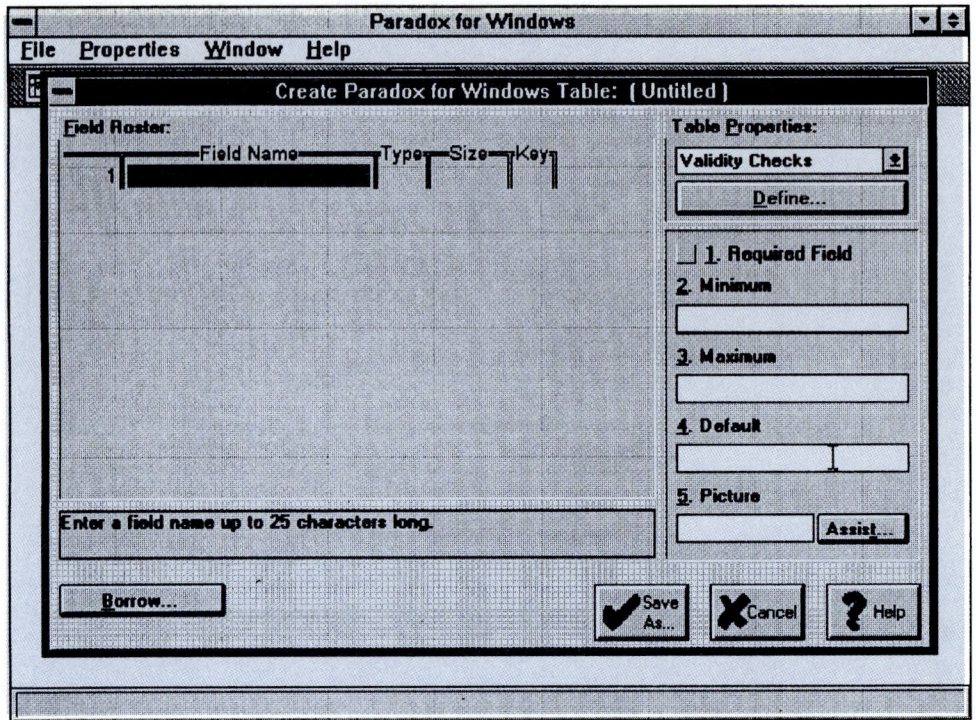

Figure 7–8
Borrow Table Structure dialog box.

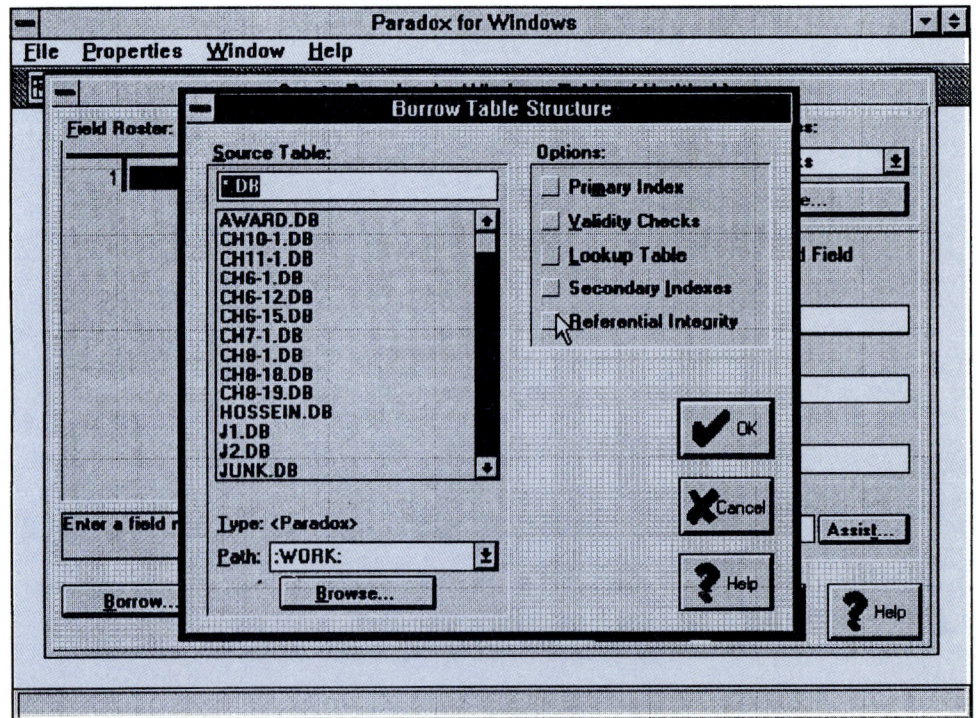

type column) and retype the new information. To delete an existing field, move the cursor to the field and press the Ctrl+Del key. When you are done with all your modifications, select the Save As option and specify a name to save this structure for your new table. Select Cancel if you are not satisfied with your modifications.

7–4   USING THE DITTO FEATURE TO REPEAT ENTRIES

When you are dealing with repeat data, you can save a lot of time by using the Ctrl+D (Ditto Keystroke) command. Suppose that in the field named DEPART-MENT, you are entering the word ACCOUNTING 15 times. This is where you use the Ditto Keystroke command. If you place the cursor in a blank field and press Ctrl+D, Paradox for Windows fills in the value used in the same field in the preceding record. This feature works only for the second record and subsequent records in the table.

In addition to using Ditto for repeating the same information from one record to another, you can use this feature to save time when entries are similar but not identical. This is very useful for long entries. Press Ctrl+D and then edit the field to make it exactly what you want.

7–5   ORGANIZING YOUR DATABASE

Often you have to organize your database table based on a field or a series of fields, for example, organizing all the students based on their GPAs, or organizing all the employees based on their salaries or their number of years of service. Once a database is sorted, the query operation is more manageable. You can see that searching for a customer in a file containing 2,000 customers would be a cumbersome task if the file were not sorted.

Sorting can be based on any number of fields available in your database. The **sort operation** can be done in **ascending** or **descending order**. It can be alphabetical, chronological, and/or numeric. The default order in Paradox for Windows is ascending.

In Chapter 6, we briefly introduced the Sort feature of Paradox for Windows, and in this chapter we will expand our earlier discussion. While you are designing a database, if you enter an asterisk in the key column (by double-clicking or pressing any character), Paradox for Windows considers this field a key, and it will automatically sort your database in ascending order based on this key. This is done as soon as you start entering data in your table.

The **key** in Paradox for Windows tables is the equivalent of an **index** in other database packages. In the next section, we will highlight important rules regarding keys in Paradox for Windows.

7–6   IMPORTANT RULES REGARDING KEYS

When you choose a key you must remember the following important rules:

1. If your database has a **single key**, this key must be the first field in the table. For example, if the account number is the only key in the database table, this field must appear in the first column of your table.

2. Paradox for Windows does not accept duplicate values in the key field. For example, Paradox for Windows does not allow two identical account numbers in the account number field *if* the field is used as a key.

3. Paradox for Windows keeps your database sorted according to the values in the key field.

4. When you select a key, data entry is slowed somewhat while Paradox for Windows sorts the table and updates the index.

5. Paradox for Windows allows you to create **multiple keys**. To do this, place an * (asterisk) after each key field in the definition table.

6. All key fields must come before any nonkey field.

7. The first key in the table is considered the primary key. This means the table is sorted based on this key first. For example, if occupation is the primary key and gender is the secondary key, all the female engineers will come first, then all the male engineers, and then all the female professors, and so forth.

7–7   EXPORT AND IMPORT CAPABILITIES OF PARADOX FOR WINDOWS

Paradox for Windows offers powerful export/import capabilities. To activate this feature, select Utilities from the File menu, then select **Import**. Paradox for Windows responds with the File Import dialog box (see Figure 7–9). If you click the down arrow icon in the Type box, you will be presented with all the file types that can be imported into Paradox for Windows (see Figure 7–10). Select the desired file type and click on OK. As soon as you do this all the file names (if there are any) with the required file type will be displayed in the File Import dialog box. Double-click the desired one. In the provided file import dialog box click on OK. The desired file will be imported into your default directory. After the importing process you can open the file by using the File Open Table command.

Figure 7–9
File Import dialog box.

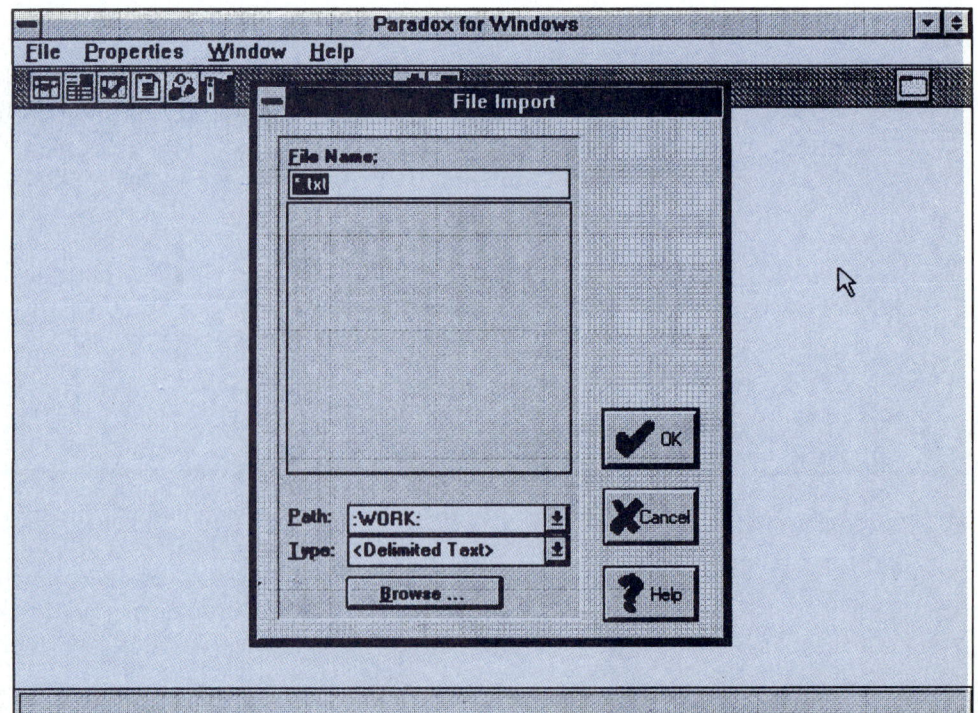

Figure 7–10
Different file types that can be imported into Paradox for Windows.

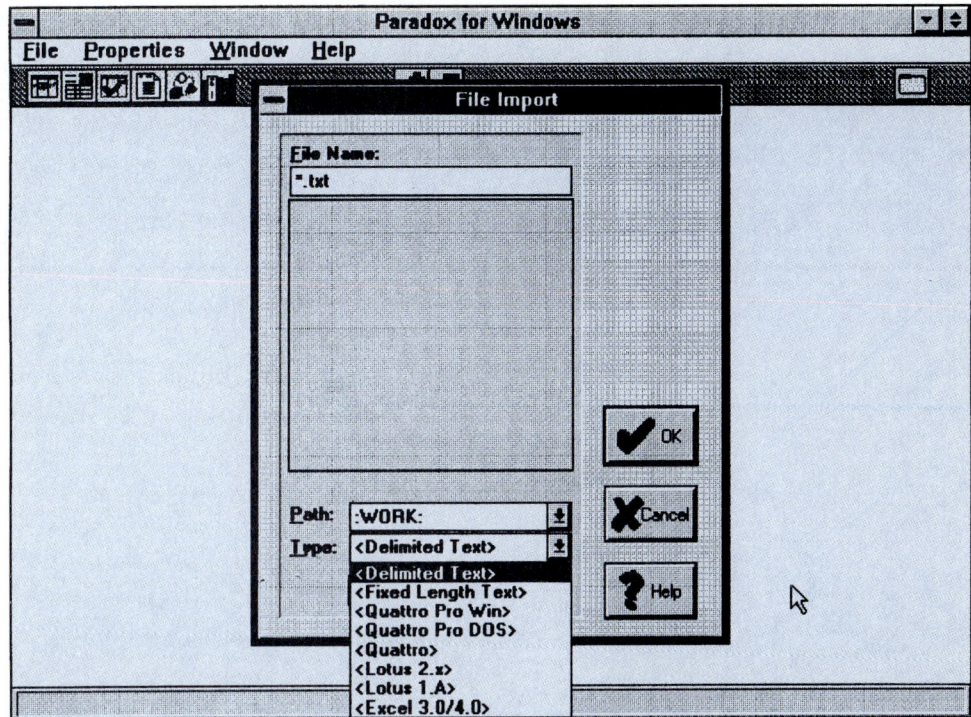

To export a Paradox for Windows table to other software applications, follow these steps:

1. Click on File, then on **Utilities**.
2. Click on **Export**. You will see the Table Export dialog box, as displayed in Figure 7–11.

Figure 7–11
Table Export dialog box.

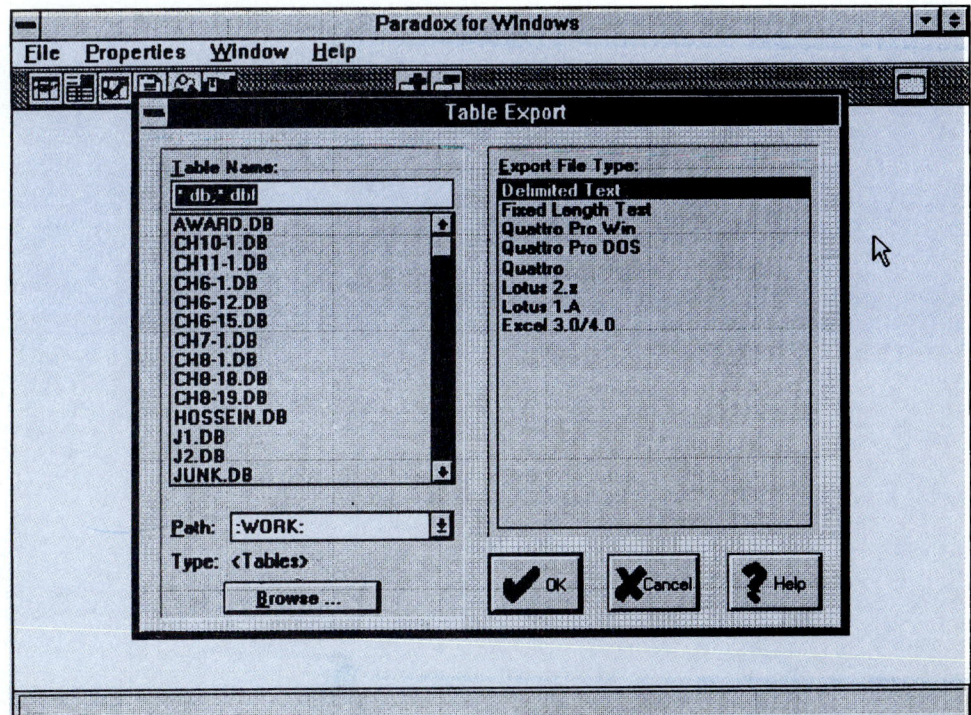

3. Choose the Table Name, highlight the Export File Type, and click on OK.
4. Click on OK again.

The exported file will be saved to the default directory with the new file extension.

7–8   ADDING AND SUBTRACTING TABLES

To combine two tables that include the same structure, follow these steps:

1. From the File menu choose Utilities and then select Add.
2. Paradox for Windows responds with the Add dialog box, as presented in Figure 7–12.
3. In the From box, type the name of the source table. You can also click on the name.
4. In the To box, type the name of the target table.
5. Click on OK.
6. To view the new table, click on View Modified Table in the Add dialog box.

When you are adding tables, remember that only unique records will be added. Duplicate records will not be added twice.

As you see in Figure 7–12, there are several options that you can choose from. The Append option adds the records from the source table to the target table. If the target table is not keyed, the records are appended at the end of existing records. If the target table is keyed, added records that meet the key criteria are inserted in their proper sort order. Records that do not meet the key cri-

Figure 7–12
Add dialog box.

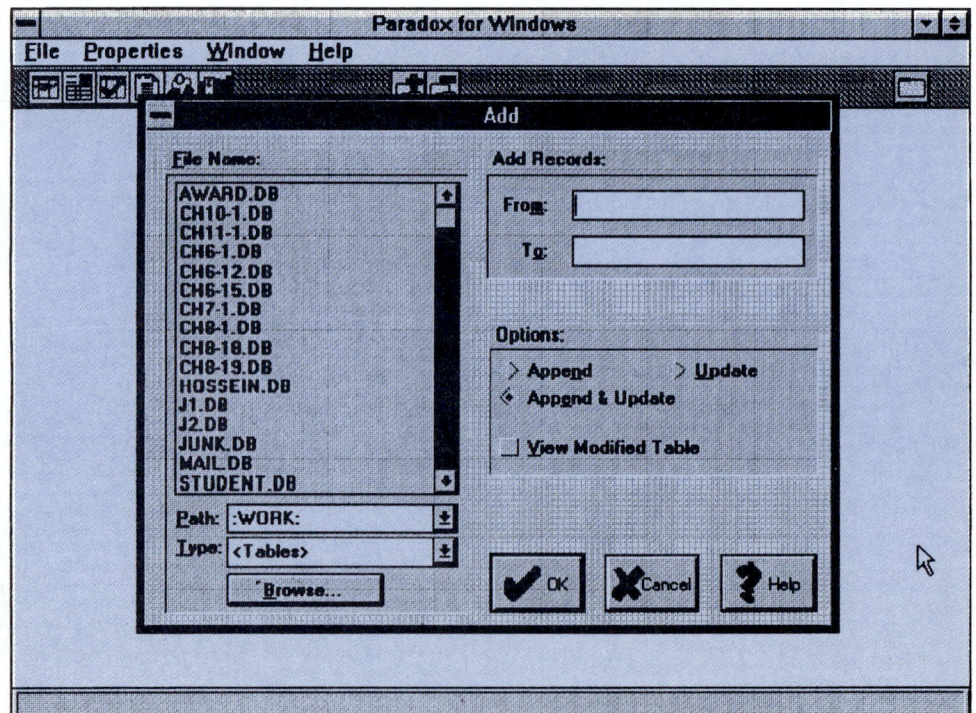

teria are stored in the temporary Keyviol table. If you want, you can edit these records to meet the key criteria, then add them to the target table.

The Update option updates records that already exist in the table you're adding to. Any records in the source table that do not match an existing record are not added. When you choose Update, the records of the source table overwrite matching records in the table you're adding records to. Paradox places the records that are overwritten in the temporary Changed table in your private directory. The table you add records to must be keyed if you want to use the Update option.

The Append & Update option adds new records to a table (following the rules stated above), and updates existing records in the target table (following the rules stated above). The table you add records to must be keyed if you want to use the Append & Update option.

To subtract two tables that include the same structure, select File Utilities Subtract, and then identify your source table in the In box and the target table in the From box (see Figure 7–13).

To view the new table, click on View Modified Table, then click on OK.

These operations have many real-life applications. For example, you may use the Add option to merge several different tables into one table. You may use the Add option to add the current mailing list to several other mailing lists in order to generate the final mailing list. Or, you may use the Subtract option to subtract what you just sold from the list in order to generate the present contents of the list.

7–9   IMPORTANT UTILITY COMMANDS

Several **utility commands** are available under the **Utilities** option of the File menu (see Figure 7–14). We have already explained some of these commands. Here we will review the new ones.

Figure 7–13
Subtract dialog box.

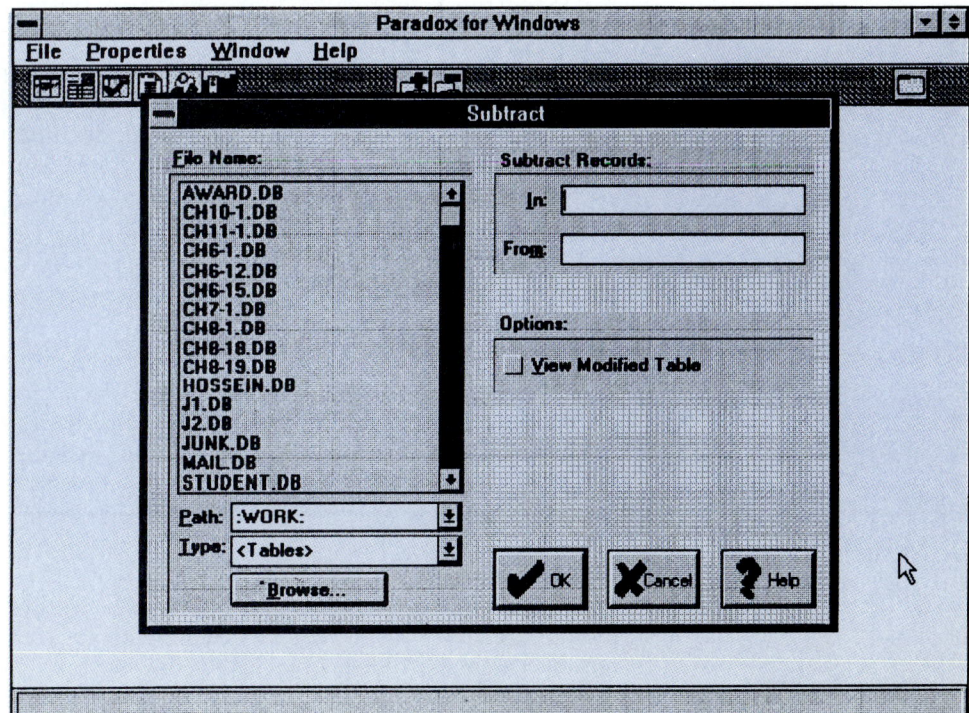

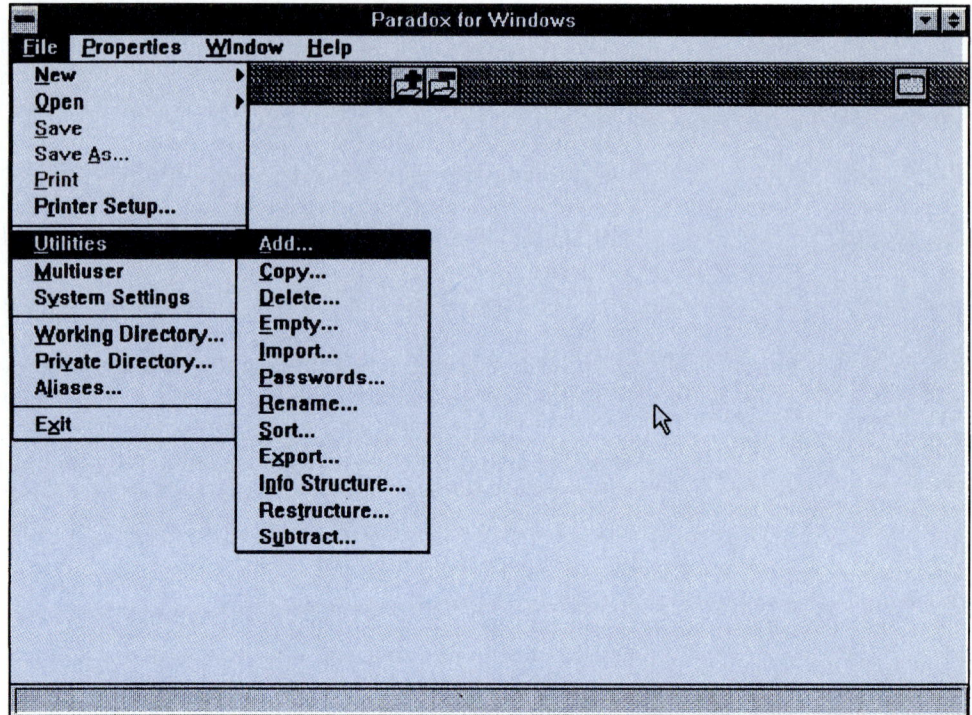

The **Copy** command is used to make a copy of an object. Objects can include tables, queries, forms, reports, scripts, or libraries. This is very helpful if you want to make a copy of a temporary table in order to make it permanent. (Certain Paradox operations create temporary tables that last only until you change your private directory or end your Paradox session. You can edit and query a temporary table as you would any other table.) You can also use the Copy command to generate a backup copy of an existing object. All you have to do is specify the source object and the destination object, and then click on OK.

Select **Delete** to delete an object if you no longer need it.

The **Utilities Passwords** option is used to specify whether to use or stop using the passwords you defined for your documents in the Create Table dialog box or the Restructure Table dialog box. The Passwords option is useful for people working in a network environment. By selecting a password you can keep unauthorized users out of your data tables.

The length of the password can be up to 32 characters. When you enter a password, Paradox for Windows displays a series of asterisks instead of the actual password. As the Enter Password[s] dialog box in Figure 7–15 shows, using this dialog box you can add or remove password(s). After specifying the exact action, click on OK.

The **Rename** option is used to change the name of an object to a new name.

Select **Info Structure** to display the structure of a table.

SUMMARY

This chapter presented various editing features of Paradox for Windows. The process of borrowing a table structure to save time in designing similar tables was introduced. Various sort rules were explained. The chapter discussed the process of adding and subtracting tables, and covered export/import capabilities and some of the utility commands.

Figure 7–15
Enter Password(s) dialog box.

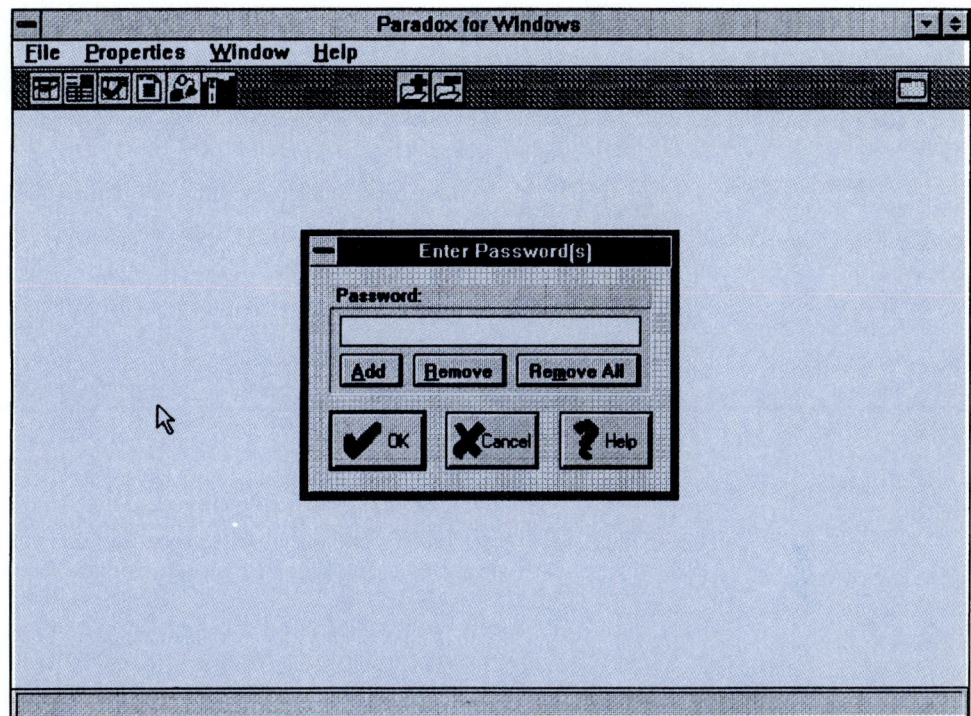

REVIEW QUESTIONS

*These questions are answered in Appendix A.

1. What are some of the Paradox for Windows editing modes?
*2. How many rows and columns are displayed in Table View?
3. What are some of the arrow movement keys in Table View?
4. How do you know which record is your active record in Table View?
5. What is the difference between Table View and Form View?
*6. Which function key switches you between Form View and Table View?
7. Which key is used to activate Field View?
8. What are some of the arrow movement keys in Field View?
9. Which key combination is used to activate the Locate Value feature?
10. Which key combination is used to activate the Locate Next feature?
11. How do you activate the Locate command?
*12. How do you borrow the structure of an existing table for a new table? How do you use the Ditto feature?
13. Why is sorting important?
*14. How many keys can you choose for sorting a table?
15. What character identifies a key field during the table construction?
16. What is the primary key?
17. Will database processing become slower or faster with keys? Discuss.
18. When does Paradox for Windows check for key violation?
19. When you sort a table, can you sort the table into itself?
*20. How many different file types can be exported to Paradox for Windows?
21. How many different file formats can be imported to Paradox for Windows?

22. Is it necessary to specify a file extension when you are exporting a Paradox for Windows table to Lotus 1-2-3?
23. What is the default file extension in the File Import dialog box?
24. What are some of the applications of the Rename command? Of Copy? Of Delete?
25. What does Info Structure do?
26. How do you generate a listing of the structure of a database table?
27. How do you establish a password for one of your tables?
28. How do you create a listing of all your tables in the working directory?
*29. How do you add two tables? How do you subtract two tables?
30. How do you change your default directory?

HANDS-ON EXPERIENCE

1. Using the sample database table presented in Figure 7–1, do the following:
   a. Using Table View, add another record to this table.
   b. Using the F7 function key, switch to Form View and change Mary's major from MIS to MGT.
   c. Using Field View, change Sue's age from 31 to 21.
   d. Using the Locate Value feature, display Sue's record.

2. By using the Borrowing structure feature of Paradox for Windows, create a sample table called SAMPLE with the same structure as Figure 7–1. Do the following:
   a. Enter the following data into this structure:

Tom	MGT	22
Susan	ACC	19
Terry	MIS	22

   b. Add a fourth field to this table called Gender.
   c. Add *M, F, M* as the data for this new field.
   d. Using the Copy command, copy this table to another table named TEST.
   e. Using the Delete command, erase TEST from your working directory.

3. Using the sample database presented in Figure 7–16, do the following:
   a. Sort this database alphabetically based on Name.
   b. Sort this database based on Gender.
   c. Sort this database based on Gender and Salary.
   d. Sort this database based on Salary in descending order.
   e. Copy this database into a new file called EXAMPLE.
   f. Display the structure of this database.
   g. Export this database to a Lotus 1-2-3 file format.
   h. By using the **Delete** command, erase the EXAMPLE table.
   i. By using the **File Open Table** command, generate a listing of all your tables.
   j. By using the **Rename** command, rename CH7-1 as TEST1.
   k. By using the **Copy** command, copy TEST1 to a new file called TEST2.
   l. By using the **Add** command, add TEST to TEST1.
   m. By using the **Subtract** command, subtract TEST1 from TEST2.

KEY TERMS

Ascending order	File export/import	Single key
Descending order	Form View	Sort operation
Editing feature	Key (index)	Table View
Field View	Multiple keys	Utilities commands

Figure 7–16
Sample table.

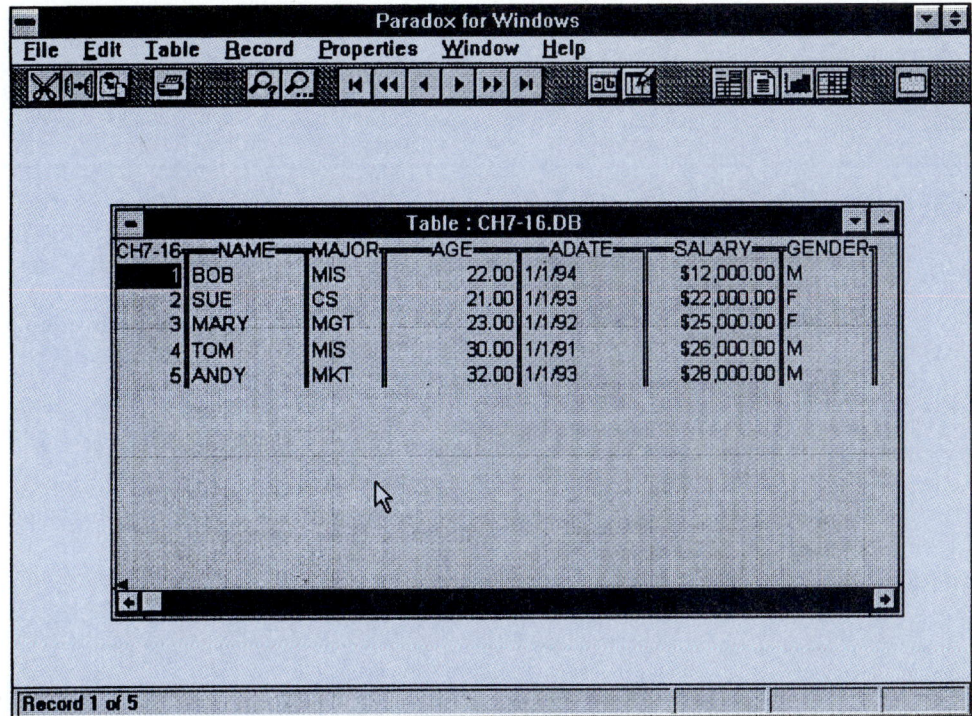

```
                              Paradox for Windows
 File   Edit   Table   Record   Properties   Window   Help

                    Table : CH7-16.DB
CH7-16    NAME     MAJOR     AGE        ADATE      SALARY      GENDER
     1   BOB      MIS       22.00   1/1/94      $12,000.00   M
     2   SUE      CS        21.00   1/1/93      $22,000.00   F
     3   MARY     MGT       23.00   1/1/92      $25,000.00   F
     4   TOM      MIS       30.00   1/1/91      $26,000.00   M
     5   ANDY     MKT       32.00   1/1/93      $28,000.00   M




Record 1 of 5
```

KEY COMMANDS

Borrow (from the Create dialog box) (to borrow the structure of an existing table for a new table)

Ctrl+A (to locate the next record with the specified criteria)

Ctrl+Z (to activate the Locate Value feature)

F2 (to activate the Field View)

F7 (to switch between Form View and Table View)

Shift+Ctrl+Z (to perform find and replace operations in Edit mode)

Utilities Copy (to copy an object into another object)

Utilities Delete (to delete an object)

Utilities Export (to export Paradox for Windows objects)

Utilities Import (to import from other software applications to Paradox for Windows)

Utilities Rename (to rename an object)

Utilities Info Structure (to display the structure of a table)

MISCONCEPTIONS AND SOLUTIONS

Misconception　You try to erase a table but you can't.

　　Solution　To erase a table you must specify the correct name as well as the correct extension and location.

Misconception　Alphanumeric data is sorted from left to right within the field, even if the data happens to "look like" numbers or even if the data happens to contain digits. For example, 625 entered into an alphanumeric field is sorted before the number 99.

　　Solution　Make these data items of equal size by adding zero (0) to the left of the number. For example, in the above example enter 99 as 099.

Misconception　You are using the Locate Value feature to locate a data item. You try over and over with no success.

Solution   Paradox for Windows is particular about whether data and search patterns are in the same case. For example, the patterns BROADWAY and broadway are not the same. To be successful you must enter the exact data item, including the case.

ARE YOU READY TO MOVE ON?

Multiple Choice

1. Using Paradox for Windows you can perform editing:
   a. in Table View
   b. in Form View
   c. in Field View
   d. all of the above
   e. none of the above

2. To switch between Table View and Form View you must press:
   a. F7
   b. F6
   c. F5
   d. F2
   e. none of the above

3. To activate Field View you must press:
   a. F1
   b. F2
   c. F3
   d. Ctrl+F4
   e. none of the above

4. To activate the Locate Value feature you must press:
   a. Ctrl+B
   b. Ctrl+C
   c. Ctrl+Z
   d. Ctrl+D
   e. none of the above

5. To locate your consecutive records after finding the first one, you must press:
   a. Ctrl+A
   b. Alt+B
   c. Alt+C
   d. Alt+D
   e. none of the above

6. The export/import operation is under which menu?
   a. Window
   b. Record
   c. Table
   d. Edit
   e. File

7. Using Paradox for Windows, you can use all of the following utilities commands except:
   a. Copy
   b. Rename
   c. Delete
   d. DIR
   e. Empty

8. One of the following characters after a field type identifies the field as a key field:

    a. + (plus sign)
    b. * (asterisk)
    c. - (minus sign)
    d. ^ (caret)
    e. none of the above

9. If your database has only one key,

    a. this key can be any field
    b. this key must be the last field
    c. this key must be the first field
    d. this key must be alphanumeric
    e. none of the above

10. Using the Paradox for Windows Import command, you can import files into

    a. Lotus 1-2-3
    b. dBASE
    c. Quattro
    d. Excel
    e. all of the above

True/False

1. You can borrow the structure of an existing table for a new table.
2. Paradox for Windows prevents duplicate values in the key field.
3. Paradox for Windows does not keep the database sorted according to the key field.
4. Databases with keys increase the processing speed.
5. Paradox for Windows allows a database with multiple keys.
6. The first key is the primary key.
7. Paradox for Windows sorts by default in descending order.
8. A Paradox for Windows table can be exported to Quattro Pro.
9. A Paradox for Windows table cannot be exported to Lotus 1-2-3.
10. Paradox for Windows does not support any DOS commands, such as Copy, Rename, or Delete.

ANSWERS

Multiple Choice		True/False	
1.	d	1.	T
2.	a	2.	T
3.	b	3.	F
4.	c	4.	F
5.	a	5.	T
6.	e	6.	T
7.	d	7.	F
8.	b	8.	T
9.	c	9.	F
10.	e	10.	F

Query by Example

8

8–1 INTRODUCTION

This chapter reviews different commands for query operation and explains different types of searches. The chapter introduces Paradox for Windows wildcard characters and discusses sorting the Answer table, in both ascending and descending order. Paradox for Windows summary operators are introduced. The chapter explains the process of saving a query and an Answer table for future use.

8–2 QUERY BY EXAMPLE: AN OVERVIEW

Paradox for Windows offers very strong **query operation** capabilities. To query means to request specific information from your database table. Query-by-example means providing a specific example and asking the application software (in this case, Paradox for Windows) to look at your example and to provide answers to your questions. When you use Paradox for Windows for query-by-example operations, two steps are involved:

1. You request specific data from a database by constructing a query statement made up of one or more Query forms.
2. Paradox for Windows responds to your request by generating the requested data in the form of a temporary table named Answer.

Performing query operations using Paradox for Windows is a very easy task. This chapter provides several examples using the sample database presented in Figure 8–1 (saved under CH8-1).

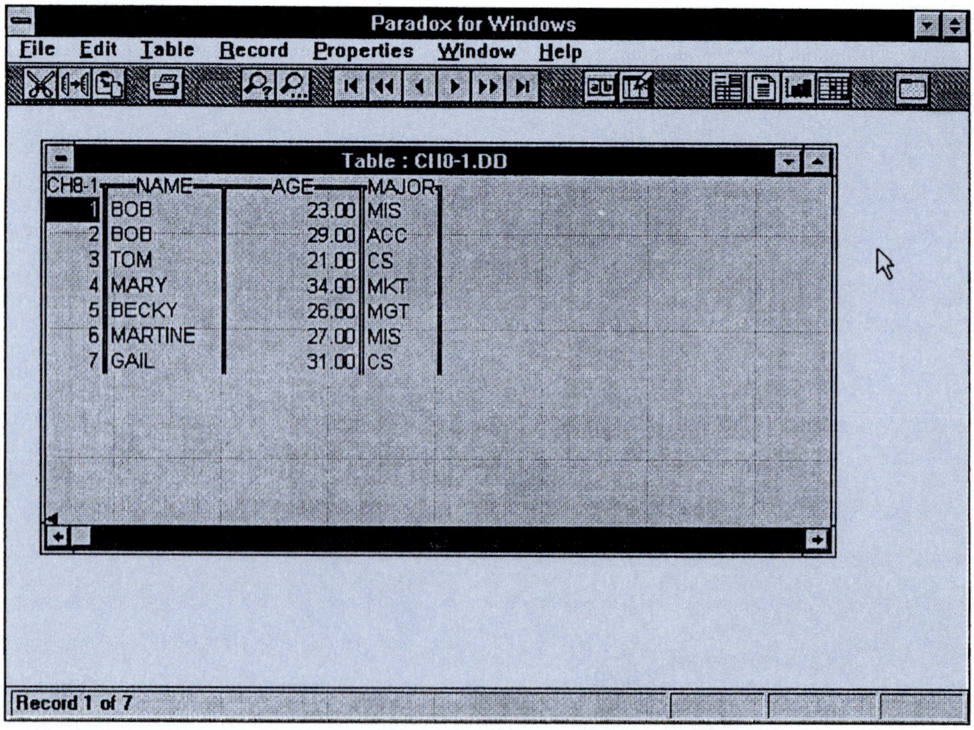
Paradox for Windows
File Edit Table Record Properties Window Help
Table : CH8-1.DB
CH8-1 NAME AGE MAJOR
1 BOB 23.00 MIS
2 BOB 29.00 ACC
3 TOM 21.00 CS
4 MARY 34.00 MKT
5 BECKY 26.00 MGT
6 MARTINE 27.00 MIS
7 GAIL 31.00 CS
Record 1 of 7

Figure 8–1
Sample database table.

8–3   DISPLAYING A QUERY FORM

To display a Query form select File New Query, or right-click on the Open Query button (the third button from the left in the Paradox for Windows desktop), then select the Open option. Paradox for Windows displays the Select File dialog box. Double-click on CH8-1. You will see a screen similar to the one displayed in Figure 8–2. As you see, Figure 8–2 shows the skeleton of the sample database presented in Figure 8–1. It gives the name of the table (CH8-1.DB) and it also presents the field names from left to right. You must decide how much of your data from the database should be included in the query. To include everything in the query, make sure the cursor is in column 1 (beneath the table name) and press the **F6** function key. You can also click the box under the table name. As you see, all fields are marked by a check mark. To perform the query press the **F8** function key or select Query, then click on Run. You can also click the Run Query button (the fourth button from the left). As you see in Figure 8–3, your entire table is displayed right below the Query form. To see the Query form more clearly, click and drag the Answer table down a little bit.

To include selected fields use the Tab key, Arrow keys, or the mouse pointer to move the cursor to the desired fields. Then press the F6 function key (or just click the desired field box). After selecting the desired fields, press the F8 function key to perform the query. Figure 8–4 shows just the NAME and AGE fields in the query. To generate this screen do the following:

1. Click on File New Query.
2. Double-click on CH8-1.DB.
3. Click on the NAME and AGE field check boxes.

Figure 8–2

Example of a Query form for the sample database presented in Figure 8–1.

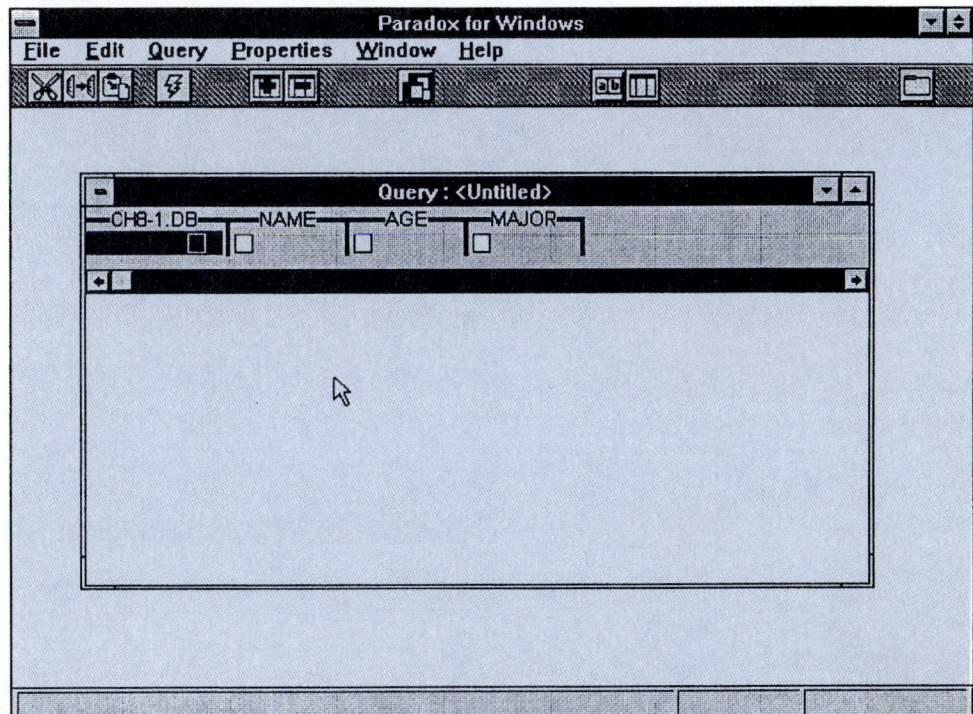

Figure 8–3
A Query that includes the entire database.

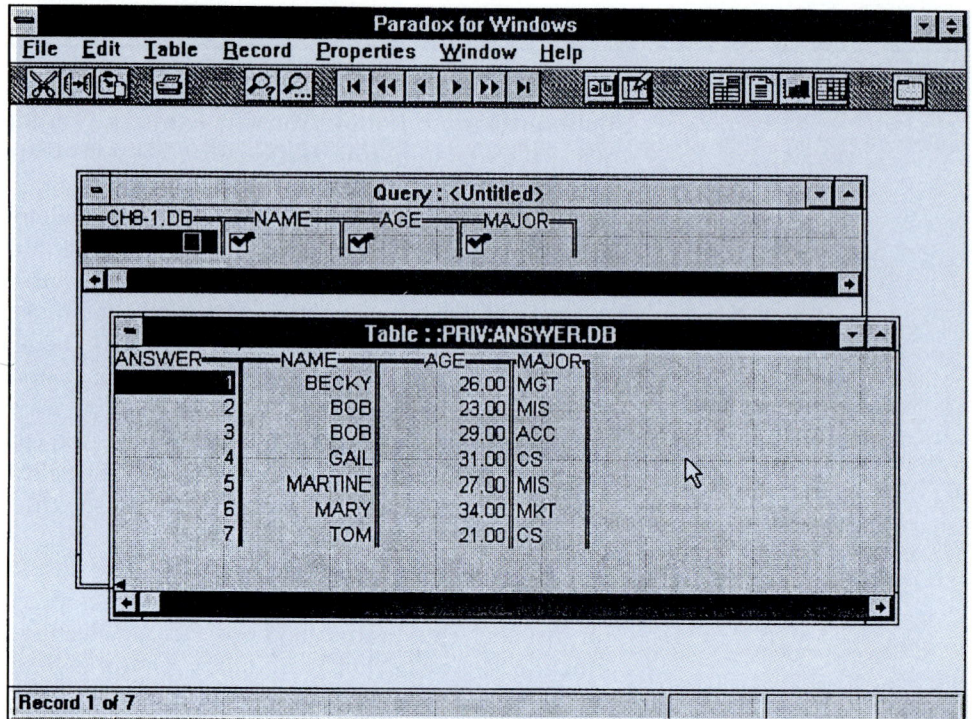

Figure 8–4
A query that only includes the NAME and AGE fields.

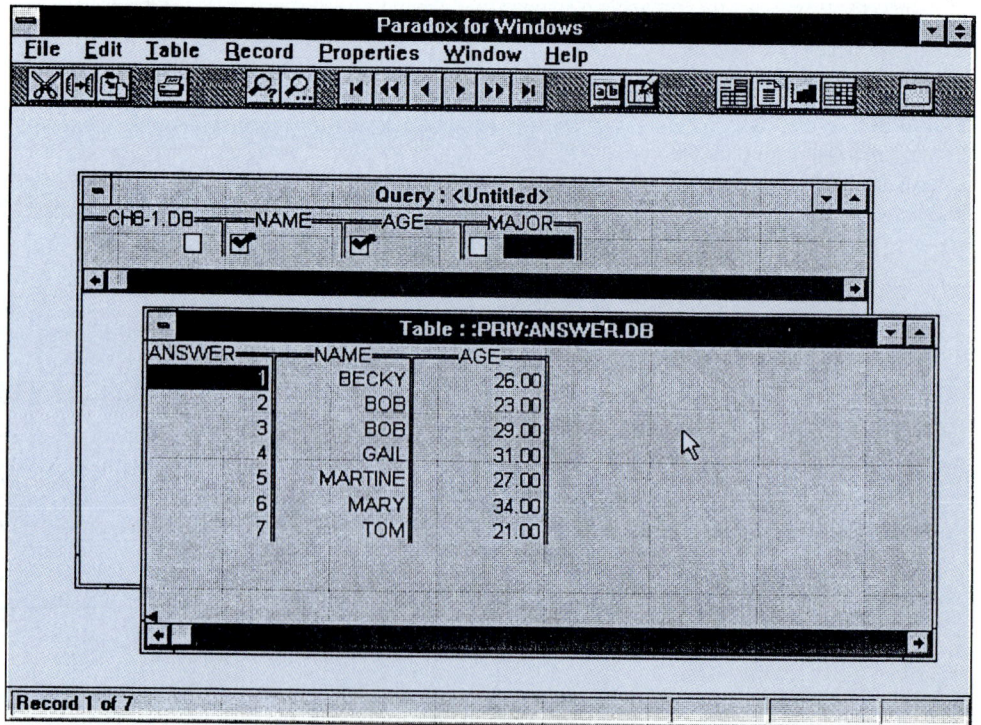

4. Click on the Run Query button or press the F8 function key.

To clear the Answer Table or any other table, double-click its menu box. Also, remember that F6 is a toggle key. After selecting a field by pressing F6, you can deselect the field by pressing F6 again.

8–4   SEARCHING FOR EXACT MATCH

To search for specific information, type the exact information in the desired field in the Query form. When you are performing an exact match, Paradox for Windows is case-sensitive. This means uppercase and lowercase characters are considered to be different. Recall the sample database in Figure 8–1 and suppose you are interested in generating a list that includes all the MIS majors.
To perform this Query start with a clear screen and do the following:

1. Click on File New Query.
2. Double-click on CH8-1.DB.
3. Click on the check box under the table name to check all the fields.
4. In the MAJOR field type *MIS*.
5. Press the F8 function key. You will see a screen similar to Figure 8–5.

8–5   HANDLING DUPLICATE DATA

If you mark certain fields to be included in the query, Paradox for Windows does not include the duplicate fields, if any. For example, in the sample database in Figure 8–1, suppose you mark the NAME field and press F8. Only one of the

Figure 8–5
A query for all MIS majors.

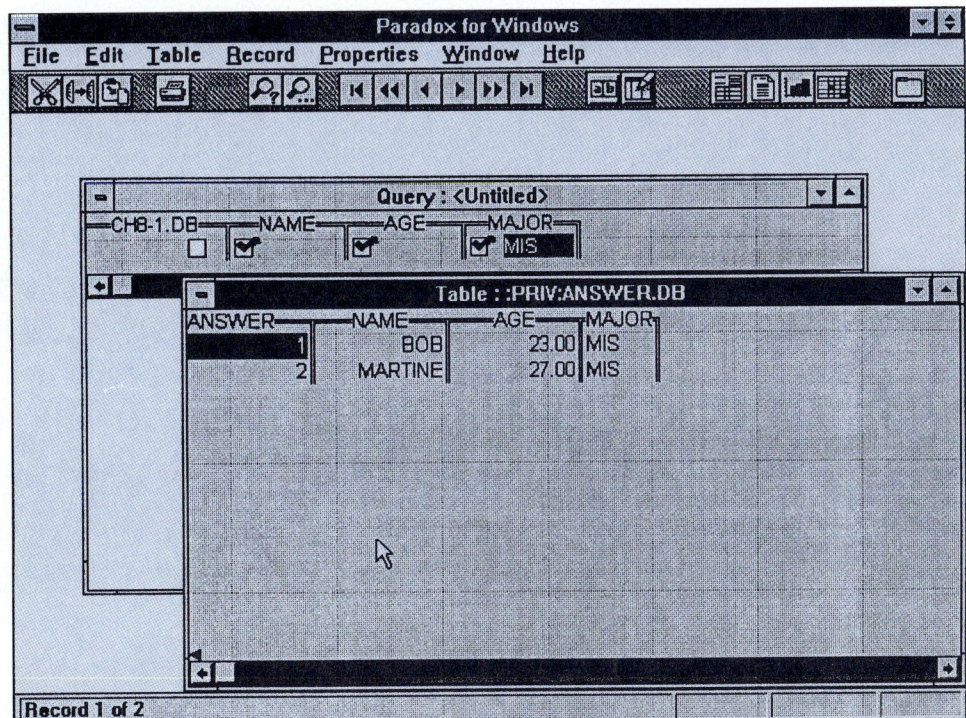

Bobs will be displayed. To display any duplicate records, use **Shift+F6** (check plus) instead of F6. (By putting a checkmark in a field, it will be included in a query. If you want the Answer table to include only unique values for the checked field, use the checkmark.) Figure 8–6 shows that the duplicate data has been eliminated, while Figure 8–7 shows that the duplicate data has been displayed. To

Figure 8–6
Using the F6 function key to avoid duplicate data.

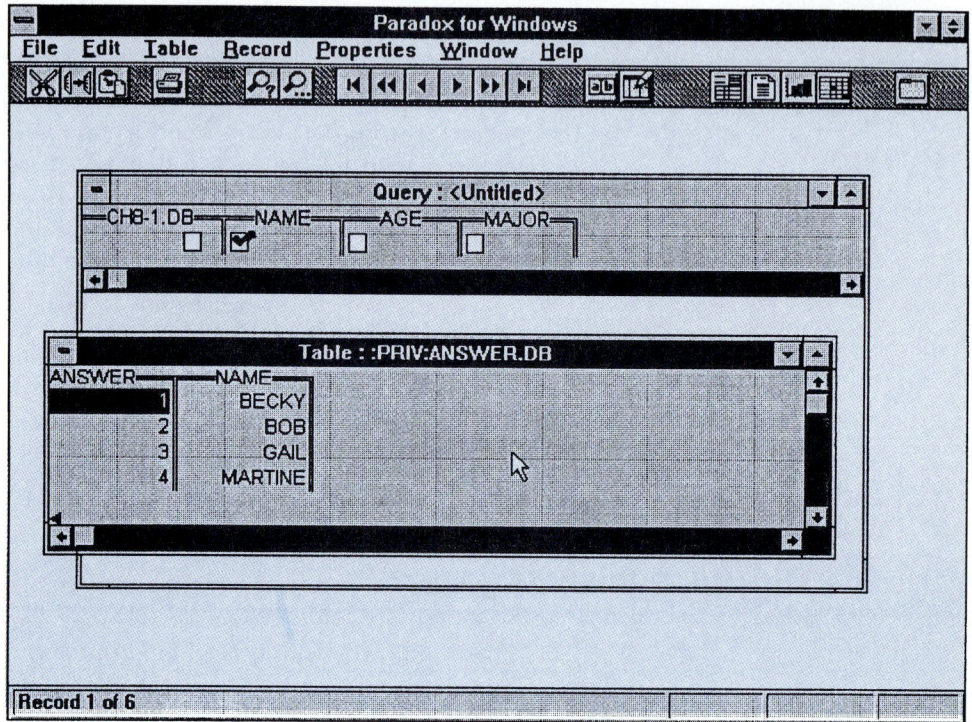

Figure 8–7
Using Shift+F6 to display duplicate data.

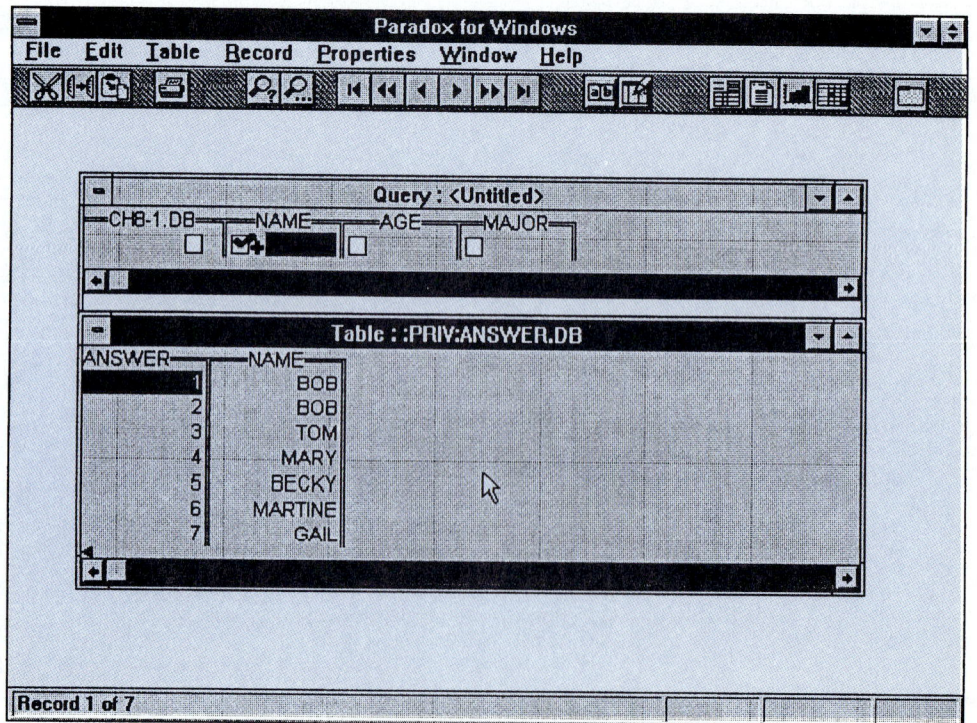

Figure 8–8
Four different check marks.

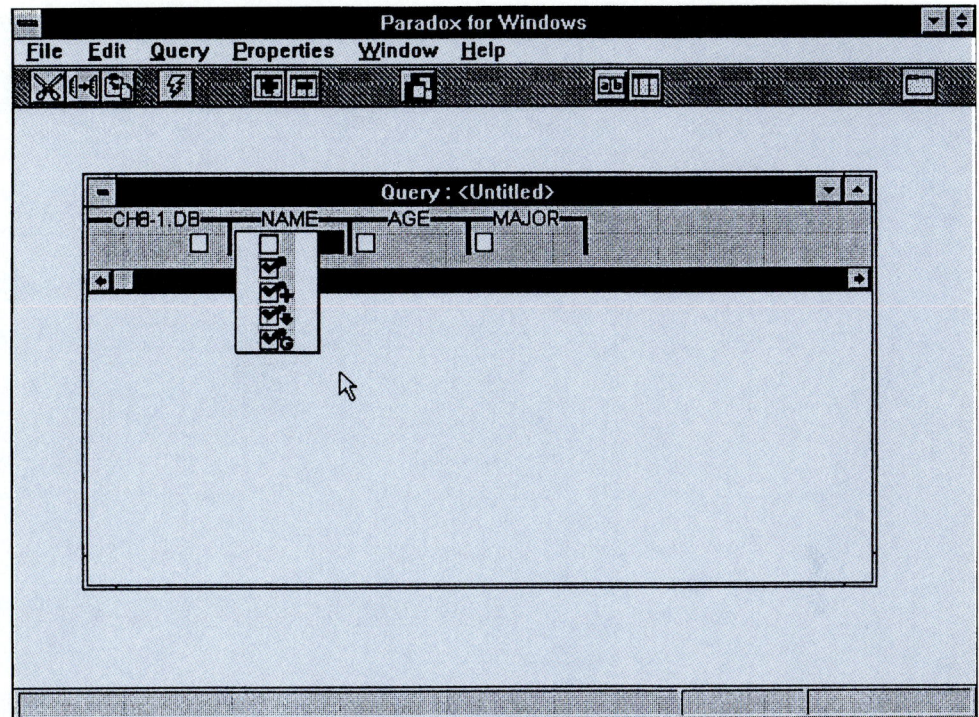

Figure 8–8
Four different check marks.

enter a check plus you can either press Shift+F6 twice or click on the check box and select check plus from the pull-down menu. Figure 8–8 shows the four different check marks used in a query.

8–6   MAKING AN EDUCATED GUESS WITH THE LIKE OPERATOR

Using the **LIKE** operator, you can locate information in your database based on your best guess as to spelling—a **"sounds like"** search. Remember, however, that the LIKE operator is your second resort if you fail to locate your desired information through the regular query operation.

To use the LIKE operator, type *LIKE* followed by your guess in the desired column (field) in the Query form. Remember that the LIKE operator doesn't work if you don't get at least the first letter correct. In Figure 8–9, we used the F6 function key to check all the fields to be included in the query. In the NAME field we typed **LIKE MART** and pressed the F8 function key. Paradox for Windows extracted two records that included names sounding like MART.

8–7   SEARCH WITH WILDCARDS

Paradox for Windows includes two powerful **wildcards**: .. (two periods) and @ (the at sign). When you use the two periods side-by-side (..) in an example field, Paradox for Windows returns any alphanumeric character, number, or date of any length. If used alone, the .. operator returns every record in the database. In Figure 8–10, in the MAJOR field, we typed *M..*, which means find every MAJOR that starts with M; the rest does not matter.

The @ wildcard represents any single character. You use @ when the position of the specific characters in the example is important. For example,

Figure 8–9
An example of the LIKE operator.

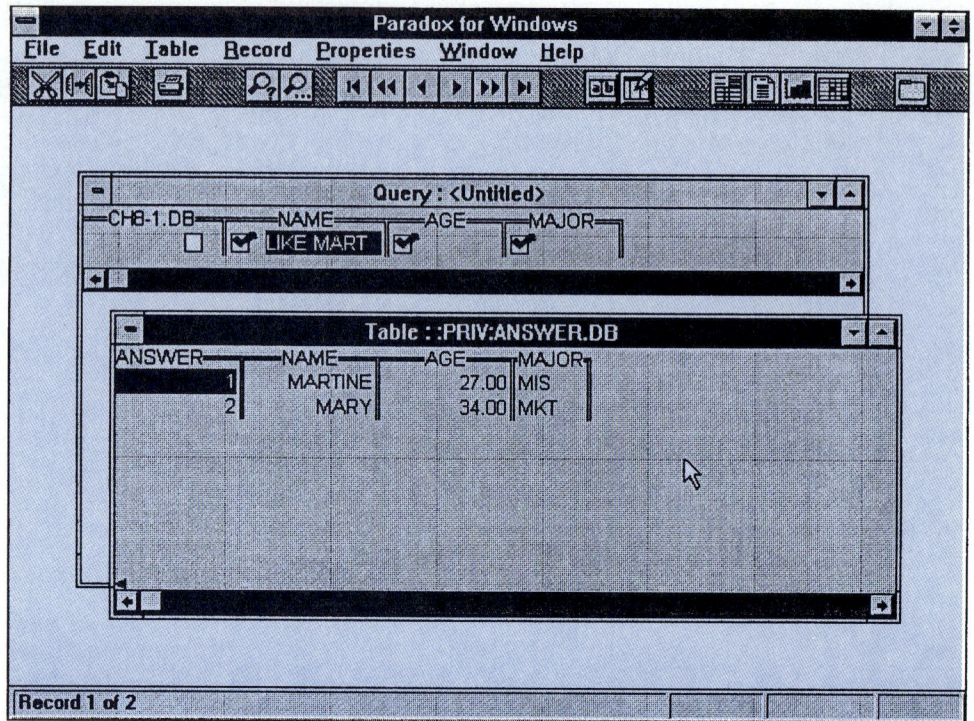

Figure 8–10
An example of the .. wildcard.

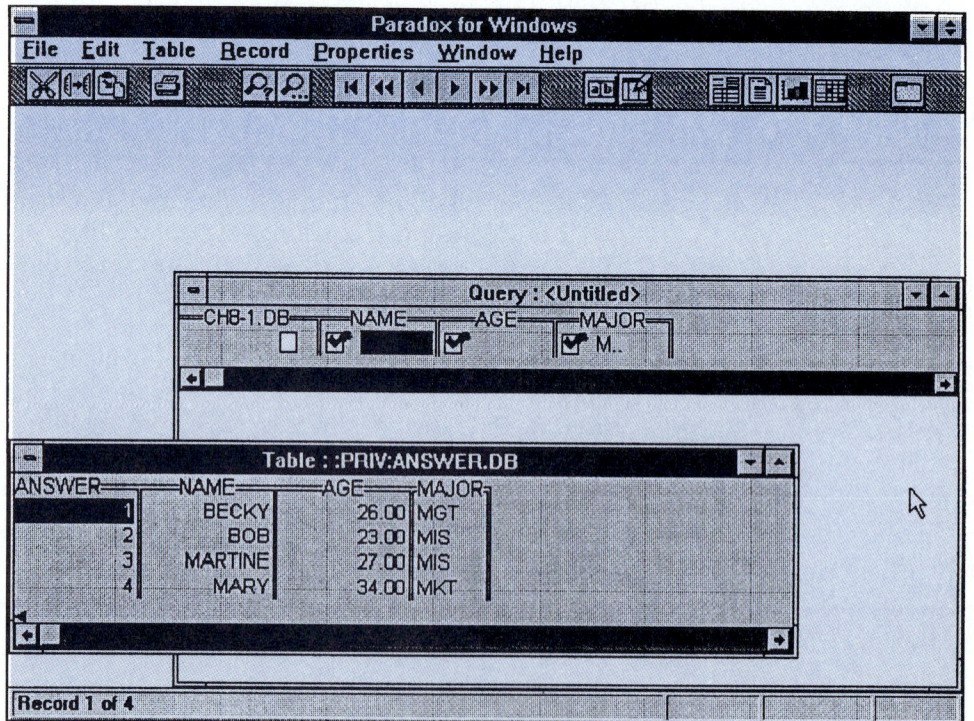

Figure 8–11
An example of the @ wildcard.

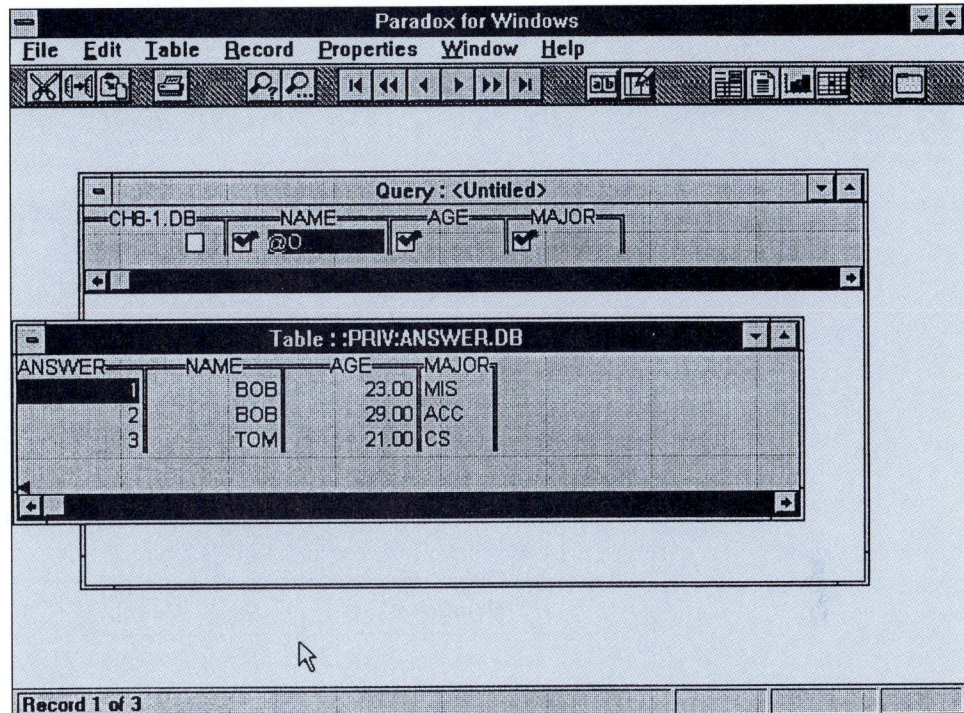

@A.. means the second character must be A, and the rest does not matter; @@C means the third character must be C, and the first two can be anything. In Figure 8–11, in the NAME field, we typed @O.., which means the second character must be O and the rest does not matter. Table 8–1 provides additional examples of wildcard characters.

8–8   WHAT ARE RELATIONAL OPERATIONS?

Relational operations are performed whenever Paradox for Windows is used for comparison purposes. In this case, the user tries to limit the scope of a command. For example, you may be interested in all the students who have a GPA of greater than 3.80 or all the employees who are engineers.

Relational operators use specific signs to perform the relational tasks. Signs for comparison operations have equal precedence and, therefore, are performed from left to right. They are summarized in Table 8–2.

8–9   SPECIAL QUERY OPERATORS

Five special operators can be used in Paradox for Windows. Table 8–3 provides a listing of these operators. Following are some figures showing examples of their use.

Figure 8–12 displays all the students who are older than 30.

Figure 8–13 displays the NAME and AGE for all the students under 25.

Figure 8–14 displays a listing of all the students whose major is MIS and who are under 25.

Table 8–1
Examples of Wildcard Characters

You type	Paradox for Windows return	Paradox for Windows does not return
AD..	ADAM ADNA ADBA ADA	MISS ADAM MR. ADNA BADA CADX
A@@B	ABTB AXYB	ATTIC XYZB
..T..	TAM TOM BUT	SAM BOB SUE
@E..	METER BED	ABE EBA

Table 8–2
Relational Symbols

Symbol	Meaning	Example
<	less than	A<B
>	greater than	B>A
=	equal to	A=B
<=	less than or equal to	A<=B
>=	greater than or equal to	B>=A

Table 8–3
Special Query Operators

Operator	Task
NOT	A true condition in the statement is changed to false and a false condition is changed to true. For example, NOT GPA>3.60 will search only students with GPAs less than or equal to 3.60. NOT ENGINEER will search all the professions except the engineers.
,	This is the logical AND. Both conditions must be true for the AND of these sentences to be true. For example, GPA>3.60, GENDER=F will search only students who are female and have a GPA greater than 3.60.
OR	If either of the condition stated is true, then the result is true. For example, GPA>3.60 OR GENDER=F will search either students with a GPA greater than 3.60 or female students.
BLANK	No data has been entered in a field or record.
TODAY	Returns system date.

Figure 8–12
A listing of the students who are older than 30.

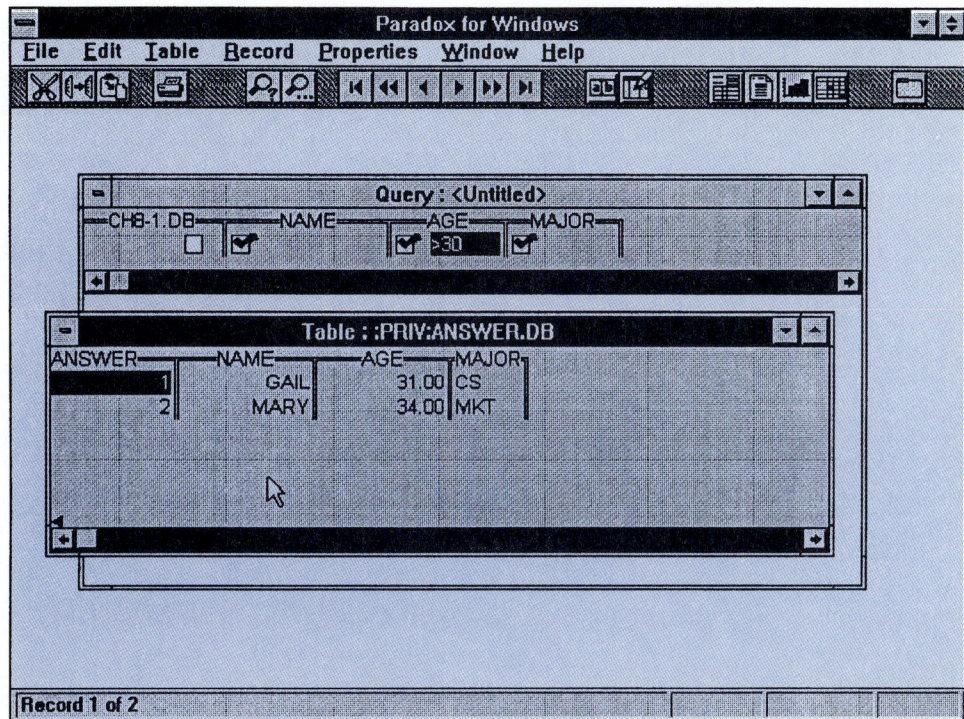

Figure 8–13
A listing of the students who are under 25.

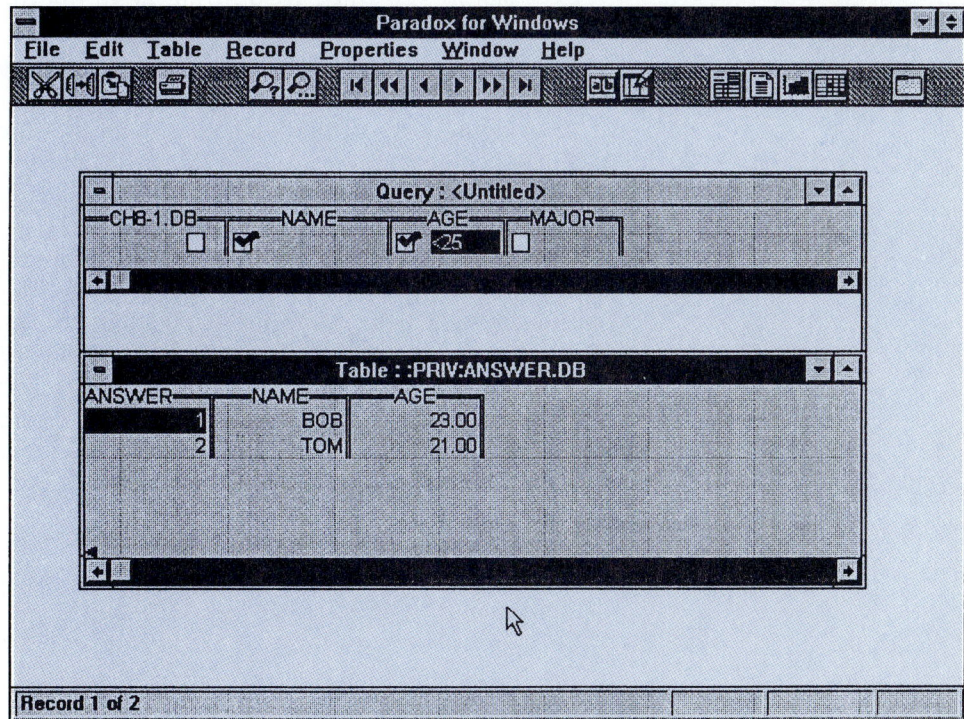

Figure 8–14
A listing of all the MIS majors who are under 25.

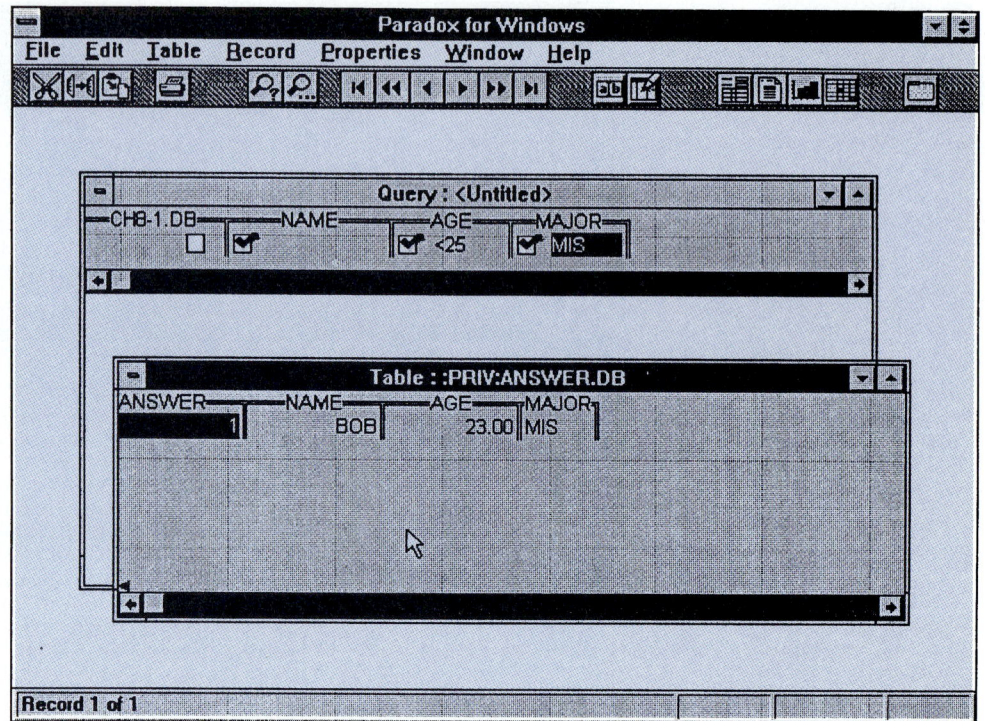

Figure 8–15 displays a listing of all the students who are either accounting (ACC) or management (MGT) Majors.

Figure 8–16 displays a listing of all the students who are between the ages of 20 and 30.

Figure 8–17 displays a listing of all the students whose major is anything except MIS.

Figure 8–18 displays a listing of all the students whose names (first name in this case) start with A, B, C, or D.

To see how the BLANK and TODAY operators work, consider the sample database table presented in Figure 8–19. Notice we have not entered any data for Sue in the AGE field. As Figure 8–20 shows, in response to a query, Paradox for Windows located the record that includes a blank field. In Figure 8–21, we used the TODAY operator in the ADATE field. The system date was set to January 1, 1994. Paradox for Windows returned the only record that matched this date.

An interesting application of the TODAY operator would be to generate a listing of overdue accounts. For example, in the ADATE field, which might be the purchase date, you could type $< = TODAY - 100$. This would generate a listing of all the customers whose accounts are overdue by 100 days or more. Figure 8–22 shows an example of this type of query. Remember that we set the system date to January 1, 1994.

8–10   SORTING THE ANSWER TABLE IN ASCENDING ORDER

By default, Paradox for Windows sorts the Answer table in ascending order by the leftmost field (in the table's structure) that is included in the query. Ties are broken by using the next field to the right in the table structure included in the query. Therefore, record sort order is not affected by the order of the fields

Figure 8–15
A listing of all the students who are either accounting or management majors.

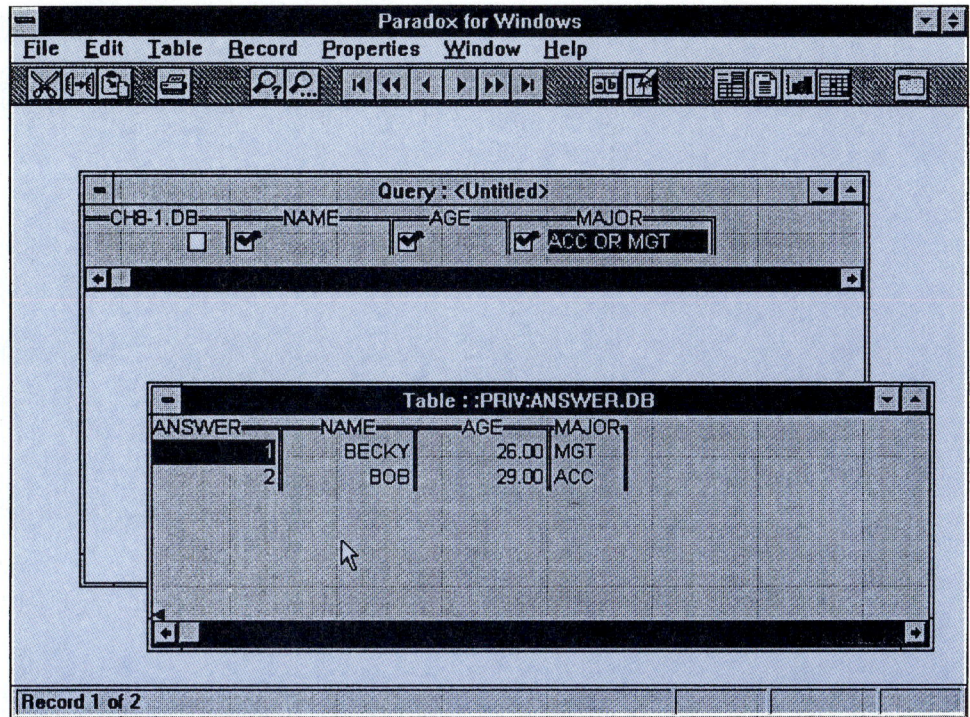

Figure 8–16
A listing of all the students between 20 and 30 years of age.

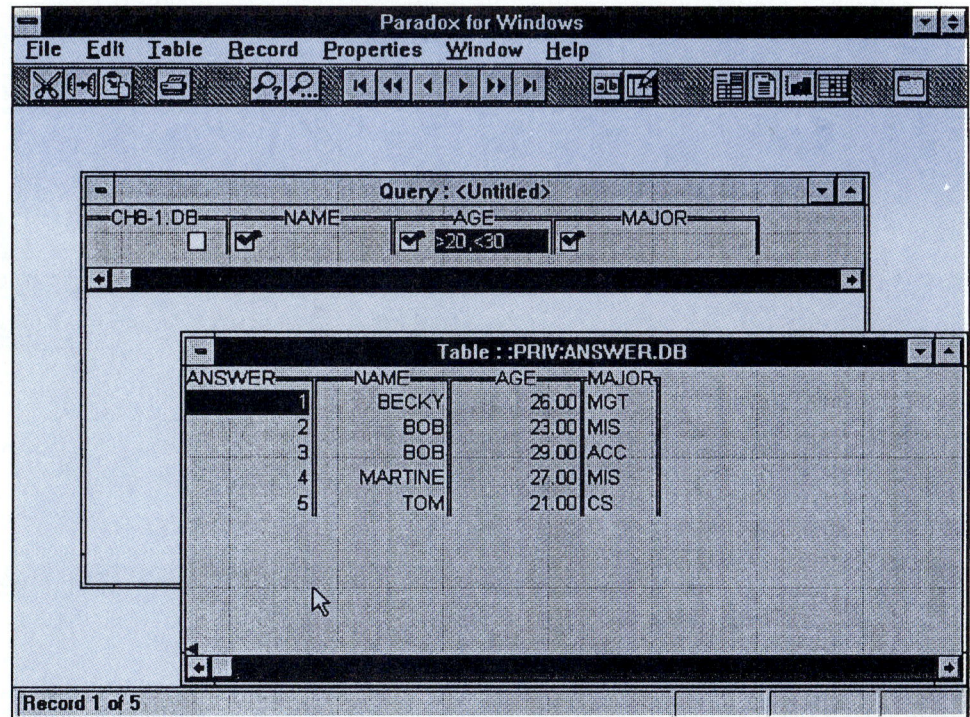

Figure 8–17
A listing of all the majors except MIS.

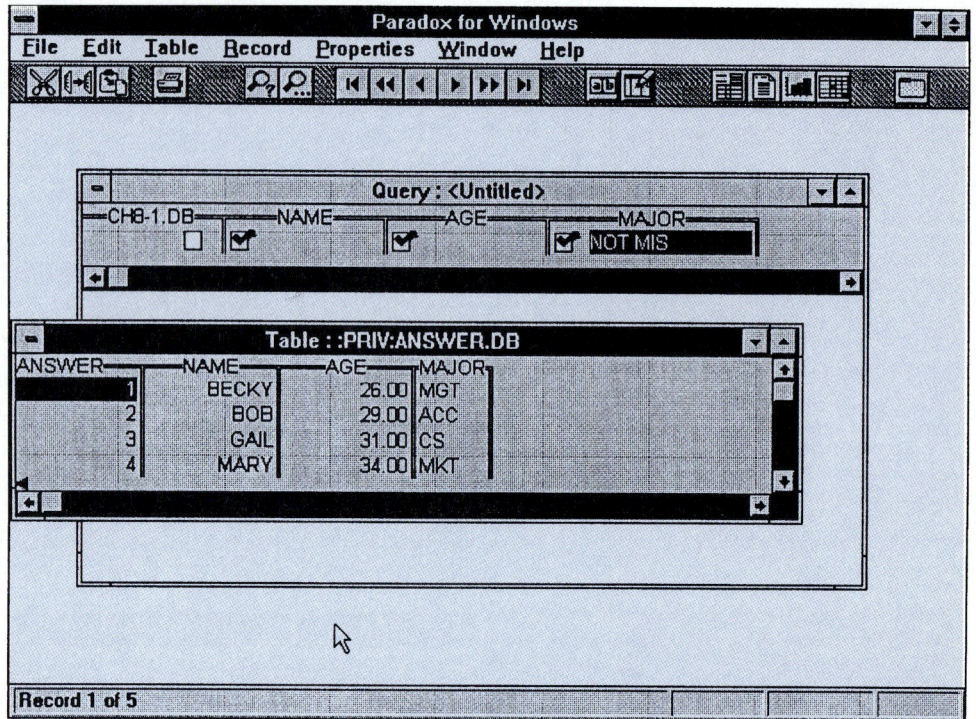

Figure 8–18
A listing of all the students whose names start with the letters A, B, C, or D.

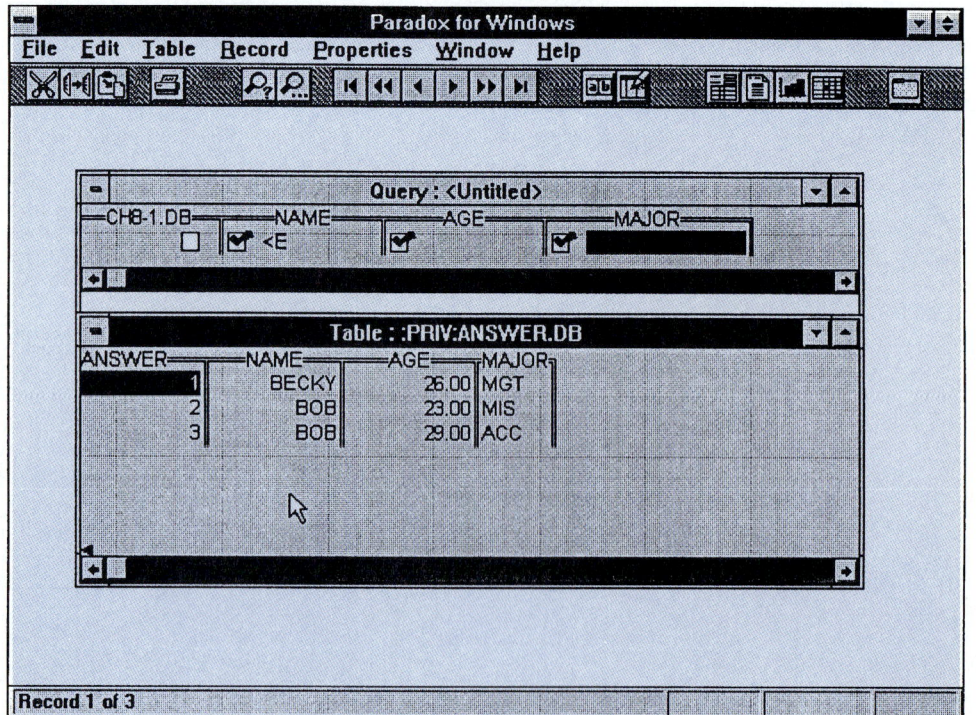

Figure 8–19
A sample database table.

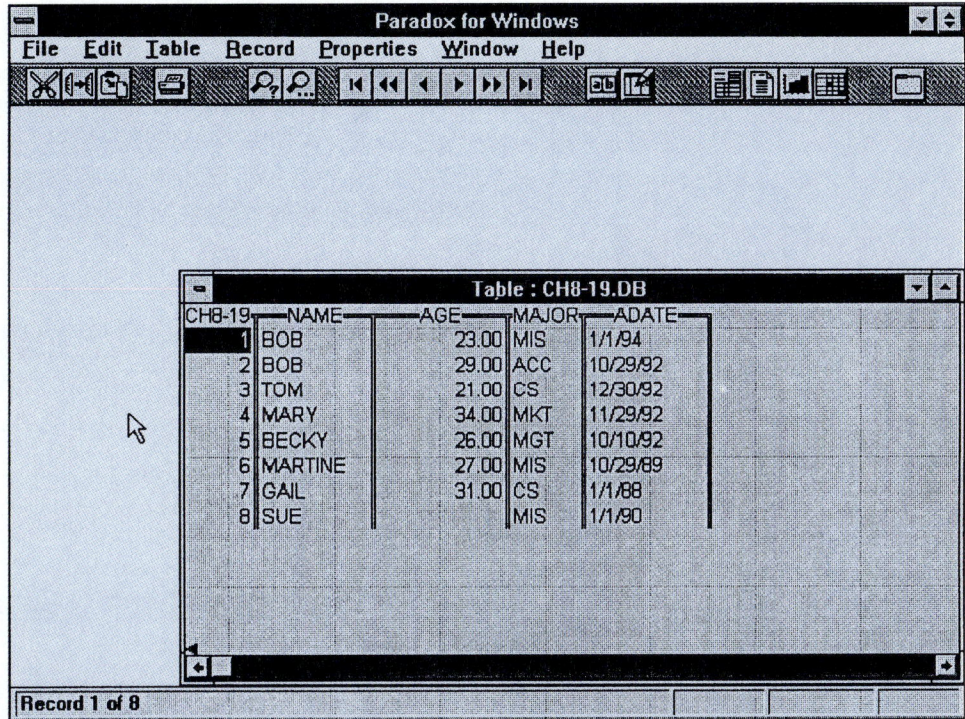

Figure 8–20
Using the BLANK operator.

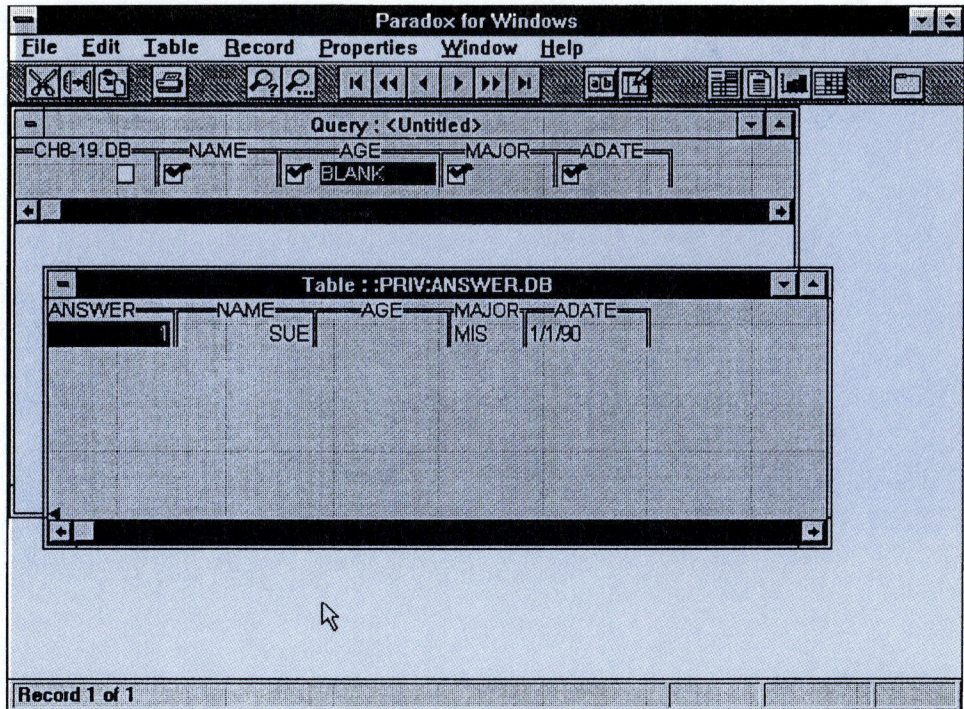

Figure 8–21
Using the TODAY operator.

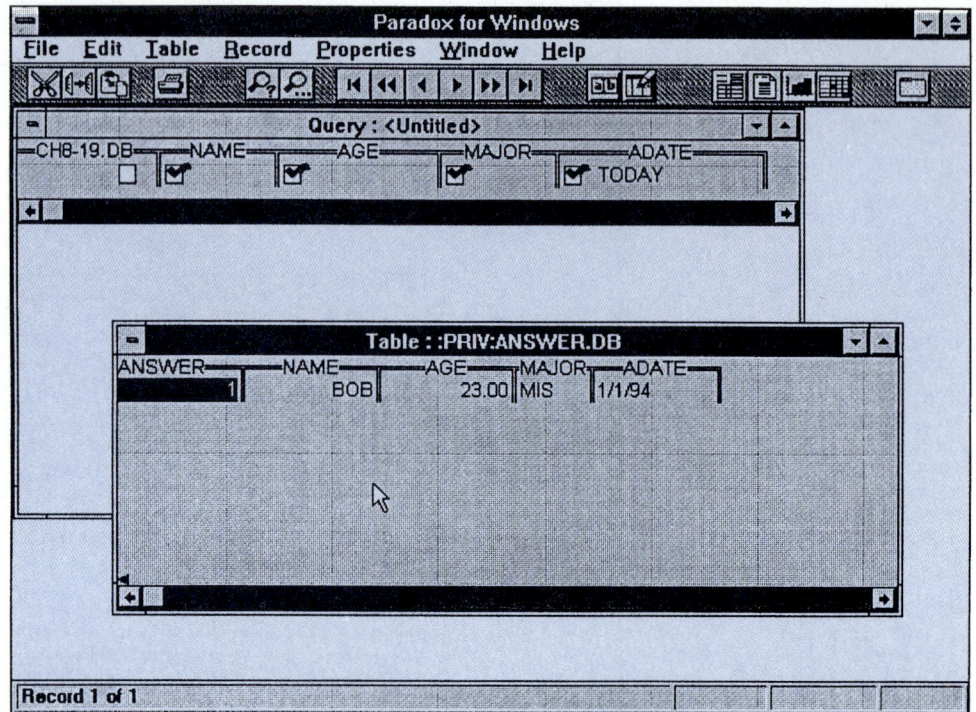

Figure 8–22
Another example of the TODAY operator.

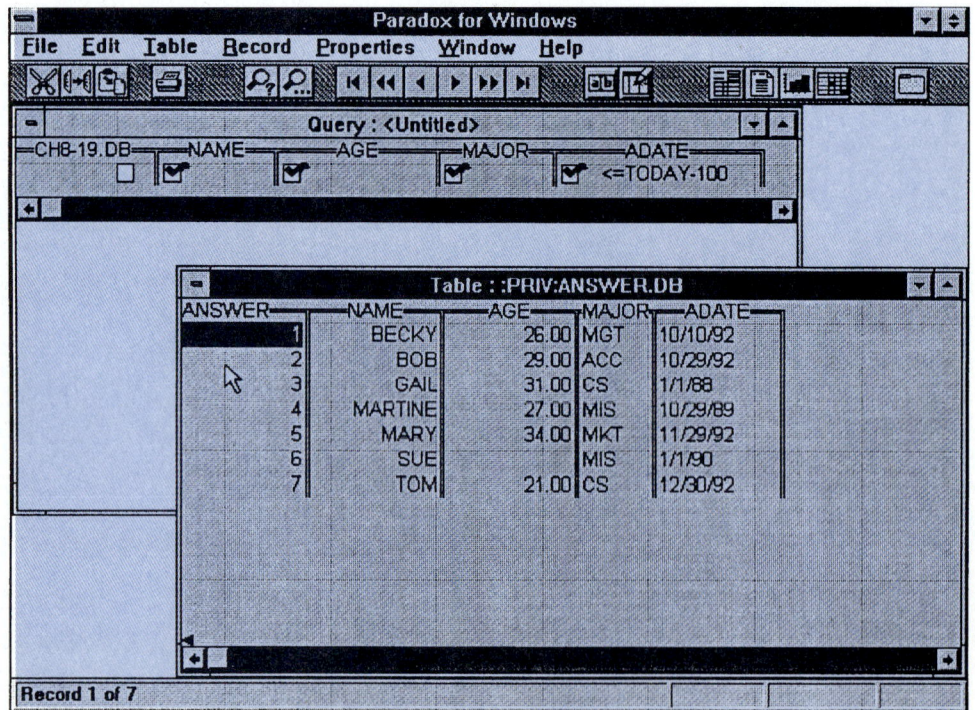

within the query. Figure 8–23 shows that by checking all the fields with the F6 function key, the Answer table has been sorted based on the first field, which is the NAME field.

In Figure 8–24, only the AGE and MAJOR fields were included in the Answer table. As you see in this figure, this Answer table is sorted based on age.

Figure 8–23
The Answer table has been sorted based on names.

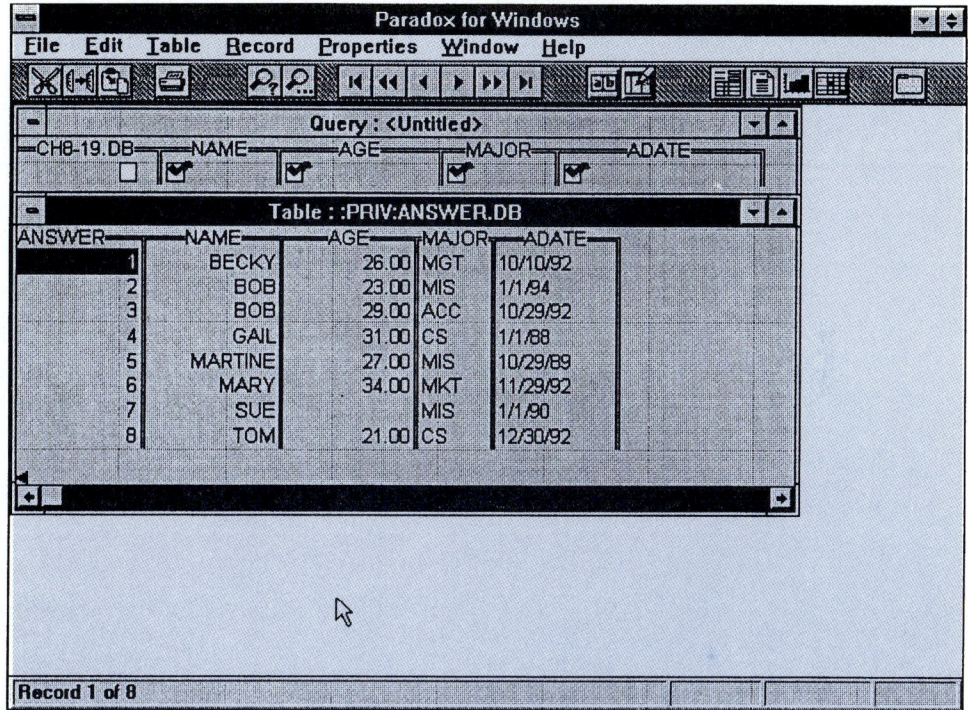

Figure 8–24
The Answer table sorted based on age (the first field included in the Answer table from the table structure).

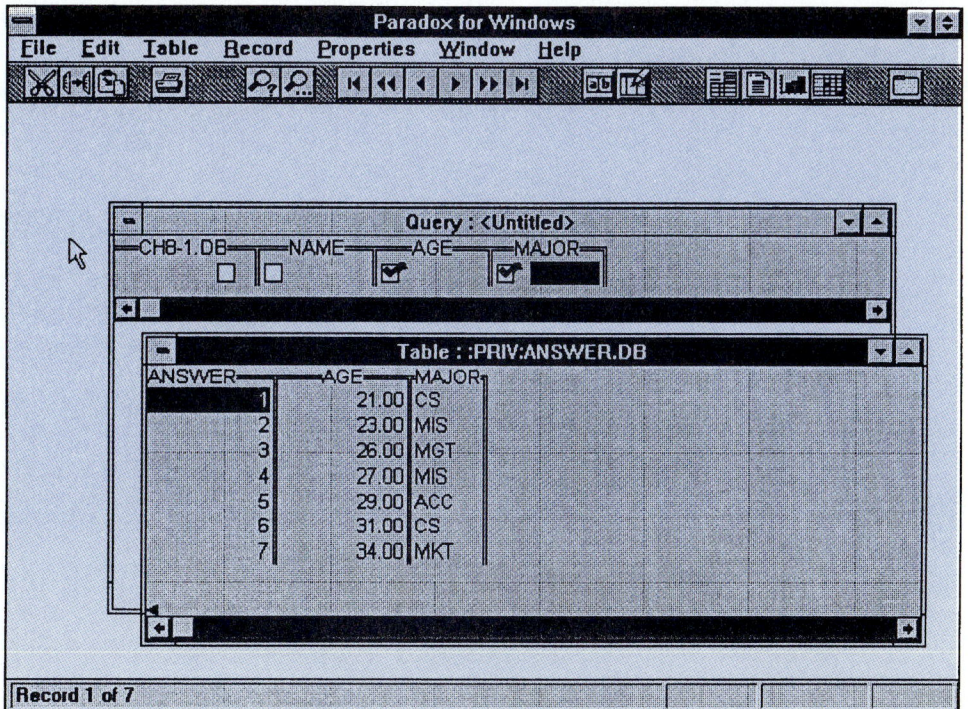

8–11   SORTING THE ANSWER TABLE IN DESCENDING ORDER

To sort the Answer table in descending order, use Shift+F6 (check descending) in place of F6. Figure 8–25 shows that the answer table has been sorted from Z to A. As you see in this figure, Paradox for Windows places a downward-pointing triangle to the right of the normal check mark symbol to indicate that the records are sorted in descending order. Paradox for Windows still sorts the records based on the first field from the table structure included in the Answer table.

8–12   PARADOX FOR WINDOWS SUMMARY OPERATORS

Paradox for Windows offers five **summary operators** that can be very helpful for generating summary information when performing query operations. Table 8–4 lists these operators.

The Default Grouping column in Table 8–4 refers to whether duplicate records are considered or not. The **SUM** and **AVERAGE** operators calculate the statistic over all the records in the group. The **COUNT, MAX,** and **MIN** operators ignore duplicate data items in the group. You can include the word All in the Query form to instruct Paradox for Windows to include duplicate records in its calculations.

To use the summary operators successfully, consider the following rules:

1. Precede the summary operator with the CALC operator.
2. Do not place a check mark in the same field in which you place the summary operator.
3. Place the summary operator in the field (column) in which the computation should be performed.

Figure 8–25
The Answer table has been sorted in descending order.

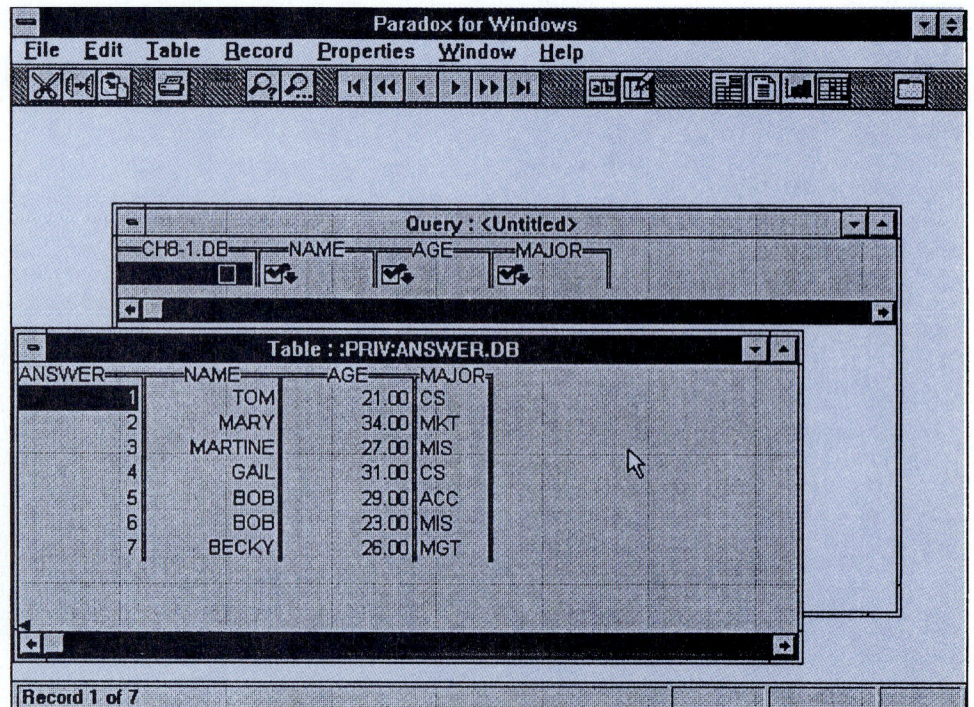

Table 8–4
Paradox for Windows Summary
Operators

Operator	Function	Applicable field types	Default grouping
AVERAGE	Calculates the average in a group	N,$,D,S	All
COUNT	Counts the number of data items in a group	A,N,D,$,S	Unique
MAX	Finds the maximum value of the data items in a group	A,N,D,$,S	Unique
MIN	Finds the minimum value of the data items in a group	A,N,D,$,S	Unique
SUM	Calculates the total of all the data items in a group	N,$,S	All

4. Place a check mark in the field or fields that you want to use to determine the grouping value. Paradox for Windows performs the summary calculation on each group of records that have identical values in the checked fields.

To understand this discussion better, study the following examples: In Figure 8–26, we are counting the number of MIS majors in our sample database (presented in Figure 8–1). In Figure 8–27, we are finding the oldest (maximum) age of the MIS majors. In Figure 8–28 we are calculating the average age for all the students. In Figure 8–29 we are looking for the youngest (minimum) student.

Figure 8–26
Counting the number of MIS majors.

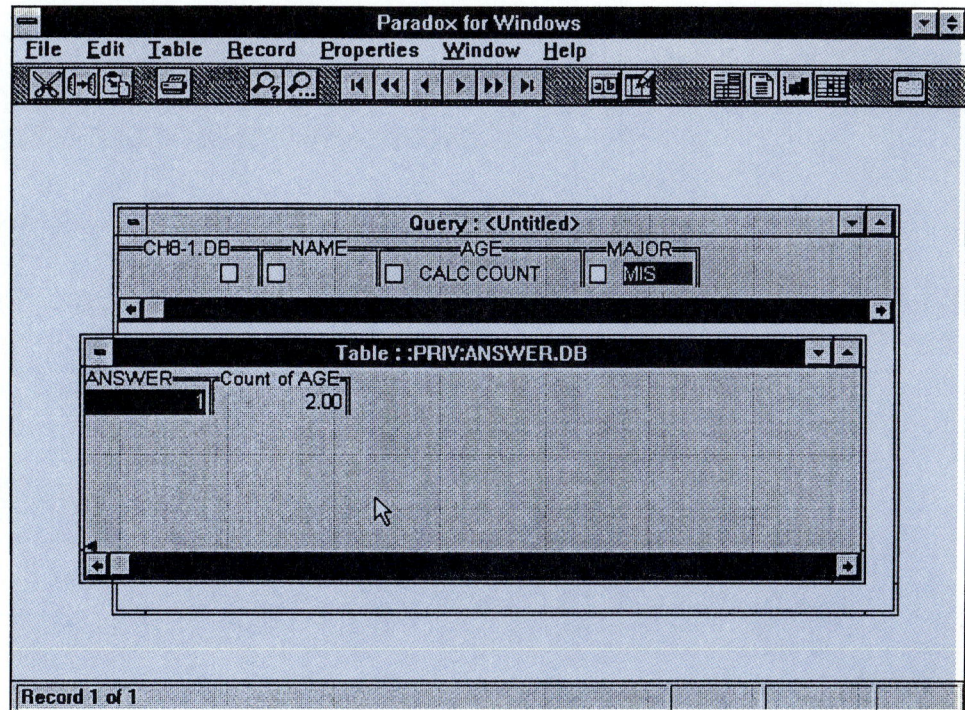

Figure 8–27
Finding the maximum age for MIS majors.

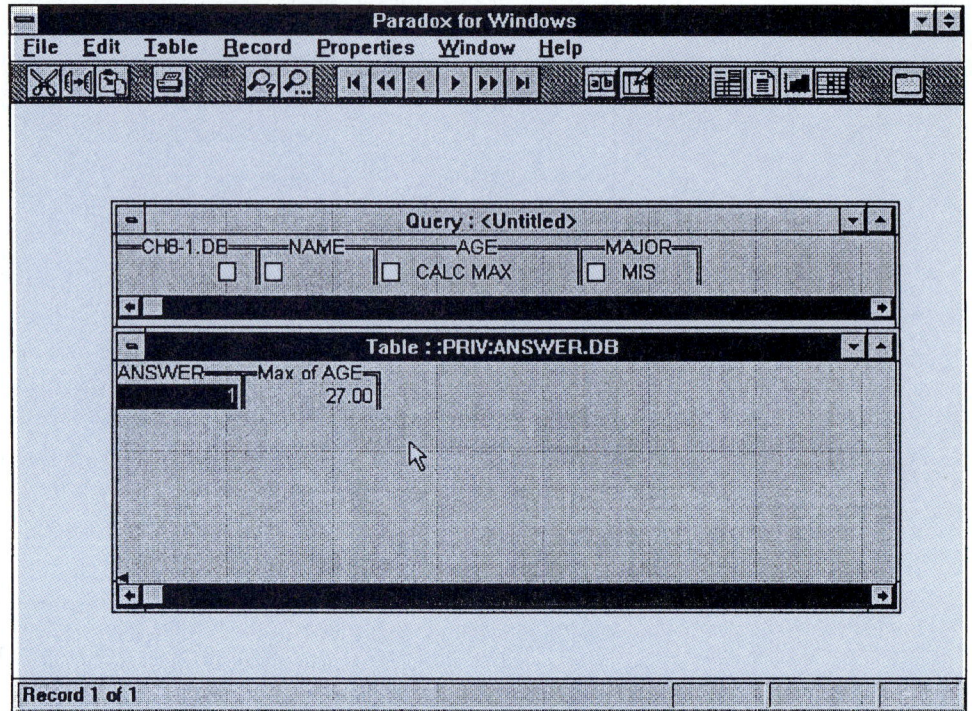

Figure 8–28
Calculating the average age of all the students.

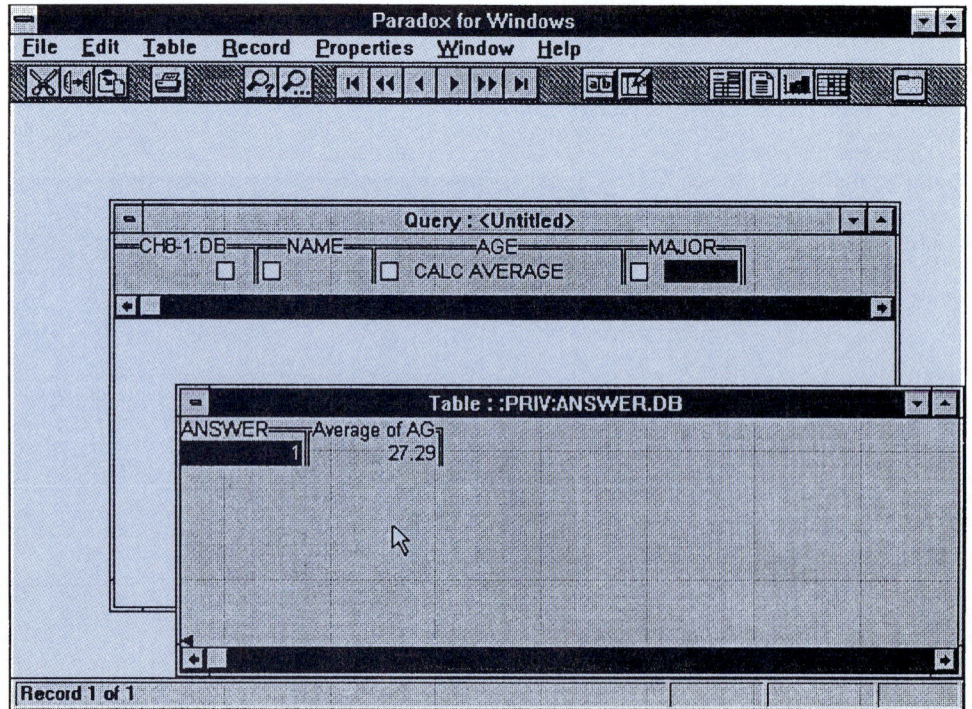

Figure 8–29
Finding the youngest student.

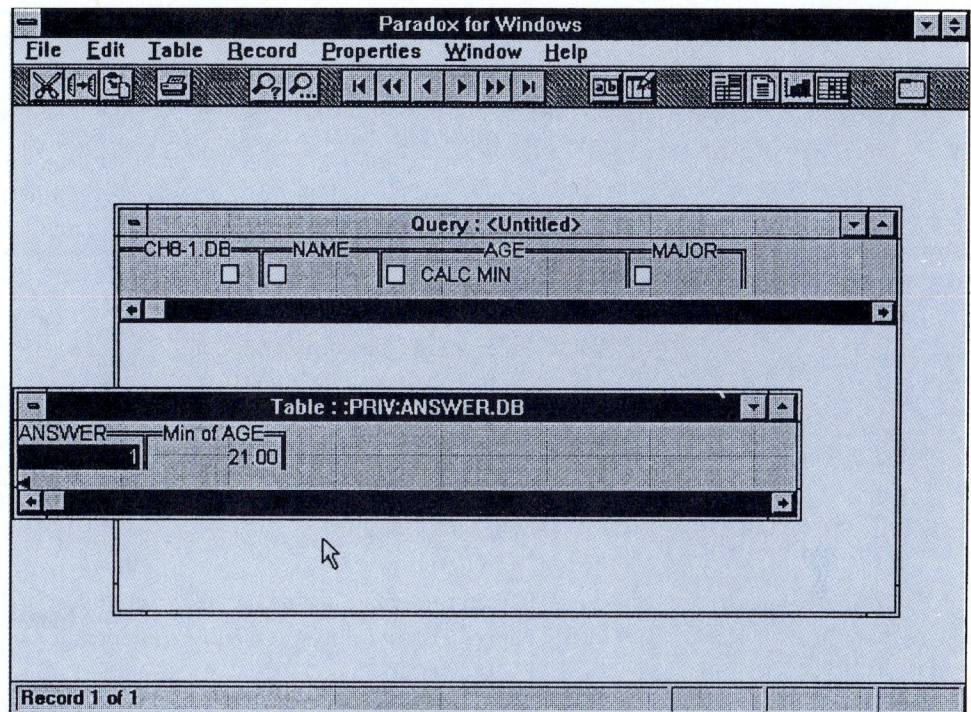

8–13   SAVING THE ANSWER TABLE AND QUERY FORM

Paradox for Windows overwrites the Answer table each time you perform a query and deletes it when you exit the program. The Answer table is one of the several temporary tables that Paradox for Windows generates. Therefore, if you want to save a specific answer table, you must rename it. You can rename an answer table after you have run the query, or you can give it a new name when you set up the query.

This is how you rename the Answer table after you have run the query:

1. Choose **Table Rename** if the Answer table is still open on the Desktop and it is an active window.
2. Enter the new name in the To Rename dialog box.
3. Click on OK.

As soon as you do this the Answer will be replaced by the new name.

To save the Answer table after setting up the query and before running it, follow these steps:

1. Choose **Properties, Answer Table Options** from the query window's menu.
2. In the Answer Name box of the Answer Table Properties dialog box, replace the file name ANSWER.DB with your new name.
3. Click on OK.

You can also save the Query form under the desired name by using the Save As command from the File menu. The Query forms will be saved with the QBE extension.

SUMMARY

This chapter reviewed different commands for query operations and discussed the relational operators. The chapter explained the process of sorting the Answer table in both ascending and descending order. It introduced Paradox for Windows summary operators, and then presented the process for saving a query and renaming the Answer table.

REVIEW QUESTIONS

*These questions are answered in Appendix A.

1. What is a relational operator?
2. What is a query operation?
3. What is a Query form?
4. In what order are the AND, OR, and NOT operators processed? What is the function of each operator?
*5. What is a wildcard?
6. What are the two wildcard characters supported by Paradox for Windows?
7. What key is used to mark all fields to be included in a query?
8. What key allows you to include duplicate data?
*9. What is query-by-example?
10. Which key is used to move from one field to another in a Query form?
11. What is the function of the F8 function key? Of F6?
12. Is Paradox for Windows case-sensitive?
13. What command is used for educated guesses?
14. What is the minimum requirement for making an educated guess?
15. What will be done by the BLANK operator?
*16. What are some of the applications of the TODAY operator?
17. How do you save a query for future use?
18. What is a Paradox for Windows summary operator? List three of the commonly used operators.
19. How many different check marks are there? How do you enter each one?
20. Can you name the Answer table before running the query? How do you name it after running the query?

HANDS-ON EXPERIENCE

1. Retrieve Figure CH8-30 (presented in Figure 8–30) from the disk or create it and do the following:
   a. Display all the engineers.
   b. Display all the engineers who are making less than $50,000 (i.e., <50,000).
   c. Display all the engineers who are making at least $50,000 (i.e., >=50,000) and have been with the company since 1989.
   d. Display all the employees except the engineers.
   e. Calculate the average salary of all the engineers, the total number of engineers, and the sum of their salaries.
   f. Display all the employees who worked during 1989 and 1993.

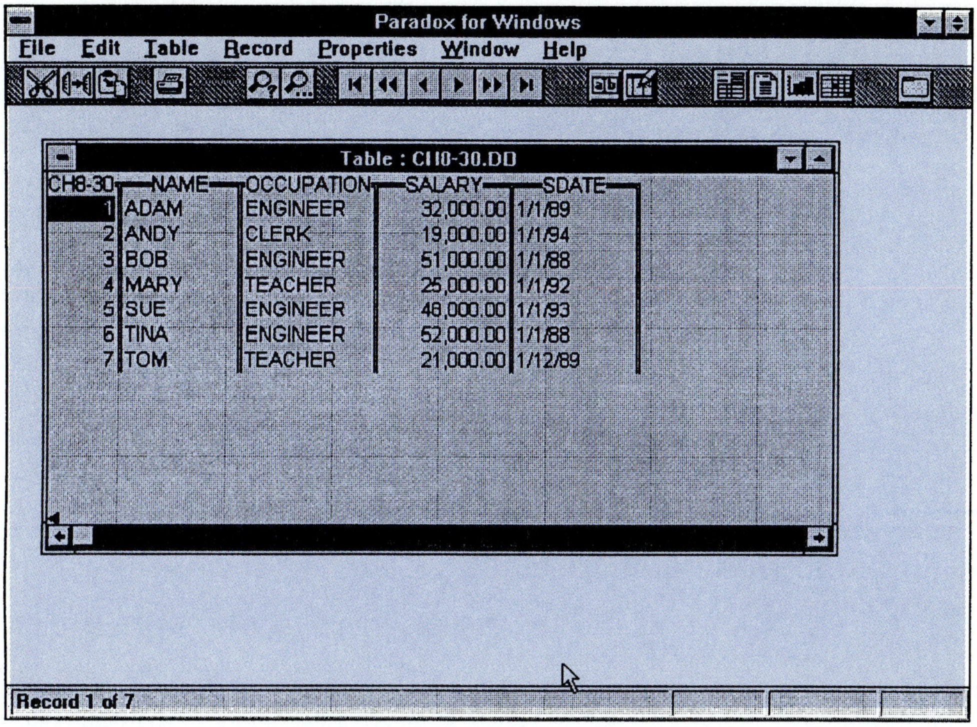

Figure 8–30
A sample database table.

        g. Display all the employees whose names start with I to Z.
        h. Display the first employee.
        i. Display the last employee.
        j. Display the structure of this database.

2. Using wildcard characters and Figure 8–1, do the following:

        a. Display all majors starting with the letter M.
        b. Display the entire database

3. Create a customer database for the Corner Grocery Store. Include three fields in this table: NAME, DATE OF PURCHASE, and AMOUNT OF PURCHASE. Do the following:

a. Enter 10 records of your choice in this database.

b. Create a query of only the names and amount of purchase.

c. Sort the Answer table in descending order.

d. By using the TODAY operator generate a listing of all the customers who are 50 days late with their account.

e. Calculate the maximum amount of purchase.

f. Calculate the minimum amount of purchase.

g. Count all the purchases between certain dates.

KEY TERMS

Condition	Relational operator	Summary Operators
Query operations	"Sounds like" search	Wildcard characters

KEY COMMANDS

F6 (to mark a field to be included in the Query)

F8 (to perform the query)

Shift+F6 (to perform a cycle check, e.g., check, check plus, check descending, and group check)

, (AND) (Logical operator—all conditions must be true)

NOT (Logical operator—the opposite condition must be true)

OR (Logical operator—either condition must be true)

AVERAGE (the AVERAGE operator)

COUNT (the COUNT operator)

MAX (the MAX operator)

MIN (the MIN operator)

LIKE (to perform a "sounds like" query)

Properties, Answer Table Options (to rename the Answer table before running it)

SUM (the SUM operator)

Table Rename (to rename the Answer table after running the query)

MISCONCEPTIONS AND SOLUTIONS

Misconception   You are performing query operations and you end up with a wrong result.

Solution   Paradox for Windows tries to relate the Query forms even if you want them to be separate. Before you start the query operation double-click the control menu box to close the current query. You can also select the Window Close All command to close all the open queries.

Misconception   Sometimes by using the F6 function key you check fields that you may not want to include in the query.

Solution   Move the cursor to the desired field and press F6 again. This will deselect the selected field.

Misconception   You press the F6 function key to check all the fields to be included in the query. This may not be the fastest method for large databases.

Solution   Press Shift+F6 (check plus) to include all the duplicate information. By doing this you are telling Paradox for Windows not to perform sorting before generating the Answer table. Since the F6 key does not include duplicate data, it performs the sort operation internally to eliminate the duplicate data.

Misconception   Sometimes you are searching for specific information but you see that some of the requested information has not been extracted by the Paradox for Windows Query operation. Probably you have mixed your data as upper- and lowercase.

Solution   Add the .. (two periods) wildcard to the end of the example. By doing this you are making the search pattern more general. However, be aware that you might get more information than you requested.

ARE YOU READY TO MOVE ON?

Multiple Choice

1. Relational operations can use all of the following special signs except:
   a. <
   b. >
   c. =
   d. >=
   e. They are all used

2. To include the entire database in the query, where do you put the cursor before you press F6?

   a. under the first field
   b. under the second field
   c. under the third field
   d. under the fourth name
   e. under the table name

3. The F8 function key:

   a. checks all fields
   b. checks all fields for descending sort
   c. checks all fields for ascending sort
   d. runs the query
   e. none of the above

4. To move the cursor to the right by one field you can press:

   a. the Tab key
   b. the right arrow
   c. both a or b
   d. none of the above
   e. the PgDn key

5. To start a query operation, select the following from the File New menu:

   a. Report
   b. Query
   c. Forms
   d. Script
   e. none of the above

6. To perform a "sounds like" search, which operator do you use?

   a. LIKE
   b. SIMILAR
   c. TRY
   d. wildcard operator
   e. none of the above

7. The Paradox for Windows check plus is achieved by pressing:

   a. F6
   b. F8
   c. Shift+F6
   d. F1
   e. none of the above

8. To rename the Answer table for future use after it has been run, select:

   a. Save As
   b. Create
   c. Scripts Rename
   d. Table Rename
   e. none of the above

9. The editing process that displays one record at a time onscreen is done in which mode?

   a. Form View
   b. Table View
   c. Edit
   d. Modify
   e. none of the above

10. To generate a total for a numeric field, you use which operator?

   a. Average
   b. Sum

c. Max
d. Min
e. none of the above

True/False

1. Relational operations are performed whenever Paradox for Windows is used for comparison purposes, to try to limit the scope of a command.
2. Paradox for Windows uses only one wildcard character.
3. There are only two logical operators.
4. There is no method available to search for a record if you have only partial information relating to the record.
5. If you are interested in viewing a particular record, you can construct a Query form.
6. When performing a search, Paradox for Windows is not case-sensitive.
7. You use the F6 function key to erase a Query form.
8. SUM, AVERAGE, and COUNT are three of the most commonly used summary operators.
9. The check plus key is used to display duplicate data.
10. A Query form can be saved for future use.

ANSWERS

Multiple Choice		True/False	
1.	e	1.	T
2.	e	2.	F
3.	d	3.	F
4.	c	4.	F
5.	b	5.	T
6.	a	6.	F
7.	c	7.	F
8.	d	8.	T
9.	a	9.	T
10.	b	10.	T

Report and Mailing Label Generation

9

9–1   INTRODUCTION

This chapter presents a detailed discussion of the report generation capabilities of Paradox for Windows. The chapter discusses the processes of generating quick reports, customized reports, and reports with grouped data. The chapter also presents the process of creating mailing labels.

9–2   REPORT GENERATION: AN OVERVIEW

Paradox for Windows gives you several options for report generation. When you design a report, you first generate a report specification, which you can save for future use. Each report specification is associated with a database table. You can design numerous reports using the same table. You can also generate reports from the Answer table.

Using Paradox for Windows you can generate tabular, single-record, multirecord, and blank reports. The one to choose depends on your specific needs; generally speaking, tabular reports are more versatile. In this chapter, we will discuss the most commonly used features of the Paradox for Windows report generator.

9–3   GENERATING QUICK REPORTS

In most cases a quick report may satisfy your requirements. As we discussed in Chapter 6, to generate a **quick report**, display your desired table, press **Shift+F7**, then click on the Print button and click on OK. Here is an example. A sample table is displayed in Figure 9–1. To generate a quick report, press Shift+F7, then

Figure 9–1
Sample database table.

CH9-1	CUSTOMER	REGION	DATE	AMOUNT
1	ANDY	9	11/11/92	$34.00
2	BARBARA	6	3/17/89	$8,434.00
3	BECKY	2	9/9/92	$7,655.00
4	BOB	9	5/11/93	$6,768.45
5	DENIS	5	9/9/91	$234.00
6	DONA	4	11/11/91	$8,888.90
7	JERRY	3	11/11/87	$9,000.05
8	JOHN	4	12/12/89	$3,452.33
9	JUDY	2	2/9/90	$780.00
10	MARY	2	3/4/91	$9,999.00
11	SAM	3	11/12/89	$8,900.00
12	SANDY	7	12/14/88	$843.00
13	STEVE	1	11/9/90	$4,300.00
14	SUE	1	9/7/91	$6,777.90
15	SUSAN	3	12/12/90	$8.00
16	TERRY	2	10/10/93	$780.00
17	TIM	2	10/10/92	$569.00
18	TOM	4	8/8/90	$43.00
19	TONIA	7	1/1/93	$4,455.00

Record 1 of 19

click on the Print button and click on OK. As you see in Figure 9–2, this report includes the system date and page number, and it also includes the table name. As you will see later, you can suppress this information if you desire.

9–4   GENERATING A REPORT FROM THE ANSWER TABLE

Let us say that from the sample database table in Figure 9–1 you would like to generate a quick report of all the customers who made purchases after January 1, 1992 and in an amount greater than $5000. To generate this report we first click on File New Query from the desktop. For the table name we type CH9–1 and click on OK. We press the F6 function key to include all the fields in the query. We type *>1/1/92* in the Date field, and we type *>5000* in the Amount field. Figure 9–3 shows the query form. We click on the Run Query button to perform the query. To generate the quick report we press Shift+F7, click on the Print button, and click on OK. Figure 9–4 displays the quick report.

9–5   DISPLAYING THE LAYOUT DESIGN SCREEN

To display the layout design screen, select **File New Report** (or right-click the Report button in the SpeedBar and select New). The Data Model dialog box is displayed, as presented in Figure 9–5.

Select table CH9–1 from the list on the left side of the dialog box and click on OK. You will see a screen similar to the one displayed in Figure 9–6. This is called the Design Layout dialog box. The majority of the report specifications will be defined in this window.

Figure 9–2
Example of a quick report.

Saturday, January 01, 1994 — CH9-1 — Page 1

CUSTOMER	REGION	DATE	AMOUNT
ANDY	9	11/11/92	$34.00
BARBARA	6	3/17/89	$8,434.00
BECKY	2	9/9/92	$7,655.00
BOB	9	5/11/93	$6,768.45
DENIS	5	9/9/91	$234.00
DONA	4	11/11/91	$8,888.90
JERRY	3	11/11/87	$9,000.05
JOHN	4	12/12/89	$3,452.33
JUDY	2	2/9/90	$780.00
MARY	2	3/4/91	$9,999.00
SAM	3	11/12/89	$8,900.00
SANDY	7	12/14/88	$843.00
STEVE	1	11/9/90	$4,300.00
SUE	1	9/7/91	$6,777.90
SUSAN	3	12/12/90	$8.00
TERRY	2	10/10/93	$780.00
TIM	2	10/10/92	$569.00
TOM	4	8/8/90	$43.00
TONIA	7	1/1/93	$4,455.00

Figure 9–3
Query form for customers who
made purchases after January 1,
1992 with a purchase amount
greater than $5000.

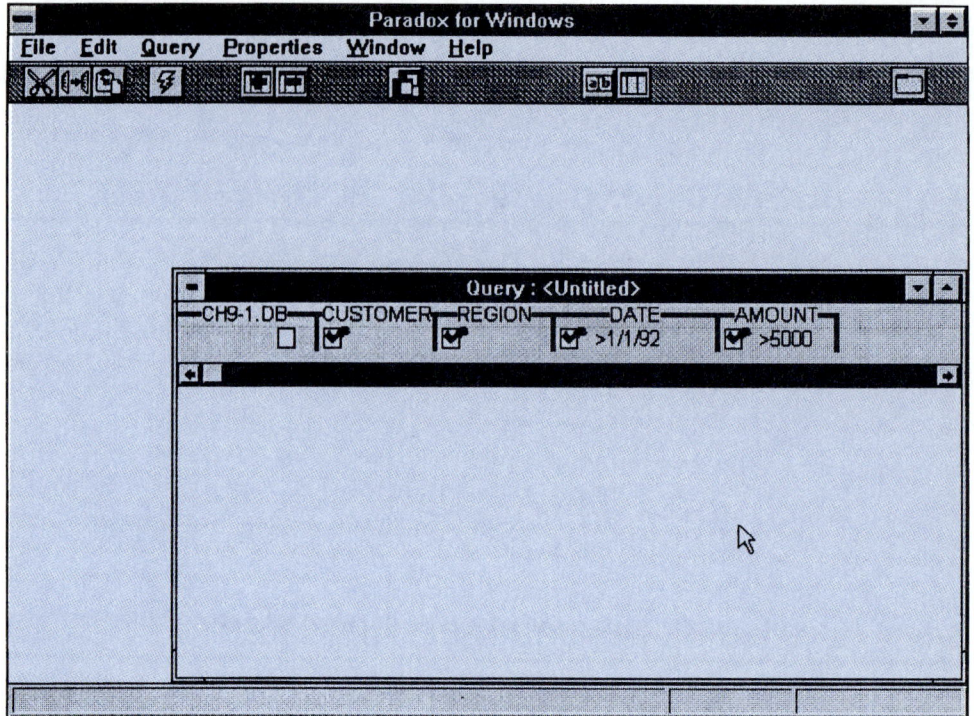

Figure 9–4
Quick report for the query in Figure
9–3.

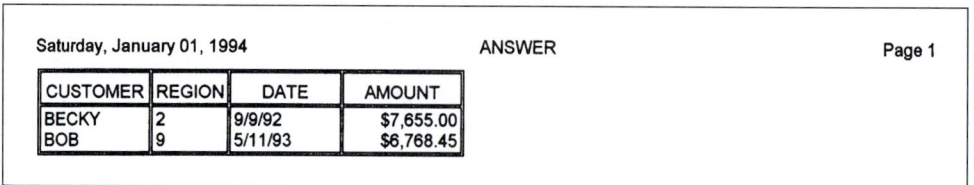

CUSTOMER	REGION	DATE	AMOUNT
BECKY	2	9/9/92	$7,655.00
BOB	9	5/11/93	$6,768.45

Saturday, January 01, 1994   ANSWER   Page 1

Figure 9–5
The Data Model dialog box.

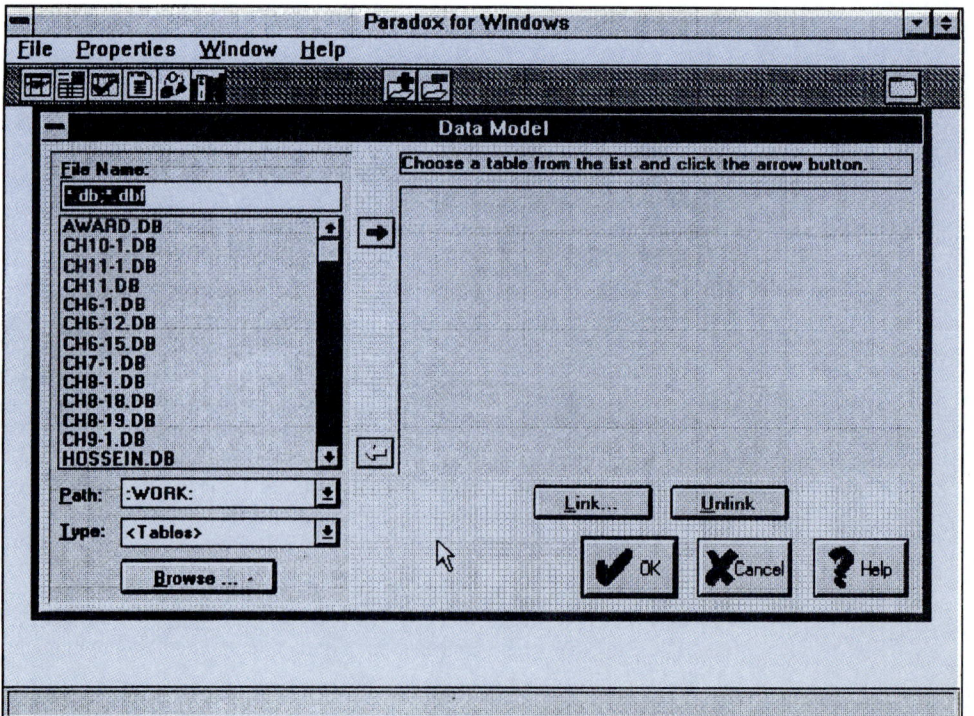

Figure 9–6
The Design Layout dialog box.

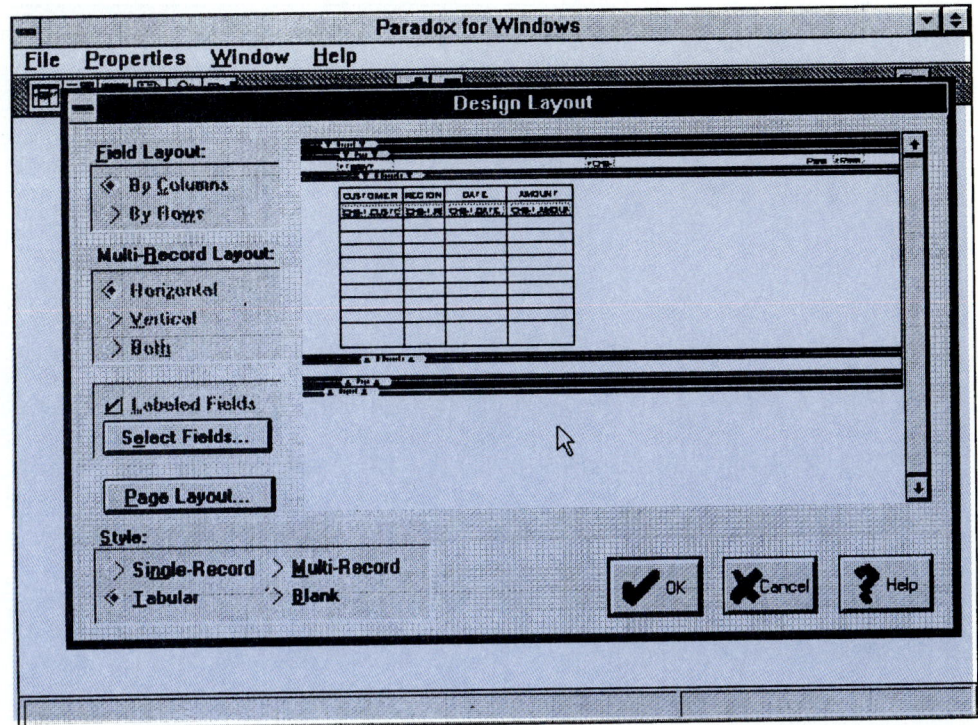

9–6   DEFINING A REPORT LAYOUT

As you see in Figure 9–6, Paradox for Windows offers several different types of reports. The default option is tabular style. This style places the table fields in the record band and includes columns, headers, and borders. This is similar to View mode in the table window.

The box on the upper right side of the Design Layout dialog box (Figure 9–6) shows a preview of the layout. If this default setting satisfies your requirements, click on OK. If not, change all the desired specifications and then click on OK.

The Field Layout box (in the upper left part of Figure 9–6) controls the order of the fields in the record band. In the default tabular style, fields are arranged in columns with field labels at the top of each column. As you see in Figure 9–6, Field Layout options are not active with the tabular style format.

The Multi-Record Layout option is active only when you select the multi-record style. Using this option you can repeat records in the record band across (horizontally), down (vertically), or both.

To see a multirecord report layout, click on the Multi-Record button in the Style box (in the lower left of Figure 9–6), and then click on the Both button in the Multi-Record Layout box. Your screen should be similar to the one presented in Figure 9–7. As you see, in this style records are displayed one after another from left to right and top to bottom. The Horizontal option displays records horizontally. The Vertical option displays records vertically and, as you see in Figure 9–7, the Both option displays records both horizontally and vertically.

The Labeled Fields check box in Figure 9–6 allows you to turn the field names on and off. In the default tabular format, field names are displayed in column headers; therefore, this option is not active.

Figure 9–7
Multirecord report style with both options.

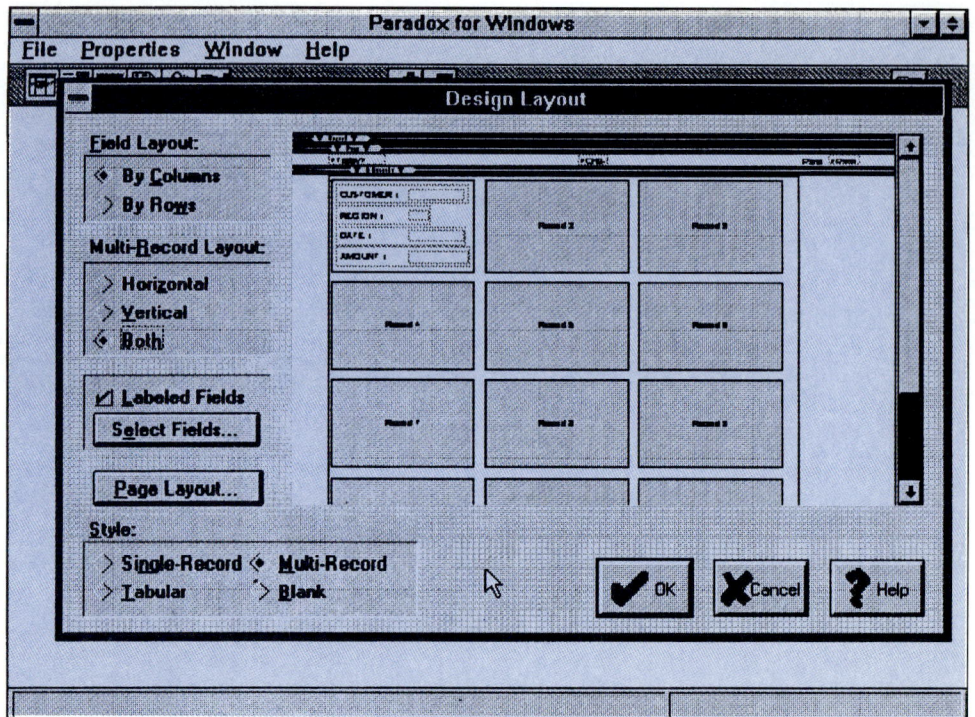

To select the fields to be included in the report, click on the Select Fields button in Figure 9–7. When you do this in our sample table, you will see a screen similar to the one presented in Figure 9–8. By default, all fields are included in the report. To remove a field, highlight the desired field and click on the Remove Field button. To add a field, click on the down arrow icon at the left side of the dialog box to display all the fields in the selected table, and then click the desired field.

Figure 9–8
The Select Fields dialog box.

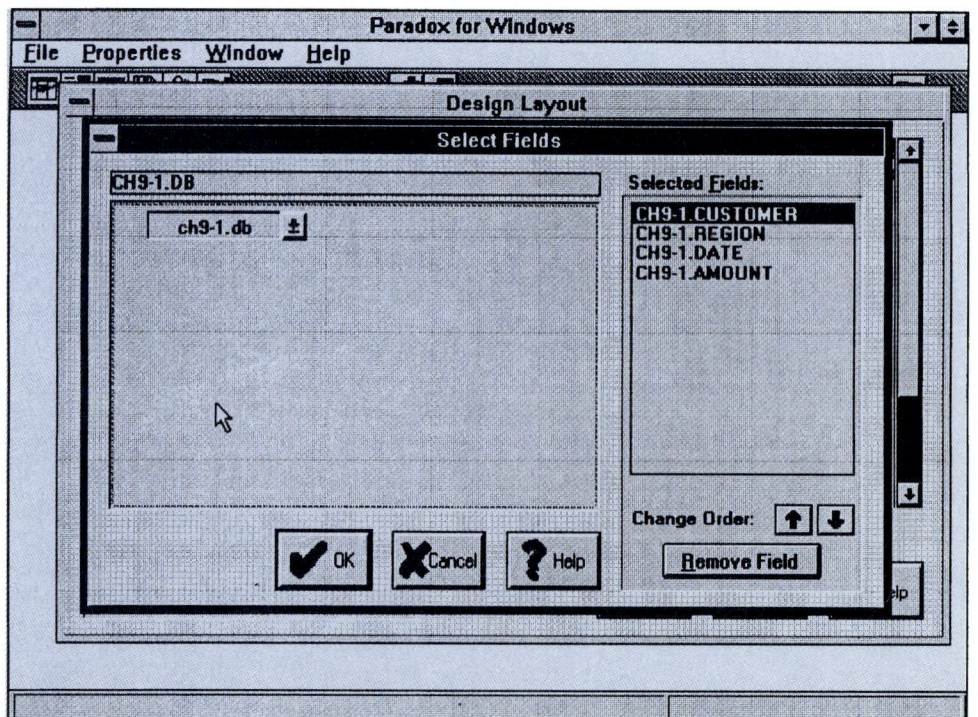

As you see in Figure 9–8, you can use the Change Order arrows (up or down) to change the order of the fields in the report.

9–7   DESIGNING THE PAGE LAYOUT

In the Design Layout dialog box (Figure 9–6), if you click the Page Layout button, you will see a screen similar to the one displayed in Figure 9–9.

As you see in Figure 9–9, you can send the output to the printer (the default option) or to the screen for viewing before printing the result. The page orientation is Portrait by default. You can select the Landscape option if you desire, which would be useful for wide tables. The paper size is letter size by default. You can change it to any of the available sizes by clicking the desired size. At the bottom of the screen in the Margins box you can change the left, right, top, or bottom margins. The unit of measurement is Inches by default. You can select Centimeters if you desire. After making all the required changes, click on OK.

9–8   SELECTING REPORT LAYOUT STYLE

As you see in Figure 9–6, Paradox for Windows offers four different styles for your reports. They are summarized in Table 9–1.

9–9   REPORT DESIGN WINDOW

After selecting the desired style (we selected the tabular style) click on the OK button. You will see a screen similar to the one in Figure 9–10. As you see in this figure, by default Paradox for Windows displays the table name at the upper right side and the system date at the upper left side. To eliminate any of these items,

Figure 9–9
The Page Layout dialog box.

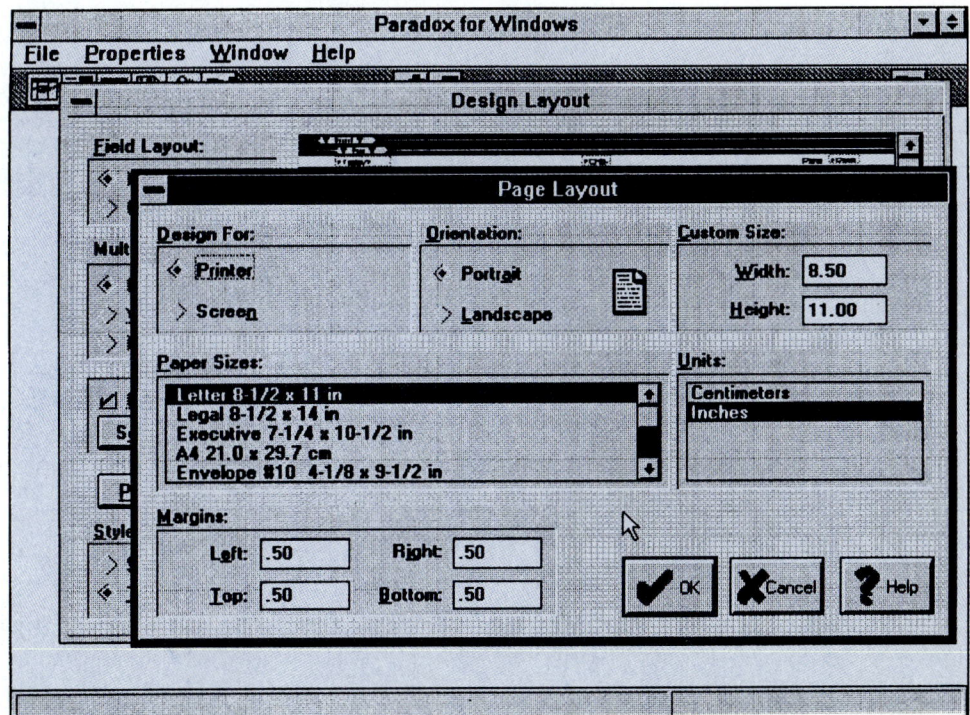

Table 9–1
Report Styles

Option	Description
Single-record	Displays one record of the table at a time. This is a useful option for tables with a large number of fields.
Multi-record	Displays several records of the table, one at a time. Records can be displayed horizontally, vertically, or both. This style can be used to generate mailing labels (discussed in Section 9–15).
Tabular	The default style for a report. It displays an image of the table you have selected. It resembles Table view in the table window.
Blank	Removes all fields from the design. The fields of the selected table are still available for placement, using the Field tool in the SpeedBar. This layout is useful when you need only a small number of fields from the table, or when field order must be significantly altered for a particular report.

Figure 9–10
The Report Design window.

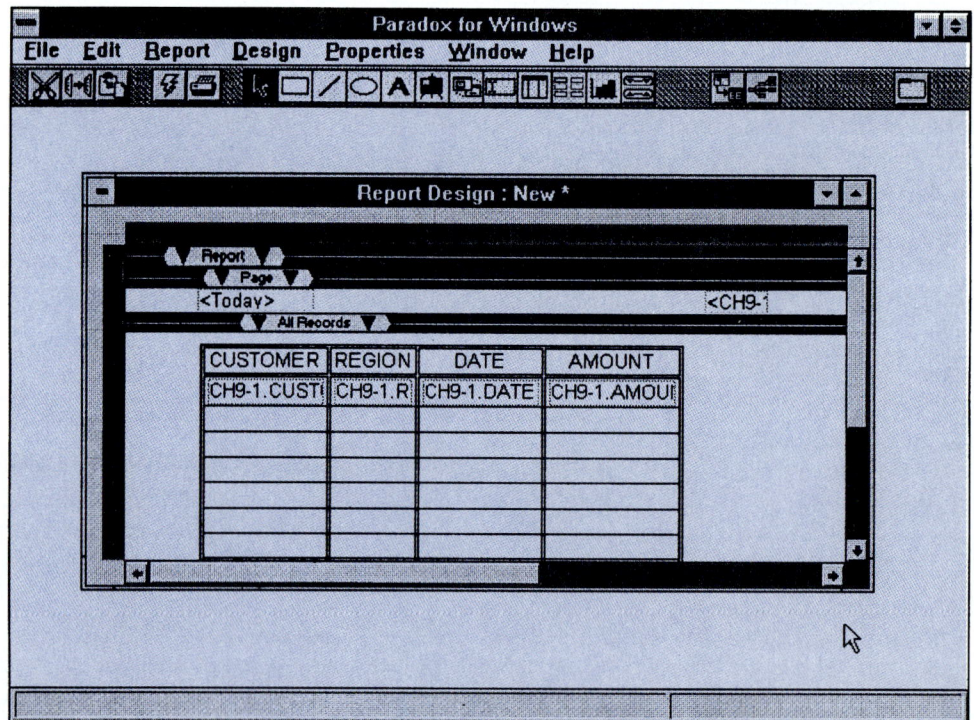

select them by clicking them, then press the Del key. As you see in Figure 9–10, Paradox for Windows displays a new SpeedBar. Table 9–2 introduces the various tools in this SpeedBar. Your actual work when designing reports starts here.

9–10   REPORT BANDS

Paradox for Windows divides the layout of a report into several areas, called bands (see Figure 9–11). Paradox for Windows has four types of bands:

Table 9–2
The Report Design SpeedBar

Button	Name	Description
	View data	Displays the report on the screen
	Print report	Sends the current report to the printer
	Selection arrow	Selects objects for moving, resizing, deleting, or editing
	Box tool	Draws boxes in report format
	Line tool	Draws lines in report format
	Ellipse tool	Draws ellipses (including circles) in report format
	Text tool	Adds text objects to report format
	Graphic tool	Adds bit-mapped graphic to report format
	OLE tool	Adds object linking and embedding (OLE) objects to report format
	Field tool	Adds fields to report format
	Table tool	Adds table objects to report format
	Multirecord tool	Adds multitable objects to report format
	Graph tool	Adds graph (bar graph, pie graph, and so on) to report format
	Add band	Adds an optional group band to the report format
	Data model	Shows the relationship of tables used in the report
	Object tree	Shows related objects used in ObjectPAL

1. The report band includes the report header and report footer. The header prints only once, at the beginning of the report. The report footer prints once, at the end of the report.

2. The page band also includes a header and a footer. These bands print at the top and bottom of each page, respectively.

3. The group band includes two parts: the table header and the body. The table header, by default, prints at the top of every page—above the fields and below the page header. The body of the report prints once for every record in the table. This band is used for generating subtotals, for example.

4. The record band prints once for each record that is presented. This is where the detail from the table prints, usually in tabular style. Summary reports do not include a record band; they print only the group and report totals.

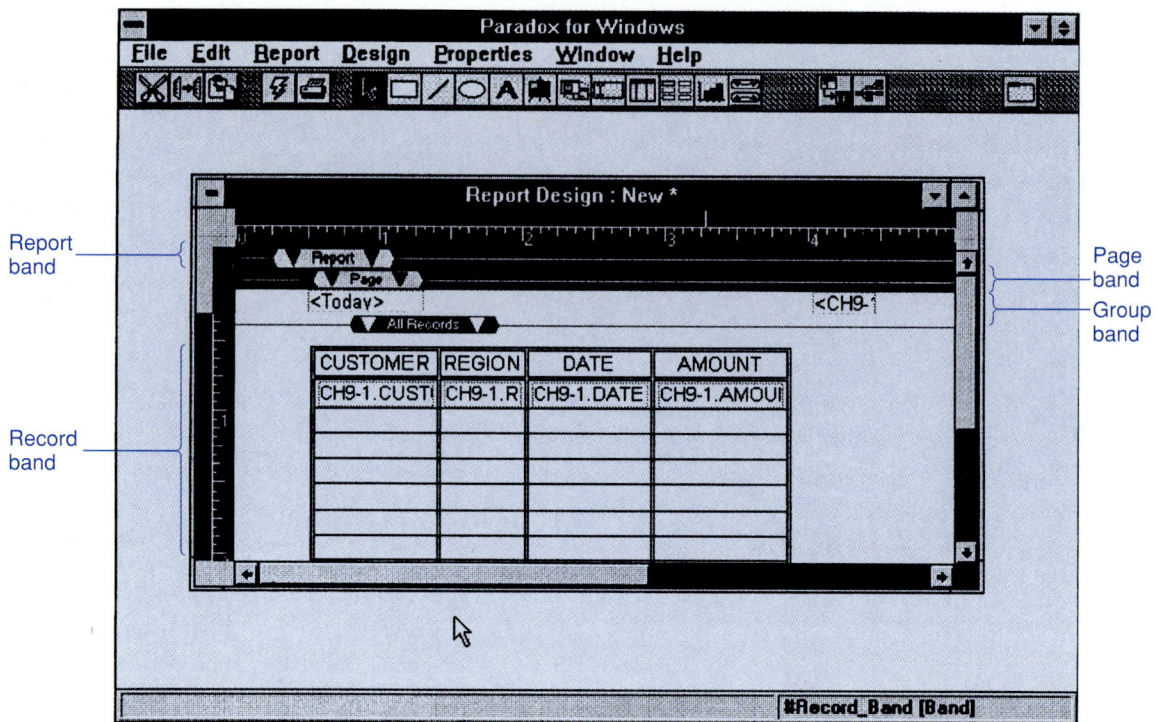

Figure 9–11
Types of report bands.

9–11   CREATING A TABULAR REPORT WITH GROUPED DATA

From our sample database table (Figure 9–1), we would like to generate a report that groups all the customers by regions, for example, all the customers in region 1, then all the customers in region 2, and so forth. These type of reports would be useful for marketing purposes. For example, you can find out the performance of each sales region. Start with a clear screen and follow these steps:

1. Select File New Report from the desktop.
2. Select CH9–1 and click on OK.
3. In the Design Layout dialog box select tabular style and click on OK. At this point you will see the Report Design window.
4. In the Report Design window, click the Add Band button (the fourth button from the right) in the SpeedBar to add a **group band** to the format. The Define Group dialog box is displayed, similar to the screen presented in Figure 9–12.
5. Click on Region and then click on OK. You will see a screen similar to the one displayed in Figure 9–13.
6. You can click and drag this field anywhere you like. By default, as you see, it is displayed toward the top center of the window.
7. You can right click on this field to display its properties and perform any desired changes, or accept it as is. We accepted it as is.
8. To include a title of your own in the report, select the Text tool (represented by the letter A). Highlight an area in the Page Band in which you want to

Figure 9–12
The Define Group dialog box.

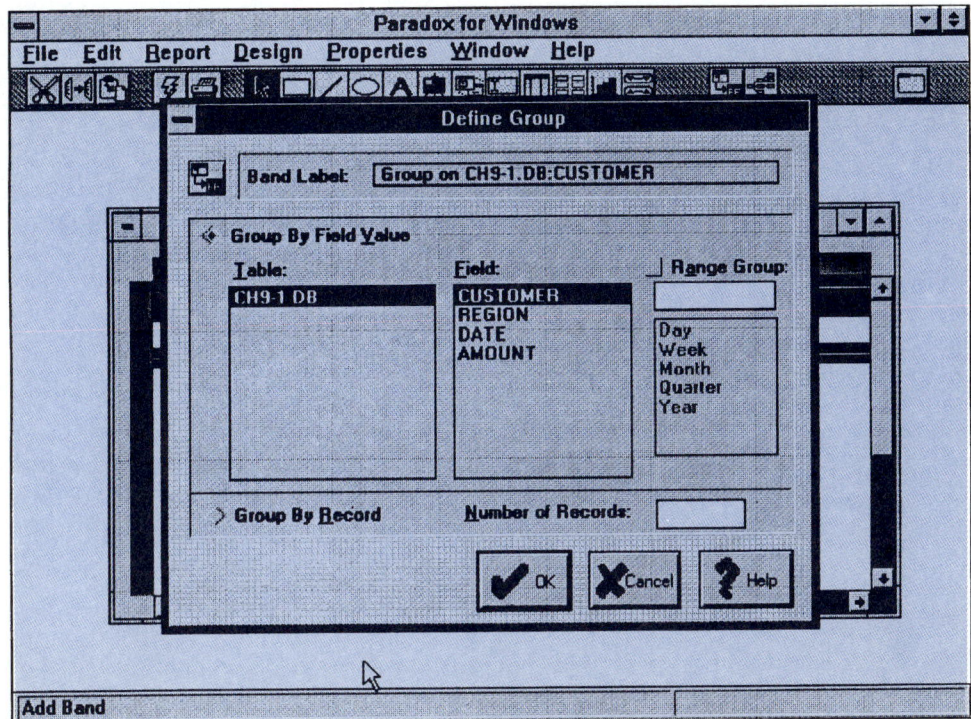

Figure 9–13
The Report Design window with a group band.

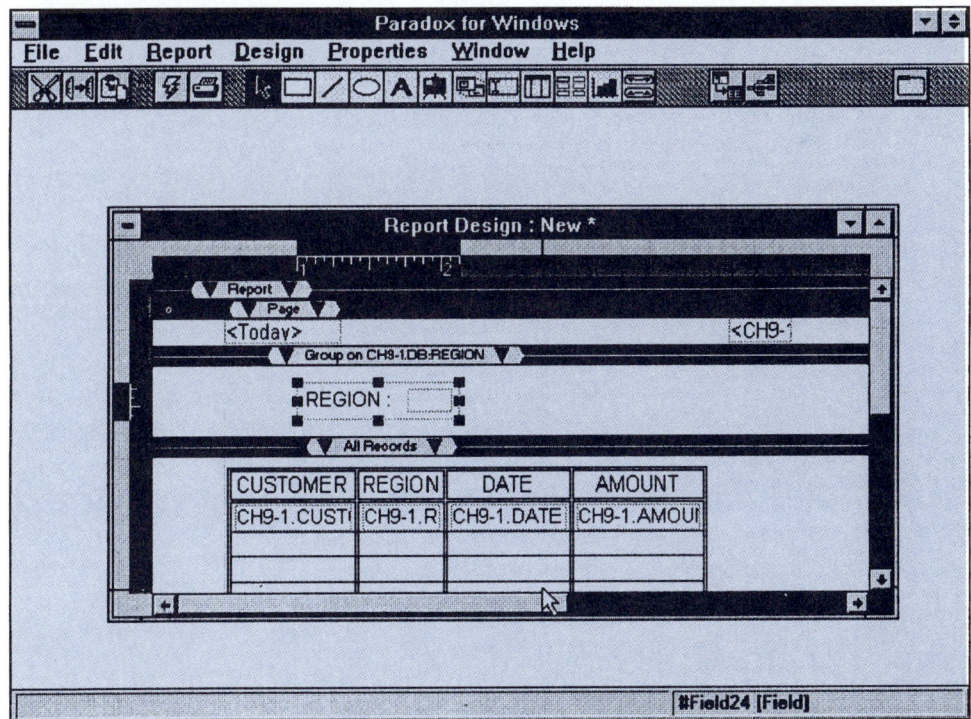

include the title and type in the desired title in the box provided. We typed *REPORT GROUPED BY REGION.*

9. Click on <TODAY> and press the Del key to remove the system date from the report.

10. Click on <CH9-1> and press the Del key to remove the table name from the report. You can click on ViewData to view your report before printing.

11. Click on the Print button and click on OK. Your report should be similar to the one displayed in Figure 9–14.

9–12   ADDING CALCULATED FIELDS TO THE REPORTS

The report that we just created would be more meaningful if we add some statistics. Paradox for Windows offers seven summary functions summarized in Table 9-3.

Suppose we want to generate a total for each region from the previous example. To do this follow the first 10 steps from the last example and then do the following:

1. Click on the Field tool in the SpeedBar.

2. Highlight the Amount by clicking on it. When the Amount field is high-lighted you will see the handle bars.

3. Click and drag the Amount field to the right of the region and then release the mouse button. At this point, your screen should be similar to the one displayed in Figure 9–15.

4. Right click on this field to display the field properties (see Figure 9–16).

5. Click on the Define Field option.

6. Click on the . . . option. You will see the Define Field Object dialog box (see Figure 9–17).

7. Click on the down arrow icon next to the table name and then click on Amount.

8. In the Summary box pull-down menu, click on Sum and click on OK.

9. If you view this design by clicking the View Data button in the SpeedBar, you will see the total of each region and the Sum(AMOUNT) label displayed to the left of all the totals.

10. To eliminate this label, in the Report Design Window right click on this field to display the field properties (Figure 9–16). Then click on the Display Type option.

11. In this pull–down menu click on Unlabeled.

12. If you print the report you will see a report similar to the one displayed in Figure 9–18.

9–13   GROUPING BY RANGE

In some cases it would be helpful to group the database table based on data ranges. For example, you might be interested in grouping all the customers who spent between $0 and $999 dollars, $1000 and $1999 dollars, and so forth. Or you might be interested in grouping all the customers who purchased between certain dates. Or you might be interested in grouping your data on some

Figure 9–14
Customers arranged by regions.

REPORT GROUPED BY REGION   Page 1

REGION : 1

CUSTOMER	REGION	DATE	AMOUNT
STEVE	1	11/9/90	$4,300.00
SUE	1	9/7/91	$6,777.90

REGION : 2

CUSTOMER	REGION	DATE	AMOUNT
BECKY	2	9/9/92	$7,655.00
JUDY	2	2/9/90	$780.00
MARY	2	3/4/91	$9,999.00
TERRY	2	10/10/93	$780.00
TIM	2	10/10/92	$569.00

REGION : 3

CUSTOMER	REGION	DATE	AMOUNT
JERRY	3	11/11/87	$9,000.05
SAM	3	11/12/89	$8,900.00
SUSAN	3	12/12/90	$8.00

REGION : 4

CUSTOMER	REGION	DATE	AMOUNT
DONA	4	11/11/91	$8,888.90
JOHN	4	12/12/89	$3,452.33
TOM	4	8/8/90	$43.00

REGION : 5

CUSTOMER	REGION	DATE	AMOUNT
DENIS	5	9/9/91	$234.00

REGION : 6

CUSTOMER	REGION	DATE	AMOUNT
BARBARA	6	3/17/89	$8,434.00

REGION : 7

CUSTOMER	REGION	DATE	AMOUNT
SANDY	7	12/14/88	$843.00
TONIA	7	1/1/93	$4,455.00

REGION : 9

CUSTOMER	REGION	DATE	AMOUNT
ANDY	9	11/11/92	$34.00
BOB	9	5/11/93	$6,768.45

Table 9–3
Summary Functions

Function	Description
Avg	Average of values
Count	Number of occurrences of a record
Max	Maximum value of all records
Min	Minimum value of all records
Std	Standard deviation of all values
Sum	Total of values
Var	Variance of all values

Figure 9-15
The location of the new field.

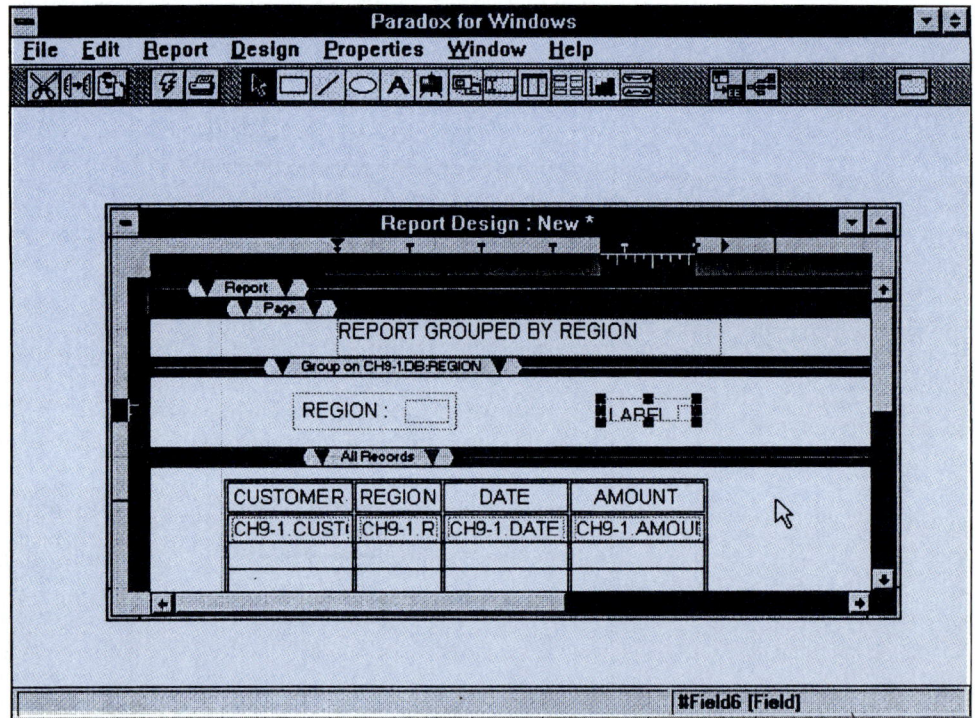

alphanumeric field, for example, all the customers who reside in certain geographical areas, or all the products whose names start with A or B, C or D, and so forth. Paradox for Windows allows you to perform all of these operations easily.

In Figure 9–10 click on the Add Band button and select a numeric field; we chose AMOUNT. Click on Range Group. Paradox for Windows responds with: 1.00. You may decide to enter 1000 in this box. This means your data items will be organized in a range with an increment of 1000. When you select the date field, Paradox for Windows responds with:

Day   Week   Month   Quarter   Year

You can select any of these by clicking the desired option.

Figure 9-16
The Field Properties menu.

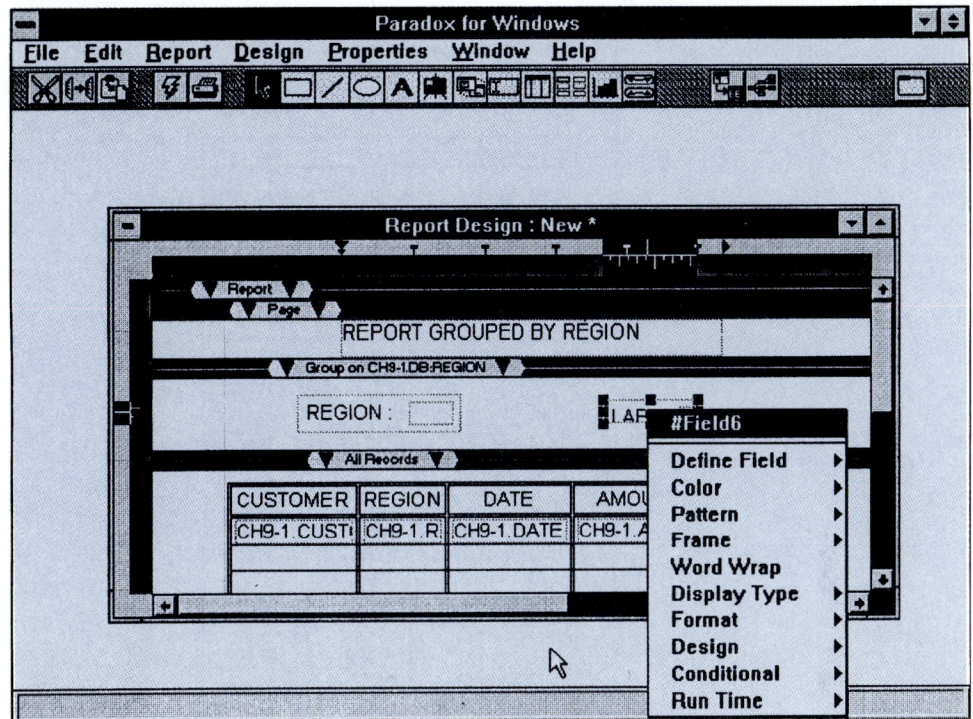

Figure 9-17
The Define Field Object dialog box.

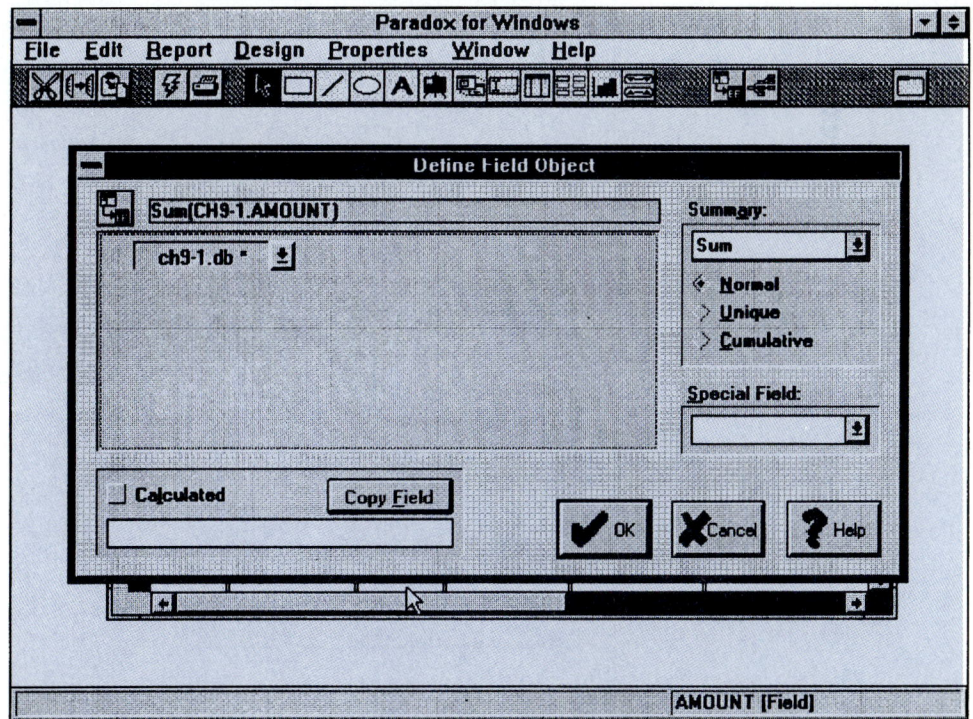

Figure 9–18
Group data with no label displayed.

REPORT GROUPED BY REGION   Page 1

REGION : 1 $11,077.90

CUSTOMER	REGION	DATE	AMOUNT
STEVE	1	11/9/90	$4,300.00
SUE	1	9/7/91	$6,777.90

REGION : 2 $19,783.00

CUSTOMER	REGION	DATE	AMOUNT
BECKY	2	9/9/92	$7,655.00
JUDY	2	2/9/90	$780.00
MARY	2	3/4/91	$9,999.00
TERRY	2	10/10/93	$780.00
TIM	2	10/10/92	$569.00

REGION : 3 $17,908.05

CUSTOMER	REGION	DATE	AMOUNT
JERRY	3	11/11/87	$9,000.05
SAM	3	11/12/89	$8,900.00
SUSAN	3	12/12/90	$8.00

REGION : 4 $12,384.23

CUSTOMER	REGION	DATE	AMOUNT
DONA	4	11/11/91	$8,888.90
JOHN	4	12/12/89	$3,452.33
TOM	4	8/8/90	$43.00

REGION : 5 $234.00

CUSTOMER	REGION	DATE	AMOUNT
DENIS	5	9/9/91	$234.00

REGION : 6 $8,434.00

CUSTOMER	REGION	DATE	AMOUNT
BARBARA	6	3/17/89	$8,434.00

REGION : 7 $5,298.00

CUSTOMER	REGION	DATE	AMOUNT
SANDY	7	12/14/88	$843.00
TONIA	7	1/1/93	$4,455.00

REGION : 9 $6,802.45

CUSTOMER	REGION	DATE	AMOUNT
ANDY	9	11/11/92	$34.00
BOB	9	5/11/93	$6,768.45

When you select an alphanumeric field, Paradox for Windows allows you to enter a number in the Range Group box. For example, you can type *1* to group by first letter, *2* to group by the first two letters, and so forth.

In our sample database table, we want to group all the customers by their amount of purchase in increments of $1000. To do this, follow these steps:

1. Click on the Add Band button in the SpeedBar. In the Define Group dialog box, click on the AMOUNT field.
2. Click on the Range Group box. Type *1000* in the Range Group box.
3. Click on OK.
4. Click on the Print button. Click on OK to print the report.

Your final report should be similar to the one displayed in Figure 9–19.

9–14   GROUPING BY RECORDS

In some cases, you may want to group a series of records together for easy reading. For example, it may be easier to read every 10 records of a large table, then a blank line, then read 10 more, and so forth.

Let us say we want to organize our sample database table by every five records. To do this follow these steps:

1. In Figure 9–10 click on the Add Band button.
2. In the Define Group dialog box, click on Group By Record (in the lower left corner of the dialog box). The default is Group By Field Value.
3. In the Number of Records box type *5*.
4. Click on OK.
5. Click on the Print button and then click on OK. Your final report should be similar to Figure 9–20.

9–15   LABEL CREATION

Paradox for Windows provides a simple procedure for creating mailing labels. The format of the printed label depends on your printer and your personal preference. You can produce single-column labels (one-up), double-column labels (two-up), and so on.

To generate mailing labels for the sample database presented in Figure 9–21, follow these steps:

1. Choose File New Report from the Paradox for Windows desktop, or right-click the Report button and select New.
2. Choose CH9-21 and click on OK in the Data Model dialog box. You will see the Design Layout dialog box.
3. Select the Multi-Record option from the Style box, uncheck the Labeled Fields, and click on OK. You will see a screen similar to the one presented in Figure 9–22.
4. To change the number of labels displayed and printed in each row, select the record band and right-click to reveal its properties. To do this, position the

Figure 9–19
A report organized by $1000 increments.

Saturday, January 01, 1994 CH9-1 Page 1

CUSTOMER	REGION	DATE	AMOUNT
SUSAN	3	12/12/90	$8.00
ANDY	9	11/11/92	$34.00
TOM	4	8/8/90	$43.00
DENIS	5	9/9/91	$234.00
TIM	2	10/10/92	$569.00
JUDY	2	2/9/90	$780.00
TERRY	2	10/10/93	$780.00
SANDY	7	12/14/88	$843.00

CUSTOMER	REGION	DATE	AMOUNT
JOHN	4	12/12/89	$3,452.33

CUSTOMER	REGION	DATE	AMOUNT
STEVE	1	11/9/90	$4,300.00
TONIA	7	1/1/93	$4,455.00

CUSTOMER	REGION	DATE	AMOUNT
BOB	9	5/11/93	$6,768.45
SUE	1	9/7/91	$6,777.90

CUSTOMER	REGION	DATE	AMOUNT
BECKY	2	9/9/92	$7,655.00

CUSTOMER	REGION	DATE	AMOUNT
BARBARA	6	3/17/89	$8,434.00
DONA	4	11/11/91	$8,888.90
SAM	3	11/12/89	$8,900.00

CUSTOMER	REGION	DATE	AMOUNT
JERRY	3	11/11/87	$9,000.05
MARY	2	3/4/91	$9,999.00

Figure 9-20
Every five records are grouped.

Saturday, January 01, 1994   CH9-1   Page 1

CUSTOMER	REGION	DATE	AMOUNT
ANDY	9	11/11/92	$34.00
BARBARA	6	3/17/89	$8,434.00
BECKY	2	9/9/92	$7,655.00
BOB	9	5/11/93	$6,768.45
DENIS	5	9/9/91	$234.00

CUSTOMER	REGION	DATE	AMOUNT
DONA	4	11/11/91	$8,888.90
JERRY	3	11/11/87	$9,000.05
JOHN	4	12/12/89	$3,452.33
JUDY	2	2/9/90	$780.00
MARY	2	3/4/91	$9,999.00

CUSTOMER	REGION	DATE	AMOUNT
SAM	3	11/12/89	$8,900.00
SANDY	7	12/14/88	$843.00
STEVE	1	11/9/90	$4,300.00
SUE	1	9/7/91	$6,777.90
SUSAN	3	12/12/90	$8.00

CUSTOMER	REGION	DATE	AMOUNT
TERRY	2	10/10/93	$780.00
TIM	2	10/10/92	$569.00
TOM	4	8/8/90	$43.00
TONIA	7	1/1/93	$4,455.00

mouse pointer in the label skeleton and right click. You will see a screen similar to the one displayed in Figure 9–23. Click on Record Layout to receive a screen similar to the one presented in Figure 9–24.

5. In the Number Across box enter *2*, then click on OK. You will see a screen similar to the one in Figure 9–25. This dialog box also enables you to select the order of printing, for example, left to right, then down or sorted down one column and then the next.

6. Click and drag the first record box to the right and arrange the layout as follows:

```
Line 1   FNAME MID LNAME
Line 2   ADDRESS
Line 3   CITY, STATE ZIP
```

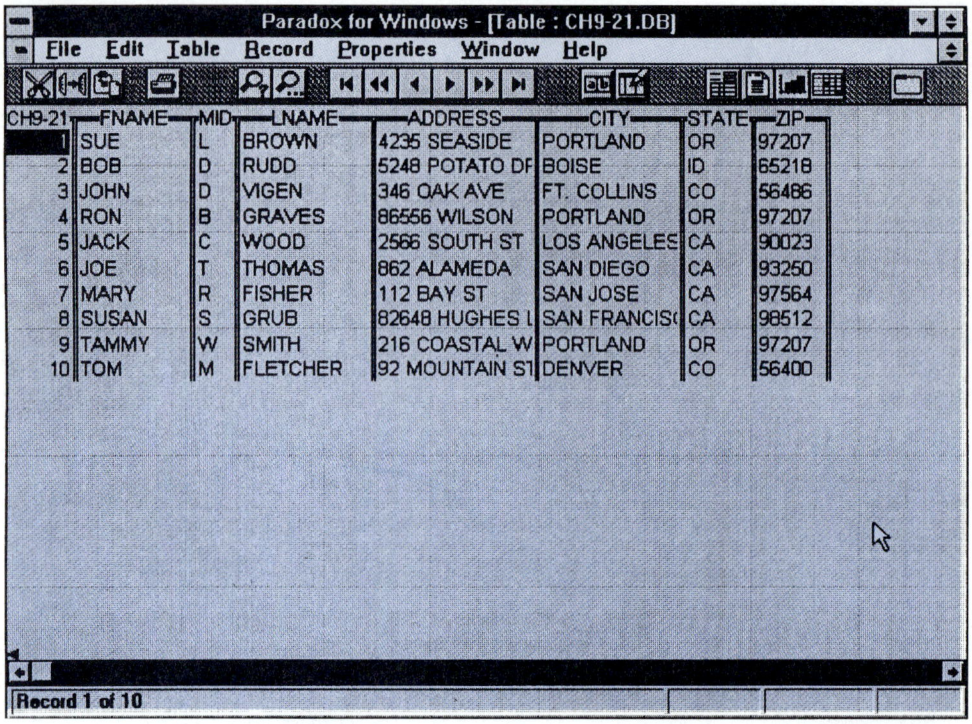

Paradox for Windows - [Table : CH9-21.DB]

File Edit Table Record Properties Window Help

CH9-21	FNAME	MID	LNAME	ADDRESS	CITY	STATE	ZIP
1	SUE	L	BROWN	4235 SEASIDE	PORTLAND	OR	97207
2	BOB	D	RUDD	5248 POTATO DF	BOISE	ID	65218
3	JOHN	D	VIGEN	346 OAK AVE	FT. COLLINS	CO	56486
4	RON	B	GRAVES	86556 WILSON	PORTLAND	OR	97207
5	JACK	C	WOOD	2566 SOUTH ST	LOS ANGELES	CA	90023
6	JOE	T	THOMAS	862 ALAMEDA	SAN DIEGO	CA	93250
7	MARY	R	FISHER	112 BAY ST	SAN JOSE	CA	97564
8	SUSAN	S	GRUB	82648 HUGHES L	SAN FRANCISC	CA	98512
9	TAMMY	W	SMITH	216 COASTAL W	PORTLAND	OR	97207
10	TOM	M	FLETCHER	92 MOUNTAIN ST	DENVER	CO	56400

Record 1 of 10

Figure 9-21
Sample table.

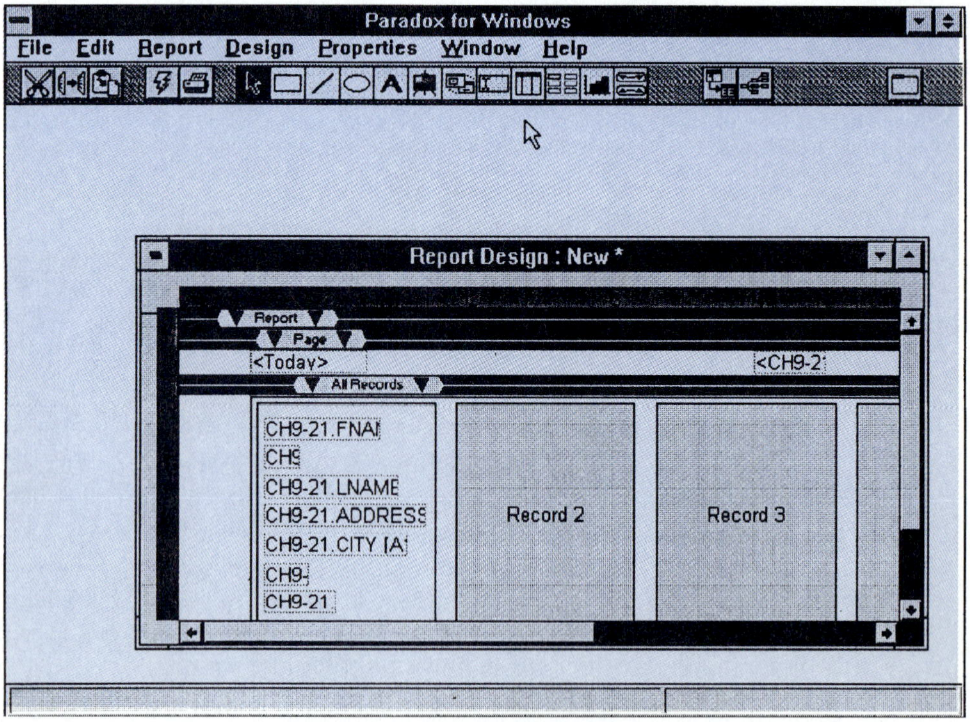

Figure 9-22
Report design layout for label creation.

Figure 9–23
Record Properties dialog box.

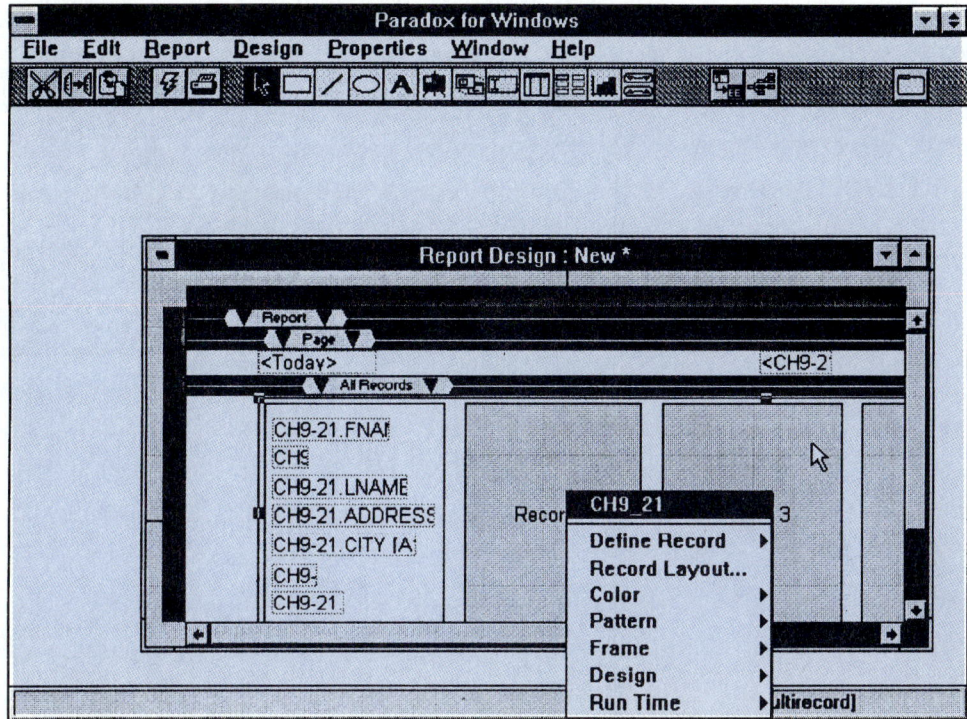

Figure 9–24
Record Layout dialog box.

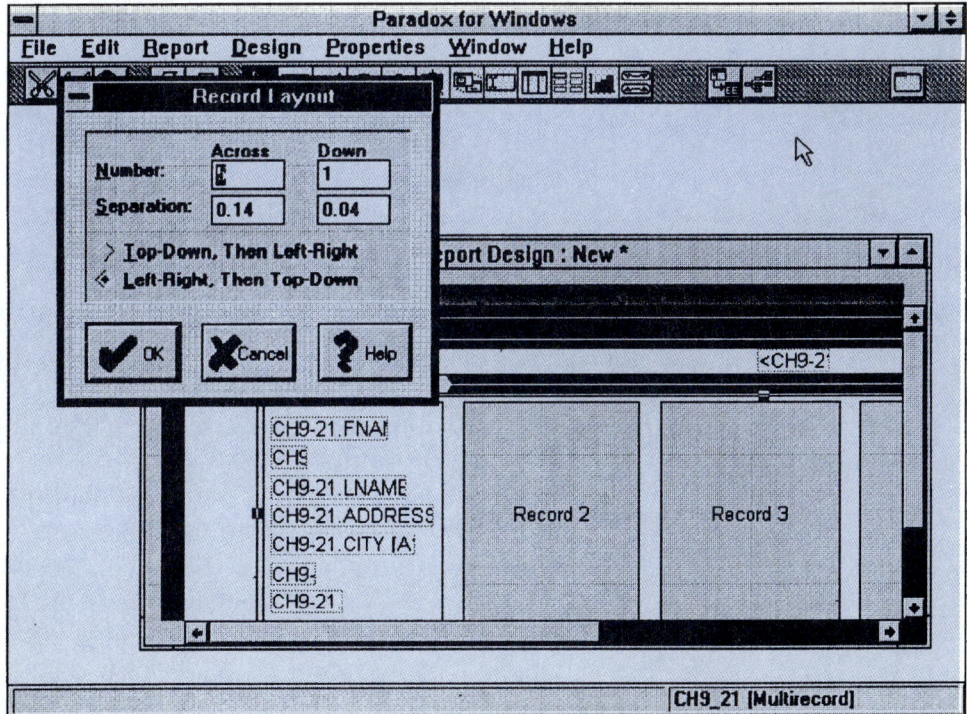

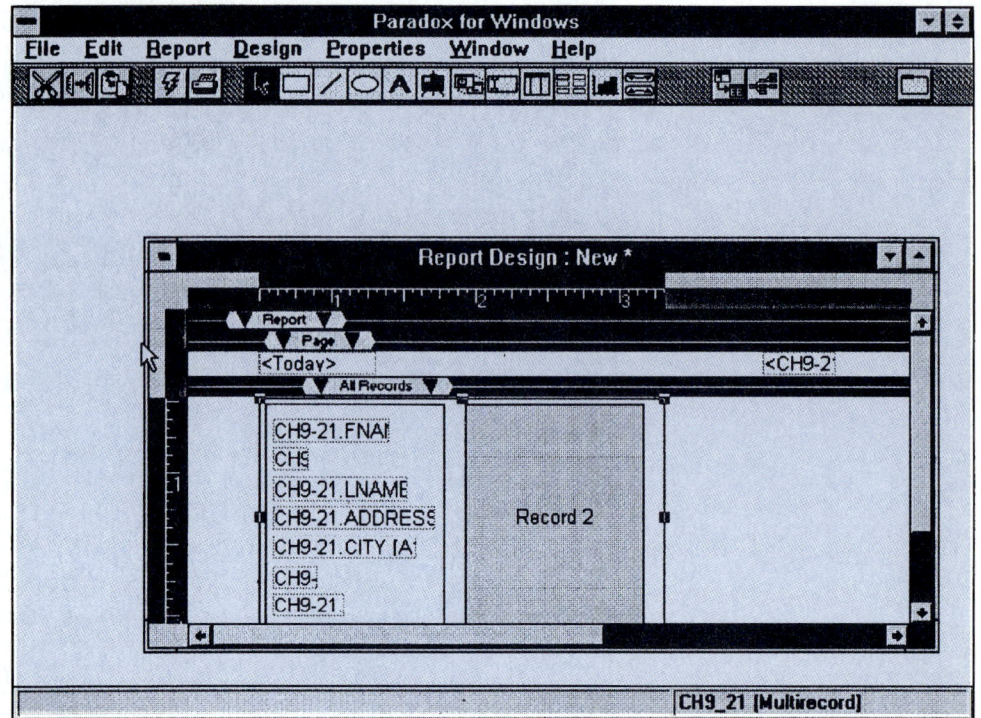

To do this click each field first to select it and then click and drag it to the correct place. To enter a comma between the city and state, first click on the Text tool in the SpeedBar and then click in the correct position and type a comma.

7. By clicking and dragging, eliminate all the unnecessary spaces. At this point your screen should be similar to the one displayed in Figure 9–26.

8. Choose File Save As to save the report. We saved it as CH9-26. Paradox for Windows attaches an RSL extension to this file.

9. To view your report, click the View Data button in the SpeedBar. To return to the design mode, click the Design button in the SpeedBar.

10. As you see, the labels are enclosed in frames. To eliminate the frame, first select the record skeleton in the design mode and then right click to display the record properties (Figure 9–23).

11. Click on Frame, then on Style. Then click on the second button from the top to change the frame style to blank.

12. To eliminate the date and file name from the report, select them individually and then press the Del key.

13. Click on the Print button and then click on OK. Your final report should be similar to the screen presented in Figure 9–27.

14. By default, Paradox for Windows displays the entire field up to its maximum length, padding any extra spaces with blanks. For the lines with more than one field, such as first name, middle initial, and last name on the first line of the label and the last line (city, state, and zip code), this creates unpleasant gaps in the report. To trim the spaces, choose the second and third field in each line one by one, inspect its properties (right-click), and uncheck Run Time Pin Horizontal. Repeat this step for other fields. Now if you print this report your final work should be similar to Figure 9–28.

Figure 9-26
Label design screen after entering fields.

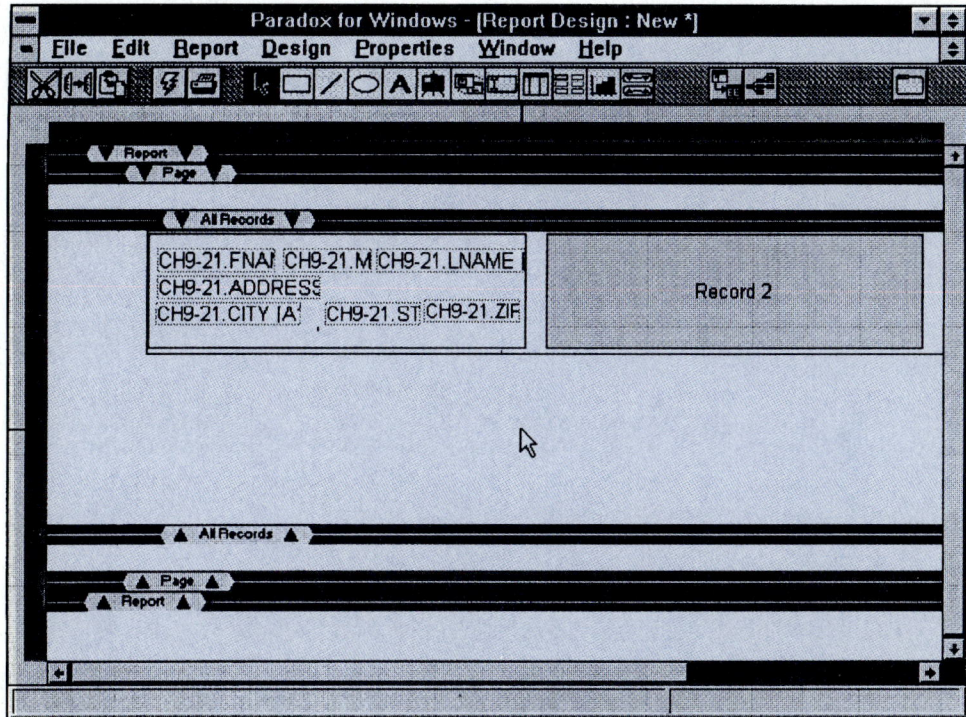

Figure 9-27
Labels printed from the sample table.

SUMMARY

This chapter reviewed the report and label generation capabilities of Paradox for Windows. The processes of generating quick reports, customized reports, and reports with grouped data were discussed. The chapter also explained the process of mailing label creation. These two features are very powerful. Practice using them to become more familiar with the operation sequences.

Figure 9-28
Final mailing list with extra spaces eliminated.

```
                                                                    Page 1

   SUE L BROWN                    BOB D RUDD
   4235 SEASIDE                   5248 POTATO DR
   PORTLAND  OR      97207        BOISE  ID            65218
            ,                          ,

   JOHN D VIGEN                   RON B GRAVES
   346 OAK AVE                    86556 WILSON
   FT. COLLINS  CO    56486       PORTLAND  OR         97207
             ,                             ,

   JACK C WOOD                    JOE T THOMAS
   2566 SOUTH ST                  862 ALAMEDA
   LOS ANGELES  CA    90023       SAN DIEGO  CA        93250
              ,                           ,

   MARY R FISHER                  SUSAN S GRUB
   112 BAY ST                     82648 HUGHES LN
   SAN JOSE  CA      97564        SAN FRANCISCO  CA    98512
           ,                                   ,

   TAMMY W SMITH                  TOM M FLETCHER
   216 COASTAL WAY                92 MOUNTAIN ST
   PORTLAND  OR      97207        DENVER  CO           56400
            ,                           ,
```

REVIEW QUESTIONS

*These questions are answered in Appendix A.

1. What is a quick report?
2. How is a quick report generated?
3. What is included in a quick report?
4. How do you start the report design process?
*5. How many bands are supported by Paradox for Windows?
6. What is included in each band?
*7. How many report styles does Paradox for Windows support?
8. How do you start the Design Layout window?
9. How do you create a report from the Answer table?
10. What are the applications of the multirecord style?
11. How do you group data?
12. How many ways can you group data?
13. How many summary operators can be used in a report?
14. What are some of the applications of grouping by range?
15. Why do you group by a series of records?
*16. What are some of the uses of subtotal reports?
17. How do you create mailing labels?
18. Up to how many labels across a row are supported by Paradox for Windows?
19. How do you print labels generated by Paradox for Windows?
*20. How do you remove the blank spaces among the fields in a mailing label?
21. What are some of the buttons on the Report SpeedBar?

HANDS-ON EXPERIENCE

1. Using the database presented in Figure 9–1, generate:
   a. A report with default settings.
   b. A report with the heading SAMPLE REPORT FOR MARKETING.
   c. A report that includes only sales amounts over $5000.
   d. A report that includes only sales amounts under $100 that were purchased in region 2.
   e. Generate other statistics in addition to the sum for this database, for example, maximum, minimum, average, and count.

2. The following is the structure of a sample database:

   Fname   (alphanumeric, width 10)
   Mname   (alphanumeric, width 1)
   Lname   (alphanumeric, width 10)
   Saddress (alphanumeric, width 25)
   City   (alphanumeric, width 10)
   State   (alphanumeric, width 2)
   Zip   (alphanumeric, width 5)
   Credit   (numeric)

   The following are 10 sample records in this database:

Suzanne	S	Smith	1912 S.W. Broadway	Portland	OR	97201	2000.00
Tom	B	Brown	1619 N.W. Gilison	Portland	OR	97209	3000.00
Terry	R	Shoemaker	1719 East Boulder	Ft. Collins	CO	92111	2000.00
Jacki	L	Thomas	1815 Rose	San Diego	CA	91291	1000.00
Mary	L	Fishler	1717 N.E. 41th	Portland	OR	97202	3000.00
Gloria	G	Gamble	1211 N.E. 50th	Ft. Collins	CO	92112	2500.00
Mike	T	Smith	707 South Haley	Los Angeles	CA	91203	6000.00
Robert	B	Bowin	1612 Truxtun	Portland	OR	97202	8000.00
Jim	T	Graves	702 Halson	San Diego	CA	91271	2000.00
Nooshin	B	Parsaei	1918 Tower	Lincoln	OR	92221	5000.00

   Create a report with the title: *Always Open Merchant* and the following elements:
   a. A report in descending order based on the credit limit.
   b. A report in alphabetical order.
   c. A report with a subtotal based on the state.
   d. A report in alphabetical order based on the city.

3. Using the sample database presented in Figure 9–21, create a mailing list with:
   a. One label across the page.
   b. Two labels across the page with the title: *A SAMPLE MAILING LIST.*

4. Create a mailing label for the customer file in question 3 in the following order:
   a. Based on the states.
   b. Based on the credit limits.
   c. Based on the last names.
   d. Based on the cities.

   In all of these examples print one label across the page.

KEY TERMS

Group band   Quick report

KEY COMMANDS

Shift+F7 (to print quick   File New Report (to start
reports)   the report design process)

MISCONCEPTIONS AND SOLUTIONS

Misconception   Sometimes you create a report that includes some unwanted data. For example, you may only be interested in seeing the names of the personnel in the accounting department, but your report includes the names of all the employees.

> **Solution**   By using the Query operation, first generate an Answer table that only includes your desired data, then generate your report from this table.

Misconception   You print your report, then find out that the specifications were not what you wanted.

> **Solution**   Click the View Data button for a screen preview of your report before printing it.

Misconception   Sometimes you may want to change the order of one or several of your fields. You can go back to your original table and use the Restructure option. This may be time-consuming.

> **Solution**   In the Define Multi-Record Object dialog box you can click the Change Order up or down arrow icon to generate the desired format. This is much faster than using the Restructure option.

Misconception   You may want to perform some changes on your report specification. Starting from scratch would be a time-consuming process.

> **Solution**   To modify a report specification, click on the Open Report icon (the fourth button from the left) in the desktop and perform the changes in this previously saved report. These files have RSL as their file extension.

ARE YOU READY TO MOVE ON?

Multiple Choice

1. A quick report by default includes all of the following except:
   a. a maximum and minimum for the numeric field
   b. a page number
   c. a date
   d. a title
   e. they all will be included

2. The design layout includes all the following options except:
   a. field layout
   b. statistics
   c. page layout
   d. style
   e. tabular

3. Paradox for Windows includes up to how many bands?
   a. six
   b. five
   c. four
   d. three
   e. two

4. One of the following is not included in the Page Layout dialog box:
   a. printer
   b. screen
   c. report style
   d. portrait
   e. landscape

5. Paradox for Windows allows you to generate:
   a. tabular reports
   b. single-record reports
   c. multirecord reports
   d. all of the above
   e. only a and b

6. Paradox for Windows includes all of the following summary operators except:
   a. average
   b. count
   c. max
   d. min
   e. they are all included

7. Paradox for Windows allows you to group your data based on:
   a. field
   b. range
   c. number of records
   d. all of the above
   e. only a and b

8. In Paradox for Windows every statement that follows is correct about mailing label creation except:
   a. you will use the Multi-Record report style
   b. you cannot trim the extra space between fields
   c. you can generate 2-up labels
   d. you can save your report specification
   e. they all are correct

9. Paradox for Windows allows up to how many reports per table?
   a. 10
   b. 11
   c. 12
   d. 13
   e. there is no limit

10. To create a subtotal, your table:
    a. must be organized alphabetically
    b. must be sorted in descending order
    c. can be in any order
    d. must be sorted by last name
    e. none of the above

True/False

1. By default, a quick report includes the system date.
2. By default, a quick report includes page numbers.
3. By default, a quick report includes the information for the maximum and minimum of data items in the group.
4. Using Paradox for Windows you can only print in portrait style.
5. Paradox for Windows allows up to seven bands.
6. The page header band is displayed first.

7. The report cannot be previewed before printing.
8. The Multi-Record Report style is used to generate labels.
9. Paradox for Windows allows you to remove extra spaces in mailing labels.
10. Your labels can be sorted in any order.

ANSWERS

Multiple Choice		True/False	
1.	a	1.	T
2.	b	2.	T
3.	c	3.	F
4.	c	4.	F
5.	d	5.	F
6.	e	6.	T
7.	d	7.	F
8.	b	8.	T
9.	e	9.	T
10.	c	10.	T

Creating Crosstabs and Graphs Using Database Tables

10

10–1 INTRODUCTION

This chapter provides a detailed discussion of crosstabs and the graphics capabilities of Paradox for Widows. The chapter defines crosstabs as a tool for analyzing various database data, and then presents an overview of various graph types and the application of each type. The chapter introduces Paradox for Windows graph elements and shows you how to create different types of graphs. Saving, retrieving, and printing graphs are explained.

10–2 WHAT IS A CROSSTAB?

A **crosstab** is a Paradox for Windows object that enables you to summarize the data in one field by expressing it in terms of one or two other fields. Crosstabs present the data in a spreadsheetlike format. For example, in our sample data table in Figure 10–1, a crosstab may summarize the number of customers in each region.

Paradox for Windows offers two types of crosstabs: one-dimensional and two-dimensional. In a one-dimensional crosstab, the data is summarized based on one field. For example, in Figure 10–1 you may summarize the number of customers in each region. In a two-dimensional crosstab, the data is summarized based on two fields. For example, in Figure 10–1 you may summarize the table based on product and region. In this example, you will be able to find out the performance of each product in each region.

Remember that the crosstab tool is available only in Paradox for Windows forms; you cannot include crosstabs in reports. To print a crosstab, select **File Print** while viewing the form.

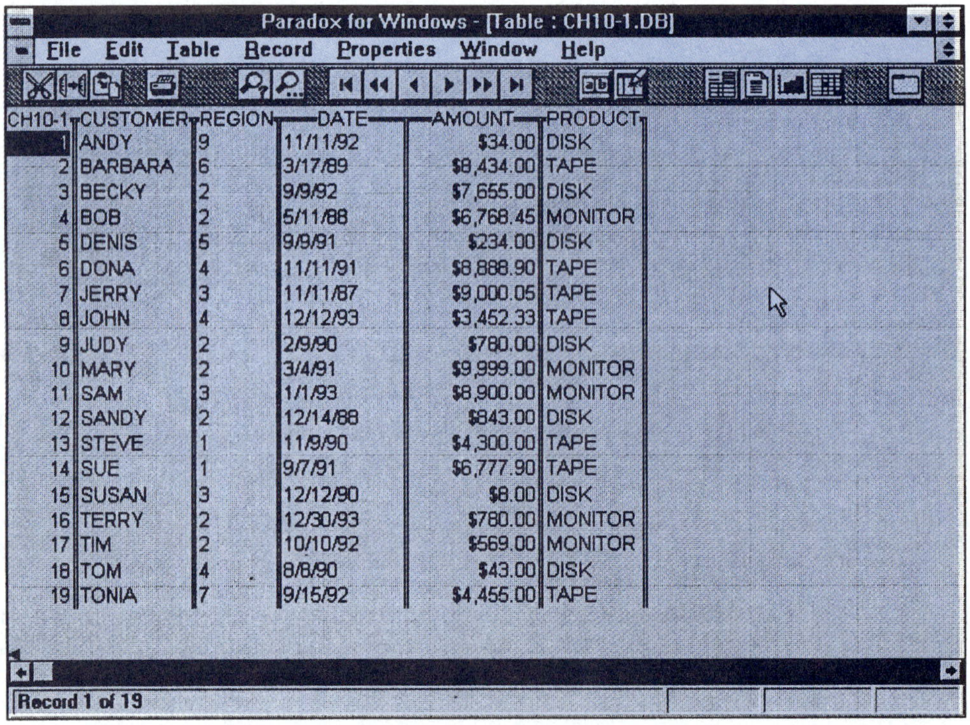

CH10-1	CUSTOMER	REGION	DATE	AMOUNT	PRODUCT
1	ANDY	9	11/11/92	$34.00	DISK
2	BARBARA	6	3/17/89	$8,434.00	TAPE
3	BECKY	2	9/9/92	$7,655.00	DISK
4	BOB	2	5/11/88	$6,768.45	MONITOR
5	DENIS	5	9/9/91	$234.00	DISK
6	DONA	4	11/11/91	$8,888.90	TAPE
7	JERRY	3	11/11/87	$9,000.05	TAPE
8	JOHN	4	12/12/93	$3,452.33	TAPE
9	JUDY	2	2/9/90	$780.00	DISK
10	MARY	2	3/4/91	$9,999.00	MONITOR
11	SAM	3	1/1/93	$8,900.00	MONITOR
12	SANDY	2	12/14/88	$843.00	DISK
13	STEVE	1	11/9/90	$4,300.00	TAPE
14	SUE	1	9/7/91	$6,777.90	TAPE
15	SUSAN	3	12/12/90	$8.00	DISK
16	TERRY	2	12/30/93	$780.00	MONITOR
17	TIM	2	10/10/92	$569.00	MONITOR
18	TOM	4	8/8/90	$43.00	DISK
19	TONIA	7	9/15/92	$4,455.00	TAPE

Figure 10-1
Sample table

10-3   GENERATING ONE-DIMENSIONAL CROSSTABS

To generate a one-dimensional crosstab from the sample table presented in Figure 10–1, follow these steps:

1. Using File Open Table, open the CH10–1 Table.
2. Click on the Quick Crosstab button (the second button from the right) in the SpeedBar. You will see the Define Crosstab dialog box, similar to the one presented in Figure 10–2.
3. Click on the table pull-down arrow icon next to the table name to display all the fields in the table.
4. Click on REGION. This will constitute the columns of the crosstab.
5. Click on the Summaries button and select the CUSTOMER field from the pull-down menu. This crosstab will generate the number of customers in each region.
6. Click on OK to run the crosstab. You will see a screen similar to the one in Figure 10–3.

You may not be able to see all the regions in this crosstab because of space limitations. To see all the regions, you can turn this crosstab around by 90 degrees. To do this follow these steps:

1. Display the table.
2. Click on the Quick Crosstab button.
3. Enter *REGION* under Categories.
4. For Summaries select CUSTOMER.

Figure 10–2
The Define Crosstab dialog box

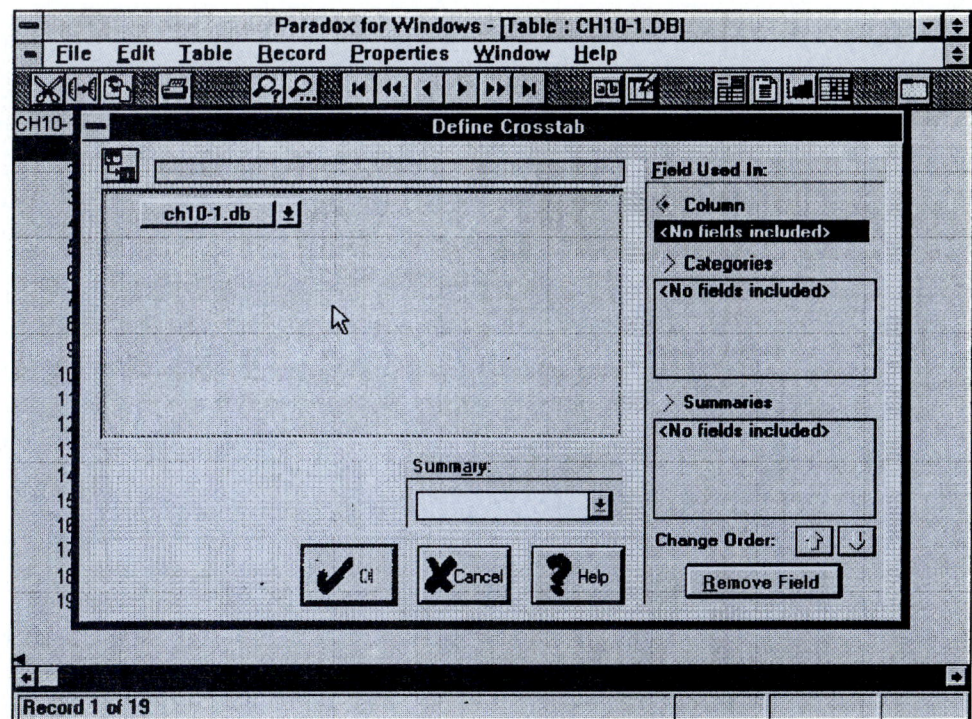

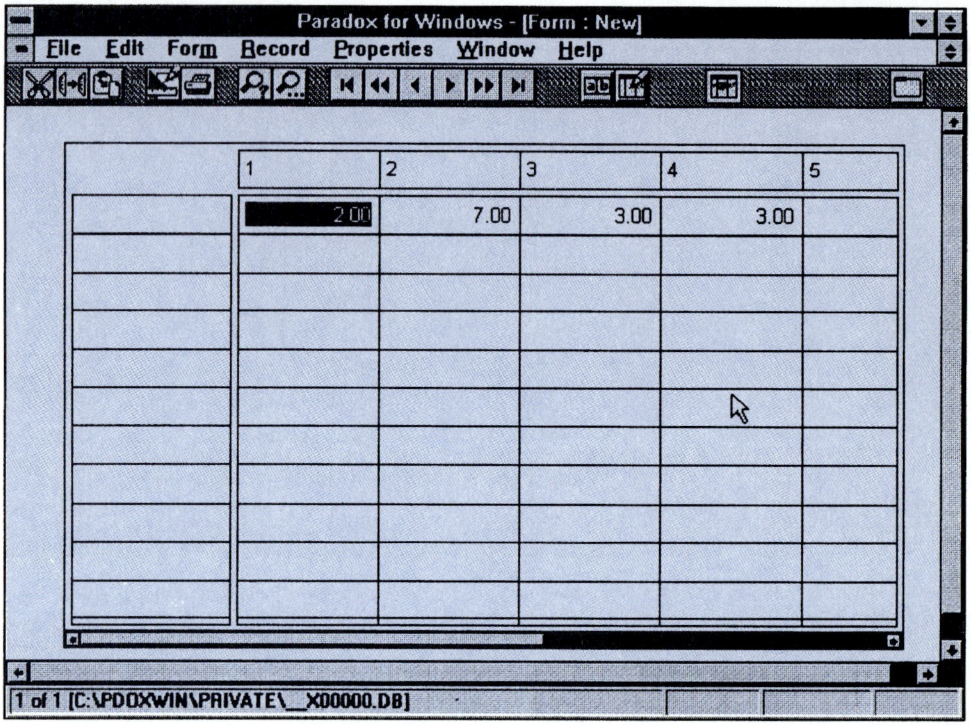

Figure 10–3
Crosstab for total number of customers in each region

5. Click on OK. Your final work should be similar to the screen displayed in Figure 10–4.

   You can always double-click the title bar or click on the maximize icon to let the crosstab fill the entire screen.

10–4   GENERATING TWO-DIMENSIONAL CROSSTABS

In two-dimensional crosstabs the data is analyzed based on two fields. For example, in our sample database table in Figure 10–1, you may want to find out how much of each product was sold in each region. To do this follow these steps:

1. By using File Open Table, open the desired table. We opened the table presented in Figure 10–1.
2. Click on the maximize button to maximize the window to its largest possible size.
3. Click on the Quick Crosstab tool. You will see the Define Crosstab dialog box, similar to the screen displayed in Figure 10–2.
4. For Column enter *REGION*.
5. For Categories enter *PRODUCT*.
6. For Summaries enter *CUSTOMER*.
7. Click on OK to run the crosstab. Your screen should be similar to the one displayed in Figure 10–5.

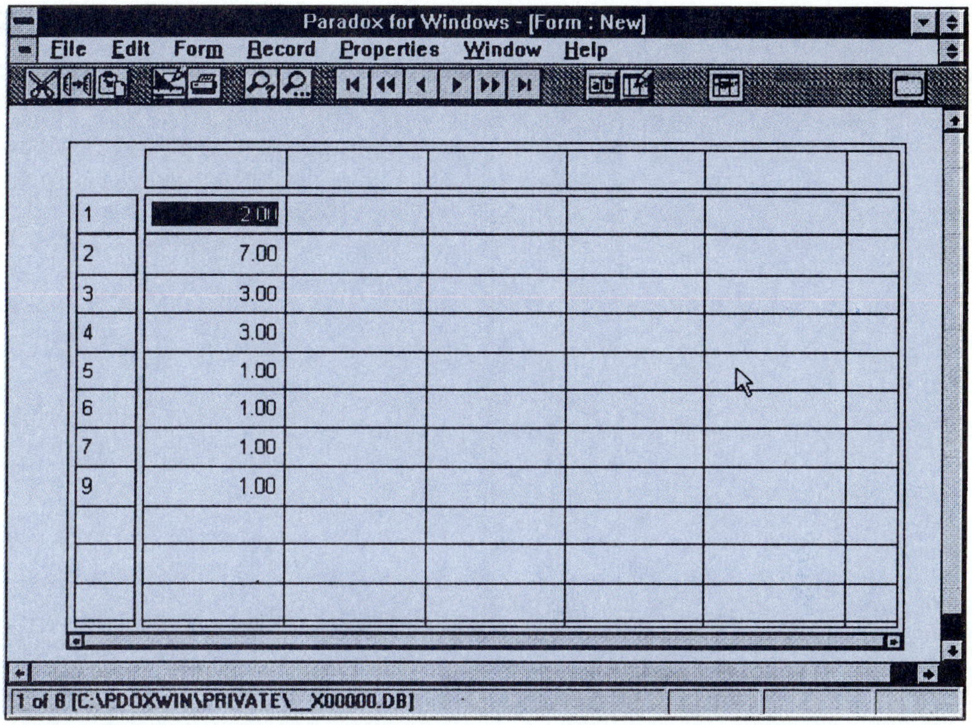

Figure 10–4
Crosstab rotated by 90 degrees

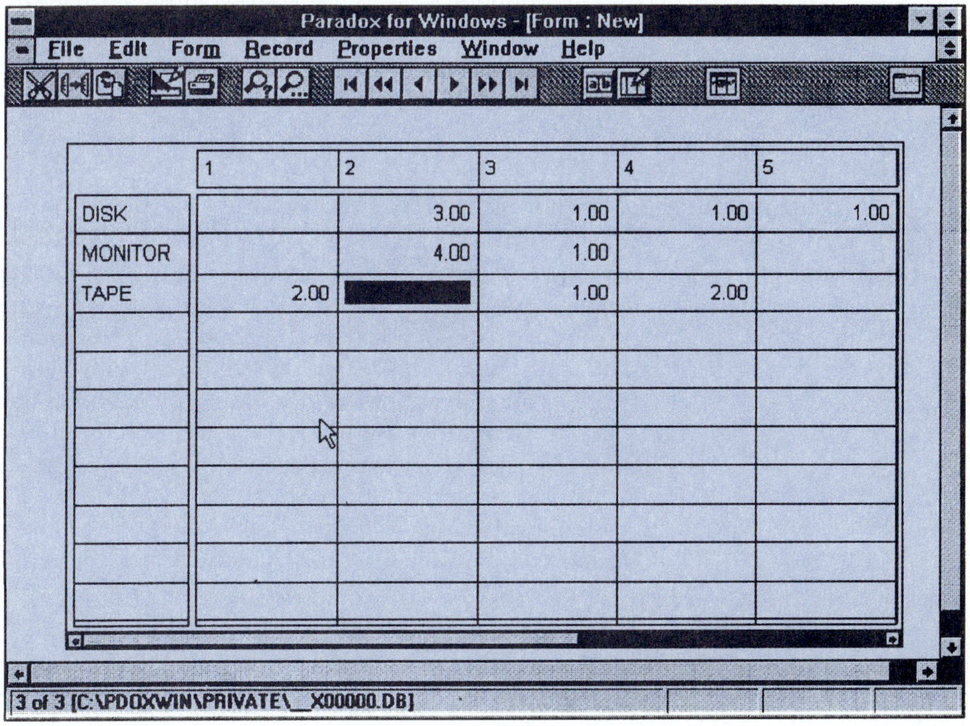

Figure 10–5
Two-dimensional crosstab

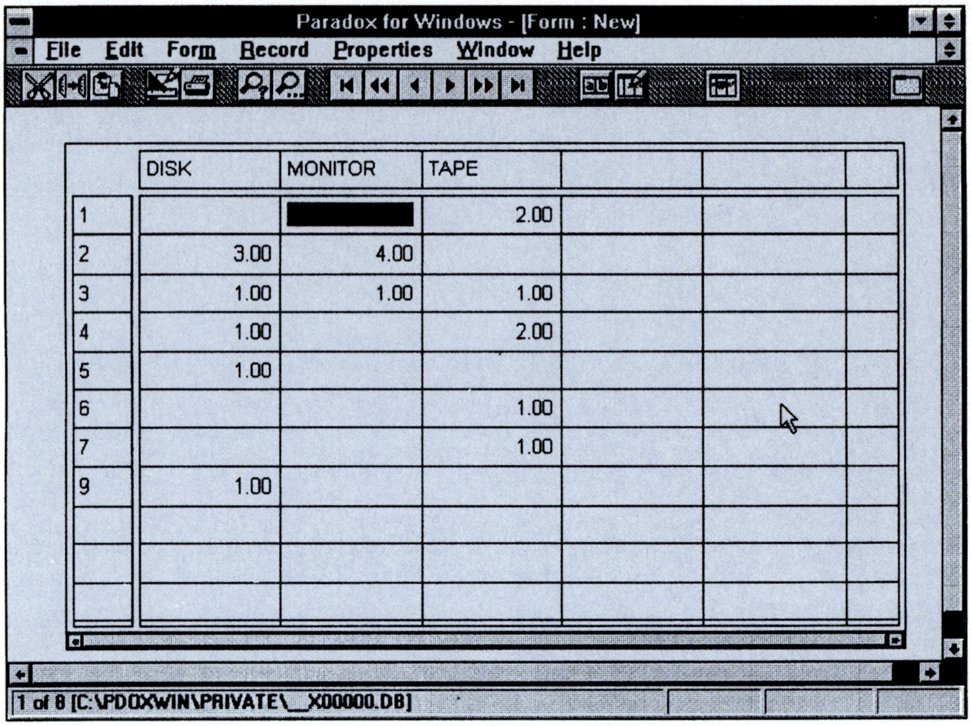

Figure 10–6
Two-dimensional crosstab rotated by 90 degrees

Again, to rotate the crosstab by 90 degrees enter *PRODUCT* under Column, *REGION* under Categories, and *CUSTOMER* under Summaries. Click on OK to run the crosstab. Your final work should be similar to the screen presented in Figure 10–6.

10–5   OTHER EXAMPLES OF CROSSTABS

Using crosstabs you can generate many different types of analyses. The summary operators—Sum, Count, Min, Max, and Avg—can be used with crosstabs. And you can analyze your data based on any of the fields in the table.

Figure 10–7 illustrates the total sales generated by each product group. To produce this crosstab, we entered *PRODUCT* under Column and *AMOUNT* under Summaries. Sum was the selected operator.

Figure 10–8 illustrates the total sales generated by each region. To produce this crosstab, we entered *REGION* under Categories and *AMOUNT* under Summaries. Sum was the selected operator. Note that this crosstab resembles a report with group subtotals, like the one we generated in the last chapter.

10–6   USING GRAPHS

In today's competitive world, business executives and decision makers need to get information in the most effective and efficient way. Graphs achieve these goals by condensing large amounts of data into a simple and easy-to-understand form.

Paradox for Windows generates seventeen different graphs (listed in Figure 10–13). The popular graph types are discussed here.

Figure 10–7
Crosstab showing total sales of each product group.

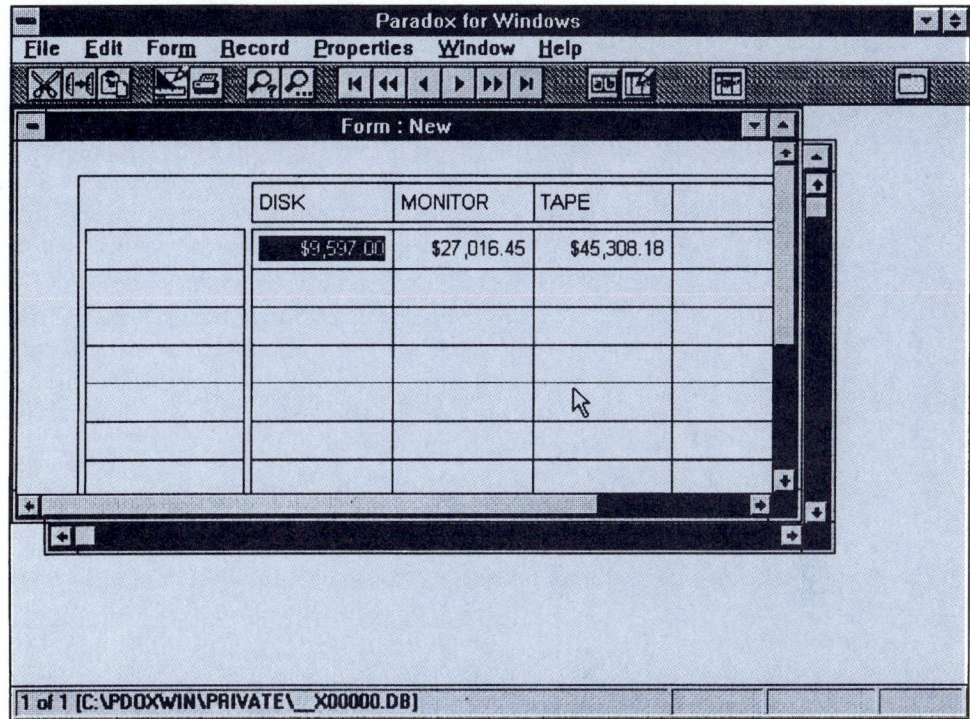

Figure 10–8
Crosstab showing total sales for each region.

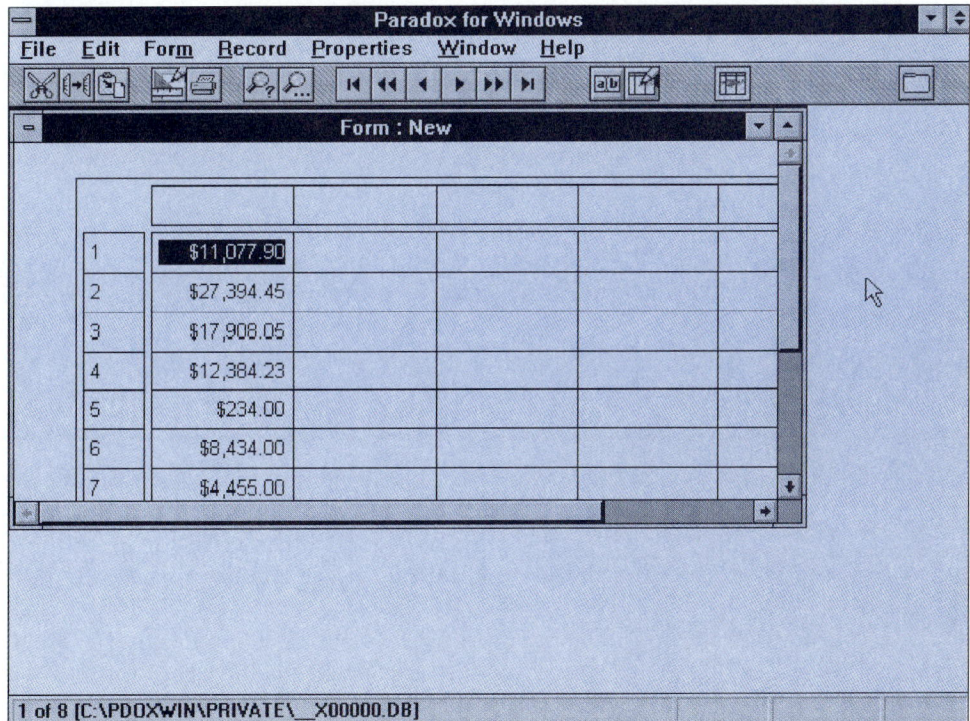

1.   **Line graphs** show changes (trends) in data over time. These graphs are suitable for time series analysis. In this type of analysis, one variable is time and the other variable can represent such things as sales, cost, or advertising budget. Using line graphs, you can easily depict advertising budget trends, total sales trends, and administrative cost trends.

2.   **Bar graphs** emphasize differences among data items. For example, you can use a bar graph when comparing such things as the sales records of five products, the oil production of two oil wells, or the student populations of six universities.

3.   **Three-dimensional bar graphs** emphasize differences among data items. For example, you could use a three-dimensional bar graph to display advertising costs for the past five years. The three-dimensional aspect creates the illusion of depth. In this manner, you will be able to see the effect of the graph better than in regular bar graphs.

4.   **Rotated-bar graphs** are useful for comparing data sets. You can compare such things as actual budget and projected budget, actual costs and budgeted costs, and so on. The bars extend from the left of the screen or printout. Rotated bar graphs are useful to depict goals.

5.   **Stacked bar graphs** compare differences among data by stacking the data items on top of each other. This may help you to better visualize data. For example, you can compare the incomes generated by different products in four regions.

6.   **XY graphs** show relationships between two sets of data, such as sales and advertising budget, height and weight, or years of education and annual income.

7.   **Pie charts** compare all the parts to the whole. For example, you can compare advertising expenses to total sales expenses.

8.   **Column graphs** are similar to pie charts; however, they show data in a vertical format. Using this type of graph, you can, for example, plot advertising costs against total costs.

9.   **Area graphs** are similar to line graphs; however, they present cumulative values. Using this type of graph, it is easy to compare and contrast several data sets, such as a company's sales in four regions.

10–7   STARTING THE PARADOX FOR WINDOWS GRAPHICS

To activate the Define Graph dialog box, first open the desired table (we opened table CH10–1 presented in Figure 10–1) and either click on the Quick Graph tool (the third button from the right) or press the **Ctrl+F7** key combination. You will see the Define Graph dialog box, similar to the one presented in Figure 10–9.

As you see in this figure, the name of the table is displayed in the upper left part of the screen. By clicking the down arrow icon next to the table name you can display a listing of all the fields in the table.

In the Data Type region you have to select one of the data types provided by Paradox for Windows. Tabular is the default data type. This type graphs the contents of a field directly without performing any summary calculations. This data type would be useful with an Answer table that already has calculated summary data. If your data series are not in proper order, use the **Ctrl+R** command

Figure 10–9
The Define Graph dialog box

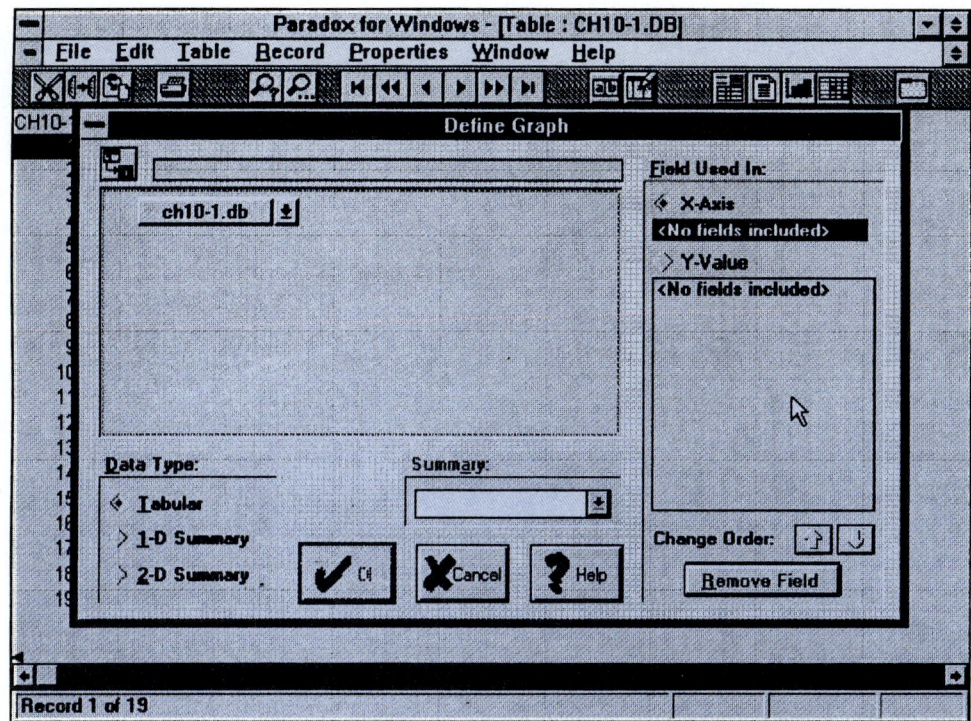

mary data. If your data series are not in proper order, use the **Ctrl+R** command to create the right order first, and then proceed with the graph design process.

The 1-D Summary option graphs the results of a one-dimensional crosstab. The 2-D Summary option graphs the results of a two-dimensional crosstab.

The X-Axis option specifies the field whose values will be used in the X-axis. Paradox for Windows allows only one X-axis field. The Y-Value option specifies the field(s) whose values will be used in the Y-axis.

The Change Order up or down arrow moves a selected field up or down in a list so that the series appears in the desired order. Remove Field is used to remove a selected field from a list.

10–8   PARADOX FOR WINDOWS GRAPH ELEMENTS

Like other graphic software, Paradox for Windows uses its own terminology in creating and manipulating different graphs. You should become familiar with the following terms (see Figure 10–10):

- The graph area is the large rectangular area containing one of the graphs, such as the pie, stacked bar, or line graph, generated by Paradox for Windows.
- The frame is the rectangle surrounding the graph area.
- Bars are solid or shaded rectangles that represent data points. Bars can be horizontal or vertical and can be stacked on top of one another, clustered, or separate.
- Axes. The horizontal line along the bottom edge and the vertical line along the left edge of the graph are called the X-axis and Y-axis, respectively. All

Figure 10–10
Paradox for Windows graph elements

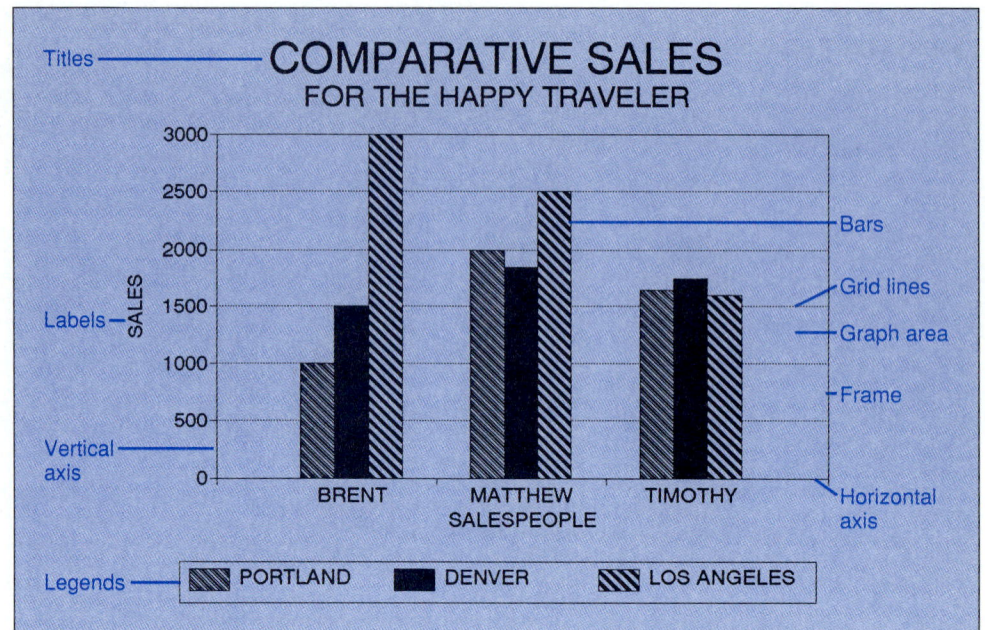

- Axes. The horizontal line along the bottom edge and the vertical line along the left edge of the graph are called the X-axis and Y-axis, respectively. All graphs except the pie graph have X- and Y-axes.
- Titles are the information displayed above the graph area, below the X-axis, or along the Y-axis.
- A **data series** includes different categories of data elements, for example, total sales in seven sales regions.
- Tick marks and grid lines divide each axis into segments of equal length. Tick marks are short line segments along the X-axis. Grid lines extend across the entire width or height of the graph area.
- Labels are the information along the X- and Y-axes. Labels describe the data graphed at the corresponding tick marks.
- **Legends** are various colored lines, shading, and markers used to illustrate multiple data series in the same graph. By studying the legends you can interpret the graph more easily.
- Scale is the distance in equal units of measurement between the tick marks or grid lines.

Figure 10–10 shows Paradox for Windows graph elements.

10–9   CREATING A BAR GRAPH

Open the sample table in Figure 10–1 and do the following:

1. Click on the Quick Graph button. The Define Graph dialog box will be displayed (Figure 10–9).

Figure 10–11
Sample Bar graph

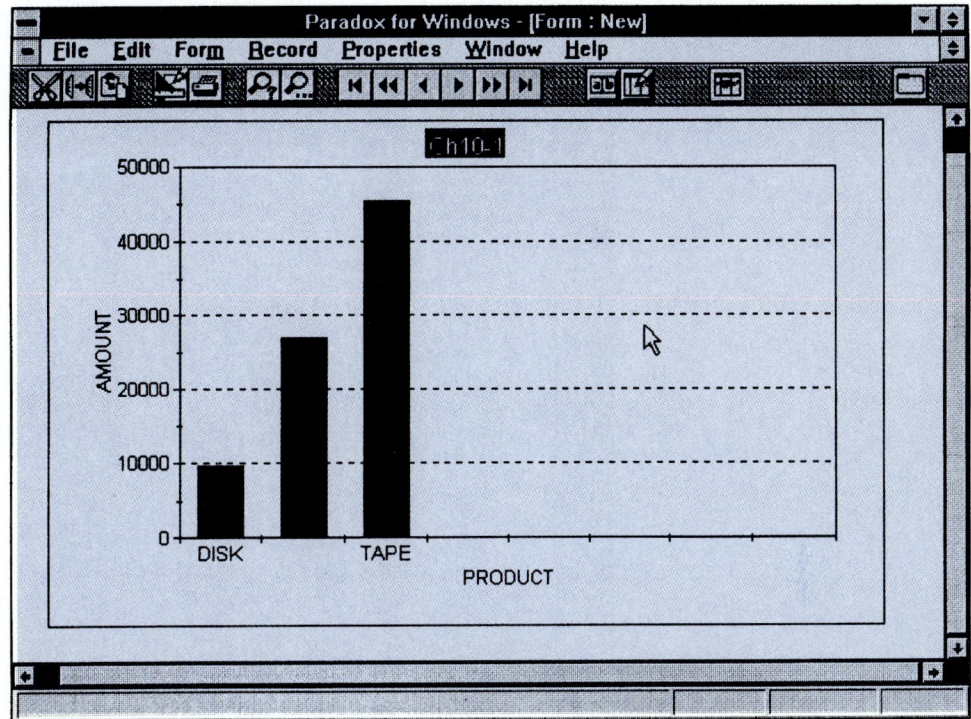

2. Click on the 1-D Summary button. For X-Axis enter *PRODUCT* and for Y-Value enter *AMOUNT*.

3. Click on OK. Click on the maximize icon. Your screen should be similar to the one displayed in Figure 10–11. (Please notice that the MONITOR label did not show up on the X-axis because it is too long!)

As you see in this figure, Paradox for Windows displays the table name as the title for the graph and displays the labels for the X and Y axes as the names of the two selected fields.

Paradox for Windows provides a great deal of flexibility for modification of all the different graph elements. To perform any modification, click on the Design button (fourth button from the left) in the SpeedBar, then right-click on any desired section of the graph. For example, to change the title of the graph in the design screen, right-click the title. To change various elements of the entire graph, right-click inside the graph border. The process of modification of the important graph elements is explained in the next few pages.

10–10 DISPLAYING THE GRAPH PROPERTIES

While the graph is displayed click on the Design button to switch to the Form design window. Right-click anywhere inside the graph border. You will see a screen similar to the one presented in Figure 10–12.

As you see in this figure, using the menu you can modify various graph elements. For example, if you click the Graph Type option you will see a screen similar to the one displayed in Figure 10–13. Click on the desired graph type to see the new graph.

Figure 10–12
The Entire Graph Properties menu

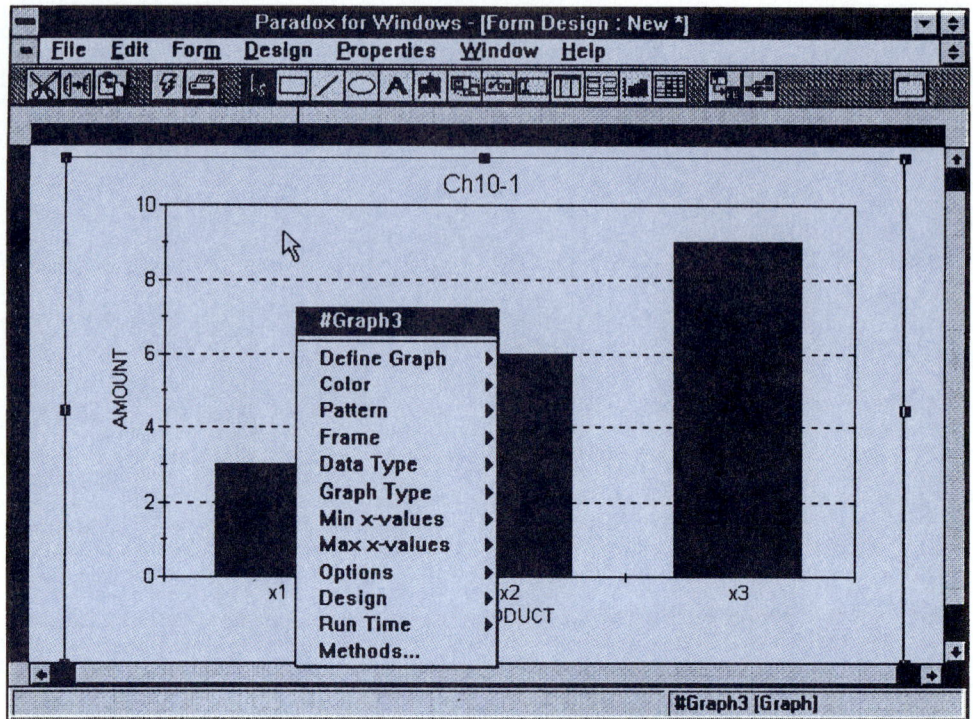

Figure 10–13
Paradox for Windows Graph Type menu

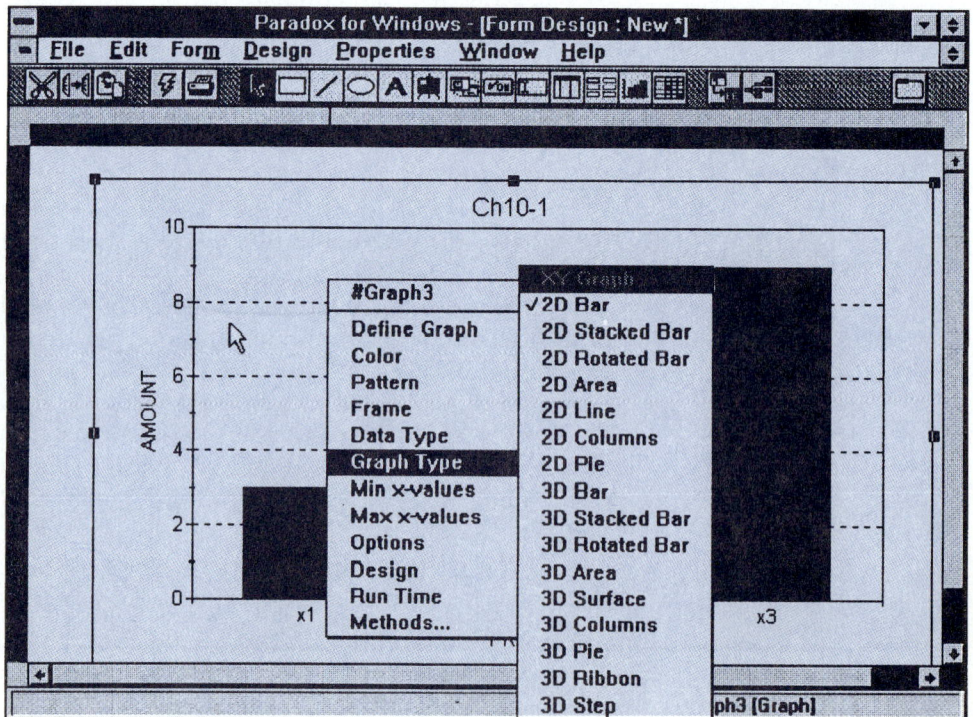

10–11   CREATING A PIE CHART

Open the table in Figure 10–1. We want to construct a pie chart that shows the percentages of total sales generated by each product. Follow these steps:

1. Using the File Open Table command, open table CH10–1.
2. Click on the Quick Graph button in the SpeedBar.
3. In the Define Graph dialog box click on 1-D Summary.
4. For X-Axis enter *PRODUCT*. For Y-Value enter *AMOUNT*.
5. Click on OK.
6. Click on the maximize icon to enlarge the graph window to the maximum size. At this point your screen should be similar to the one displayed in Figure 10–11.
7. Click on the Design button in the SpeedBar.
8. Right-click inside the graph border to display the entire Graph Properties menu. You will see a screen similar to the one displayed in Figure 10–12.
9. Click on Graph Type (see Figure 10–13).
10. Click on 2D Pie. At this point your screen should be similar to the one presented in Figure 10–14.

Suppose you want to enter a new title for this graph. Position the mouse pointer on the graph title (on CH10–1). As soon as you see a small up arrow, right-click. The Title box is displayed (see Figure 10–15). Click on Title and then click on Text. Enter *SALES BREAKDOWN BY PRODUCT* and click on OK. Position the mouse pointer on the new title and right-click. Click on Subtitle and then click on Text. Type *For 1994* and click on OK. Your new graph should be similar to the one displayed in Figure 10–16.

Figure 10–14
Sample pie chart

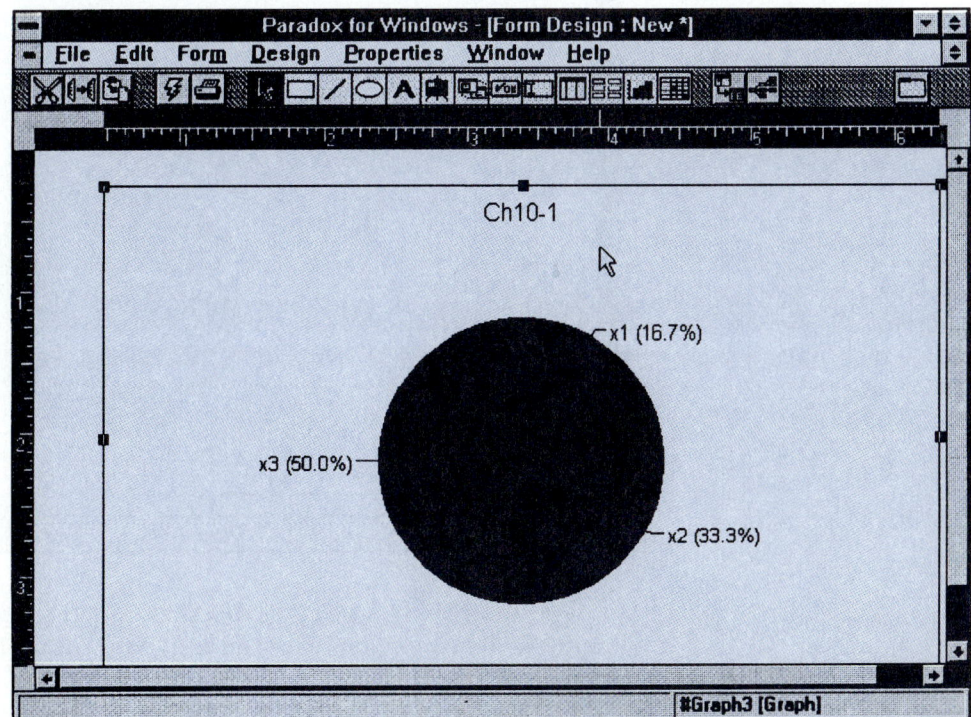

Figure 10–15
The Title box

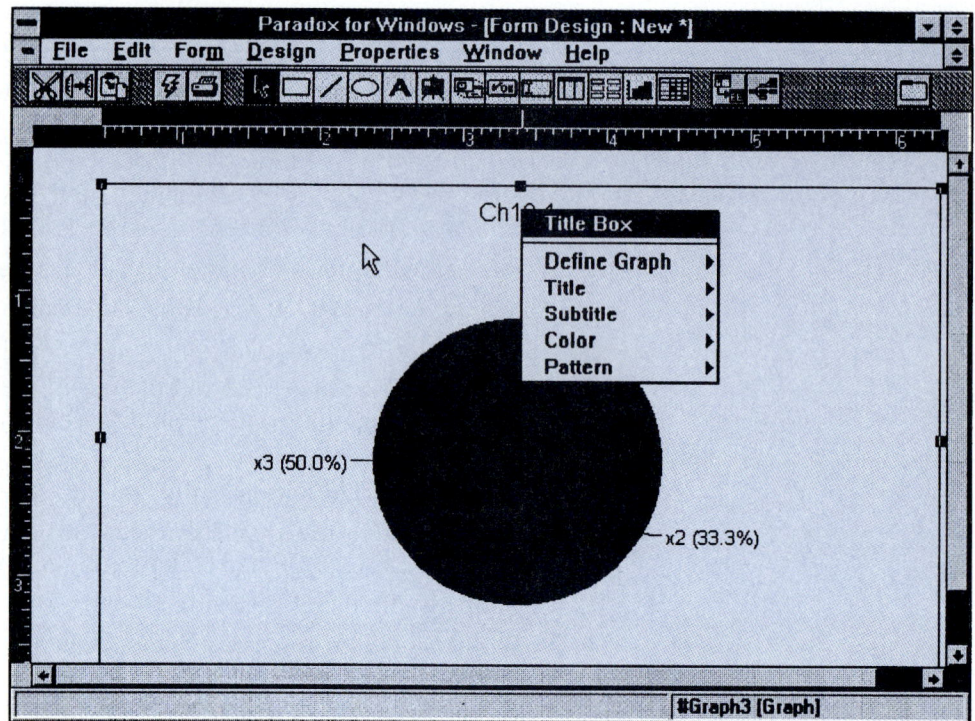

Figure 10–15
The Title box

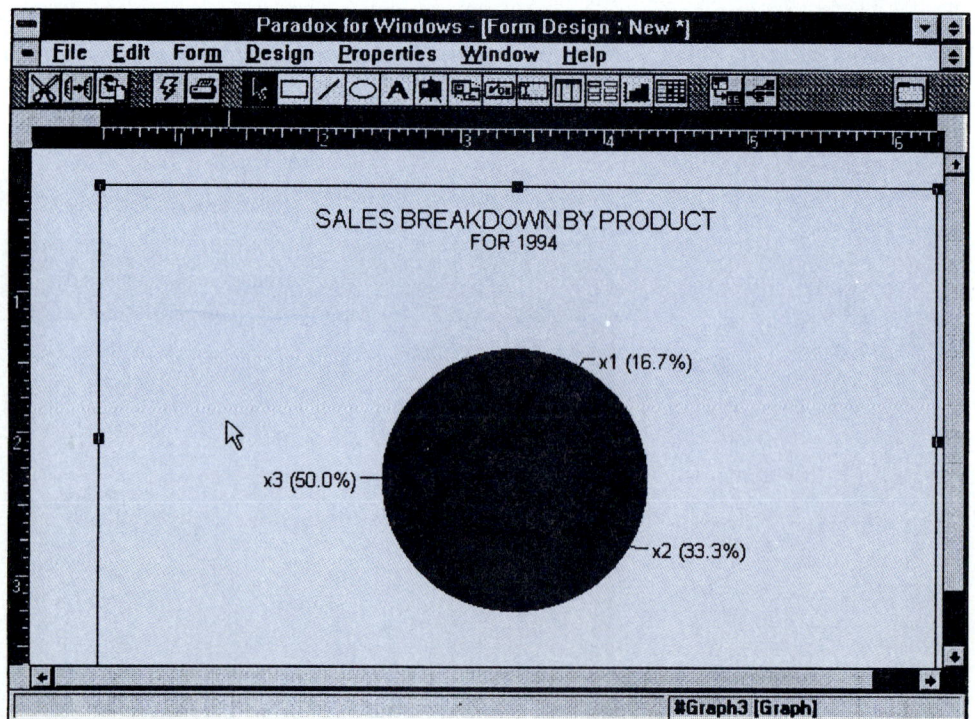

Figure 10–16
New title for the pie chart

To explode a piece of this pie chart (to draw attention to it), right-click on the desired piece and click on Explode. Figure 10–17 shows an **exploded pie chart**.

Figure 10–18 illustrates a 3D Bar graph for the same data.

Figure 10–17
Exploded pie chart

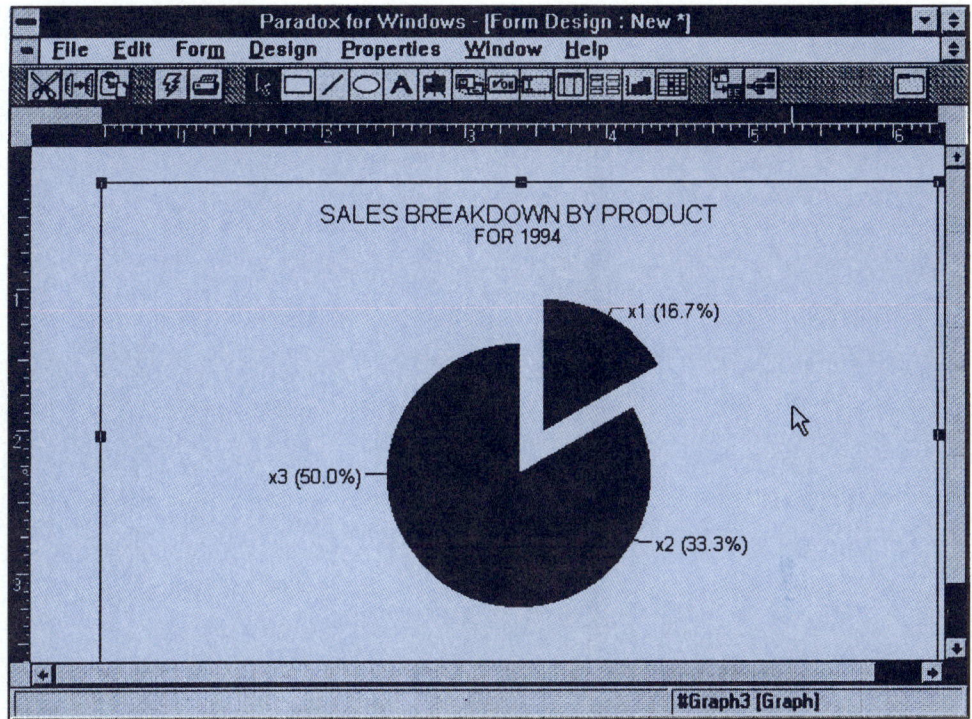

Figure 10–18
3D bar graph

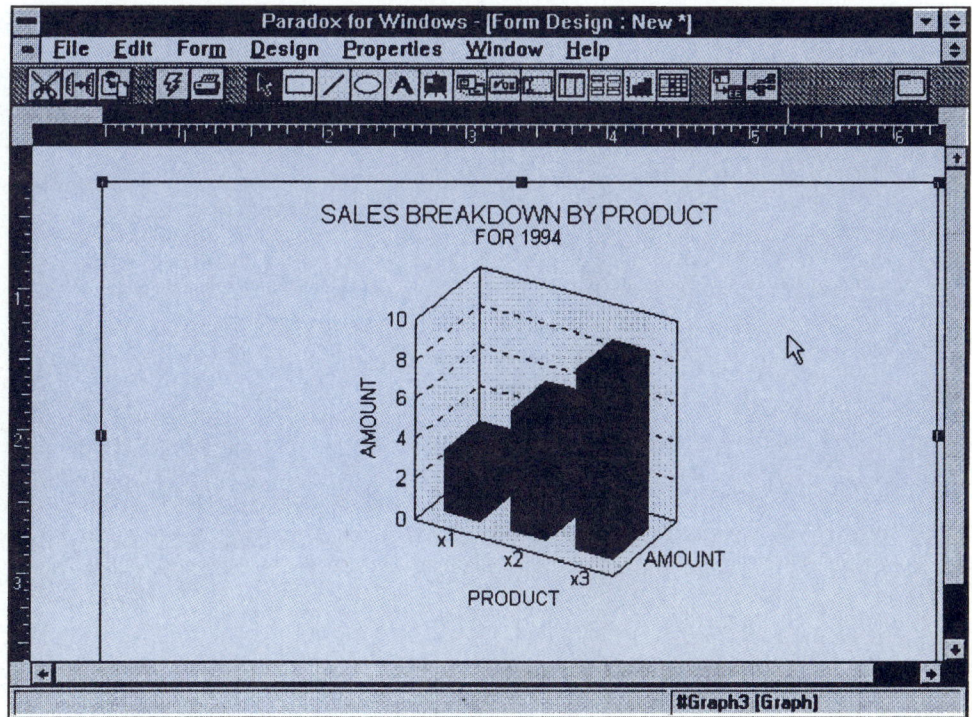

Figure 10–19 illustrates a 2D Columns graph for the same data.
Figure 10–20 illustrates a 3D Pie chart for the same data.
Figure 10–21 illustrates a 2D Line graph for the same data.
Figure 10–22 illustrates a 3D Area graph for the same data.

Figure 10–19
2D Columns graph

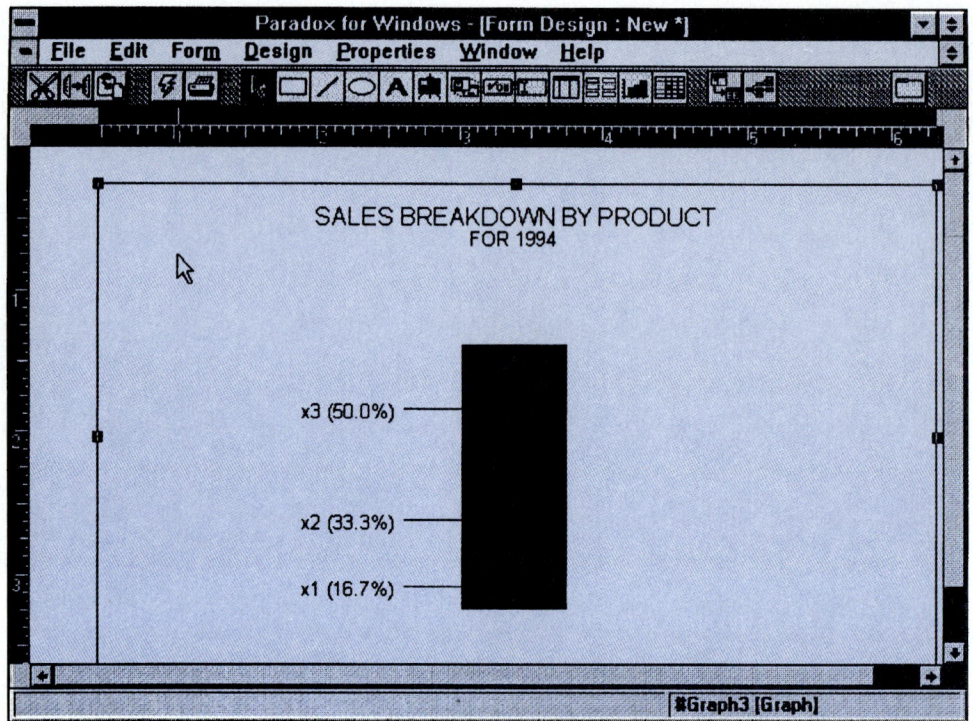

Figure 10–20
3D pie chart

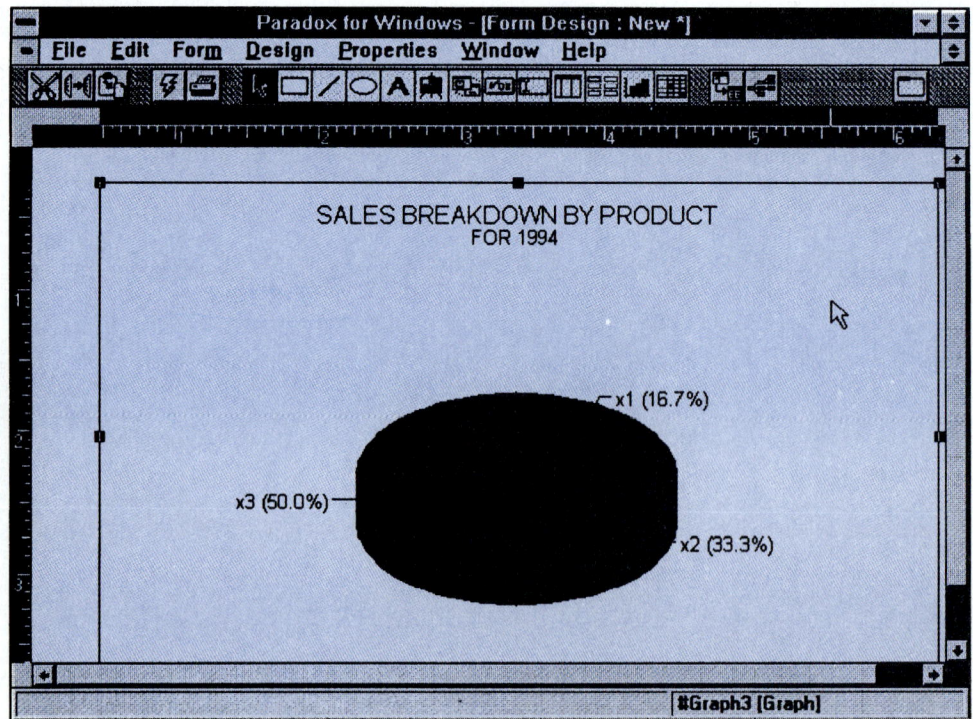

Figure 10–21
2D line graph

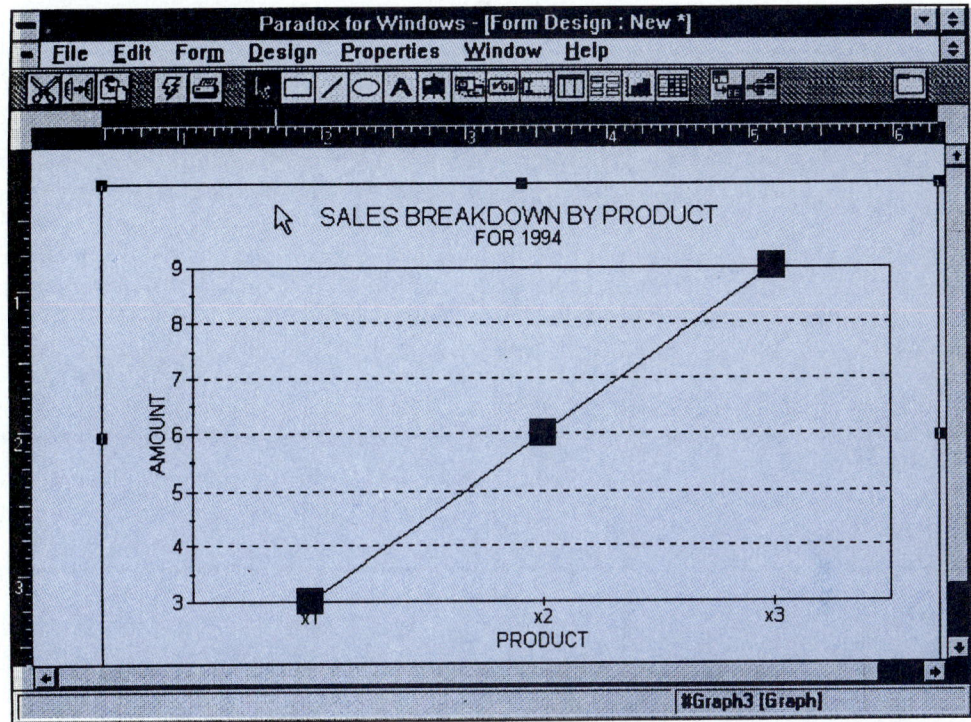

Figure 10–22
3D area graph

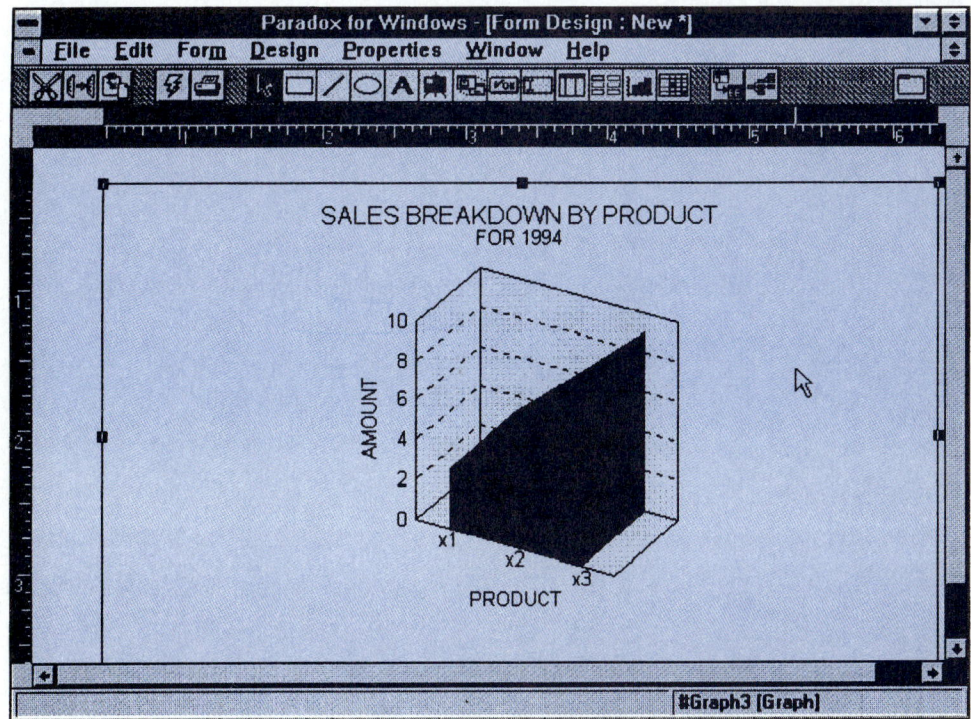

10–12   SAVING AND RETRIEVING GRAPH SPECIFICATIONS

To save the specifications of a graph to your disk for future use, in the design screen choose the File Save or File Save As command. Type in a name up to eight characters, then click on OK. If you are not saving to your default drive and directory, you must also specify the desired drive and/or directory path along with the file name.

To retrieve a saved graph, click on File Open Form, then specify the graph name, and then click on OK. Remember, graphs are saved as forms with the FSL extension.

10–13   PRINTING GRAPHS

To print a graph while the graph is displayed, select File Print from any menu and click on OK. The graph will be printed as it is displayed on the screen.

SUMMARY

This chapter provided a detailed discussion of crosstabs and graphic capabilities in Paradox for Windows. The chapter presented an example of popular Paradox for Windows graph types. The processes of saving, retrieving, and printing graphs were explained.

REVIEW QUESTIONS

*These questions are answered in Appendix A.

1. What is a crosstab?
2. How many types of crosstabs are supported by Paradox for Windows?
*3. Which summary operators can be used with crosstabs?
4. How many different types of graphs can be generated by Paradox for Windows?
5. What is the application of each graph type?
*6. What is the difference between a line graph and an XY graph?
7. Which key combination is used to create a crosstab?
*8. Which key combination is used to generate a graph from the crosstab?
9. What is the default graph title?
*10. How do you change the default graph title to a title of your choice?
11. How do you display graph properties?
12. How do you display the Graph Type pull-down menu?
13. What is the default title for the Y-axis? For the X-axis?
14. What are some of the Paradox for Windows graph elements?
15. What are legends? Why are legends important?
16. Where in the graph area are legends displayed?
17. How do you start the Define Graph dialog box?
*18. What are the options in the Define Graph dialog box?
19. Can you change the pattern of the pieces of a pie chart? If yes, how?
20. How do you explode a pie chart?
21. Why might exploding a pie chart be helpful?
22. How do you modify graph titles?

23. How do you print a graph?

*24. What is the file extension when you save a graph?

25. How do you save the graph specifications?

26. How do you retrieve a graph?

27. How are crosstabs and subtotal reports similar?

HANDS-ON EXPERIENCE

1. Using the database table presented in Figure 10–1, generate as many different crosstab and graph types as possible.

2. Using the table presented in Figure 10–23, do the following:
   a. Generate a pie chart.
   b. Generate an exploded pie chart.

3. Using the database table presented in Figure 10–23, generate a rotated bar graph.

4. Create the first and second titles for the graphs in question 3. For the first line type *SALES*. For the second line type *FOR 1994-1995*.

5. Using the database table shown in Figure 10–23, generate a line graph.

6. Using the right-click technique, investigate the different graph properties.

KEY TERMS

Crosstab	Graph types (line, bar, three-dimensional bar, rotated bar, stacked bar, XY, pie, and area)	Legend
Data series		
Exploded pie charts		

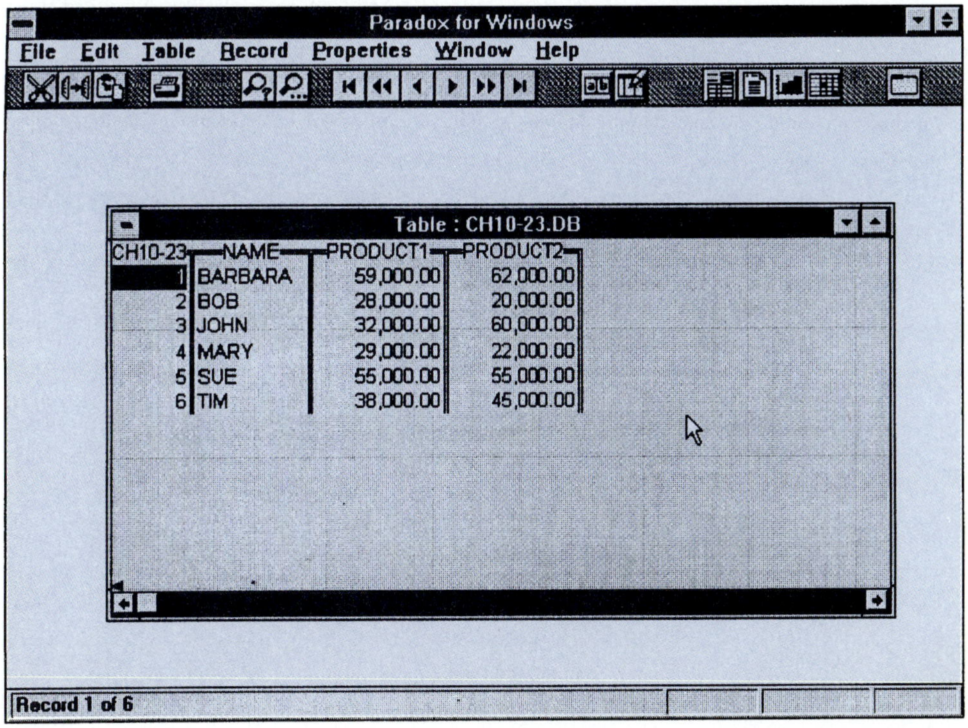

Figure 10–23
Sample database table

KEY COMMANDS

Ctrl+F7 (to generate a
graph)

Ctrl+R (to switch or rotate
columns of a table)

File Print (to print a
graph)

MISCONCEPTIONS AND SOLUTIONS

Misconception   You are trying to generate a graph from a table but the columns of the
table are not in the order that you want. You may think you have to construct the table
from scratch.

Solution   By using the Ctrl+R (Rotate) command, switch the columns around.

Misconception   You click on OK at the end of your graph session, and you think your
graph has been saved. Paradox for Windows does not save the graph specification to disk
when you click on OK.

Solution   From the displayed menu, select File Save or File Save As.

ARE YOU READY TO MOVE ON?

Multiple Choice

1. How many different graphs can Paradox for Windows generate?
   a. 17
   b. 16
   c. 15
   d. 14
   e. 13

2. The Define Crosstab dialog box includes all of the following except:
   a. Column
   b. Categories
   c. Graph Type
   d. Summaries
   e. Change Order

3. To generate a graph from a crosstab, you must press:
   a. Alt+X
   b. Alt+B
   c. Graph Image
   d. Ctrl+F7
   e. none of the above

4. To change the default graph title, which menu do you use?
   a. Graph Title Box Properties
   b. Graph Legend Box Properties
   c. Entire Graph Properties
   d. Graph X-Axis Properties
   e. none of the above

5. Paradox for Windows allows up to how many titles on the top of each graph?
   a. five
   b. three

  c. four
  d. one
  e. two

6. Using crosstabs you can use all of the following summary operators except:
   a. Average
   b. Variance
   c. Sum
   d. Count
   e. Max

7. By default, what does Paradox for Windows assign as the graph title?
   a. sum
   b. average
   c. sales
   d. table name
   e. year

8. To switch the columns of your database table you must use:
   a. Ctrl+S
   b. Ctrl+R
   c. Ctrl+W
   d. Ctrl+M
   e. none of the above

9. Paradox for Windows graph elements include all of the following except:
   a. graph area
   b. frame
   c. titles
   d. axes
   e. all are included

10. The Define Graph dialog box includes all of the following except:
    a. Tabular
    b. 1-D Summary
    c. Graph Title
    d. 2-D Summary
    e. Y-Value

True/False

1. Using Paradox for Windows, you cannot generate stacked bar graphs.
2. The Graph Type option in the Graph Properties menu allows you to change the currently specified graph type.
3. Pie charts cannot be exploded.
4. You can either view a graph on the screen or you can print it through the printer.
5. Paradox for Windows allows up to two titles on the top of your graph.
6. By default, pie charts are presented as percentages.
7. Paradox for Windows does not allow you to generate three-dimensional graphs.
8. Paradox for Windows graph specifications can be saved for future use.
9. Paradox for Windows supports only one-dimensional crosstabs.
10. Only one piece of a pie chart can be exploded.

ANSWERS

Multiple Choice		True/False	
1.	a	1.	F
2.	c	2.	T
3.	d	3.	F
4.	a	4.	T
5.	e	5.	T
6.	b	6.	T
7.	d	7.	F
8.	b	8.	T
9.	e	9.	F
10.	c	10.	F

Advanced Features

11

11–1   INTRODUCTION

This chapter presents some of the advanced features of Paradox for Windows. It introduces the CHANGETO operator for changing the contents of your database tables, discusses building multitable queries, and explains linking different tables with common fields. The chapter also shows you how to perform calculations on multiple tables.

11–2   MAKING GLOBAL CHANGES WITH THE CHANGETO OPERATOR

The **CHANGETO** operator performs the same task that the Find and Replace command performs in the majority of word processing programs. With the CHANGETO operator you can change the contents of a specific field or fields or the contents of the entire database table. Suppose that in the sample database table presented in Figure 11–1 you want to increase the salary of all the employees by 20 percent. To do this, follow these steps:

1. From the desktop, click on File New Query, select CH11–1, and click on OK. The Query form is displayed.
2. Press the Tab key twice to move to the Salary field.
3. Press the **F5** key (to give an example). Then type *SALARY* followed by a comma. Notice that SALARY is displayed in reverse video.
4. Type *CHANGETO* followed by one space. Notice that as you type, the width of the field is extended to accommodate your data.
5. Press the F5 key and type *SALARY*1.20*. At this point your screen should be similar to the one displayed in Figure 11–2.

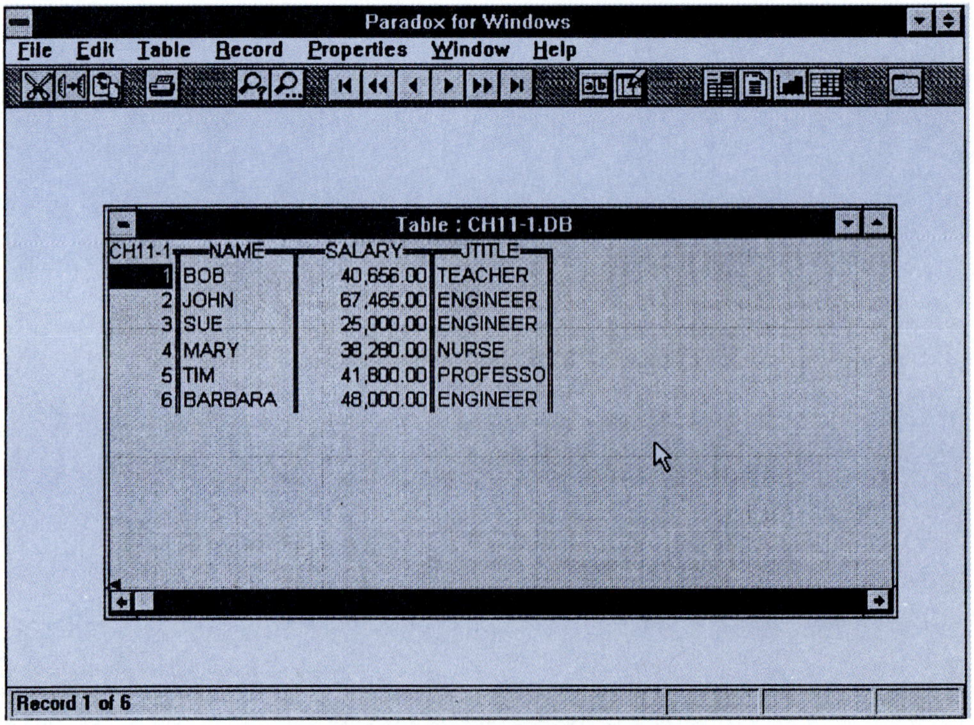

Figure 11–1
Sample database table

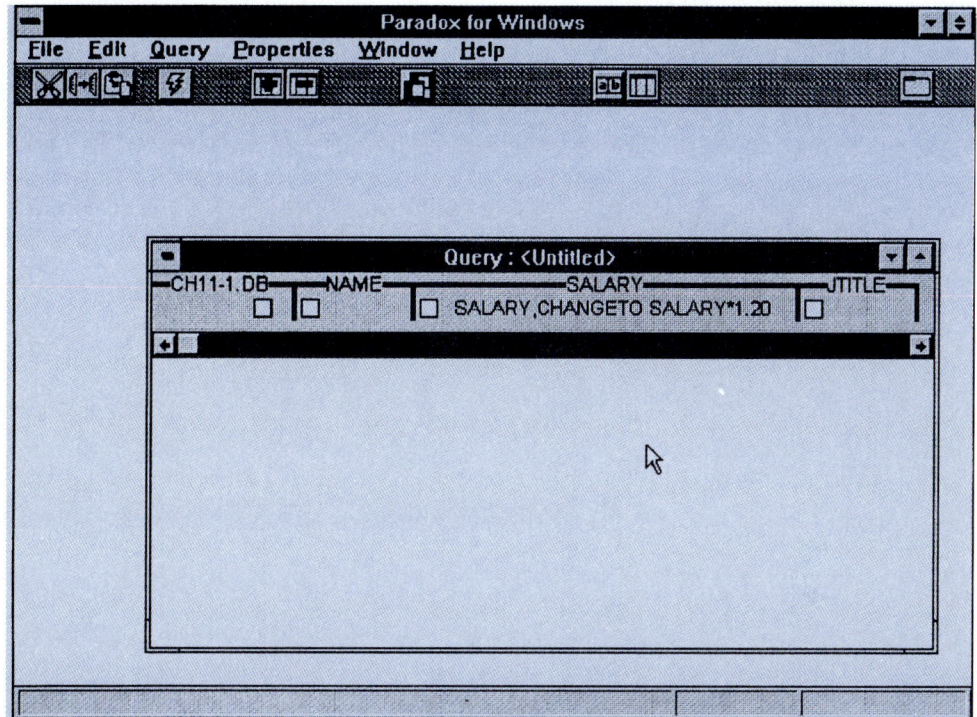

6. Click the Run Query button in the SpeedBar (fourth button from the left). Your screen should be similar to the one displayed in Figure 11–3.

As soon as you click the Run Query button, you are presented with a CHANGED table. The CHANGED table displays all the records that have been

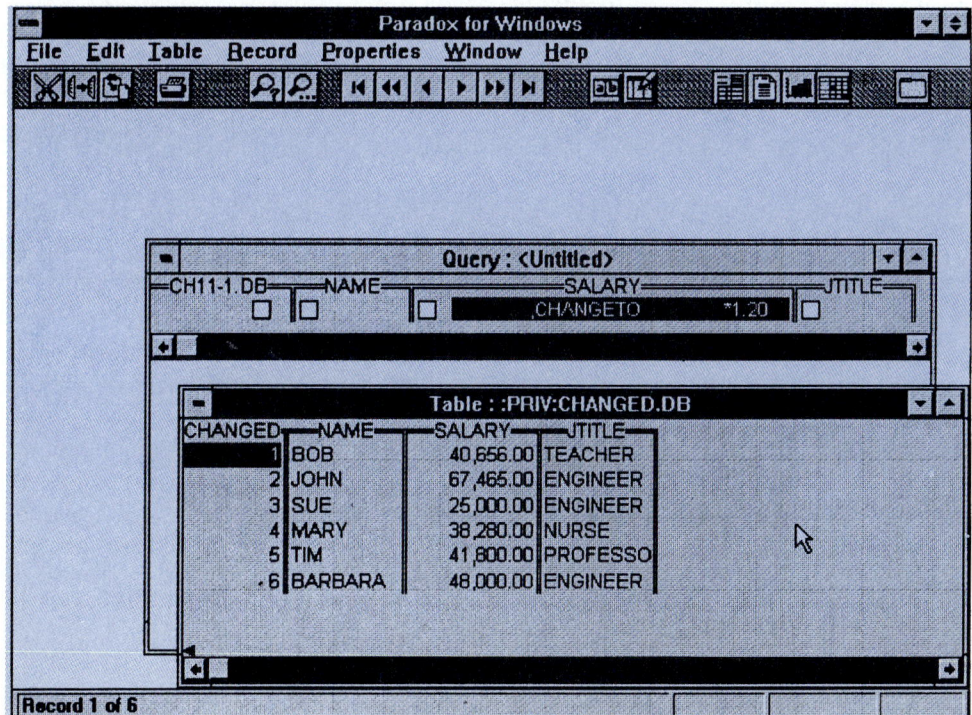

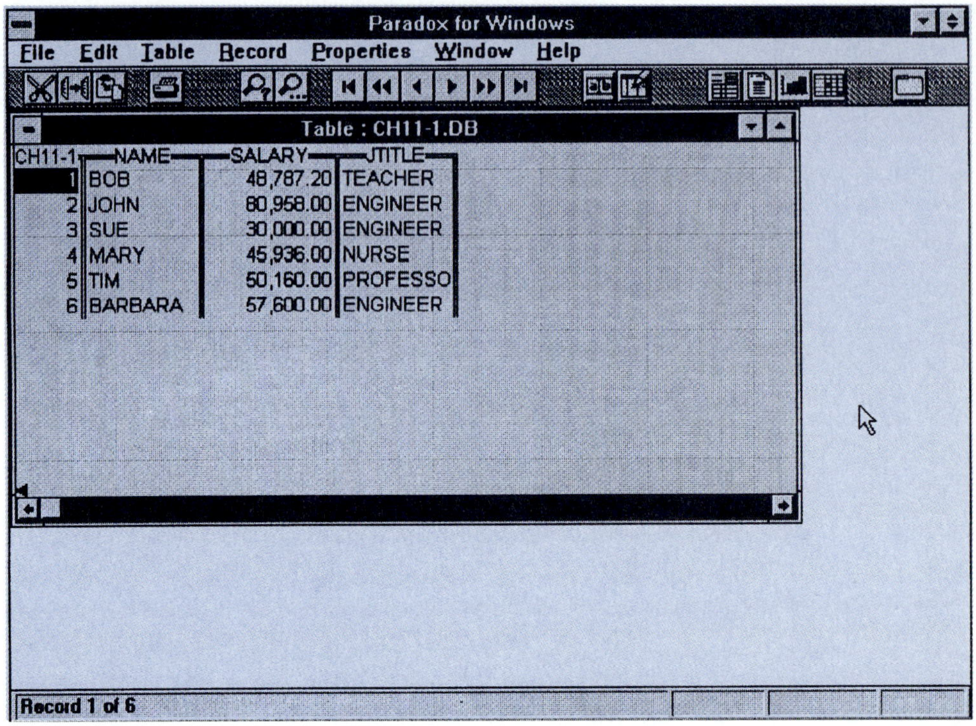

Figure 11–4
The new table CH11–1 after the salary increase

changed with their original values. In our case, all the records are changed. If you are not satisfied with the modifications, you can use the File Utilities Copy command to copy the CHANGED table to the original table. If only the selected records are changed, you can use the Add option from the File Utilities menu to add the CHANGED table to the original table. Your table must have a key for you to see the correct result of the Add command.

The CHANGED table is a temporary table. It will be replaced by the next CHANGED table as soon as you execute another CHANGETO operation.

If you view the CH11–1 table (in Figure 11–4), you will see that, indeed, all the salaries have been increased by 20 percent.

11–3   CHANGING SELECTED RECORDS USING THE CHANGETO OPERATOR

Suppose that in the table presented in Figure 11–4 (the new CH11-1.DB) you want to increase the salary of all the engineers by 10 percent and of all the teachers or professors by 15 percent, and not raise the salary of other employees. To do this, follow these steps:

1. Click on Window Close All and No to close all the open queries.
2. Click on File New Query.
3. Specify the table name and click on OK. In our case, we specified the table in Figure 11–4 that is saved under CH11–1.
4. Move the cursor to the Salary column and press F5 (to give an example).

5. Type *SALARY1* followed by a comma.

6. Type *CHANGETO* followed by one space.

7. Press the F5 key, then type *SALARY1*1.15.*

8. Move the cursor to the Jtitle column and type *TEACHER OR PROFESSOR.* Since both teachers and professors receive the same raise, we put them in one row.

9. Move the cursor to the Salary column again in the second row and press the F5 key.

10. Type *SALARY2* followed by a comma.

11. Type *CHANGETO* followed by one space. Then press the F5 key and type *SALARY2*1.10.*

12. Move the cursor to the Jtitle column and type *ENGINEER.* At this time, your screen should be similar to Figure 11–5.

13. Click the Run Query button in the SpeedBar. You can also press the **F8** function key. If you view the CH11-1 table (presented in Figure 11–6), you will see that indeed the teachers' and professors' salaries have been increased by 15 percent and the engineers' salaries have been increased by 10 percent.

In this example we used SALARY1 and SALARY2 in the Query form. This might be a bit confusing. You must make these two examples unique. Since you are in the Salary column, Paradox for Windows will consider whatever you type as a variable for Salary. We changed the second one to Salary2, to make it unique. In place of this variable, you could type anything you want.

Figure 11–5
The completed query form

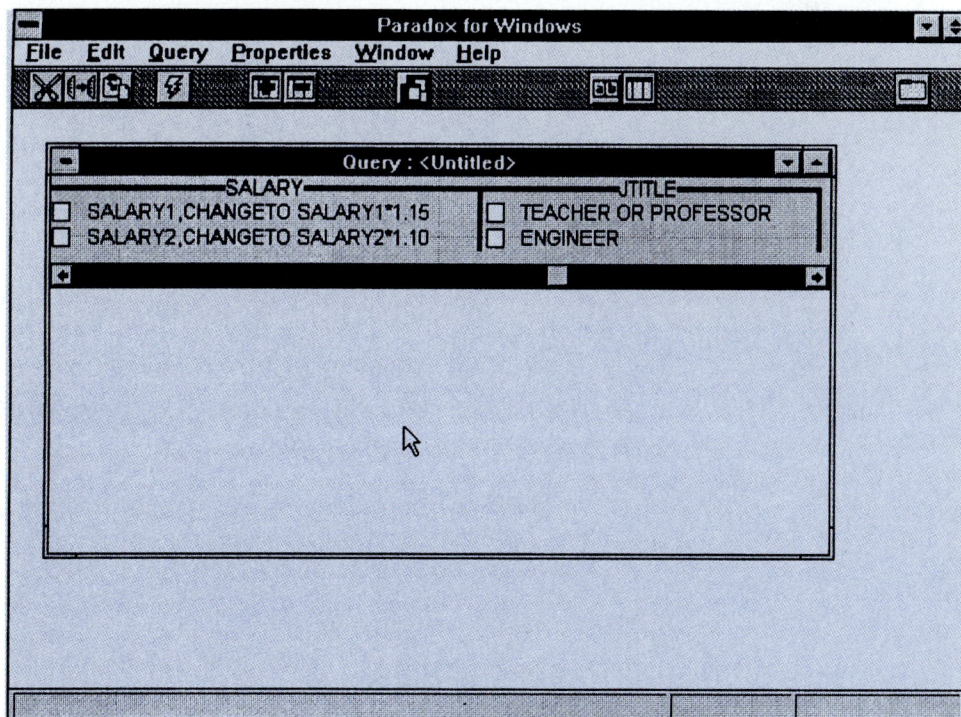

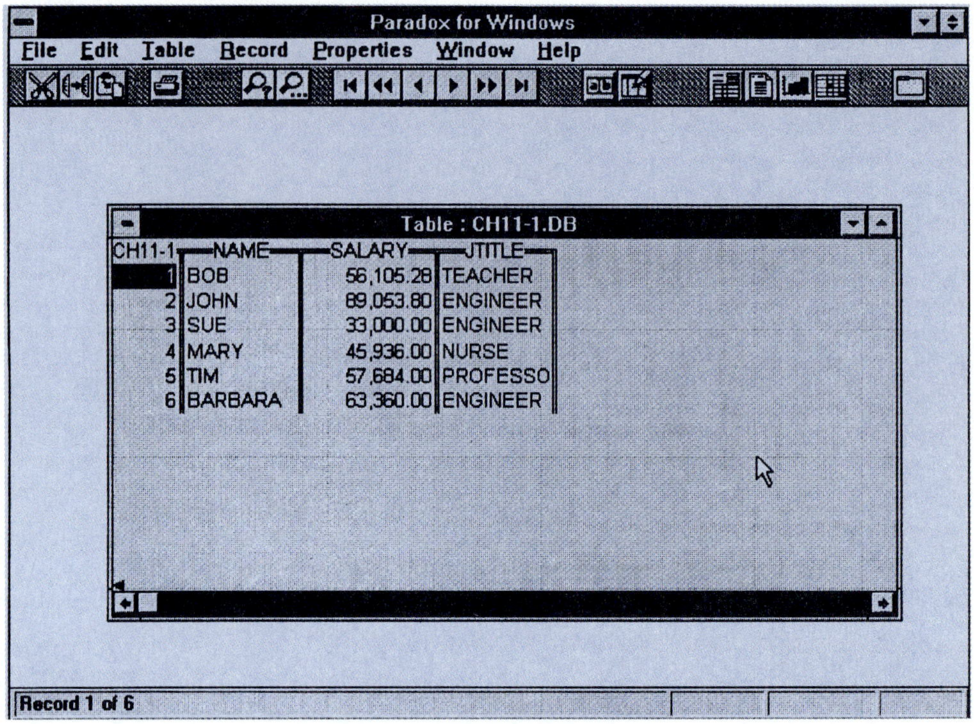

Figure 11–6
Table CH11–1 after the salary increase for teachers, professors, and engineers

11–4   USING THE CHANGETO OPERATOR WITH ALPHANUMERIC DATA

The CHANGETO operator can be used with alphanumeric data as well as with numeric data. Let us say in table CH11-1 presented in Figure 11–6, you would like to change the job title of all the engineers to STAFF. To do this, follow these steps:

1. Click on Window Close All No to close on the open queries.
2. Click on File New Query.
3. Identify your table. We selected table CH11–1 presented in Figure 11–6. Click on OK.
4. Move the cursor to the Jtitle column and type *ENGINEER* followed by a comma.
5. Type *CHANGETO STAFF*.
6. Click on the Run Query button. If you view your table, you see that all engineers have been changed to staff. Figure 11–7 shows all the changed records.

Please notice that while working with alphanumeric data you do not need to press the F5 key to provide an example. Just type your example element followed by a comma, then the CHANGETO operator, and then the new data item.

11–5   BUILDING MULTITABLE QUERIES

Often you may want to create a report based on several tables. Paradox for Windows, through its **multiple query** operations, allows you to **link tables** to perform such tasks. Let us walk through an example. Figure 11–8 is a sample student file.

Figure 11–7
Changing the alphanumeric data using the CHANGETO operator

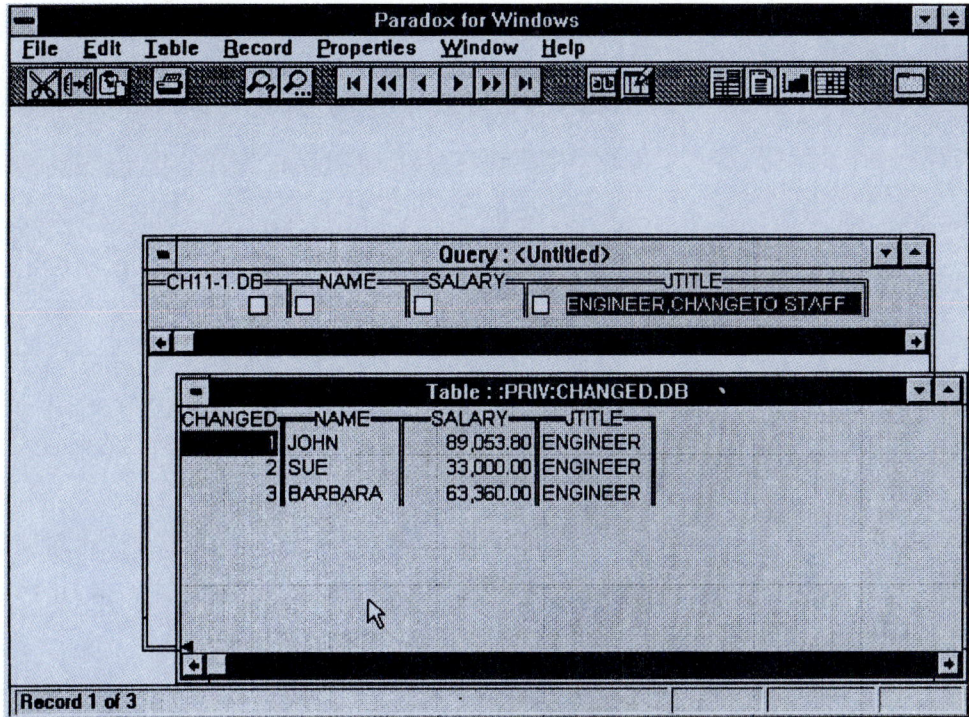

Figure 11–8
Sample student file

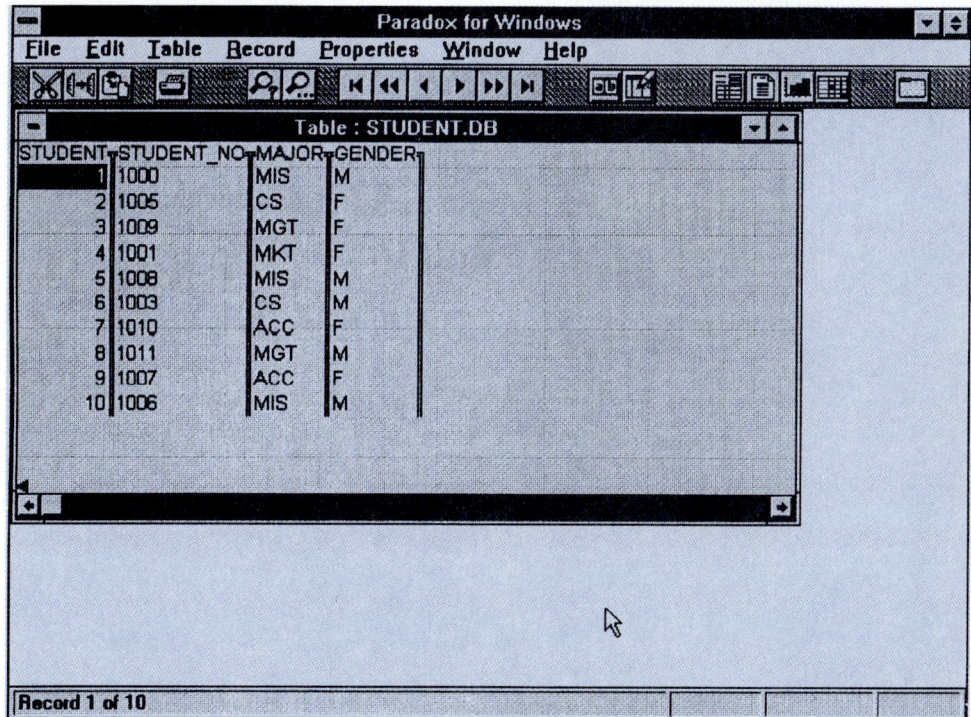

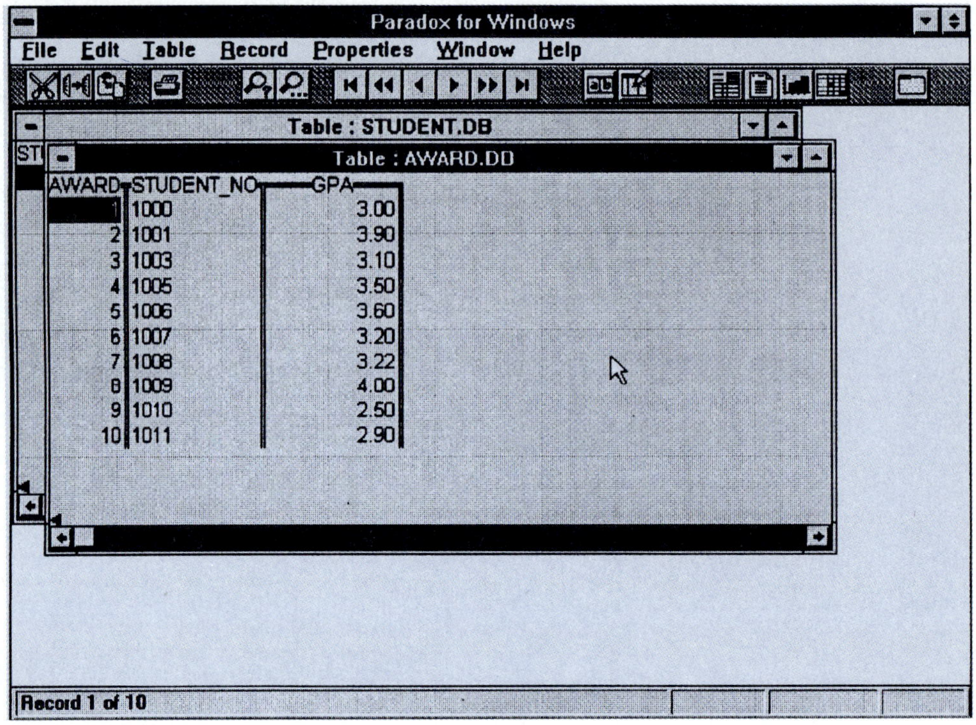

Figure 11–9
Sample award file

Figure 11–9 is a sample award file. You would like to create a table that borrows Major and Gender from the student file and GPA from the award file.

Files to be linked must include a common field. In our example, the common field is the STUDENT_NO. It is up to you to include or not include the common field in the Answer table. Follow these steps:

1. Double-click the control menu box to close all the open tables and queries one by one. You can also click on Window and then click the Close All option to close all the open tables and queries.

2. Click on File New Query.

3. Highlight STUDENT and click on OK.

4. Click on Query and then on Add Table. Double-click the AWARD file. Now the Query screen includes two queries (see Figure 11–10).

5. Press the **F6** key to put check marks in all fields in STUDENT.DB and put a check mark in the GPA field of AWARD.DB.

6. Click on the Join Tables button (fourth button from the right) in the Speed-Bar and click in the STUDENT_NO column of the STUDENT.DB file.

7. Click in the STUDENT_NO column of AWARD.DB. You will see EG01 in the STUDENT_NO field of both tables. At this point your screen should be similar to the one displayed in Figure 11–11.

8. Click on the Run Query button.

As soon as you click on Run Query, the Answer table is created (see Figure 11–12). As you see, the two tables have been joined based on the common key, which is the STUDENT_NO.

You can remove a table from the Query form. To do this click on the Remove Table option in the Query menu. As soon as you do this the Remove

Figure 11–10
Query screen with two blank query images

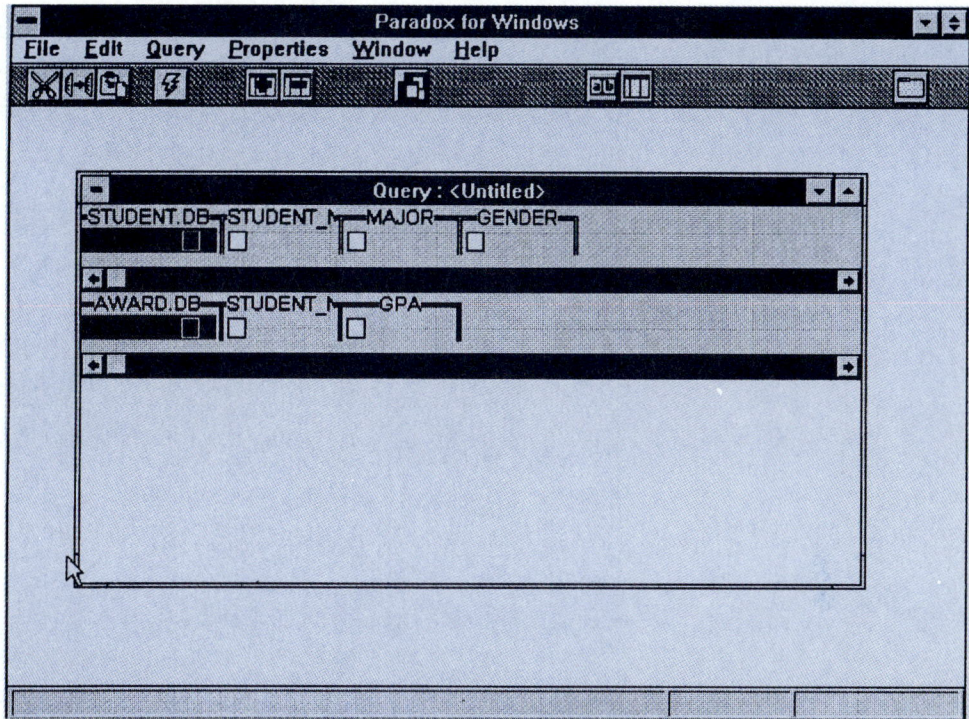

Figure 11–11
Query screen with common fields linked

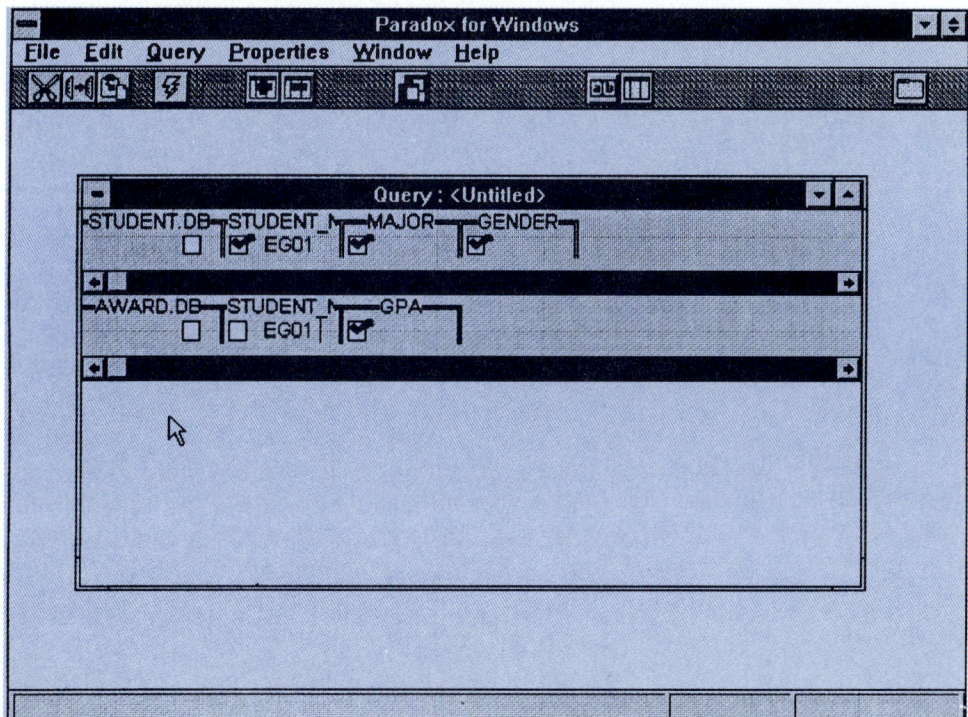

Figure 11–12
The Student and Award tables are
joined in the Answer table

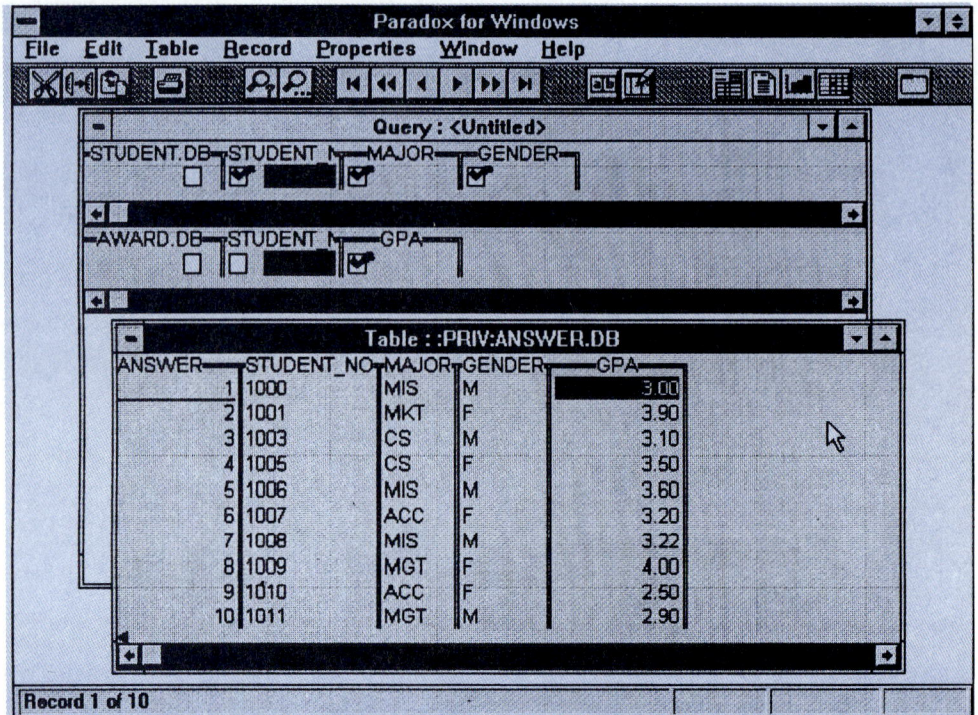

Table dialog box is displayed. Click on the desired table, then click on OK. The
selected table is removed from the Query table.

11–6   IMPORTANT RULES FOR JOINING TABLES

To perform a successful **join operation**, consider the following rules:

1. The maximum number of tables that can be joined is 24.
2. In a Paradox for Windows query-by-example (QBE), you use an example element to link tables manually. The example element is a unique example that appears in the linking field. The name does not have to match the field type or field name. For example, in an alphanumeric field, you can type *567*, and in a numeric field, you can type *XYZ*. You can also use the Join Tables button in the SpeedBar to enter in the example mode.
3. The order of the tables that you call for the linking is not important; however, fields will be selected from top to bottom and from left to right.
4. The linking field (for example, the STUDENT_NO) does not need to be included in the query.
5. If you want to include the linking field in the Answer table, place a check mark in the linking field of *only one* of the query forms. Otherwise, the Answer table will include the linking field more than once.
6. If other Query forms on the Query screen are not related to your query, Paradox for Windows attempts to link them. Make sure that you close all the unwanted Query forms by double-clicking their control menu box.

11-7   USING LINK OPERATIONS FOR JOINING SELECTED RECORDS

Let us say that in the previous example, you would like to create a report just for MIS majors that includes the STUDENT_NO, MAJOR, GPA, and GENDER. To do this everything stays the same as before, except you type *MIS* in the student query in the MAJOR field. (See Figure 11–13.)

Remember that the relational operators such as AND, OR, and NOT, discussed in Chapter 8, work with multiple tables. For example, to create a query that includes all MIS or MGT majors, all you have to do is to type *MIS OR MGT* in the MAJOR column of the student query form. (See Figure 11–14.)

11-8   PERFORMING CALCULATIONS IN MULTIPLE TABLES

Using the query operation with multiple tables you can perform numeric calculations. Let us walk through one example. Figure 11–15 is a Product table. Figure 11–16 is a Price table. We would like to generate an Answer table that includes Product Name, Quantity, Unit Price, and Total Price of each item. Do the following:

1. Click on Window and then on Close All to close all the open tables and queries.
2. Click on File New Query.
3. Double-click on PRODUCT as the name of the table presented in Figure 11–15.
4. Click on Query Add Table and double-click on PRICE to add it to the query screen. This is the name of the table presented in Figure 11–16.

Figure 11–13
Selecting certain records by using the linking operation

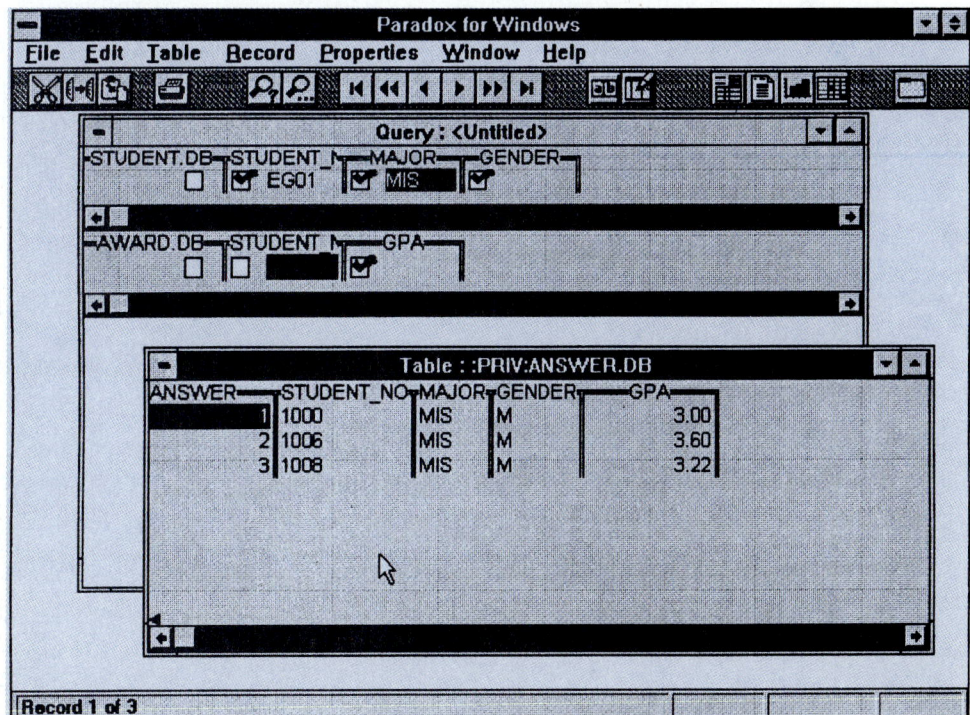

Figure 11–14
All the MIS or MGT majors

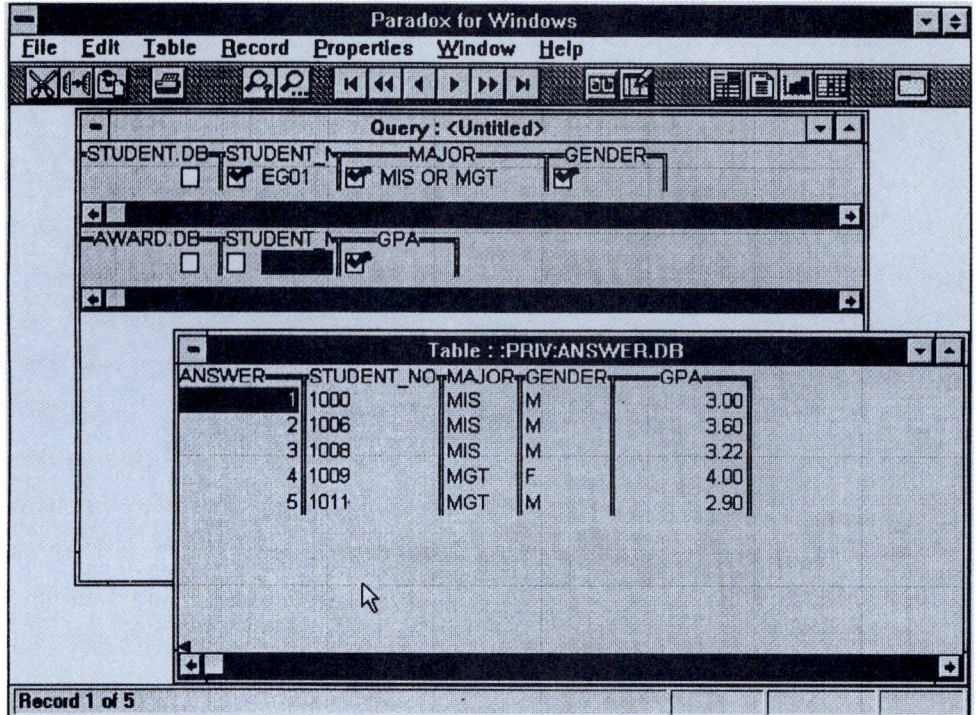

Figure 11–15
The Product table

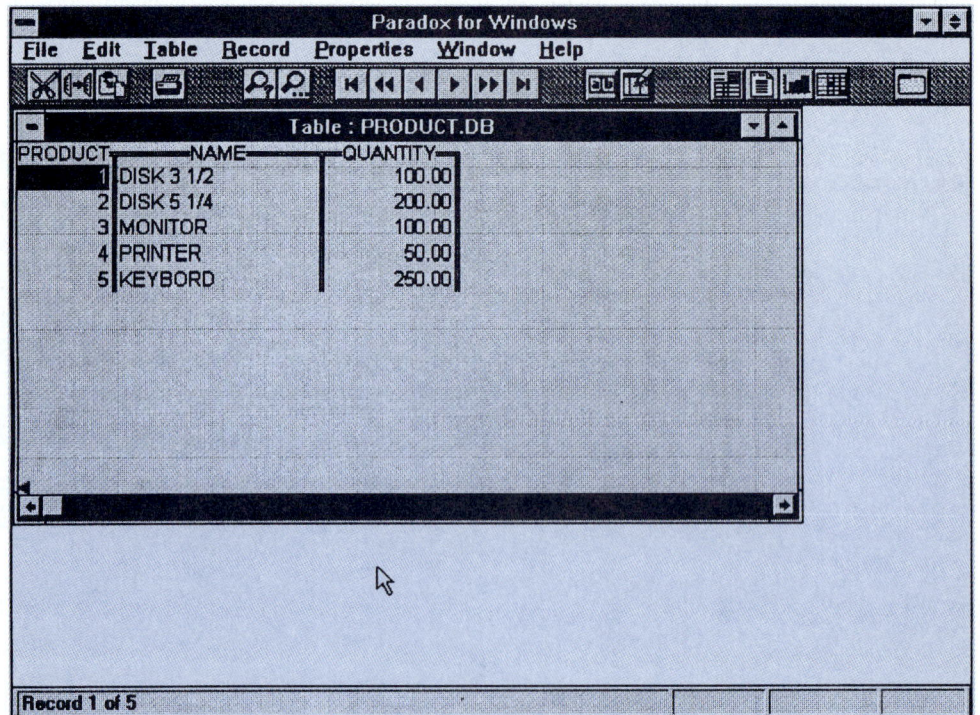

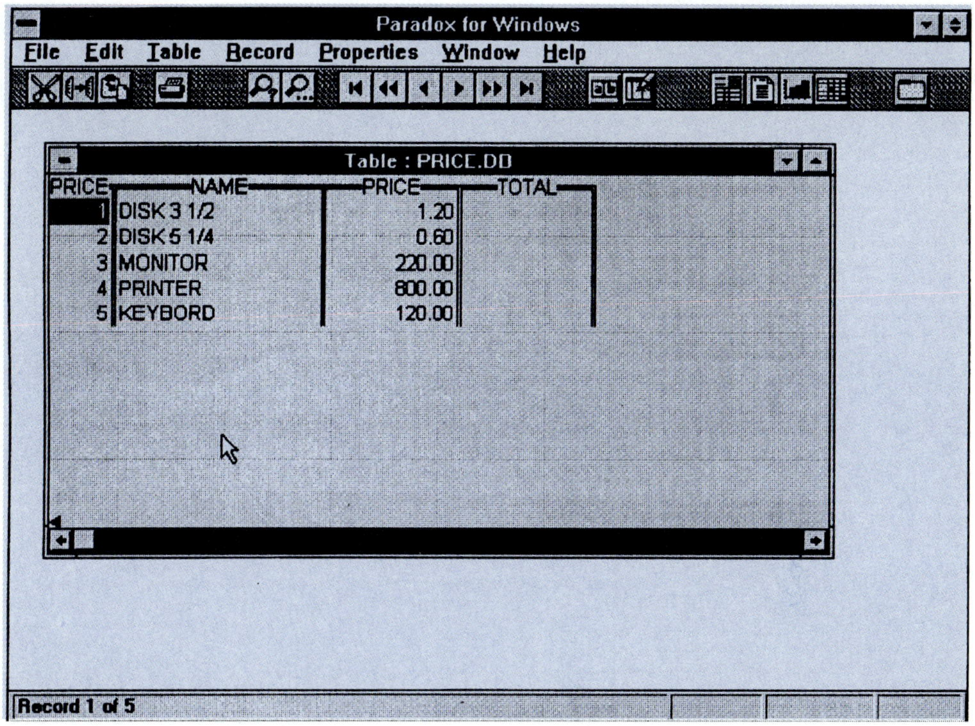

Figure 11–16
The Price table

Figure 11–16
The Price table

5. By pressing the F6 key, place check marks for all the fields of the PROD-UCT.DB table.

6. Move the cursor to the Name column of the PRODUCT.DB table and press F5 (for giving an example). Then type *XXX*. This is used as the link element.

7. Move the cursor to the Quantity column and press the F5 key. Then type *QUANT*. We will use QUANT for our numeric calculations. You could type any other variable.

8. Move the cursor to the Name column of the PRICE.DB table and press the F5 key. Then type *XXX*. Again, this is the link element for linking the two tables.

9. Move the cursor to the Price column and press the F6 key to check this field.

10. While you are in the Price field, press the F5 key and then type *PRICE*.

11. Move the cursor to the Total column and type *CALC*, then press the spacebar once. Press the F5 key and then type *QUANT*. Notice that QUANT is displayed in reverse video. Press the spacebar once again and type an asterisk for multiplication. Press the F5 key again and type *PRICE*. Press the spacebar and type *AS TOTAL PRICE*. The **AS** operator allows you to enter a descriptive title. If you do not use the AS operator, the QUANT*PRICE will be displayed. By using the AS operator the TOTAL PRICE will be displayed. At this point your screen should be similar to the one displayed in Figure 11–17.

12. Click on the Run Query button in the SpeedBar. You will see a screen similar to Figure 11–18. As you see in this figure, the price is multiplied by the quantity and the results are displayed in the TOTAL PRICE column.

Figure 11–17
Query screen for performing calculations

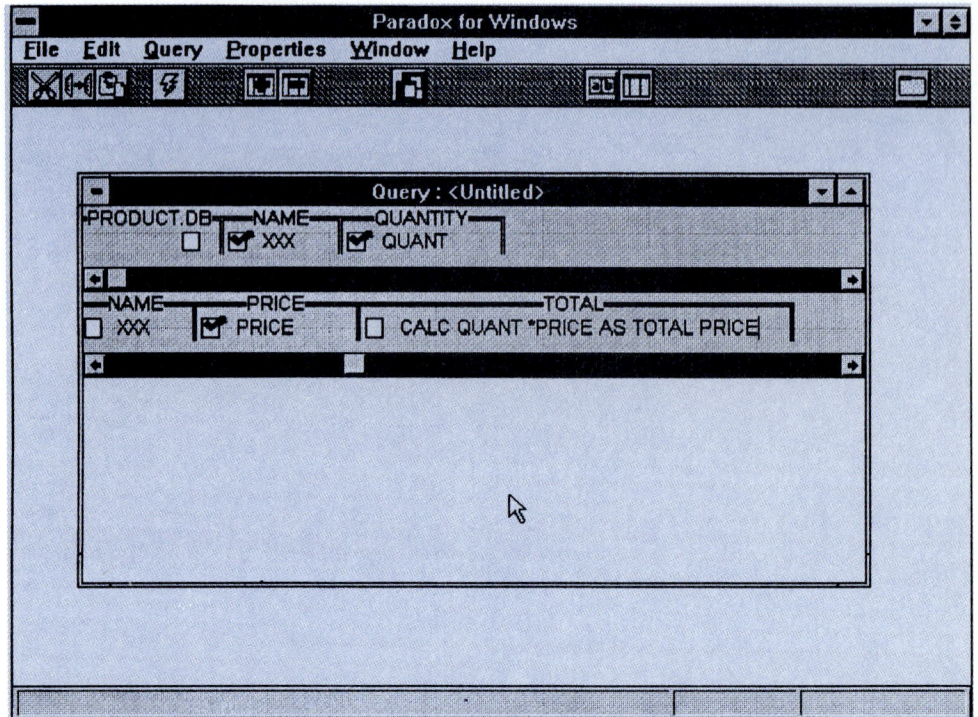

Figure 11–18
The result of numeric calculations on two tables

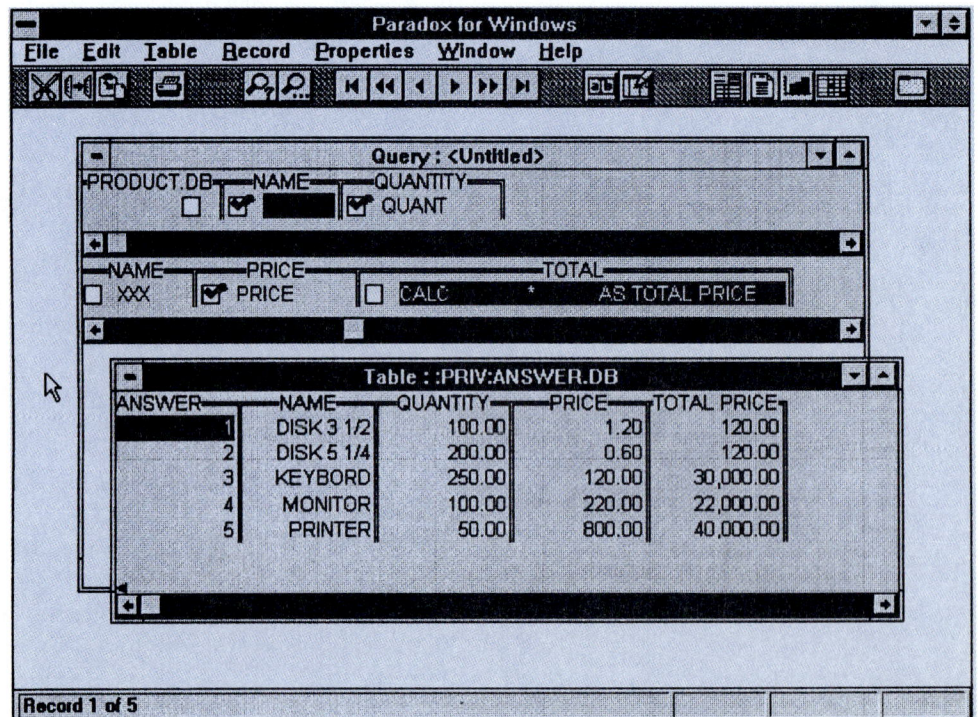

SUMMARY

This chapter introduced some of the advanced features of Paradox for Windows: the CHANGETO operator for changing the contents of your database table; multiple table queries; file linking by using unique examples in Query forms; and performing calculations in multiple tables.

REVIEW QUESTIONS

*These questions are answered in Appendix A.

1. What are some of the applications of the CHANGETO operator?
2. When are you supposed to press the F5 key in query operations? What button in the SpeedBar performs the same task?
3. What records are displayed in the CHANGED table?
*4. How can you convert the CHANGED table to a permanent table?
5. After performing the CHANGETO operation, can you change your mind and return to your original table? If yes, how?
6. Can you perform an OR operation with the CHANGETO operator? If yes, how? The AND operation?
7. Do you need to press the F5 key when you want to provide an example for the alphanumeric data?
8. What are the requirements for tables to be linked?
9. How do you tell Paradox for Windows that a specific field is used for linking?
*10. Is there any limit on the number of tables for linking?
11. Is there any particular order for specifying your tables for linking?
12. Can you use link operations to select certain records? If yes, how?
13. Can you perform calculations on multiple tables?
*14. When do you use the AS operator?
15. How do you add more tables to the query window? How do you remove a table?
16. What is the application of the CALC operation?
17. Can you use the AND, OR, and NOT operators with multiple queries?
18. How do you run a query? What function key runs a query?

HANDS-ON EXPERIENCE

1. Using the database table presented in Figure 11–1, use the CHANGETO operator to do the following:
   a. Increase the salary of all professors by 14 percent.
   b. Increase the salary of all professors or teachers by 20 percent.
   c. Using one Query form, increase the salary of all professors by 10 percent and the salary of all engineers by 20 percent.
   d. Using the File Utilities Copy command, copy the last CHANGED table to a table called A:TEST2.
   e. Reduce all the salaries by 17 percent.
   f. Change all the "Engineers" to "Technical Staff."

2. Using the Award and Student tables presented in this chapter, do the following:
   a. Create an Answer table that includes all the Majors and GPAs.
   b. Create an Answer table that includes all the Genders and GPAs.

c. Using the link operation, create an Answer table that includes all the CS and MKT majors.

d. Create an Answer table that includes all the MIS or CS majors.

3. Using the Price and Quantity tables presented in this chapter, do the following:

a. Create an Answer table that includes only Name, Quantity, and Price.

b. Create an Answer table that includes Name, Quantity, and Price*Quantity under the heading Asset. (Hint: You have to use the AS operator.)

KEY TERMS

Join operation	Linking tables	Multiple queries

KEY COMMANDS

F5 (to give an example)	CALC (to calculate a new field)	OR (to perform the OR operation; one of the conditions must be true)
F6 (to check fields to be included in the query)	CHANGETO (to change the contents of a table)	
F8 (to run a query)		
AS (to specify a more descriptive heading)		

MISCONCEPTIONS AND SOLUTIONS

Misconception You type your example element and do not receive the correct information when you click the Query button.

> **Solution** For nonnumeric data you must first press the F5 function key, then type your example element.

Misconception You are linking two files and receive information that other files in addition to your two files have been linked.

> **Solution** Before you start the linking operation by using the Window Close All command, close all the open queries.

Misconception You are performing calculations and receive a wrong result.

> **Solution** All your calculations must be preceded with the CALC operator.

ARE YOU READY TO MOVE ON?

Multiple Choice

1. To provide a unique example in query operation, what key must you press before you type in your unique example?

a. F1

b. F2

c. F5

d. F10

e. F9

2. The example element will be displayed:

a. in reverse video

b. in capital letters

   c. in lowercase letters
   d. with stars
   e. none of the above

3. After using the CHANGETO operator, a temporary table will be generated called:

   a. TEMPORARY
   b. PERMANENT
   c. TEST
   d. CHANGED
   e. none of the above

4. If two professions in your employee database receive the same salary raise:

   a. you can put them in the same line by using the AND operator
   b. you can put them in the same line by using the OR operator
   c. you can put them in the same line by using the NOT operator
   d. you must put them in two lines
   e. none of the above

5. When you work with multiple tables, all of the following is correct except:

   a. the limit on number of the tables is 24
   b. the two tables must have a common field
   c. the order of the tables that you bring in does not matter
   d. the second table must be sorted in descending order
   e. they are all correct

6. When you work with multiple tables, all of the following are correct except:

   a. the linking field must always be included in the Answer table
   b. to include the linking field you use a check mark
   c. you must always use the F5 key to specify the unique examples with numeric fields
   d. they are all correct
   e. they are all wrong

7. A Query image includes all of the following except:

   a. table name
   b. field names
   c. field type
   d. control menu box
   e. the maximize and minimize icon

8. To add a table to the Query Window you must select which menu?

   a. File
   b. Edit
   c. Properties
   d. Window
   e. Query

9. One of the following operators cannot be used with multiple query operations:

   a. AS
   b. CALC
   c. AND
   d. OR
   e. they all can be used

10. The limit on the number of tables that can be joined is:

   a. 10
   b. 24
   c. 5
   d. 34
   e. none of the above

True/False

1. To perform a global change in your table you can use the CHANGETO operator.
2. The CHANGETO operation works only with numeric data.
3. To provide an example element you press the F5 function key.
4. There is no button in the SpeedBar that performs the same task as the F5 function key.
5. After performing the CHANGETO operation the entire actual table with no changes will be displayed.
6. There is a method to return the changed table to the original table.
7. The Run Query button is one of the buttons in the SpeedBar.
8. To come up with a more descriptive name you must use the CALC operator.
9. To close all the open queries you can use the Window menu.
10. Using the Window command is the only method for closing a Query.

ANSWERS

Multiple Choice		True/False	
1.	c	1.	T
2.	a	2.	F
3.	d	3.	T
4.	b	4.	F
5.	d	5.	F
6.	a	6.	T
7.	c	7.	T
8.	e	8.	F
9.	e	9.	T
10.	b	10.	F

Answers to Selected Review Questions

A

Chapter 1

2. Keyboard and mouse.

6. Floppy disk and hard disks.

13. It varies: 1 to 4 megabytes and higher.

17. Keep it in a dust-free environment. Protect it against excessive heat and humidity.

22. Every application program provides an editing feature so you can edit your mistakes. Or, in the worst case, you can retype your mistakes.

27. Priority of mathematics operations are:

   • Expressions inside parentheses have the highest priority.

   • Exponentiation (raising to power) has the next highest priority.

   • Multiplication and division have the third highest priority.

   • Addition and subtraction have the fourth highest priority.

   • When there are two or more operations with the same priority, operations proceed from left to right.

Chapter 2

3. Because all your programs and data files will be saved with that information. Later, you can determine when a document was created, which version of a document is the most recent one, and so on.

7. Type *A:* and press Enter. Type *C:* and press Enter.

15. A batch file is a disk file that includes a series of commands and statements. To execute this file you must type the file name. An autoexec file starts execution as soon as you get your computer started.

16. Internal commands: COPY, DATE, TIME. External commands: FORMAT, DISKCOPY, DISKCOMP.

Chapter 3

2. Type *CD WIN31* and then press Enter. Then type *WIN* and press Enter.

8. Restore, Move, Size, Close, and Minimize.

12. Press the Ctrl+Esc key combination to activate the Task List, then double-click the desired application in the Task List dialog box.

Chapter 4

3. Designing and implementing a database, establishing security measures, documenting the database, and so forth.

7. A data model is a procedure for creating and maintaining a database. The popular data models are relational, hierarchical, and network.

13. Union compatibility means that two relations (tables) must include the same type and the same number of fields.

16. A distributed database should increase the responsiveness of a CBIS by providing localized access. The user receives data in an immediate mode.

20. Database machines improve the efficiency of database processing by devoting an entire CPU to the database tasks. This should improve the overall data processing operations by freeing the main computer from database processing and devoting its entire processing power to other data processing tasks.

Chapter 5

2. Speed and accuracy.
6. Four.
11. Press the F1 function key.
15. Ten.
22. The File option.

Chapter 6

3. The New Table command from the File menu.
7. The Save command saves the existing file under its present name. The Save As command allows you to specify a new name if you so desire.
11. In the Edit mode move the cursor to the desired record and press the Ctrl+Del key combination. To erase all records from the Table menu, choose the Empty command and then click on Yes.
15. No. No.
18. Press Shift+F7.

Chapter 7

2. Twenty rows and up to 80 characters.
6. The F7 function key.
12. Choose the Borrow button from the Create Paradox for Windows Table dialog box. To use the ditto feature, press the Ctrl+D key combination in a blank field.
14. As many fields as you have.
20. See Figure 7–11.
29. To add, use the Add command from File Utilities. To subtract, use the Subtract command from the File Utilities command.

Chapter 8

5. A wildcard represents one or several characters. For example, the @ wildcard represents any single character. The .. (two periods) returns any alphanumeric character, number, or data of any length.
9. Query-by-example means you provide an example, and based on this example Paradox performs Query operations on your database.
16. The Today operator can be used for any date manipulation task such as calculating the overdue listing of customers.

Chapter 9

5. Four.
7. Four.
16. Sales analysis, regional analysis, and various grouping of your database data.
20. Inspect its properties (right-click) and uncheck Run Time, Pin Horizontal.

Chapter 10

3. Sum, Count, Min, Max, and Avg.
6. Line graphs show trends. XY graphs show relationships.
8. Ctrl+F7.
10. Choose the Tile option, then choose Text.
18. See Figure 10–9.
24. FSL.

Chapter 11

4. Use the File Utilities Copy or File Utilities Rename command.
10. The limit is 24.
14. The As operator is used to create a more descriptive title for the table columns.

Appendix B:
Sharing Information Among
Windows Applications

B

B–1   INTRODUCTION

This appendix provides general guidelines for sharing information among Windows applications. The appendix first briefly reviews the commands and capabilities available within various Windows applications for sharing information. Then it describes the Windows Clipboard as a tool for exchanging information among Windows applications. Object linking and embedding are introduced as two prominent techniques for sharing information among applications. This presentation should assist you in making your data more portable, and it should increase your efficiency and effectiveness in using Windows applications.

B–2   BUILT-IN CAPABILITIES OF SELECTED SOFTWARE

Several Windows software packages include Export/Import commands that enable you to share information over a wide array of Windows applications. Quattro Pro and Paradox for Windows are two examples of such applications. All you have to do is to select the Export/Import command and follow the prompts.

Other Windows application packages such as Excel, Word, WordPerfect, and Lotus 1-2-3 for Windows allow you to save a file in a variety of formats. This is done when you are using the Save or Save As commands. As soon as you save a file under a given format, that file can be readily available to the target application.

More powerful information exchange is available through the Clipboard and object linking and embedding, which are the main topics of the rest of this appendix.

B–3   THE WINDOWS CLIPBOARD

Windows Clipboard serves as a temporary location for storing information. You can copy or move information from one application to the Clipboard; then you can copy (paste) the contents of the Clipboard to another application. The information that you copy to the Clipboard stays there until you clear the contents of the Clipboard or copy other information to it.

The Clipboard can also serve as a buffer for exchanging information among several applications. When you exit Windows or turn your computer off, the contents of the Clipboard is erased.

B–3–1   Moving or Copying Information to the Clipboard

When you are using a Windows application, you can easily move or copy text to the Clipboard. You can also move or copy an image to the Clipboard. To copy or move information to the Clipboard, follow these steps:

1. Highlight or select the text or the information that you want to move or copy. Remember, you can copy or move text, graphics, or both. In most applications, clicking left anywhere on a graph will select it for moving or copying.

2. From the application's Edit menu (e.g., the Edit menu of Lotus 1-2-3 for Windows), select Cut or Copy. Cut removes the selected text or image from its current position. Copy only takes a snapshot—the existing information remains intact.

To copy the contents of an entire screen to the Clipboard, display the desired screen and press the Print Screen key (or Shift+Prtsc or Alt+Prtsc). This process puts a snapshot (also called a bitmap) of the screen onto the Clipboard.

B–3–2

Transferring Information from the Clipboard

To transfer the contents of the Clipboard to another Windows application, follow these steps:

1. Start the desired application.
2. Position the insertion point at the place that you want the information from the Clipboard to appear.
3. From the application's Edit menu, select Paste.

B–3–3

Working with the Clipboard Viewer

By means of the Clipboard Viewer, you can view, save, retrieve, and delete the contents of the Clipboard. To view the contents of the Clipboard, follow these steps:

1. Switch to the Program Manager (if you are not already there). You can do this by pressing the Ctrl+Esc key combination to display the Task List; then double-click on the Program Manager option.
2. Open the Main group window (if it is not already an open window).
3. Double-click on the Clipboard Viewer icon. Click left on the maximizer button to let Clipboard fill the entire screen. You will see a screen similar to the one shown in Figure B–1. The sample text was copied to the Clipboard from the Write application. Write, one of the accessories available in Windows 3.1, is a word processing program.

Figure B–1
Clipboard Viewer menu.

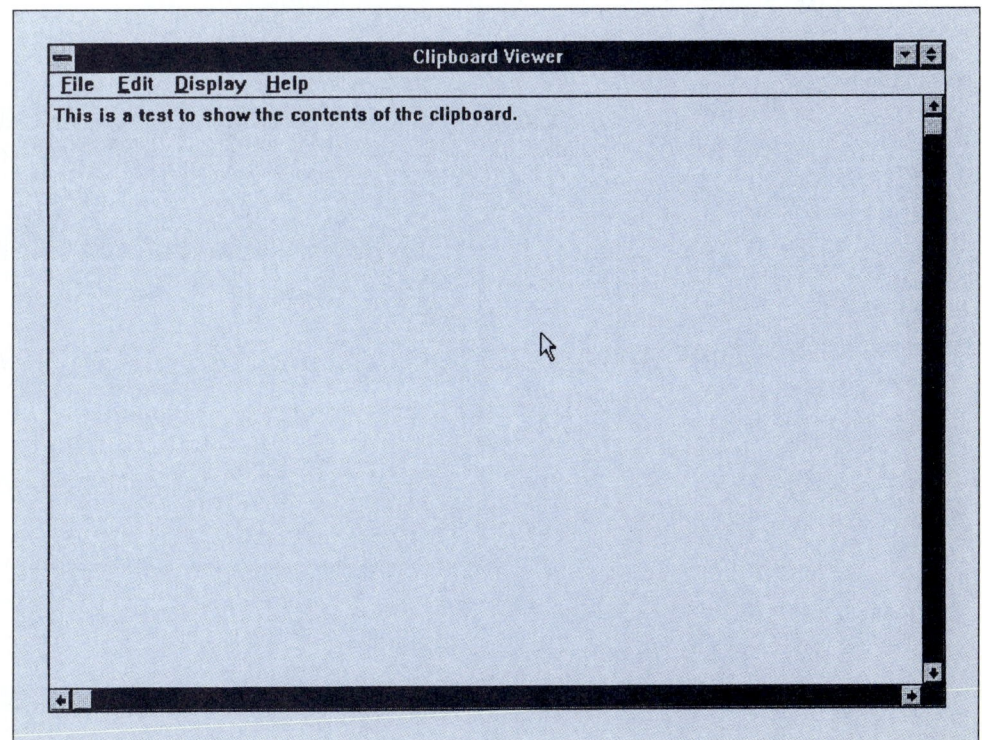

You can view the information in the Clipboard in any of the formats that were supplied by the original application. To view a format from the Display menu, select the desired format; for example, choose Text. The Auto option displays the Clipboard contents in the format that it had when it was placed on the Clipboard. The other options are different formats supported by Windows and a specific Windows application. To return to the previous format that was displayed, from the Display menu, select Auto.

B–3–4

Saving the Contents of the Clipboard to a File

The contents of the Clipboard can be saved in a file for future use. To do so, follow these steps:

1. From the File menu in the Clipboard Viewer, select the Save As option. The Save As dialog box appears; see Figure B–2.
2. Type in a name of up to eight characters. You must specify the complete path if you are saving to a directory and drive different from the default one. The Clipboard automatically attaches a CLP extension to the file name.
3. Select OK to finalize the save procedure.

B–3–5

Retrieving a Clipboard File

To retrieve a clipboard file, follow these steps:

1. Select Open from the File menu in the Clipboard Viewer. The Open dialog box appears; see Figure B–3.
2. Select the .CLP file that you want to retrieve.
3. Select OK.

Figure B–2
Save as dialog box of the Clipboard Viewer.

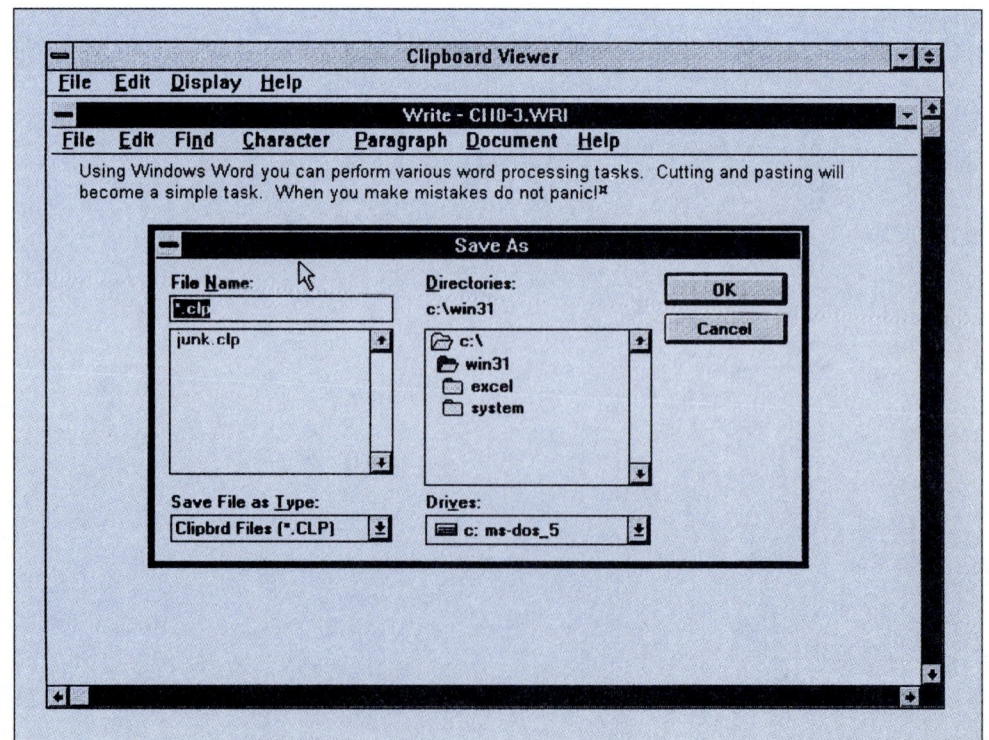

Figure B–3
Open dialog box of the Clipboard
Viewer.

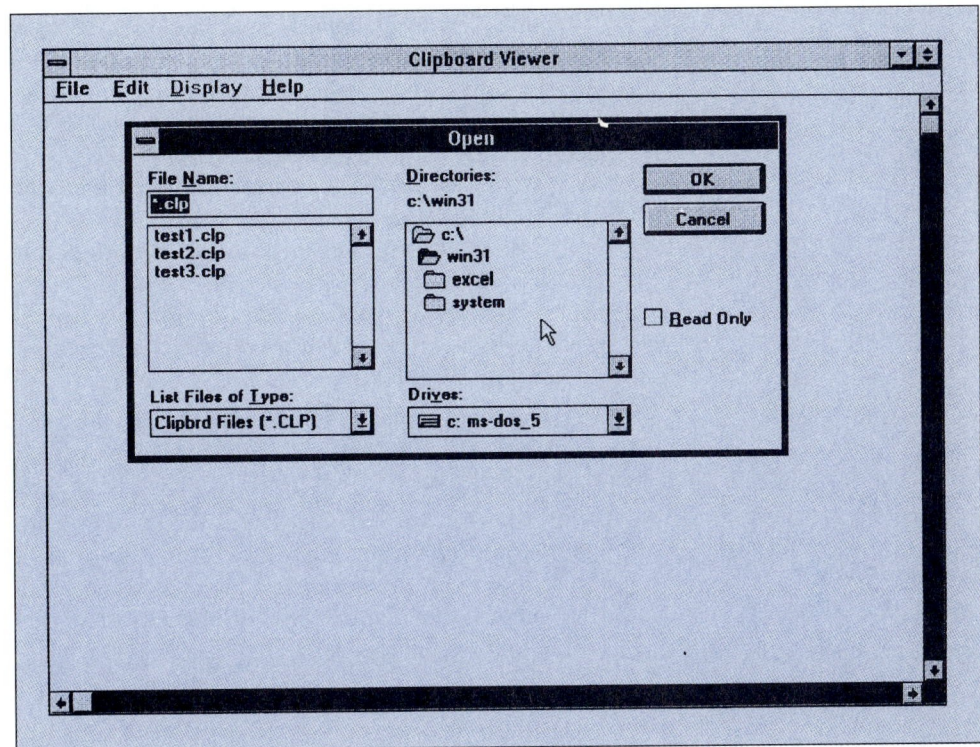

B–3–6

Clearing the Contents of the Clipboard

To clear the contents of Clipboard, follow these steps:

1. Select Edit from the Clipboard Viewer menu.
2. Select Delete. You will be prompted with the Clear Clipboard dialog box displaying Yes and No options. Selecting Yes will erase the contents; selecting No will not erase the contents of the Clipboard.

When you are in Clipboard Viewer, simply pressing the Del (Delete) key will also clear the contents of the Clipboard. Clearing the contents of the Clipboard frees up some of your computer resources. Remember, however, that placing new contents into the Clipboard automatically erases the old contents regardless of any differences in size.

B–4   OBJECT LINKING AND EMBEDDING

Windows 3.1 offers a powerful tool in the form of object linking and embedding (OLE—pronounced "oh-lay"). Windows has always allowed users to copy graphics or other objects between applications. With earlier versions of Windows, however, if you decided that you wanted to change a Paintbrush graphic, for example, that had been copied into a Write document, you had to delete it from your Write document, reload Paintbrush, load and edit the graphic to make the desired changes, save the graphic, and then copy it back into the Write document. Now, by means of OLE, you can create the graphic using Paintbrush, embed the graphic into your Write document, and edit the graphic from within the Write document—you don't have to delete it!

To be more specific, you can open the Paintbrush application automatically from within the Write document by double-clicking on the graphic. In this scenario, Paintbrush appears on the screen with the graphic already loaded and ready for editing. Any changes that you make to the graphic in Paintbrush are automatically made to the graphic in the Write document, because a dynamic link exists between the Paintbrush application and the graphic that is embedded in the Write document.

Several terms are important for understanding OLE:

1. Object—any graphic or item of information. For example, a spreadsheet, a range or a single cell from within a spreadsheet, a table, and a graph are all examples of objects.

2. Server—any application whose objects can be linked or embedded into other applications. Paintbrush and Sound Recorder are examples of server applications.

3. Client—any application capable of accepting objects that are created by a server application. Write and Cardfile are examples of client applications. Cardfile is an accessory available in Windows 3.1. The Cardfile can help you manage names, addresses, phone numbers, and other information critical to your daily activities.

4. Source document—the document in which the object was created

5. Destination document—the document into which the object is embedded or linked

B–4–1   Embedding an Object Versus Linking an Object

There is an important distinction between embedding an object and linking an object. When you embed an object, you are actually making a copy of the object from the server application and placing the copy into the client application. You may then make editing changes to the object from within the client application simply by double-clicking on the object. The server application that was used to create the object is automatically loaded, with the object ready for editing.

Now here is the distinction. Any changes that you make to an embedded object do not change the original object that was copied from the source document in the server application. Any editing changes appear only in the destination document of the client application; the source document object is left in its original form. On the other hand, linking an object involves creating a link, or reference, to the original object in the source document. Once an object is linked into the destination document, simply double-clicking on the object automatically loads the server application that was used to create the object, with the object ready for editing. At this point, changes made to the linked (client) object do change the source object in the source document.

B–4–2   Example of Object Linking

Let's say that you are the business office manager for a school district and you maintain budget data using a spreadsheet application. At some point during the year, you must send a budget report containing a copy of the spreadsheet to your school district board, the county office of education, and the state department of education. The three reports contain the same spreadsheet data, but each report also contains other pieces of information relevant only to the respective entity.

You create the three reports using Write, and in each of the reports (destination documents) you create a link to the spreadsheet (source document). You finish the reports and suddenly remember that you forgot to add a budget item into the spreadsheet (source document). No problem! Retrieve any one of the three reports (destination documents) into Write (the client application) and double-click on the spreadsheet (object). Automatically, the spreadsheet application (server) appears with the spreadsheet (source document) loaded on the screen. Make your editing changes, save the spreadsheet (source document), and exit the spreadsheet application (server). The links automatically update each of the three spreadsheets contained within the reports with the missing piece of information, and you can print reports and send them on their way.

B–4–3 Hands-On Example of Object Embedding

We will now walk through an example of how to embed a graphic created in Paintbrush into a Write document. Follow these steps:

1. Open Paintbrush. To do this, double-click on the Accessories group icon then double-click on the Paintbrush icon.
2. Click on the maximize button at the upper right of the screen to allow Paintbrush to fill the entire screen.
3. Select the hollow circle tool from the toolbox and create a circle in the upper-left corner of the drawing area.
4. To save the drawing, select Save from the File menu and specify TEST as the name; then click left on OK.
5. Using the pick tool (the second tool from the top) from the toolbox, select the drawing by clicking left above and to the left of the drawing; then drag the mouse down and to the right so that a dashed box surrounds the circle.
6. From the Edit menu, select Copy. This places a copy of the drawing in the Clipboard.
7. Exit Paintbrush by selecting the Exit option from the File menu.
8. Open Write. To open Write double-click on its icon in the Accessories group.
9. Click on the maximize button at the upper right of the screen to allow Write to fill the entire screen.
10. Move the insertion point to the location where you would like to position the embedded object.
11. From the Edit menu, select Paste. A copy of the drawing is placed (or embedded) into your Write document.

Now let's say that you want to jazz up the drawing a little. To do this, double-click left anywhere on the object (the circle). Paintbrush will open with a copy of the drawing already displayed and ready for editing. Follow the steps outlined next to modify the object:

1. Click left on the paint roller (the fourth tool from the top left) tool in the toolbox.
2. Click left on a different color in the color palette at the bottom of the screen.
3. Click left anywhere inside of the circle. Your circle should fill with the selected color.

4. Select Update from the Paintbrush File menu. The circle in the Write document ment should instantly fill with the selected color. As mentioned earlier, editing an embedded object does not change the appearance of the object in the source application. Editing changes made to an embedded object change only the appearance of the object in the destination application. You can verify this by opening the Test.bmp file. You will see that all the improvements are not reflected here.

5. Select Exit and return to [Untitled] from the Paintbrush File menu. Paintbrush will close, and you will be returned to your Write document so that you can continue working. Click left anywhere outside of the circle to deselect it; then you may continue editing your Write document. When you are finished editing, save your document under TEST and exit the Write application.

B–4–4   ## Hands-On Example of Object Linking

Follow the steps outlined next to link an object from Paintbrush to a card in Cardfile and a document in Write.

1. Open Paintbrush.

2. Click on the maximize button at the upper right of the screen to allow Paintbrush to fill the entire screen.

3. Select the hollow square (the seventh tool from the top left) tool from the toolbox and create a square in the upper-left corner of the drawing area.

4. Save the drawing by selecting the Save option from the File menu; then specify TRY as the name and click left on OK.

5. Using the pick tool (the first tool from the top right) from the toolbox, select the drawing by clicking left above and to the left of the drawing; then drag the mouse down and to the right so that a dashed box surrounds the square.

6. From the Edit menu, select Copy. This places a copy of the drawing in the Clipboard.

7. Switch back to the Program Manager by means of the Ctrl+Esc key combination.

8. Open Cardfile.

9. Click on the maximize button at the upper right of the screen to allow Cardfile to fill the entire screen.

10. Select Picture from the Edit menu.

11. Select Paste Link from the Edit menu. A copy of the drawing will be placed in the upper-left corner of the card.

12. Exit Cardfile by selecting the Exit option from the File menu; then click left on Yes to save your changes. Cardfile will respond by displaying the Save As dialog box.

13. Type *LINKTEST* and click left on OK to give the file a name. After saving the file, you will be returned to the Program Manager.

14. Open Write.

15. Click on the maximize button at the upper right of the screen to allow Write to fill the entire screen.

16. Select Paste Link from the Edit menu. A linked copy of the drawing will be placed in the upper-left corner of the document.

17. Exit Write by selecting the Exit option from the File menu; then click left on Yes to save the changes. Write will respond by displaying the Save As dialog box.

18. Type *LINKTEST* and click left on OK to give the document a name. Don't worry about the document having the same name as in the Cardfile—the extensions are different. After saving the file, you will be returned to the Program Manager.

You have now created and saved an object in the source application (Paintbrush) and placed a linked copy of the object into a Cardfile card and a Write document. In addition to placing a copy of the drawing into the Cardfile card and Write document, Windows also created a direct link between these two drawings and the application that created the drawing (Paintbrush). We will now test the links by making a change to the original object in Paintbrush, and opening the LINKTEST.CRD card file and LINKTEST.WRI document to see if the objects in these two files are updated with the changes.

19. Switch to Paintbrush by using the Ctrl+Esc key combination or by clicking anywhere on its Window (if it is already on the screen).

20. Select the roller tool from the toolbox.

21. Click left on a different color in the color palette at the bottom of the screen.

22. Click left anywhere inside the box that you created. The box should be filled with the specified color.

23. Select Exit from the File menu; then click left on Yes to save your changes. You will be returned to the Program Manager.

24. Open Cardfile.

25. Click on the maximize button at the upper right of the screen to allow Cardfile to fill the entire screen.

26. Select Open from the File menu. Cardfile will display the Open dialog box.

27. Double click left on LINKTEST.CRD to open this file. Cardfile will display a screen similar to Figure B–4 to alert you that this card file contains links to other documents and that the links may need updating.

28. Click left on OK. Your Cardfile with the object inside the card will be displayed. Notice that the change we made to the original object in Paintbrush has not appeared.

29. Select Picture from the Edit menu.

30. Select Link from the Edit menu. Cardfile will display the Link dialog box (Figure B–5). This screen allows you to update your links, change or cancel your links, and view link information.

31. Click left on Update Now; then click left on OK. The link will be updated, and you should now see the changes that you made to the original object in Paintbrush.

32. Select the Exit option from the File menu; then click left on Yes to save your changes. You will be returned to the Program Manager.

33. Open Write.

34. Click on the maximize button at the upper right of the screen to allow Write to fill the entire screen.

35. Select Open from the File menu. Write will display the Open dialog box.

Figure B–4
Cardfile link warning dialog box.

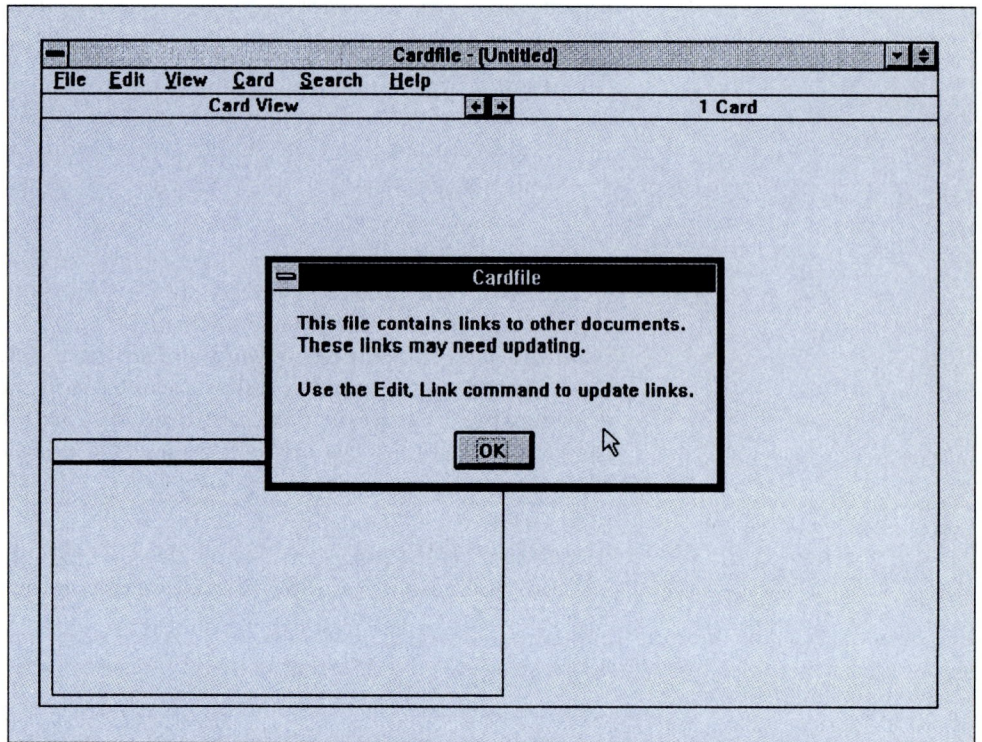

Cardfile - [Untitled]
File Edit View Card Search Help
Card View   1 Card

Cardfile

This file contains links to other documents.
These links may need updating.

Use the Edit, Link command to update links.

OK

Figure B–5
Cardfile Link dialog box.

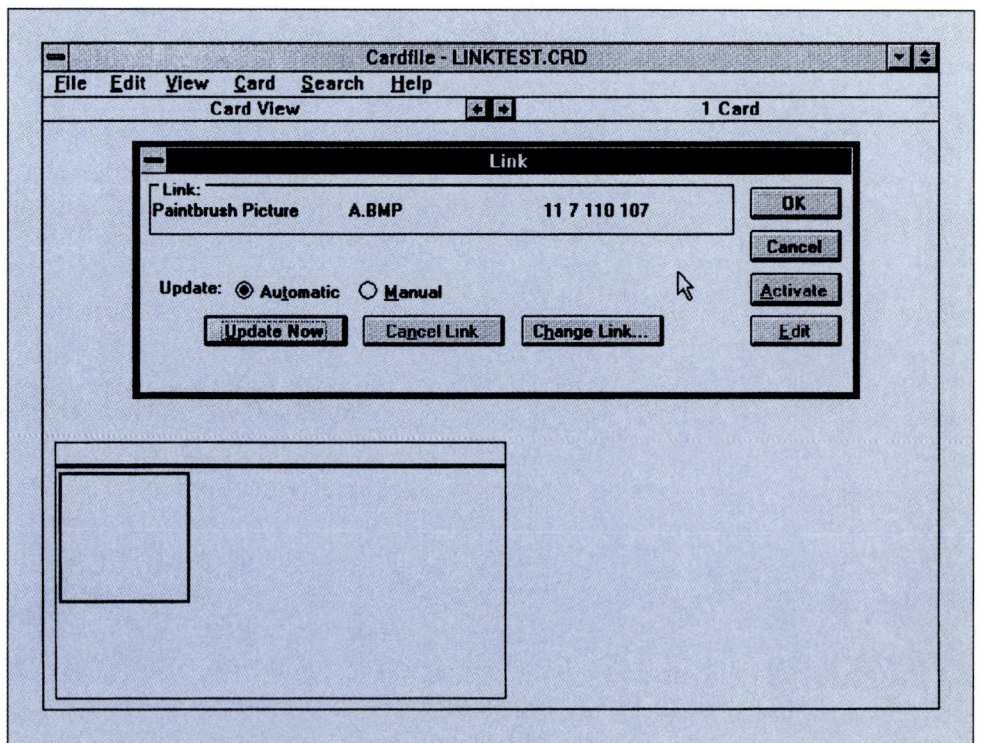

Cardfile - LINKTEST.CRD
File Edit View Card Search Help
Card View   1 Card

Link

Link:
Paintbrush Picture   A.BMP   11 7 110 107

Update: ⦿ Automatic ○ Manual

Update Now   Cancel Link   Change Link...

OK
Cancel
Activate
Edit

36. Double-click left on LINKTEST.WRI to open this file. Write will display a screen similar to Figure B–6 to alert you that this file contains links to other documents and to prompt you about whether to update the links now.

37. Click left on Yes. Your document will be displayed on the screen with your changes already displayed.

38. Select the Exit option from the File menu; then click left on Yes to save your changes. You will be returned to the Program Manager.

At this point, you may not be sure about the difference between linking an object (as we just did) and embedding an object as we did in the first example. When would you use one method and not the other? As you already know, double-clicking on the drawing automatically loads the application that created the drawing (Paintbrush) with the drawing ready for editing. If the drawing is linked in the destination application, any changes that you make to the drawing using the server application alter both the original object and all linked copies of the graphic in any client application (Cardfile, in this case). Alternatively, if the drawing were embedded, any changes that you made to the embedded drawing in the Cardfile would not alter the original file in the server application. In any case, you may edit the linked object using the same sequence of steps used to edit an embedded object.

B–4–5

Dynamic Data Exchange Versus OLE: What's the Difference?

The OLE feature of Windows 3.1 represents a significant improvement over the way that previous versions of Windows allowed the exchange of data between applications. In versions of Windows prior to 3.1, the capability to move objects among applications as we have been discussing was called dynamic data exchange (DDE).

Figure B–6
Write Link dialog box.

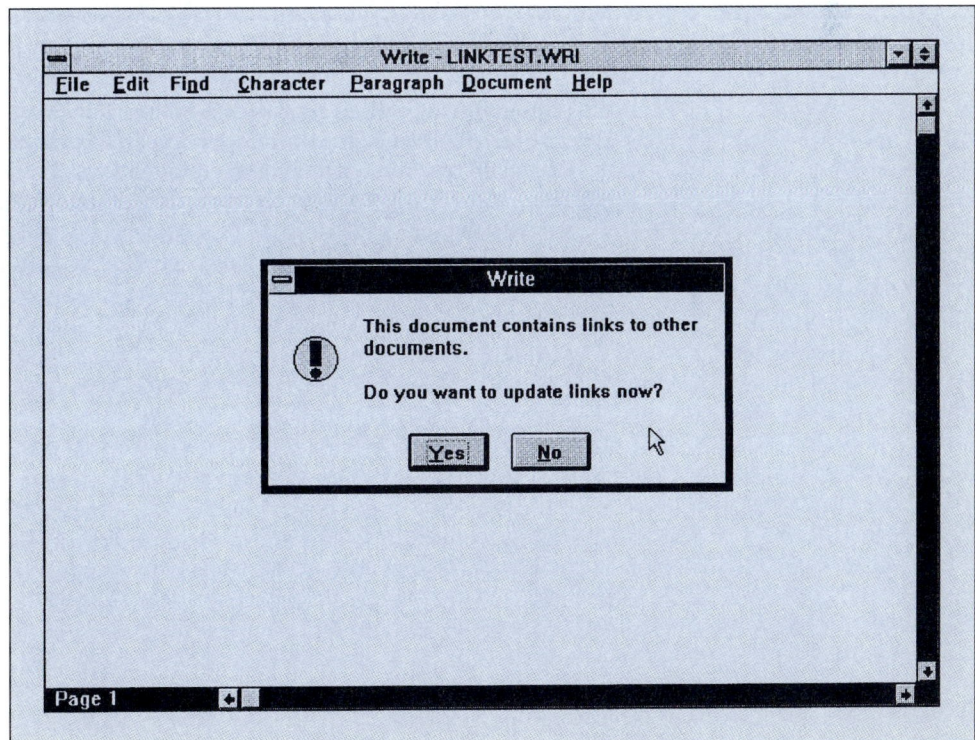

To share information among different applications using DDE, all the applications must be running on the Windows desktop and the related files must be opened. And more important, the updating process occurs only one way: from the server to the client. The data can only be edited in the server application. So, OLE is the next logical step in technological progress beyond the DDE capabilities. By means of OLE, sharing information among different applications becomes document driven rather than application driven. Updating can take place in either direction.

The OLE feature also represents an improvement over DDE in its use of dynamic link libraries to maintain the link information used between applications. In previous versions of Windows, DDE link information was stored within the linking (server) application itself. This created overhead for each server application and opened the door to problems because such a wide variety of linking protocols existed between the various server application programs. With OLE, linking information is stored within dynamic link libraries, thereby freeing the various server application programs from having to store the information. Instead of many applications each storing link information, all link information is now stored under the single umbrella of dynamic link libraries. The application programs are free of the overhead and simply refer to the libraries as necessary to gain access to the link information they require. Thus, OLE is more application independent and flexible and forms a more reliable platform for using its powerful capabilities.

In our discussion of object linking and embedding we used Paintbrush, Cardfile, and Write. They were selected because any Windows application has access to them. You can apply the same principle to the application of your choice. Also, you should consult the documentation of your desired software to see if it supports OLE. The older versions of Windows applications support DDE, whereas the newer versions mostly support OLE in addition to DDE.

SUMMARY

This appendix provided general guidelines for sharing information among Windows applications. It discussed export/import capabilities and saving with different file formats, the Clipboard, and object linking and embedding. This information should improve your efficiency and effectiveness as you use various Windows applications.

Index

ISBN 0-02-309571-7